*more . . .*

# THE GREATEST WAR

## VOLUME II

### D-DAY AND THE ASSAULT ON EUROPE

## GERALD ASTOR

**WARNER BOOKS**

A Time Warner Company

WARNER BOOKS EDITION

This Warner books edition is published by arrangement with Presidio Press.

*Cover design by Jerry Pfeifer*
*Cover flag photo by Philip James Corwin*
*Cover inset photo by U.S. ARMY Signal Core*

Warner Books, Inc.
1271 Avenue of the Americas
New York, NY  10020

Visit our Web site at
www.twbookmark.com.

For information on Time Warner Trade Publishing's online publishing program, visit www.ipublish.com.

 A Time Warner Company

Printed in the United States of America

First Warner Books Printing: October 2001

10 9 8 7 6 5 4 3 2 1

*For the late Donald I. Fine*

# CONTENTS

# PREFACE

When I told Gen. George Ruhlen that I intended to write a book covering the battles fought by Americans during World War II, he wrote to me, "How many pages are you projecting, 5,000 or squeeze it into 3,000?" His comment was well taken, for an encyclopedic account of what happened to Americans in World War II would require many volumes and in fact the historian Samuel Eliot Morison produced something on the nature of twenty books covering just the engagements of the Navy and the Marines.

However, my intention was not to cover the war from objective to objective nor was it to describe the details of strategy and tactics. I freely confess that, even in an oversize manuscript, I have omitted many hard-fought battles, units, and individuals who underwent the same hardships, terror, and sorrow, and who, in spite of their ordeals, overcame. Instead I hope to present a sense of what the American fighting man (women in World War II were restricted to clerical and service positions although as the book indicates, some nurses underwent much of what the men did) experienced in terms of what he thought, felt, saw, heard, and tried to do. Words on a page cannot match those moments under fire but by their own voices the soldiers, sailors, and airmen reveal the nature of that war well beyond anything shown in films or TV, except perhaps for *Saving Private Ryan*. (Even here one might quibble about the premise upon which the story unfolds.)

Having written six books on World War II, I am well aware that eyewitness accounts or oral histories have their weaknesses due to faulty memories, skewed perspectives, and the common human resort to self-service. On the other hand, these same deficiencies also afflict official reports. In his letter to me, George Ruhlen remarked that a friend of his named Brewster commanded a task force whose mission was to regain possession of a crossroads during the Battle of the Bulge. "Some 20 accounts were written by 'historians' who were never there, most inaccurate, but only one writer ever contacted Colonel Brewster for his recollection of that action."

I expect there will be some who will dispute an individual's version of some events in this book, but I believe that by relying on as many sources and veterans as I have the essential truth of the experiences is correct. Although many of the sensations and the reactions of those on the scenes seem similar—the most replicated comment was "Suddenly, all hell broke loose"—there were significant differences from year to year, from campaign to campaign, from area to area.

It was the biggest of all wars and those who fought the battles deserve to be heard.

# ACKNOWLEDGMENTS

So many people have shared their memories and experiences with me that I cannot cite them individually. Their words are credited to them in the text and to some extent through Roll Call.

I received special help from Paul Stillwell of the United States Naval Institute in Annapolis; Joseph Caver of the United States Air Force Historical Research Center at Maxwell Field, Alabama; Dr. David Keough at the United States Army History Library at Carlisle Barracks, Pennsylvania; the United States Naval Historical Center; Debbie Pogue at the United States Military Academy Library; Jim Altieri; William Cain; Tracy Derks; Len Lomell; Benjamin Mabry; Jason Poston.

Small portions of this book appeared in some of my previous writings on World War II.

# 1

## Husky

AT CASABLANCA WHEN THE ALLIED LEADERS HAD CONGRATU-
lated themselves on the start of Torch they had also agreed
upon the capture of Sicily. Initially Eisenhower favored by-
passing that island in favor of Sardinia and Corsica as better
suited for a campaign in Italy. On the flank of Italy, operations from these islands would require the enemy to disperse
his forces rather than concentrate them against an attack
from Sicily. But Sicily guarded Mediterranean sea lanes and
the size of the island suggested that once captured it could
be more easily held against a counterattack. The port city of
Messina, separated from the mainland by a narrow strait,
could serve as a base for an assault upon Italy proper.

To carry out Husky, the Allies amassed a huge army. The
Americans contributed the 1st, 3d, and 45th Infantry Divisions, the 2d Armored, elements from the 82d Airborne, and
the Rangers. They would be joined by Canadian and British
soldiers as well as the naval and air forces. General Sir
Harold Alexander, respected even by Patton, assumed com-

of ground troops. Montgomery would lead his countrymen while Patton drew the honors for the GIs.

Studies convinced the Allies that the small island of Pantelleria between Tunisia and Sicily if under enemy control would allow Axis aircraft to hammer the Husky forces. In friendly hands it would provide a base for air operations. A rocky coastline, however, boded ill for a seaborne invasion and the rugged countryside denied opportunities for paratroopers. Perhaps because of its apparent impregnability, the enemy high command stationed a garrison of 11,000 Italian defenders, even though the growing disaffection of Mussolini's legions for the war had become obvious in North Africa. The Allies gambled that an all-out series of air raids might discourage any resolute defense. For six days and nights in the early days of June 1943, the combined air forces rained some 5,000 tons of high explosives upon the area inhabited by most of the Italian soldiers. On 11 June, as assault troops started to climb into the landing craft, Pantelleria capitulated, the bastion falling without a single casualty for the invasion force.

Among the outfits that engaged in the aerial attacks on Pantelleria was the 99th Fighter Squadron, the first of the unique African-American Air Corps units known as the Tuskegee Airmen. The tradition of segregation in the armed forces, and restriction of blacks to largely service and labor organizations, afflicted the U.S. military throughout World War II. Pressure from African-American leaders like Walter White, A. Philip Randolph, and Mary Bethune along with the support of whites like Eleanor Roosevelt breached the military color line in a few places. With great reluctance, the Air Corps had agreed to form what was sneered at as a *Spookwaffe*, in an experiment to see whether "Negroes" possessed the intelligence and ability to fly combat.

Under the command of Benjamin O. Davis Jr., a 1936 graduate of the USMA, the first of his race in more than forty years, the 99th reported to the fighter command in North Africa. They were not regarded as qualified nor were they welcomed by most on the scene. However, Phil Cochran, now part of the Training Command, said, "I found that they were a delightful group of guys to be with; they were a lot of fun. I found out that they could fly formation beautifully. They could land an airplane with more expertise than any young pilots I ever saw. They were trained to the hilt. When I converted them to new formations, they caught on quicker than other squadrons.

"But they lacked aerial judgment. Physically they could fly the airplane exceptionally well, but if they were to be criticized—it wasn't their fault—they were lacking in such things as navigation. They didn't know how to get from here to there properly, and especially in a tough district where there isn't a lot of civilization. It's easy to fly from Buffalo to Cleveland, because you followed the damn lake. But when you get on one of those desert things, and get a little disoriented, there aren't any rail lines to follow and there aren't any highways to follow and there aren't any towns to look down on and say that is [such and such] city. So they would get lost." In fact, because of the hostility to them at air bases around the States, the Tuskegee Airmen rarely had an opportunity to hone their navigational skills in cross-country flights.

Cochran noted, "They were exceptionally eager. Man, if there was a group that ever wanted to prove themselves, they were it. And they would get embarrassed when one of their men would do something that any young, inexperienced pilot would do. They would say, 'We are not supposed to do that; we can't afford to do that.' They didn't want to make mistakes because they had been made special. I always kind of felt for them. I had a fine time of just sitting with those guys. I got to know their wives. I drank beer with them at night. I just lived right with them and I kept talking to them and talking to them, and then going up with them, taking them up one at a time, two at a time, and making them fight each other and fight the winner. They were just so anxious to learn something, and eager to go and eager to fight."

Cochran's affection for the 99th was reciprocated. "He was a great guy," said Spann Watson, one of the original twenty-six pilots of the 99th. "At Tuskegee we more or less trained ourselves. They would just send you out to practice. But Cochran helped the 99th learn how to fight." In their P-40s, the African-Americans were in the skies over Pantelleria and the area commander, Col. J. R. Hawkins, offered them "Heartiest congratulations for the splendid part you played in the Pantelleria show." Nevertheless, the naysayers never shut their mouths throughout the war nor after, no matter what the achievements of the Tuskegee Airmen.

The Pantelleria success enabled Husky to go forward on schedule. But no one believed that the experience would be replicated at Sicily. While the Italians had not shown great determination in North Africa, in Sicily they would defend their native turf. To overwhelm the stalwart defenses, which included a substantial number of first-rate German soldiers backing up the Italians in coastal positions and supported by the *Luftwaffe*, the biggest airborne effort ever launched would begin on the night of 9 July. The attack would include both paratroopers and gliders.

Bill Yarborough expected his own regimental command after the drop in North Africa, but he received only the 2d Battalion of the 504th Parachute Regiment under Ruben

Tucker. Aside from his hurt feelings, Yarborough said there was another aspect to Husky that perturbed him. "The planning was done by the staff of the 82d Airborne, a part of which were not airborne officers but straight legs. My distress was even greater when the debacle occurred, because I felt I had something to say about recognition signals, maps, and even equipment."

The order of battle for Husky I scheduled the 505th Parachute Infantry Regiment, commanded by then-Col. James Gavin, reinforced with the 3d Battalion of the 504th, to jump east of Gela, on the southern coast where the 1st Infantry Division expected to come ashore. The remembrances of paratrooper Bill Dunfee indicate the appalling vagueness of the plot. Dunfee, an Ohio high school dropout, led a rifle squad for Company I, 3d Battalion in the 505th RCT (Regimental Combat Team). "Our CO was Capt. Willard Follmer and I jumped in Follmer's plane. Major Edward Krause, the battalion CO, had informed Follmer of I Company's mission, giving him an airphoto of the area where they were to land. He didn't tell him where but instructed him to pick a drop zone two or three miles from where the 1st Division would be landing and about the same distance from the drop zone of the rest of the battalion. I Company's mission would be to reduce several pillboxes in the area, kill or capture the Italians manning them, set up roadblocks, and then light bonfires to signal the 1st Division offshore that was clear. After studying the airphotos, Follmer picked a narrow valley just over and north of Lake Bivier. Krause approved and said the Troop Carrier Command would be notified.

"Despite Krause's order to the contrary, Follmer, remembering all too well the misdrops and mishaps that had occurred in practice jumps, took it upon himself to contact the

Air Corps. In the middle of the night he left our camp in the olive grove and went to the airfield about a mile away. Locating the lieutenant colonel who was to lead the I Company flight, getting him out of bed, showing him the airphotos, Follmer was not surprised to learn that the colonel knew nothing of our mission. He was very cooperative. They agreed to put I Company at the rear of the 3d Battalion's flight and [travel] in a line of three Vees, instead of the standard nine-plane-wide Vee. This would put I Company into the narrow valley. Follmer thanked the colonel and returned to the olive grove, with no one the wiser as to his circumvention of Krause's order.

"July ninth started with an early breakfast. We were issued a basic combat load of ammunition, grenades, and rations. Two items were unique to the Sicily operation, Mae West life preservers and gas masks. The Mae Wests were left on the planes and the gas masks discarded shortly after landing. We had an early supper at 1600 hours. Trucks carried each group to their C-47s. After the equipment bundles were checked and loaded, we crawled in the shade to relax. At this time we were given the password and countersign, 'George'—'Marshall' and told our destination in a mimeographed note to each of us from Gavin. Time came to chute-up and board the planes. The first took off at 2010 hours and by 2116 the complete combat team was airborne. Since my squad was jumping [from] Captain Follmer's plane, I was put at the end of the line as the last man out. I was concerned when Follmer put one of the new men between me and the rest of the squad. We had a direct order from Krause to shoot any man that refused to jump. That presented a problem since my M1 was in a canvas container under my reserve chute."

To protect the transports, gliders, and troopers, Husky I

exploited the cover of darkness. Unfortunately, nighttime operations exposed the airborne armada to jittery gunners aboard the great invasion fleet moving through the Mediterranean. Antiaircraft crews tended to regard the sound of motors in the sky as a signal to open fire. As a consequence the transports took off from North African fields but instead of a straight northeast course to the island, they flew east to pass over the small island of Linosa and then the British outpost of Malta before a turn north toward the southwest corner of Sicily, and the ultimate leg, northwest to Gela. Unfortunately, a thirty-five-mile-per-hour wind blew many aircraft off course, carrying numerous planes beyond Malta, and the pilots approached Sicily well off the mark.

"The pilots were as green as ourselves," said Dunfee, "and the navigation pretty primitive. They established a heading and flew for it X number of minutes and then turned as indicated to another heading. This did not take into account the gale over the Mediterranean. Many flights became separated and missed the check points of the small island of Linosa and the larger island of Malta [from where Eisenhower and his staff saw them in the sky]. Most of the flight that missed the checkpoints dropped our guys along the southeast coast of Sicily in the British zone." A worse fate met the British gliders destined for Siracusa. In spite of the scheme to avoid friendly fire, Allied ships shot down ninety of the flimsy craft, which crashed in the sea.

"As we approached Sicily," said Dunfee, "for reasons unknown, the others of the 3d Battalion flight turned back out to sea, subsequently returning to drop on the wrong DZ. Our pilot and Follmer, seeing the Acate River, were satisfied we were on the proper course. As we crossed the coastline, Follmer told me to pass the word back, 'Stand up, hook up, and check equipment.' This done, we sounded off the equipment check, starting with me and moving toward the door. About this time, over Lake Bivier, Captain Follmer, moving by me, said, 'About five minutes,' and took his position by the door. Being crowded when we stood up, it became necessary for me to step through the bulkhead into the radio operator's area. My attention was called to the new man who had sat down. I told him to stand up and he started giving me conversation. I made it very clear to him in four-letter words that he damned well better stand up.

"I had noticed the green light was on when Follmer yelled, 'Let's go!' We started moving toward the door. The man in front of me went past the door into the tail section of the plane. I grabbed his back pack and pulled him back to the door. He started to back off again so I grabbed the sides of the door opening and pulled us both out. I had no more felt the shock of the parachute opening when I was going through pine trees, hitting the ground going downhill. Getting down so fast, my thought as I hit the ground was that I'd had a malfunction but I was able to stand, get rid of the parachute harness, and, securing my equipment, move out.

"Being unable to find the man that went out ahead of me I thought he may not want me to find him. I started back the way we flew in to 'roll up the stick,' but I couldn't find anyone. I spent the night searching for my company. Since I had no idea how far the plane had traveled during the mixup at the door, my assumption was I had landed over the crest of a mountain beyond the valley. By daylight I traveled back over the crest and headed downhill into the valley. By noon of D day I noticed movement on the far side of the valley that I thought to be part of my group. Not sure of who they were I took a route that would eventually intersect their path. By early evening I'd made contact with four men from the 2d Battalion. They too were lost and after comparing notes we decided we didn't know where we were. Being tired, hungry, and frustrated, we sacked out for a few hours. On awakening, we could not agree on our next move. My suggestion was to move south, believing we would contact either I Company, friendly troops, a road, or the Mediterranean. My idea was dismissed and they had none better, so I took off by myself. I found a larger group of troopers, what was left of the 3d Battalion, and finally my company. Less one planeload and myself, I Company had accomplished its mission. Although Follmer had broken his leg, he directed the troopers from the back of a confiscated mule."

Husky I strewed paratroopers from Licata to Siracusa, a distance of eighty miles. The demolition team that was to prepare the Acate River bridge for demolition was dropped sixty miles east in the British zone. The 3d Battalion, less I Company, was scattered between Scoglitti and Vittoria, a few miles southeast of the Acate River. Gavin himself landed twenty miles from his drop zone. He, two of his staff, and three equally lost troopers spent the night wandering in search of the main body of the regiment. They blundered into an enemy position that cost them their first dead man, then sneaked off to hide during daylight. While Gavin, Dunfee, and similarly lost souls could contribute little or nothing to the operation, others among the 3,400 troopers in Husky I, mostly in small groups, improvised to disable the local communications network, knock out some objectives, occasionally call in effective naval support, and delay the rush of the Hermann Goering Panzer *Fallschirmjäger* Division to reinforce beach defenses.

Eisenhower's "eyes," Maj. Gen. John Lucas, reached the Gela beachhead at about 7:30. He was disturbed to see enlisted men and officers crouched in slit trenches rather than moving inland. He told his diary, "If I ever command troops again I will teach them nothing about digging. The slogan 'A soldier's best weapon is his shovel' has taken a lot of fight out of our Army.' He shared this sentiment with Patton, who habitually excoriated GIs for resorting to foxholes. Neither man seemed to appreciate the difference between the general officer's behind-the-lines vantage point and that of the combat soldier exposed to artillery, mortars, and small arms.

On his second night in Sicily, Gavin located as many as 250 paratroopers under Krause along with units from the 45th Infantry Division. He struck out for Gela but enemy troops barred the way. Tanks from the Hermann Goering Panzer Division clanked to the front, oblivious to bazooka rounds that bounced off their thick skins. A fierce firefight at Biazza Ridge stalled Gavin's people and they were in danger of being overwhelmed. With only a single 75mm piece from the Parachute Artillery plus a pair of 81mm mortars, Gavin and cohort were severely outgunned. In his book, *On to Berlin*, he wrote, "About four o'clock a young ensign who had parachuted with me the first night came up with a radio and said he could call for naval gunfire. I was a bit nervous about it because we didn't know precisely where we were and to have the Navy shooting at us would only add to the danger. . . . We tried to fix our position in terms of the railroad crossing over the road, and he called for a trial round. He then called for a concentration, and from then on the battle seemed to change." Not for the last time would the big guns of the Navy aid the invaders. The tide in this encounter turned with the arrival of half a dozen Sherman tanks.

Gavin ordered an attack, employing anyone who could carry a weapon, riflemen of the paratroops, engineers, clerks, cooks, truck drivers. The Germans withdrew but not before they killed forty-two Americans, including the forward observer from the Navy, and wounded another hundred. The enemy losses were greater, but more important, the beachhead had remained intact.

Jay D. Northrup, son of a Wall Street executive and an OCS graduate, volunteered for the Rangers after he reached North Africa. He joined the 4th Battalion. "For the invasion of Sicily at Gela we sailed from North Africa on British Commando invasion boats. They were great to work from since each platoon was assigned its individual LCP (Landing Craft Personnel) and was boarded from the main deck simultaneously by all platoons and when loaded dropped to the sea at one time." Other systems required men to climb down cargo nets to landing vessels or travel across the Mediterranean on the boats that would beach them. The Commando boats allowed better coordination among groups traveling separately.

Northrup explained, "When loaded, the boats were ready to head for the beach in Vee formation following a submarine with a red light. When near the beach, the sub left and the LCPs fanned out in a straight line to land on the beach simultaneously. At Nemours a fellow kidded that they were going to tie a rope with fishhooks on it to my belt so that when we hit the beach, I, going first, would have the opportunity to trip the mines on the beach. I never gave this a second thought until I hit the beach at Gela. I was a few feet on it when I went face first to the ground, thinking about the rope and fishhooks. [I had tripped] over a cable of some type that took me out of the antiaircraft searchlights that were covering the beach and soon to be taken out by the Navy. There was no hesitation of the Rangers hitting the beach and moving into the city. The heavy storm that preceded our landing [which had so disorganized the airborne] was a blessing as the waves brought considerable sand onto to the beach and packed it tight over the Teller mines, saving many lives, I am sure."

While rampant surf neutralized mines in the sector of the 4th Ranger Battalion, the surge of the first wave from the 1st Ranger Battalion carried it into a very live field of anti-personnel Bouncing Bettys. The first explosion shredded platoon leader Lt. Walter Wojic. In swift succession more mines detonated, killing and mutilating. First Sergeant Randall Harris, his stomach held in only by his tightened cartridge belt, assumed command. He picked a path through the deadly ground, moving the men to positions where the Rangers seized an opportunity to wipe out pillboxes and machine-gun emplacements that were firing on compatriots still pouring ashore.

Among those in the 4th Battalion now hitting the beach was F Company platoon sergeant Jim Altieri. His boat had been delayed when it slowed down to pick up Rangers dumped from a craft hit by fire from defenders. He was surprised when his ramp dropped and he waded through two feet of cold water to the shore. "I couldn't believe it. Nobody was shooting at us; no mines were exploding. It was not supposed to be this easy. Before I knew it we were safely across the beach, climbing a wide path leading up to the cliff. A path, unguarded, unmined! Right past two pillboxes still acrid with grenade smoke, we climbed. Some outfit had beaten us to the punch." At terrible cost, D Company had preceded them and eliminated potential heavy opposition.

Darby, who apparently seldom missed an opportunity to personally combat the enemy, had met up with a Ranger unit assaulting Italian defenders barricaded inside a hotel. The painstaking rehearsals for house-to-house, room-to-room operations featuring grenades and submachine guns paid off and the Americans overcame the *fascisti*. Meanwhile, Altieri and his platoon approached their objective, the cathedral square at the center of Gela. A burst from a machine gun cut down the point man. "Every building bordering the square seemed to be crawling with persistent Italian gunners," remembered Altieri. "It was still pitch-black night and we could hardly see the Rangers alongside us, let alone the Italians. But we knew the difference between a Ranger walking or running and an Italian; we knew the distinctive contrast between our automatic fire and theirs, our grenade bursts and theirs; even the sounds of our men reloading their clips."

In the darkness, Altieri heard Italians talking and then the distinctive noise of leather footwear approaching. "On an inspiration, I held [Corporal James] Hildebrant's arm and yelled, *'Veni qua subito!'* [Come here quickly]. Within seconds four stocky Italians carrying their rifles at the port double-timed up to us. Their leader, thinking I was an Italian officer, actually clicked his heels to attention. Hildebrant and I jammed our rifles at them and quickly disarmed them."

Allen Merrill, the Ranger dropout assigned to an engineer battalion, had rejoined the Rangers as a scout for Altieri's F Company. He recalled the first moments of the operation as his boat bounced and splashed toward the shore. "A new replacement in our squad, Ben, whispered that he was scared shitless. I told him we all were but that didn't seem to help him. He told me he had a gut feeling he wasn't going to make it. I lied and said most of us had that feeling going into combat for the first time. As 1st Scout I was to be first man out. It was 0425 hours as we ground ashore and the ramp slapped the water. Muzzle fire from machine guns echoed in staccato blasts and tracers seemed to float overhead at the waves of troops behind us. In addition to my Thompson sub-machine gun I carried extra ammo, a pouch of grenades, both high-explosive and smoke, thirty feet of half-inch rope, a pair of wire cutters, and a nasty-looking four-foot pipe, three inches in circumference, called a bangalore torpedo, in the event we needed to blow anything up that impeded our advancement. My normal weight was 160. With this gear I weighed 220.

"I stepped off the ramp and into three feet of water. A wave covered me before I regained my footing and I spit out the water I'd swallowed and started forward, waist deep, then thigh and knee and finally onto the sandy shores of Gela Beach. Flares lit and floated above in the night sky. As we moved toward the cover of a seawall and a series of small structures, the machine gun found our range and its fire swept across the landing area. Our platoon made it to the structures along the road that slanted from the beach upward toward the town of Gela, some two hundred yards ahead." Merrill encouraged Ben, "See, you made it."

Merrill continued, "From the eerie light of bursting shells and flares I could see the face of my platoon huddled among the rubble of structures along the beach road. It was the composite face of fear, mine undoubtedly included. But there was no time to be fearful. Orders were quietly passed down. As we moved up the road keeping a low profile, the platoon leader called me and the second scout to lead the column some fifty feet ahead. I moved out; Bob [second scout] followed. The platoon moved out a few seconds later." Merrill reached the town square, but darkness hid the fountain, promenade, and marble benches carefully carved in the sand replica. Dawn broke, outlining buildings in the square, including the cathedral, across from where the Rangers huddled.

"The CO summoned Ben to act as company runner between us and those still moving up the beach road. He issued instructions for the rear company. Ben took the message and seemed to turn toward the rear. Then before anyone was aware, he ducked low and started running. But he ran in the wrong direction. In momentary confusion he ran past the wall I was behind and right across the open area. I was ready to call out but before I could he had taken perhaps three steps when a machine gun opened fire and cut him down in midstride. It was just one rapid series of shots and then all was silent again. I was looking straight ahead when he zipped past me. I saw where the shots came from across the square. There was no doubt about it; they came from the cathedral. I reported what I observed."

Quickly the Rangers devised a plan for the two squads to attack the church gunners. As daylight brightened Merrill said he plainly saw the machine gun on a tripod in the main doorway with some figures behind it. According to Merrill, he crept to within five feet. "There was still almost about ten minutes till our planned synchronized convergence on the doorway. I took one step up the three steps to the doorway. I reached out with my left foot and lifted the barrel [of their machine gun] high in the air as I tossed the grenade into the doorway. They were so surprised they never got off a single shot. When the smoke and debris settled, I stood in the doorway with my submachine gun ready. There had been three men nestled behind the gun, all were sprawled in death. Men ran from the cathedral holding their ears. I let one quick blast go from my Thompson. More men ran toward me, yelling something in Italian I did not understand. Most of them had their hands up high over their heads. My squad ended up taking more than forty prisoners."

For nearly an hour the Rangers besieged the church where

a hard core of defenders answered shot for shot. Captain Walter Nye directed Altieri, "Clean 'em out." The order shook Altieri momentarily. "Now I must spill blood on consecrated ground in a holy cathedral. Of all the situations a soldier can face, this to me was the most unpleasant. But Rangers can't waste time debating moral issues. A few more rifle pings from the tower apertures were convincing reminders that the enemy inside the holy ground was very much alive and very tenacious. I kicked the door open wide, threw in a grenade, flung myself back as the grenade exploded and, before the debris had cleared, fired eight fast rounds into a corner of the cavernous cathedral. Wincompleck, followed by McKiernan, Merrill, and Big Pruitt, rushed by me, bounded over the altar rails, shot it out with two Italians holed up in a sacristy, then fought their way up the winding tower stairs. When it was all over we had flushed out three diehard Fascists of the Livorno Division; sprawled grotesquely by the altar were two dead Italian soldiers." Altieri crossed himself, knelt, offered a silent prayer before the altar, then returned to the fighting. In the glow of morning at 6:00 A.M., the Rangers counted more than fifty prisoners and untold numbers of dead. Medics began to patch up the wounded including Randall Harris with his exposed innards. Evacuated to a hospital ship, Harris earned a Distinguished Service Cross and a battlefield commission for his leadership at Gela.

With the Gela beachhead seemingly secure, the GIs of the 1st Infantry Division waded ashore. Bill Behlmer, as an anti-tank crewman for the 1st Infantry Division, recalled, "We moved inland after the first day and the Hermann Goering Panzer Division encircled us. Tanks everywhere. We stood our ground and thought we could outlast them. The 57mms [cannons copied from the British 6-pounder] that had replaced our 37mm cannons performed beautifully. Finally their big guns had us zeroed in and the German armored infantry was advancing. We knew we had to change our positions, but we couldn't get the trucks up the hill to move our guns. I could see we were surrounded and got going. The Germans captured our guns and spiked them. The heavy cruiser *Savannah* and our own artillery saved the day. The *Savannah* steaming back and forth off the beach knocked out the tanks."

The 3d Infantry Division zeroed in on Licata for its objective. William Rosson with the 7th Regiment noted an extremely high sea. One officer on his LCI (Landing Craft, Infantry) was washed overboard. He was saved by the next boat. Sailors swam to the beach and set up lines that the troops used to struggle ashore. The opposition was light and the soldiers captured Agrigento quickly. Bill Kunz, with Headquarters Company of the 39th Field Artillery Battalion (3d Infantry Division) as part shore fire-control section, on 9 July sailed from Bizerte on an LCT (Landing Craft, Tank). "A severe storm separated us from the main convoy and we were in danger of sinking for some time. A destroyer found us and we headed for the beach at Licata very early in the morning of 10 July. Our LCT beached and was disabled by gunfire. The tank moved out to Green Beach and so did we with some Rangers and the 3d Division, 15th Infantry. We received welcome fire support from the *Nicholson, Edison, Buck, Ludlow, Roe, Swenson, Woolsey, Wickes* [destroyers] and the cruisers *Brooklyn* and *Birmingham*. The Navy ensign in charge of our disabled LCT went with us and marched the 120 miles to Palermo, on the northeast coast. He had a rough time and remarked he would never leave a Navy ship again if he lived to return to one."

Toward afternoon, a Ranger outpost noticed tanks backed

by foot soldiers, some eighteen to twenty miles off, making their way toward the Ranger perimeter. Some 1st Division troops appeared to be retreating from the armor. Binoculars identified the tanks as Renaults, lightweights used by the Italians. About ten feet from Merrill, a high-level conference of brass at Darby's command post appraised the situation. Patton, immaculate, a necktie neatly tucked into his pressed gabardine shirt, his trademark ivory-handled pistols hanging at his sides, shod in knee-high brightly burnished boots, sur-veyed the scene with Terry Allen, Teddy Roosevelt Jr., Lucian Truscott, and others. Biographer Carlo D'Este said Patton glimpsed a naval officer with a radio and shouted, "Hey, you, with the radio!" Extending his arm in the direction of the Italians, he ordered: "If you can connect with your Goddamn Navy, tell them for God's sake to drop some shell fire on the road." Soon the cruiser *Boise* obliged and began hammering the enemy tanks. Before departing, Patton instructed a captain to "kill every one of the Goddamn bas-tards."

The general, however, left the area before the armor came within range of the Americans in Gela. According to both Merrill and Altieri, Darby commandeered a lone 37mm gun in the possession of some engineers and as the first tank rat-tled up the road fired the cannon. He knocked off a tread and then put a second round through the thin-skinned vehicle. The crew climbed out to escape but Ranger sharpshooters picked them off. Darby and his 37 victimized a second tank while Ranger bazooka shells knocked out a third. A Ranger leaped atop the disabled Renault tank, lifted the hatch, and dropped in a grenade. "In the stark silence of my soul," said Merrill, "I can still hear those men scream, momentarily, and then nothing." A ricochet off the concrete roadway by one of Darby's missiles stopped a fourth tank. When a crewman emerged from the hatch with a burp gun in hand, a Ranger BAR decapitated him. Now a barrage of 4.2 chemical mortars with white phosphorus shells, "liquid fire," landed among the enemy troops and remaining armor. The soldiers fled. "In the field glasses," said Merrill, "you could see them panic and a look of terror filled their agonized faces, as they ran helter-skelter trying to avoid the spreading smokelike substance. The weapon was operated by men from the 1st Division."

Having fought off the Germans at Biazza Ridge, Gavin, expecting a renewed attack, deployed his troopers for the remainder of the night. "It must have been about 2200 hours," he said, "when all hell broke loose in the direction of the beaches. Antiaircraft fire was exploding like fireworks on the Fourth of July, tracers were whipping through the sky, and as we were observing the phenomena, the low, steady drone of airplanes could be heard. They seemed to be flying through the flak and coming in our direction. Everyone began to grasp their weapons to be ready to shoot at them. A few of us cautioned the troopers to take it easy until we understood what was going on. Suddenly at about 600 feet the silhouettes of American C-47s appeared against the sky— our own parachute transports! Some seemed to be burning; and they continued directly overhead in the direction of Gela. From the damaged planes some troopers jumped or fell. At daylight, we found some of them dead in front of our positions."

Yarborough's choice of the word "debacle" was most appropriate for Husky II. Whatever could go wrong did, and much was due to ignorance and error rather than the uncertain weather or bad luck. Yarborough remembered, "I went into the Sicilian operation on the second lift and from a personal view it was a traumatic experience. I didn't even have a map as Battalion CO. Ruben Tucker had the only one in the outfit. The briefing consisted of drawing on the ground with a stick. 'We're here. They're there. You're going to do this and they're going to do that.' "

During the daylight and early evening hours of Husky's D day, the vast array of Allied Navy ships and transports coped with repeated forays of German aircraft. There was word of German parachutists dropped as reinforcements against the British. Allied antiaircraft batteries on the ships were primed for attacks from above. Anxious not to miss the designated drop zones of Husky I, the air fleet attempted to use the invasion armada as the reference point for passage over Gela. On the night of D plus 1, a burst of gunfire from an Allied warship at the convoy of C-47s bearing the remainder of the 504th signaled open season to other vessels. The slow-moving airplanes broke formation, wheeled in desperation, tried to veer away from the deadly friendly fire. Altogether twenty-three planes were shot down, killing 318 troopers along with the air crews. Among the dead was the 82d Airborne's assistant division commander, Brig. Gen. Charles Keerans.

The surviving airplanes dispersed over the island, scattering troopers in their wakes. Tucker's airplane, with 2,000 flak holes, traveled the length of the coast twice before finally dumping the regimental commander and his stick reasonably close to his drop zone. Wherever they landed, the troopers ambushed enemy soldiers, blew up defenses, transport, and communications. As would occur in the future, the widespread dispersal of the men fooled enemy intelligence into the belief that the attackers numbered many more than actually landed.

A graduate of the Civilian Conservation Corps, Ed Sims, as a twenty-two-year-old second lieutenant and platoon leader for Company F of the 2d Battalion, remembered standing by the open door as his aircraft neared Sicily. "The night was calm and the light from the quarter moon reflected off the whitecaps of the Mediterranean Sea below. Suddenly against the dark background of the sky, a gradual buildup of fiery red tracers from below were engulfing our formation. I felt a shimmy go through our plane and then pandemonium reigned as antiaircraft guns of our own forces at sea and on the beaches were blasting our slow-flying aircraft.

"As my plane flew through the heavy flak, I could hear the hits as they penetrated. From my door position, I scanned the sky for other planes but could see only those going down in flames. My plane developed a distinct shudder and banked away from the flak with one engine starting to sputter. I had my men stand up and hook up then, before going forward to talk with the pilot. I instructed my platoon sergeant to get the men out fast if the plane started to go down.

"From the pilot I learned he had lost the formation and had a damaged starboard engine. We decided, since there was land below, that he would stay our present course and allow me a few seconds to return to the door, then turn on the green (go) light when in jump attitude. We both realized that with the heavy load he had, it would be difficult for him to fly back to North Africa. [He did make his home field with a badly damaged plane.] I rushed back to the door yelling to my men to get ready to jump. As I arrived at the door, the red (warning) light came on followed within seconds by the green light just as I hooked up. I immediately released the equipment bundles from under the plane, then jumped into the darkness with my men following.

"Landing was quick and rough. My parachute had just

opened seconds before landing. The plane must have been less than 300 feet above the ground. When assembled, I learned that one man had been injured when he hit a stone fence. I sent patrols in opposite directions on a nearby road to look for signs and landmarks. One patrol located a road sign indicating that Augusta was forty kilometers. This was sufficient to locate our general position on the map as about twenty-five miles from where we planned to land in the vicinity of Gela. Also we were several miles behind the German forces opposing the landing of the 45th Division. I had fourteen men with me so we moved in a southwesterly direction toward Gela. At one point we had a short firefight with a small German force, but they soon fled. Later we spotted a company-size German force moving north but since they did not see us, we held our fire and let them pass. Our next contact was with advance elements of the 45th Division. They opened fire on us and for a few moments the situation was dangerous. We had a tough job convincing them we were U.S. paratroopers."

Lucas offered a highly negative appraisal of the air drops, four days after Gavin and his regiment struck Sicily. "Judging from this operation, I am extremely doubtful of the value of airborne troops. The losses in men and planes are heavy and not paid for by the results accomplished. The results would be of great value, of course, if the Air Corps could put these people where the plan calls for them to be. They don't seem able to do this.

"The paratroopers knocked out a Mark VI tank with a 75mm howitzer. It must have been a lucky shot. The bazooka didn't hurt it. The other Mark VIs we got were knocked out by the 75mm antitank guns. We lost six tanks to their three. The paratroopers spread over a huge area and many of them like Gavin's battalion [that of Dunfee] east of

Gela did excellent work. . . . But they were not landed where they were supposed to be. . . . Some paratroopers were shot by an outpost last night when they did not know the proper countersign."

Lucas attributed the Husky II disaster to the tardiness of the Air Corps in providing the routes for their planes and for them being so far off course. "These planes have a knack for coming over at the worst possible time. One group came over a unit that had just been bombed and strafed by the Germans and the poor devils thought, which I can understand, that the Hun was on their backs again so they opened fire." He added the comment, "Air refused to bring any more airborne in, because of the unfortunate fact that some planes had been shot down by ground troops." [Lucas ignored the major source of friendly fire, the navy ships.]

Although the first counterattacks had been beaten back by the paratroopers and the Rangers, the infantry divisions seeking to drive deeper into Sicily coped with stiff resistance and the ambitions of British and American generals. The Husky chief, Alexander, considered the GIs inferior combat soldiers. He sought to use them as a blocking force to protect what he considered the superior army under Bernard Montgomery. The top brass bickered over who should attack along which axis, without regard for which units enjoyed the best opportunity to hammer the foe. The squabbling cost lives as American artillery that could have aided a Canadian brigade held its fire rather than trespass across the demarcation line separating the Allied armies.

John Lucas scorned the ally: "The British are rather surprisingly slow. Two reasons . . . 1. Strong opposition. 2. Montgomery is notorious for the meticulous care with which he prepares for his operations. This virtue . . . can become an obsession that finally defeats its object. He will not move until everything, every last ration and round of ammunition, is ashore and in its proper place. This was needed in the desert against Rommel. Here [Sicily] speed would seem to be the better part of wisdom. Destroy the enemy before he can be reinforced from the mainland.

"Patton has done a splendid job in this operation but neither Eisenhower nor Alexander have mentioned that fact as yet." Indeed, D'Este notes that the supreme commander had reservations about his Seventh Army commander, whom he blamed for both the airborne disaster and the inadequacy of communications to Malta about the progress of Husky. To individuals like Lucas who found fault with Alexander, Eisenhower confided, "[that] he had never seen a case where the British tried to put anything over on us. He said, put myself in Alexander's place. He first came in contact with American troops when the fighting at Kasserine and Gafsa was going on. They did so poorly that the British lost confidence in us as offensive troops. Later the same division [the 1st] did well in Tunisia but in Sicily there were two new divisions, the 45th had no combat experience and the 3d with only a little. . . ."

According to Lucas, Eisenhower felt Patton should stand up to Alexander. "He would not hesitate to relieve him from command if he did not do so." When Eisenhower praised Bradley [II Corps commander] and Truscott [in command of the 3d Division], Lucas disagreed. "Terry Allen's 1st Division had done most of the fighting. I pointed out that while other division COs received Distinguished Service Medals, Allen, who had been much more involved, did not."

While the generals politicked and sniped at one another, the men in the field hustled forward. Bill Dunfee's airborne regimental combat team marched up the west coast. "It was increasingly obvious," said Dunfee, "that the Germans were sacrificing the Italian Army in a delaying action. This allowed them to evacuate most of their units across the Strait of Messina into Italy. The Germans did abandon huge quantities of materiel. The Italians were something less than enthusiastic fighters, and gave up after a token effort of defense. This was of little comfort to our wounded and was very frustrating to those of us that had to take them prisoner."

The American foot soldiers, reinforced by the arrival of the 2d Armored Division, steadily advanced. Bill Kunz of the 3d Division was with an infantry column bound for Palermo on the northwest coast. "We were learning some hard-taught lessons. The enemy were masters with booby traps. Enemy bodies may explode if moved. Also equipment, and the same went for enemy weapons. Any likely looking resting place is dangerous. One GI picked up a soap bar and gave it to a family. Later it went off. We took a lot of casualties from mines and booby traps."

Patton's Seventh Army rolled up the western half of Sicily rapidly and within two weeks occupied Marsala on the extreme western tip and Palermo on the north. Montgomery's Eighth Army to the east moved slowly against defenders protected by emplacements on towering Mount Etna and their determination to buy time for the evacuation of men and gear through Messina. Montgomery, aware of the strength that prevented his army from breaking through to Messina, invited Patton to cross the hitherto sacrosanct boundaries and capture the prize of that port. For all of the flak about "God Almonty" and the image of an overbearing, conceited Briton, Montgomery was a general who, said Carlo D'Este, abhorred the "senseless waste of men so casually practiced by the British leadership [of World War I]." Patton, who had uncharacteristically bided his time, snatched the opportunity. He sent the 3d Division along the northern edge of the island toward Messina while the 45th and 1st battered the enemy from the center of Sicily. The going was particularly difficult for Terry Allen's GIs, who received help from the 9th Division.

Patton himself raced back and forth to the various fronts and on 17 August, less than six weeks after the beginning of Operation Husky, he led a convoy into Messina, where an advance guard from the 3d Division beat an amphibious force dispatched by Montgomery. The city was in ruins from constant shelling and aerial bombardments and now the new residents ducked incoming from the Germans in Calabria, just across the strait.

More than Sicily was devastated at the end of Husky. Bill Dunfee remarked on the anger against the supposedly unenthusiastic Italian defenders who nevertheless inflicted serious casualties. Because of the killed and wounded, as well as the unpleasant experiences with booby traps, attitudes harshened and triggered at least one war crime. At Biscari a sergeant and a captain from the 45th Division murdered seventy-three Italian prisoners. The shooters faced separate court-martials. The sergeant offered a defense that combined the claim of extreme emotional stress with an impression that Patton and lesser officers had directed the troops to take prisoners only under limited circumstances. Found guilty, he received a sentence of life but higher authorities commuted the term, simply stripping him of his stripes.

The captain argued that his actions reflected instructions from superiors and cited his memory of a Patton speech. "When we land against the enemy, don't forget to hit him and hit him hard. We will bring the fight home to him. When we meet the enemy, we will kill him. We will show him no mercy. He has killed thousands of your comrades and he must die. If you company officers in leading your men against the enemy find him shooting at you, and, when you get within two hundred yards of him, he wishes to surrender, oh, no! That bastard will die. You will kill him. Stick him between the third and fourth ribs. You will tell your men they must have the killer instinct. Tell them to stick him. . . . We will get the names of killers and killers are immortal. When word reaches him that he is being faced by a killer battalion, a killer outfit, he will fight less. . . ."

Subsequently, a soldier swore, "We were told that General Patton said, 'Fuck them. No prisoners!' " An officer reported Patton as having said, "The more prisoners we took, the more we'd have to feed, and not to fool with prisoners." In a letter to his wife Beatrice, Patton wrote, ". . . these Boches and the Italians that are left are grand fighters, [they] have pulled the white flag trick four times. We take few prisoners." The officer in the dock insisted, "I ordered them shot because I thought it came directly under the general's instructions. Right or wrong, a three-star general's advice, who has combat experience, is good enough for me and I took him at his word." Acquitted, the captain later was killed in action.

While engaged in the final campaign to capture Messina, Patton visited the tents of the 15th Evacuation Hospital outside Nicosia. In the wards lay the latest casualties of the fighting, mostly GIs from the 1st Division. Among the patients, Patton encountered Pvt. Charles H. Kuhl with no visible wounds. When Patton inquired why Kuhl was there, the soldier answered, "I guess I can't take it." Patton instantly flew into a rage, berated Kuhl as a coward, and ordered him from the tent. When the soldier failed to move, the general slapped him in the face with his glove, grabbed him by the collar, shoved him out, and kicked him in his backside. On the scene, John Lucas noted in his diary, "We stopped at an evacuation hospital to visit the wounded and try to cheer them up. Brave, hurt, bewildered boys. All but one, that is, because he said he was nervous and couldn't take it. Anyone who knows him can realize what that would do to George. The weak sister was really nervous when he got through."

Patton's ire still raged when he wrote in his diary that night, "Companies should deal with such men, and if they shirk their duty, they should be tried for cowardice and shot." Two days later, he distributed a memo decrying the presence in hospitals of soldiers "on the pretext that they are nervously incapable of combat. Such men are cowards and bring discredit on the army and disgrace to their comrades, whom they heartlessly leave to endure the dangers of battle while they, themselves, use the hospital as means of escape." He ordered commanders to prevent them from hospitalization and arrange courts-martial "for cowardice in the face of the enemy."

His rampage against GIs diagnosed with "battle fatigue," "shell shock," "combat neurosis" continued at the 93d Evacuation Hospital. There he blasted Pvt. Paul G. Bennett, a shivering artilleryman who confessed his problem was "my nerves." The general snarled, "Your nerves. Hell, you are just a goddamned coward, you yellow son of a bitch. Shut up that goddamned crying. I won't have these brave men here who have been shot seeing a yellow bastard sitting here crying." Patton went so far as to draw one of his ornately handled pistols from his holster and threaten, "I ought to shoot you myself right now, God damn you." He ordered the quivering Bennett out of the tent, slapped him in the face, and heaped curses upon the bawling soldier. The general started to walk off, then turned and smacked Bennett a second time with such force that he knocked his helmet liner off. Before he finally left, Patton addressed the hospital commander: "I won't have those cowardly bastards hanging around our hospitals. We'll probably have to shoot them sometime anyway or we'll raise a breed of morons."

Patton was anything but regretful about the incident. He drove to the II Corps command post and breezily told Omar Bradley he had just slapped around a malingerer. When the hospital authorities through the chain of command notified Bradley, he filed the papers in his safe on the grounds he would not approach Eisenhower over Patton's head. But too many individuals had witnessed these scenes for them to pass without notice, and the press picked up the story.

Subsequently, Patton would confess to an associate he had been "a damn fool" in both cases. But his admission of an error in his behavior never meant that he believed battle exhaustion acceptable, but only that he had lost his composure in striking an enlisted man. Ironically, he himself may well have been a victim of the same type of emotional distress he despised in others.

John Lucas continued to dismiss the occurrence, referring to it as "the slapping incident which created so much furor in the papers in the States. I saw nothing serious about it at the time. There are always a number of such weaklings in any army." He added, "George has never grown up and is still about eight years old. He can't see that commanding an army is different from commanding a division. All the men in a division know the commander and understand his peculiarities."

After an investigation into the facts, Eisenhower tried to save Patton's career. "I felt that Patton should be saved for service in the great battles still facing us in Europe." He tried to lift him off the hook through a strong reprimand and directed he apologize to the patients. Patton complied, although D'Este says it was on the advice of John Lucas, rather than because of a demand by Eisenhower. However, the furor in the States forced Eisenhower to relieve him.

The ax also fell on Terry Allen. According to Omar Bradley, "Early in the Sicilian campaign I had made up my mind to relieve Terry Allen at its conclusion. This relief was not to be a reprimand for ineptness or for ineffective command. . . . Under Allen the 1st Division had become increasingly temperamental, disdainful of both regulations and senior commands. It thought itself exempted from the need for discipline by virtue of its months on the line." Bradley added, "Allen had become too much of an individualist to submerge himself without friction in the group undertakings of war. The 1st Division under Allen's command had become too full of self-pity and pride. To save Allen both from himself and from his brilliant record and to save the division from the heady effects of too much success, I decided to separate them."

As early as 28 July, Lucas's diary reported, "I gave [Eisenhower] a letter from Patton recommending the relief of Allen and Roosevelt from the 1st Division. Terry's relief is to be 'without prejudice' and I hope he will be given a command at home. The boy is tired." Why the knives were honed for Terry Allen is a matter of conjecture. He was never a part of the club, having quit the Military Academy just short of graduation. His enjoyment of carousing with his staff in off-duty hours would not have endeared him to the straight-laced Bradley. As D'Este points out, the public thought of Bradley as a "plain, soft-spoken general with whom the average civilian could readily identify. If truth is the first casualty of war, so was the pretense that Omar Bradley was a general of the masses, an image that Bradley himself gladly encouraged for the remainder of his life. The real Omar Bradley was somewhat narrow-minded and utterly intolerant of failure." Physically, Bradley may have appeared almost grandfatherly and he never displayed the flamboyance of Patton, but he was equally demanding for the niceties of the profession.

Although Allen was respected by Patton, who demanded he have the 1st Division for the critical attack on Gela, theirs was a testy relationship, perhaps a natural result of competition and ambition. Allen would have proudly agreed that he had enormous concern for the welfare of his people. He would have had compassion for those who broke down under stress; it is difficult to imagine that he would ever have struck a hospitalized soldier. Indeed, when Allen returned to combat in Europe to command the 104th Division he received a letter from a father worried about his son. Allen wrote back, "I can readily understand your worry regarding him and your anxiety to secure accurate information regarding his welfare. I have just sent for your son, have talked to him and find he's in fine shape and doing well. The division has been fighting hard since 23 October and so far have had marked success without excessive losses when their accomplishments are considered. Your son and the other boys like him have been largely responsible for the combat success of the division." There are no similar letters to be found in Patton's file and very few if any among the papers of other World War II commanders.

The choice for Allen's successor, Maj. Gen. Clarence Huebner, probably delighted all of Allen's detractors. Lucas had noted with approval that the British "fired Huebner who was on duty at General Alexander's headquarters. Too virile an American." Bradley praised the new commander as "a strict disciplinarian." The GIs in the 1st Division, however, felt they had lost a fine leader and the Rangers attached to the Big Red One agreed.

# 2

# Island Ventures

ON 8 DECEMBER, MARINE GENERAL ALEXANDER ARCHER VAN-degrift, taking with him the 1st Marine Division, relinquished his command over the ground forces on Guadalcanal to Army general Alexander M. Patch. To root out the remaining Japanese, Patch would field all of the components of the Americal Division, some lingering Marine units, and troops from the 25th, 37th, and 43d Divisions. The quality of American air power in the Pacific improved dramatically. The twin-engine P-38 fighter replaced many of the P-40s. The Lightning flew high enough and fast enough to contend with the Zero even if it gave away some advantage in turns. The F4U Chance-Vought Corsair, a misfit for carrier warfare, gave Marine pilots at Henderson Field a weapon superior to the Wildcat. The latter was itself supplanted by the much faster F6F Hellcat. The Army bomber command accepted the futility of high-altitude attacks against ships and innovated low-level skip-bombing by the two-engine B-25s and B-26s, much to the detriment of enemy shipping.

The capture of islands and advances in New Guinea allowed greater use of land-based planes and participation of the Air Corps along with the Marine and Navy flyers who used flattops. Robert DeHaven, a P-40 replacement pilot, wore the wings given his father for World War I. In Australia, he entered a combat replacement training unit [RTU]. "We had about three or four weeks working on combat formation and tactics before we were sent up to the line at New Guinea. When I got to the squadron and actual combat I had just shy of fifty hours in the P-40."

The indoctrination was rudimentary. "You didn't try to dogfight with a Zero. We had a lot of classes in aircraft recognition. One of the major discussions about the war in New Guinea was the problem of survival. If you went down in the water you could expect sharks. Everybody had shark repellent, which didn't work. If you went down [over land] you hoped to find friendly natives. Living in the jungle, escape planning and routes was essentially meaningless. The idea of anybody trying to walk out by himself was just ridiculous. We carried little pidgin English books, where, if we could find a friendly native and talk to him, the chances of getting out were improved. The .45 we wore in a shoulder holster was meaningless. In twenty-four hours the gun would be so rusted it would be useless. If you used it you gave yourself away. The Aussie liaison officers, former territorial wardens or representatives of mining companies before the war, emphasized that the jungle is a harsh place but also your friend. If you felt you had to fight your way out, use a knife. Keep it quiet. Strike and get back in the bush. Five feet off a trail you couldn't be seen."

To discourage Japanese soldiers in the wilds of New

Guinea, the natives received bounties in mother-of-pearl shells, their medium of exchange, for each set of Japanese ears brought in. DeHaven said he saw local people hiking down roads with a string of such trophies, as many as two dozen hanging from their loin cloths as they went to collect. "But as far as intimate combat information, we got very little until we reached our squadrons. Then the older heads in the outfit [got] us into innumerable sessions about tactics, strategies, conditions, engagements, etc."

DeHaven joined the 7th Fighter Squadron, 49th Fighter Group at Dobodura. "The first thing we had to do was build our own house. All of the quarters were sixteen by sixteen pyramidal tents set up on six-foot posts so the insects and snakes couldn't get in. The posts and platform for the tent had to be built by somebody and that somebody was the fellows going to occupy them. They had a practice of putting one old head in with three new pilots." DeHaven recalled the chief amenity was a fresh egg once a month and no matter how late an individual had stayed up or how severe his hangover, when the ration of eggs arrived, every man was roused from bed.

The 49th Group consisted of two P-40 squadrons and one P-38 unit. The limited range of the P-40 required the enemy to meet the Americans halfway in most instances while the P-38s flew and fought over much greater distances. DeHaven remarked that the kill ratio for the P-38 9th Squadron was greater by almost two to one. "The 9th had as many, if not more, aces than any other squadron in the Pacific. The 49th Fighter Group became the highest-scoring fighter group in the history of the Air Force. That is strictly in aerial kills. In the Pacific we did not count aircraft destroyed on the ground, half victories, quarter victories. If there were two people that had shot at an airplane and it was a question of who was to get credit, they flipped a coin."

DeHaven remembered his elation when he was given his own P-40 and allowed to paint his name and personal insignia on it. "I was the proudest son of a bitch in the world. Here I am in combat. My own airplane, my very own crew chief. The crew chief was a very helpful force facing into combat. For instance, the kind of damage that he had seen, what he knew the airplane could absorb. We had an armament section but the armorers only worked on the airplane with the forbearance of the crew chief, as did radio or anyone else. When he said the ammunition was loaded and he'd checked out the guns, you didn't have to fire a burst. You knew they were going to work. He was God on that airplane. When he said it was ready to fly, you didn't make a walkaround check. That would have been insulting. You got in and you flew."

For most of his first half-dozen missions, DeHaven flew under a leader named Ray Melikian, the operations officer, who apparently was blessed with superkeen eyesight. These first sorties carried DeHaven toward Lae, in search of shipping, but the newcomers all yearned for a crack at enemy fighters. "On occasion, Ray called in 'bandits high' when nobody else could see them. After a fast circle climb eventually the rest of us would see the gaggle, eight or ten Zeroes or Oscar fighters. We would continue circling full bore but we didn't attack and pretty soon Ray decided he just couldn't get an advantage and took us home.

"We young bucks would get excited as hell and irritable because we hadn't taken them on. He would sit us down and say, 'Gentlemen, give me just one tiny advantage—airspeed, altitude, or both—to make one run through them and you'll get your shot . . . and we're going to keep right on going, nobody turns around.' He wanted that flight intact. He didn't want people scattering on their own and getting picked off. He drilled firmly on formation integrity."

Melikian reiterated the common wisdom that advised against trying to climb away from a Zero or seek to turn into one. He warned against solo combat but in DeHaven's first opportunity to shoot at an enemy plane, he violated the precept. Along with the operations chief he dove on a pair of low-flying Val bombers. DeHaven remembered, "Ray came in astern of the Val, snapped off a shot with no apparent effect and pulled up as we overran him. There was scattered cloud cover, and we busted out on top of that, made a big fast turn and came around again. As we did I saw a P-40 go by underneath me, almost inverted and shooting at the second Val. It was also in a turn so the P-40 overshot him. Ray didn't appear to see this, so I broke formation and made a descending roll. I was directly behind the Val—overtaking him. I pulled the power back some and as I slowed down, I noticed these funny-looking little red balls zipping by over my canopy. The Goddamned gunner in the back of the Val was shooting at me. First time I'd ever been shot at and at first I didn't realize what it was. I was really surprised. Not scared, just surprised—and indignant. The adrenaline was really flowing. I settled slightly below and behind him, watched him fill the sight, then cut loose. In the barrage I burned up five out of six guns, but he slowly rolled over and went straight into the water. Later, I got my ass chewed royally and rightly. I was forcefully reminded but gratefully not belabored about it. The older heads recognized that there was a degree of impetuousness about youngsters in combat—you could expect many were going to get excited and do something they had been told not to do."

That same encounter also saw a veteran of the squadron

forced to bail out after the rear gunner on a Val shot out his coolant. "When Bob Lee went into the water, we saw him inflate his vest but not his seat raft. We all had both. We didn't know at the time but one of his arms was broken and he had tucked it inside his vest. He couldn't get to the lanyards on the raft with only one good arm. We put in a call back to base to try to get a PT boat to pick him up. There were one or two that were working along the coast. Then we started circling to begin our shark-strafing session. It was inevitable, those waters are loaded with sharks and, good God, some are massive. We got a couple. You would see a big splotch of red and then a great thrashing as other sharks tore into the one that was hit. It only took a moment and then they would go back to circling Bob. We tried other things. I got my seat raft out from underneath me and started down. I wound back the canopy, laid the raft on the crook of my left arm, holding the lanyard in my hand. I got the airplane just as slow as I would get it and level about twenty feet off the water. I got lined up on Bob and when I thought I was over him, I flipped that raft out, holding onto the lanyard so the raft would open up as it fell down to him. What I didn't consider was that the raft was packed in a preservative powder. I had on a pair of sunglasses. When the raft went out, the powder flew back and the world disappeared. There I was, sitting five knots above stall and maybe twenty feet off the water. I jammed the throttle forward and, as frequently happens when you jam a throttle, the engine coughs momentarily. Mine did and that got my attention." While Lee was unable to retrieve the raft, a PT boat rescued him while DeHaven cleared his glasses and made it home.

There, in addition to the scolding from his superiors, he also absorbed a lecture from the crew chief. "He explained to me how one could become defenseless with frozen guns.

It meant you fired in bursts too long, causing the barrels and breeches to overheat. When the shells slammed into the chamber, they'd expand and jam. The eject mechanism would not pull open the spent cartridge shells. So concentrate on firing in short bursts.

"When you've got one in your sights and you know you're hitting him, it's the most difficult thing in the world to release that trigger. The tendency is to keep pouring it on. Soon you've got four guns firing, then three, then two . . . that really doesn't take very long. In a P-40, a five-second burst would put all six guns out of commission. You never wanted to fire more than one or two-second bursts if you wanted to stay in business. Another lesson the crew chief gave was getting the guns out and changing all those barrels. He made me attend the entire procedure."

Like most fighter pilots, DeHaven found air-to-ground work less rewarding than aerial combat. "There's rarely anything to score in air-to-ground," he remarked. "It's not a mano-a-mano situation. For the most part, at least in the jungle, you are shooting at a blind target. You can't see anything; you are shooting at a grid mark, a set of coordinates, or a smoke bomb. Once in a while, early in the war, 1943, we had many opportunities for shipping targets. That was fun because, if good enough, you could sink a boat with P-40 gunfire. We did an awful lot of dive-bombing. The basic problem was you never knew where your opposition was. There's nothing more irritating or distracting than to suddenly see 20mm or 40mm bursts coming up on you right out of a clump of coconut trees and you can't shoot back because you can't see the guns. You might see some smoke coming out of the bush, go down and strafe it but while you're doing that another clump over there suddenly opens up. It's distracting and hardly fun.

"Air-to-air is something else. This is essentially a man-to-man proposition. Actually, I can't say man-to-man because you never consider an airplane as occupied by an individual or human. It's just a piece of machinery. There were times when air-to-air combat was a little more personal, when a man bailed out, a rare occurrence in the Pacific. It was quite common in Europe and the Mediterranean. But in the Pacific, I don't think I saw more than half a dozen enemy pilots bail out during two tours. The situation was magnified by the brevity of Pacific combat. You rarely engaged more than a minute or two. Ninety percent of your fights were hit and run."

The limited number of parachutes observed by DeHaven may have had something to do with increasing savagery. He admitted shooting one enemy in his chute. "They actually started the parachute strafing in China. They pulled it on us first, too. Moreover, since most of our combat was over enemy territory, the possibility of a Jap who bailed out getting safely home was pretty good. The rationale was, why give him a second chance to come back and get you? If we bailed out, we expected to get shot at and the possibility of coming home was nil. If you were captured by the Japanese you were essentially dead. They didn't ship prisoners from New Guinea all the way back to a prison. They couldn't afford to do it. They executed prisoners; that was well documented. Those they didn't [kill] they starved or beat to death. The farther they were from the home island, the less likely they were to keep prisoners because they were a burden. They had to feed them, care for them, and the Japs were having enough trouble feeding their own troops."

The dismal prospects if shot down bothered some airmen enough so they were sent home. "We had two," recalled DeHaven. "They had chronic engine trouble—almost every flight they would turn back before they got fifty miles from the field. Back on the ground, the crew couldn't find anything wrong with the engines."

The code breakers scored a great coup when they intercepted a radio message from Rabaul detailing a forthcoming inspection of Japanese facilities on Bougainville by the architect of the Pearl Harbor attack, and the man considered the guiding light of Imperial Navy warfare, Admiral Yamamoto. Nine Zeros accompanied the two bombers bearing the admiral and his staff. Eighteen P-38s ambushed the covey, scattering the escorts. The U.S. flight leader, Capt. Thomas G. Lamphier Jr., blasted Yamamoto's plane with his 20mm cannon. The aircraft burst into flames and crashed in the jungle. There were no survivors.

Having occupied Guadalcanal and turned away the Japanese seeking to expand their hold on New Guinea, the American forces in the Pacific pursued the strategy of island hopping. The losses at sea while trying to land soldiers on Guadalcanal set the Imperial Navy far enough back on its heels to allow bloodless conquests of the Russell Islands close to Guadalcanal. Admiral Nimitz and his staff agreed the next logical target was New Georgia, another link in the Solomon chain bordering the Slot. New Georgia, and a clump of islands closest to it—Rendova, Arundel, Kolombangara, and Vangunu—were obvious stepping-stones for the offense, not only because of the location, but also because the enemy had chosen to build an airfield at Munda Point on New Georgia. That base could threaten the American forces on New Guinea as well as block progress toward points closer to the Philippines and eventually the home islands.

Over a period of months small groups of Americans slipped ashore on New Georgia to scout out the terrain, examine the beaches, pinpoint optimum locations for artillery, and pick up intelligence on the deployment of the enemy troops. Although the turf came under the jurisdiction of Nimitz, the most available ground force was the Army's 43d Infantry Division, which went ashore on Guadalcanal too late to encounter the Japanese. Also scheduled for the initial assault on New Georgia were some Marine Raiders and elements of the 37th Infantry Division that had been dug in around Henderson Field to protect the base against infiltrators or snipers.

On 22 June 1943, leathernecks from the 4th Marine Raider Battalion, carried by destroyers, stepped onto a secluded beach at Segi, where a small enclave of native constabulary under Maj. Donald Kennedy, a New Zealander, acted as coast watchers and guerrilla fighters. After getting their bearings, a company led by Tony Walker, a Yale graduate, in rubber boats and canoes set out for an objective, the harbor at Viru along the coast away from the Slot. Raider Roger Spaulding recalled, "The third night ashore, we assembled in the quiet lagoon waters for the raid on Viru. Fifty assorted boats gathered in the darkness, were boarded by the Raiders and about thirty natives. Heavy equipment like the radio and mortar shells were loaded on a magnificent native canoe that carried about twenty men, mostly native paddlers and the native sergeant.

"Under the mangrove trees at times and under the brilliant stars, we paddled until well past midnight and finally landed at a tiny shore village [some eight miles from Segi] where huts had been built above the water on stilts. We pushed our rubber boats through the mud and pig pens and moved on up to dry land. The boats were quickly pulled back on the water and tied to each other. They were towed back to Segi before sunup. We tried to eradicate any evidence of our passing by wiping the mud behind ourselves and praying there would be a heavy rain before dawn [to conceal their presence], but it did not rain. The Japanese did find our tracks and a small patrol harmed the natives even though the natives participated not at all either for or against us. Truly hapless innocents of the war.

"As miserable as was the edge of the swamp outside the village, the place was a Garden of Eden compared with what we went through the next four days. Mud was ankle- to knee-deep all the way. Every step was slippery and the muscular action required to stay afoot was exhausting. The farther back in the column a Raider was, the harder [it was]. Hundreds of feet stirred up the mud and made it deeper as we went. Then, too, the rains came and went and the trail became a long necklace of small, deep mud puddles. Rivers were almost welcome as a time to cool off and rinse off the muck. We crossed one river, the Choi, at least three times, as we went in sort of a straight line, but the river coiled like a snake through the jungle. At each crossing the banks were a special hardship because entry and exit slopes on the banks became a mud pit waist-deep. It had to be crossed for several feet before the bank dropped off into shoulder-deep water.

"Only Raiders who were close to six feet tall could cross with head above water. Shorter Raiders were lifted by the man in front and behind to keep their heads up. Rifles, machine guns, and BARs were hoisted above our heads to keep out the mud and water. All else went underwater, packs, bullets, and all. Things like cigarettes, matches, and coffee grounds were tied tightly in rubberized pouches to keep dry and usable." Through the pitch-black nights, the Marines, led by their native guides, tied pieces of phosphorescent twigs and pieces of luminous rotting wood to the person in front in order to follow him.

"I was on the point with Corporal Tower and Private Harbord," said then-private Milton J. "Cajun" Robert. "We crossed the river [Choi] and kept going until we came to the crest of a hill where the native threw up his head as he smelled the Japs and said, 'Japs come.' He took off immediately on the right of the trail and so did Harbord and I. Tower was killed immediately on the trail. Harbord emptied his M1 from behind a large banyan tree. I turned my BAR sideways so it would not walk up as I fired and let the first twenty rounds go. I think we were about fifteen minutes ahead of our outfit. The Nips were chattering a hell of a lot. A hell of a lot of them went to my left as I continued firing. Could even hear their hobnail shoes hitting the roots of trees. They opened up with a machine gun no more than thirty-five to forty yards away. I threw grenades, holding [them] three to four seconds because they were so close.

"[I] was about to raise up and fire again as a head started to rise on the other side of the root I was behind. Backed up a little and shot his head off! I also popped a shot at a Jap officer with a sword, shot at his head as he came up behind his men. Horse Taylor later told me that I shot the back of his head off and that he, Horse, had placed his machine gun right by him and shot him again with his .45 because he was still alive." That firefight cost the Raiders five dead and one wounded, but with further resistance suppressed, Tony Walker's company continued toward Viru Harbour. After Cajun Robert killed the enemy machine-gun crew he saw a boat below a 150-foot cliff begin to pull away. He immediately opened fire and Taylor joined in with his machine gun. Robert learned later that seventeen Japanese soldiers, accompanied by three pregnant Tonganese women, had been aboard.

Private First Class Bill Thompson, in the antitank section, participated in the attack. His leader ordered, "Bill, go back and tell Captain Walker to knock off the mortar fire. We now have men in the enemy positions." Thompson zigzagged toward the captain's position and a sniper put a bullet clean through his pack. When he reached Walker's approximate location, Thompson said he called out the code name for the commander, " 'Cold Steel! Cold Steel!' I received no response so I kept yelling. Finally, I committed the unpardonable sin—I yelled, 'Captain Walker! Captain Walker!' I heard him yell back at me, 'Right here, Major, what the hell do you want?' That was the fastest promotion and demotion I ever had."

Cajun Robert cautiously explored the scene. "Corporal Green called to me about the machine-gun position I shot out and said, 'Cajun, this one is alive and playing dead. What are we going to do with him?' I told him to stick him. Just then Father Redmond [the battalion chaplain] came up and I said ix-nay to Green. Father Redmond wanted to know what was the matter and we told him that this one was still alive. He made the sign of the cross and said, 'May God have mercy on his soul,' and kept going. Green then looked at me and I said, 'Stick him, dammit!' We then threw him over the cliff. Before leaving, we formed a seven-man squad and fired a twenty-one-gun salute to our dead." Altogether the expedition to Viru and environs left thirteen Americans dead and another fifteen wounded.

On 30 June, the first elements of the U.S. invasion force occupied Vangunu and effectively eliminated the garrison. The Japanese, apparently unaware of the American success, dispatched three barges packed with reinforcements and supplies to Vangunu from New Georgia. Marines from the 4th Raider Battalion and infantrymen from the 103d Regiment of the 43d Division ambushed the landing craft, killing all but a few of the 120 estimated passengers.

On 1 July, GIs from the 43d's 172d Regiment and elements from the 103d widened their beachhead on Rendova. Separated from New Georgia by a narrow strait, Rendova had been chosen as a staging area for the invasion to capture the Munda Point air base. Because the distance between Rendova and New Georgia was so small, the former could provide a platform for long-range shelling of the Japanese. No one, however, had counted on what the rain would do to such well-laid plans. Seabees from the Navy labored to create roads over muck that drowned huge logs and steel mats. Foxholes became bathtubs as the rains pelted down. Artillerymen struggled to dig firm emplacements and clear the towering palms for fire lanes. A surprise attack by Japanese bombers killed a number of Seabees, destroyed earthmovers, and blew up supplies. A covey of enemy warships that pumped hundreds of shells onto the water-logged tenants of Rendova inflicted much less damage.

On 2 July, just after midnight, the 1st Battalion of the 172d Regiment loaded into landing craft to cross the treacherous, reef-ridden channel to New Georgia itself. The soldiers expected to wade ashore at Zanana Beach, undefended according to intelligence. When the canoeborne native guides vanished with their signal lamps, chaos followed. Boats piled up on a reef. In the blackness of night, coxswains bawled questions and directions to one another; engines reversed and then thrust forward; boats collided. The disorder so appalled the commander that he ordered a return to Rendova, while sending a couple of hardy souls to furtively examine Zanana.

A few men never got the word to head home and together the Americans scouted the area, coming away with the knowledge that no enemy troops protected the shores of Zanana. To avoid another nighttime fiasco, on Independence Day 1943, the 1st Battalion stepped onto the beach during daylight hours and quickly advanced far enough for a perimeter some 500 yards beyond the water. By 5 July, the 43d Division could commence its drive to Munda Field. At the same time, the Japanese commander, now fully aware of the American intentions, drew in whatever troops he could to repel the Americans.

Private First Class Sam LaMagna, who as a former National Guardsman remembered wrap leggings, World War I rifles, and stove pipes to represent mortars, at Zanana wore and bore the latest equipment, but nothing had prepared him for the ordeal. "The first couple of nights gave us a taste of what jungle warfare was all about. The Japs were experts. They were Imperial Marines, the elite armed forces of Japan who had fought in China for many years. Munda Trail was thick with trees, brush undergrowth, vines. Sound was more important than sight. You could hear someone before you could see him. After many casualties, we learned to fight a Jap war. At night, stay in your hole until the surrounding area has been sprayed with machine gun and BARs. Sort of like spraying for mosquitoes. You can't see them but they're there. At first daylight, Jap snipers would shoot anyone walking around or into our foxholes. They tied themselves up in trees and it was a great morale booster to see Japs hanging after machine-gun and BAR bursts.

"At night it was an individual war with everyone fighting for his life. The screams pierced the jungle night and sent chills up my spine. Art Delorge, Syl Bottone, and Gildo Consolini stayed in different foxholes. Farmer Bederski and

I shared one. At first break of dawn we'd peek over and wave, as if to say, 'Hey, I'm okay.' One morning Syl and Gildo waved back but not Art. Farmer came back and notified us Art was killed by his foxhole buddy who thought Art was a Jap and panicked. Art was bayoneted. Later Gildo was killed by a Jap at night. Every morning I'd hear who was killed or wounded. Company F [172d Reg.] had about 30 percent casualties and the men were getting jittery. Rumors went around that the Japs were yanking GIs out of their holes by the helmets and to keep helmets unbuckled. At night I could hear teeth chattering."

LaMagna remembered a soldier he called Joe who clearly showed signs of distress. When LaMagna shared a foxhole with Joe one night, he awoke to find his companion about to toss a grenade, followed moments later by a loud tirade that pinpointed their position. LaMagna eventually quieted him by rapping him in the mouth with a .45 pistol and threatening to blow his head off. The platoon sergeant volunteered to control Joe the following night. Shots erupted from the sergeant's foxhole along with cries of "Shoot him! Shoot him, or he'll kill us all!"

"By now all the Japs knew our positions," said LaMagna, "and sent in a barrage of artillery and mortar rounds. My first thought was Joe and when shells started to explode all around me I drew my knees up against my chest and prayed. A shell landed near my hole and felt like someone hit me across the head with a baseball bat. My hole caved in and I passed out. In the early morning, two guys dug me out. I was covered with dirt, my nose stuffed with mud and blood, a cut on my right shin and knee. I was dazed, glassy-eyed. I passed out on a litter and was sent to a hospital on Guadalcanal.

"I awoke on a cot next to the platoon sergeant. I asked

him what happened. 'Joe grabbed my .45, thought he saw Japs, and started shooting. A bullet went through my knee into my chest. The other sergeant had to shoot and kill Joe or they both would be dead.' " His injuries kept LaMagna under treatment for five weeks. Tagged for shipment to the States, he begged to return to his company. When the medics agreed and discharged him as fit for duty he rejoined his outfit, down to less than one-third of its complement because of the fighting on New Georgia.

To fill up the ranks, replacements like Leonard Glenn Hall, who hailed from Oklahoma and Texas, became members of Company F, 172d Regiment. He and other newcomers picked up their weapons from a salvage pile a few hundred yards from the front. The best that Hall could find was a Springfield with a rope sling that replaced the standard leather one. Each replacement received only a single canteen but they threw away their gas masks. On his first day on the line, a well-concealed machine gun zipped bullets along the trail. "No one had told the replacements that the first rule of survival," said Hall, "was to get off the trail." The enemy fire stitched his trousers, burning his calf with a grazing shot. Veterans offered no sympathy but scorned them for not having immediately formed a defense.

Within a few days, Hall and another novice, Trinidad Borrego, drew assignment as lead scouts. "Only the depleted condition of the company," said Hall, "could justify two green soldiers as advance men on an unknown, forbidding ridge. Both of us knew something was wrong when we reached a rusted, barbed-wire fence, but neither wanted to be considered a coward, so we kept moving forward. Ten feet into the clearing behind the fence were pillboxes. Suddenly shots rang out and I saw smoke curling from the rifle pointing out of the nearest emplacement. Quickly raising the old bolt-action '03 I placed a shot at the butt plate of the Japanese rifle without ever seeing the enemy. The rifle fell and a thrashing sound came from the enclosure."

From his vantage point Hall saw more Japanese soldiers entering the pillboxes. He continued to fire, providing cover for Borrego, who leaped to his feet and raced back to the safety of the jungle. The gunfire died out and Hall saw a Japanese helmet on a stick, a lure for him to fire and show his position. He held back. Tiny pebbles struck the ground around him, and Hall, who said he was already resigned to his death, summoned the courage to glance backward. He saw Borrego beckoning him to retreat. The 6'4" Hall sprinted to the rear, leaped the barbed-wire fence, and tumbled into a half-dug foxhole as machine-gun bullets whizzed overhead. "Repeated attempts to capture this strong point in the days ahead," said Hall, "were disastrous. This ridge became the final resting place for many American soldiers."

With the 43d Division stymied by the enemy, the American leaders committed the 37th Infantry Division to the New Georgia enterprise. Cletus J. Schwab, who would put his ability as a high school baseball pitcher to good use with hand grenades, climbed the ranks, rising to staff sergeant, second in command of a forty-two-man platoon in the 148th Infantry Regiment. He had been under fire from snipers and air raids while guarding Henderson Field at Guadalcanal. Again that did little to ready him for the resistance on New Georgia. "The first day, to gain over a hundred yards we faced twenty-five machine guns, small and large mortars, and 75mm fieldpieces. During the night we dug foxholes while ships brought in more supplies. As we moved northeast we met the 5th Marine Raider Battalion of about fifteen hundred men. Their mission was the same as ours and the 145th Regiment [a 37th Division unit] was moving in from the southeast. It took twenty-eight days to secure the island. When the battle started we had only ten days' rations. For eighteen days we lived on jungle plants, Japanese rice, and fish."

The advance on the Munda Point objective stalled in the face of fierce opposition and counterattacks. The battle planners inserted parts of a third Army division, the 25th. To envelop the foe, the 4th Marine Raider Battalion returned by sea to Enogai, New Georgia. Their objective was Bairoko, a village that barred the way to the Japanese air base. The attack opened with rebel yells or, according to one participant, an Indian war whoop. John Dennis Hestand, a member of a fire team in C Company, recalled, "After we'd gone about a mile or maybe two, we stopped and formed a skirmish line across the trail. Until then everything was real quiet, but after we all got into position, it sounded like every gun within miles went off and everybody was screaming and hollering. We started moving on. We'd run a little way, hit the deck, shoot some, get up, and go it again. On one of my get-up-and-run periods I felt like I'd been kicked in the stomach by a mule. I grabbed my stomach and went down. Corporal Harold Pickett saw me go down, came over and said, 'Let me see.' I took my hands away and smoke was coming from my cartridge belt just to the left of the buckles, the left half of which was gone. We finally figured a bullet or something had hit an M1 clip, blew it up, and set my belt afire. My belly-chest stung some, but there was no big-hole penetration. So we got up and continued on.

"Some time later, I was on my belly shooting some and I felt like somebody had hit me on the right leg just above the knee with a red hot poker. There were mortars bursting in the treetops and on the ground all around us and all kinds of other stuff was flying around, coming from all directions, twinging, whirring, and thunking. A lot of our guys were getting hit and needing corpsmen. Pickett was again nearby and heard me yip, came over, dumped some sulfa in the hole on the side of my leg, bleeding pretty bad, tied on a big bandage, and I took off for the aid station.

"After a while I found it and there must have been a hundred guys, bleeding, hurting, being bandaged. One I saw was Captain Walker. He was on his belly and a corpsman was picking at something in the captain's right hip pocket area. He said, 'Hi, Hestand. Where'd they hit you?' I told him in the leg and he said, 'The dirty little bastards shot me in the ass.'

"A corpsman said they were sending about fifty of the walking wounded and some of the litter cases back to Enogai for evacuation. He asked if I thought I could walk it. I was hurting but could still walk. We formed up and started back down the trail. Before we left, somebody took my M1 away and gave me a BAR with a bunch of ammo so I could sort of ride shotgun as most of the other guys were arms and chest wounds.

"We started back later in the afternoon, going real slow with the litter cases, and got maybe half a mile or so when it got dark. We settled down but didn't sleep or rest much because there were still a lot of explosions around with flares [and from] planes. During the night my leg started getting stiff and really hurting. Come daylight we started moving back to Enogai but I couldn't walk anymore. I tried to keep up but, hobbling and crawling, wasn't doing so good. Wasn't alone because there were some other troops on the trail. After what seemed like forever, and me not getting very far, two big, fuzzy-haired natives came down the trail from Enogai and made a chair with their crossed hands, got me aboard supporting my stiff leg, really hurting now, and being real gentle and easy, got me back to Enogai. There they checked my leg, put on a new bandage, and then onto a rubber boat to a PBY. Some Zeros came over and strafed. Some of the wounded guys were wounded again and some of the plane crew, too."

Cajun Robert, armed with an automatic rifle, labeled Bairoko "one hell of a fight." He remembered "running out of ammo four times that day and got more from the dead and wounded. On the last time looking for more ammo I came across Pfc. [Jeff] Watson dead, turned him over, took his ammo and drew my Ka-Bar [knife] and cut his belt to see where he was hit. He was hit in the stomach and I tried to see if he had any life in him." Robert paused to give water to a wounded leatherneck, "then went forward again and put out a machine gun that had my outfit pinned down. I'm proud to say I put that gun out with ammunition taken from Watson. Watson was my friend and he had begged me to arrange for him to carry a BAR."

The company received orders to retreat. Roger Spaulding noted, "We had just barely enough men still standing to carry out the wounded and protect ourselves while we did so. Further attacks were impossible. On the way out those with rifles walked the flanks, protecting the column of stretchers that dripped blood all the way back to Enogai."

Among those limping in retreat was Robert, hit in the legs by a mortar burst. For all of his scavenging he was down to his last seven rounds but he shot the head off a lurking sniper with one of those few bullets. Robert climbed into a PBY with a crew of six and forty wounded leathernecks. He flinched as a Japanese fighter sprayed the PBY with its machine guns. Although six on his ship incurred more wounds, Marine Corsairs shot down the interloper.

Having repulsed the initial Marine assault at Bairoko, the

Japanese astonishingly mounted a furious counterattack, punching away at the ridge position occupied by Cletus Schwab and others from the 37th Division. "There was a storm of rifle, machine gun, and mortar fire coming from the direction of our company outpost," recalled Schwab. "Snipers were moving in on us. They had filtered along the ridge during the dark of the night. We heard Japanese firing weapons from several new directions. They were all around us, trying to break through our barbed wire.

"We were only protected by jungle grass. The Japanese were firing from the cover of the jungle. One of my sergeants reported to me that six or seven of his men had been hit by machine guns and mortars and two were dead." Only the intercession of another company from Schwab's battalion relieved the pressure. "Six Japanese made banzai suicide charges with bayonets. They were all killed. We had stopped the attack and I estimate about 800 or 900 Japanese were killed or wounded. A patrol reported that forty or fifty of their dead were lying in the barbed-wire fence. I had forty-two men in my unit when the battle for New Georgia started. At the end I had twenty. The rest were either dead or wounded. I was wounded in the back but remained with my platoon."

The combined forces of the Americans ground up the defenders of Munda Point, with the field listed as officially captured on 5 August. The Japanese had lost another valuable outpost. Neighboring Kolombangara, a refuge for some of the Japanese facing extinction on New Georgia, was effectively neutralized. When the American strategy indicated that Halsey and MacArthur intended to bypass the place, the Japanese removed some 12,000 soldiers to fight elsewhere.

The Marines also learned a lesson; the light infantry of Raider battalions that brought to bear nothing larger than a

60mm mortar could not defeat a well-dug-in enemy without heavy support from artillery, navy ships, or airplanes. The concept of the Raiders lost currency and, in a reorganization, their four battalions reconstituted the 4th Marines, a regiment lost when the Japanese overran the Philippines.

Meanwhile, the campaign against the Japanese on New Guinea continued. MacArthur plotted to seize Lae, a port on the northeast coast of the island, and another enemy center, Salamaua. His script involved an attack by the Australian 9th Division transported to within twenty miles of the city by air. The operation depended upon seizure of an airdrome at Nadzab, and the 503d Parachute Infantry Regiment on 5 September 1943 would drop on-site.

"It was a delicate operation involving the first major parachute jump in the Pacific War," said MacArthur. "I inspected them and found, as was only natural, a sense of nervousness among the ranks. I decided that it would be advisable for me to fly in with them. I did not want them to go through their first baptism of fire without such comfort as my presence might bring to them." He observed the drop from a B-17.

Hugh Reeves, a Mississippi youth, had volunteered for airborne after being told he was ticketed for military police duty in New York. Rod Rodriguez, a former Florida National Guard soldier, volunteered for paratroops because, he said, "The challenge of testing myself in an elite unit appealed to me. Also the jump pay of $50 a month seemed a princely sum when a private's monthly pay had just jumped from $21 to $31 a month."

"There were bombers above us, fighter planes above them, and A-20s all around us," said Reeves. "As we approached our destination we could hear the B-24s with their machine guns chattering away, strafing the jungles below. I was in the sixth plane in our group, and when I went out the door I could see nothing but treetops. My chute opened, made one pendulum swing, and I felt myself crashing through limbs. All I could do was fold my arms to cover my face, keep my feet together, point my toes down, and say a quick prayer that I would not hit a large limb, for, just as I reached the outer edge of that one swing, I saw my chute collapse like a busted paper bag as it hit the top of the tree before I did.

"When I came to, there was a medic standing over me, pointing a Tommy gun and saying, 'Lager.' Our answering password was 'Label' because the Japs had trouble with the ell sound. I looked up at my chute still hanging to a large pine with thousands of one-inch needles sticking out. My guardian angel had looked after me for that tree was well over a hundred feet high and that would have been a free fall had that pine not been there to slow me down."

His good friend Rodriguez said, "The airfield was seized without opposition, being manned by service personnel who fled on our arrival. I quickly became a jump casualty when I landed in a tall tree and drove a branch sharp as a spear completely through my thigh, emerging in my groin area. Doctors later told me it had grazed the main artery flowing into my right leg, and had it been cut I would have bled to death in seconds. For two days I was kept hopped up on dosages of morphine, until the airport was opened and I could be evacuated."

The Australian infantrymen aided by troopers from the 503d hacked and shot their way toward Salamaua and Lae. The two towns yielded on 12 and 16 September. It was Halsey's turn to expand American control and his goal was Bougainville, a big island at the northern head of the Solomon chain. Its airfields could support Air Corps bombers from New Guinea bases and Navy torpedo bombers from Munda against the huge depot of Rabaul.

Adroit raids by Halsey's forces, flying from carriers and shore bases, along with the heavyweights contributed by the Air Corps, battered enemy vessels and diverted the Japanese from interfering with the landings at Empress Augusta Bay by the 3d Marine Division on 1 November. The beachhead grew and within three weeks the 37th Division had joined the leathernecks. The Americans on Bougainville consolidated their positions, leaving the way clear for MacArthur to make his move on the island of New Britain and its vital center, Rabaul.

# 3

# Pointblank, Blitz Week, and Ploesti

THE 56TH FIGHTER GROUP OFFICIALLY DEBUTED ON 8 APRIL 1943 with a rodeo along the French coast near Dunkirk, but nothing of consequence occurred. An original pilot with the 56th Fighter Group was John McClure, an instructor with a class of students at the time of the Pearl Harbor raid. The group had originally flown P-35s, P-36s, and the P-39 but, when, in 1943, it arrived at Horsham Saint Faith airdrome in Great Britain, the pilots occupied the roomy cockpits of P-47 Thunderbolts. "We'd started our operations in early April and I was on my seventh mission, the 29th of April," recalled McClure. "It was our first major contact with the enemy. In the mess we had a little confusion and we got separated. I got hit and managed to get back out over the coast. The one set of instructions we had was for heaven's sake don't let 'em get a hold of a Jug [P-47].

"I got out over the North Sea and I was down to about 400 feet when I bailed out. A German coastal patrol picked me up. In the water like that you lose your sense of time, but from my watch, which stopped when I hit the water, and the Germans figuring from their own watches, it was about an hour and a half. They shook their head, 'No way,' because at that time of the year, twenty minutes is about average survival time. I had discovered that my life raft was full of holes and my Mae West had a puncture. I pulled the emergency kit off the raft and proceeded to float. I didn't have time to be afraid on the way down because there are so many things to do, you don't have time to think. And you suffer from shock. I couldn't move, almost paralyzed, they drug me up over the side of the boat and took me to an island along the Dutch coast."

McClure was issued a skimpy blanket and then taken by train to Amsterdam with a trio of guards. There he was imprisoned in solitary confinement. "It was absolutely black, no light, about six feet long, three or four wide with an iron bench on one side. You lose all concept of time under such circumstances but I later figured out I was there a little over two weeks. I'd get a little piece of ersatz bread—half sawdust—and a cup of ersatz coffee, twice a day. That was it.

"Periodically, they'd take me up for an interrogation by an officer who spoke very good English. He didn't mince too many words. They asked questions and beyond name, rank, and serial number, they wanted to know what you were flying, who was your CO, where you were located, what kind of armament does this aircraft have, and technical questions. They seemed particularly interested in organization, who was there, and how many. When you didn't go beyond name, rank, and serial number, they encouraged you with the old rubber hose. When you didn't answer, they'd say, 'We'll give you a little time to think this over.' This was repeated, every day or so.

"They came down at the end of about two weeks and took

me for interrogation. The guy told me that if they didn't get some answers out of me, they'd call in the firing squad. They weren't going to fool with me any more and he'd give me a couple of hours to think it over. They pulled me back after some hours and it was almost a repeat of the same thing and then the third time there were three guards with bayonets drawn. They herded me up and out into the courtyard of the prison. About then, here comes a ten-man rifle squad and they lined up just opposite me. They led me down a flight of steps and suddenly turned, took me out the gate, placed me on a train for Frankfurt, and *Dulag Luft* [the center for interrogation of downed Allied flyers]."

Another member of the 56th Fighter Group was Robert Johnson, a twenty-three-year-old Oklahoma native. Said Johnson, "The P-47s were like big Cadillacs, a super big old Cadillac. It would fly itself." When one landed a Jug, which seemed to come into a field and squat, Johnson said, "It was just like you were approaching a cold toilet seat." Johnson struggled to learn gunnery. "One training technique was for another guy to fly 100 to 200 feet over the water and then we'd come in and shoot at his shadow. It was a matter of a quick burst and then a break because you could be in the water real quick. We did a lot of skeet shooting to teach us how to lead a target. From time to time, they took us to shoot at flying targets. I never did **qua**lify because I could not hit the flags. I learned my combat shooting, firing at airplanes."

When the 56th Fighter Group arrived in England, he listened to an RAF pilot who advised, "If a German gets on your tail, don't sit still. Move, shake your airplane, get all over the sky. Don't sit still because then he's got you." Men who'd flown with the Eagle squadrons taught some tactics. "The P-47 was a very comfortable airplane—big cockpit, very warm, so we wore our typical woolen OD [olive drab] uniform. We put a silk scarf around our necks inside the shirt collar to keep from cutting our necks on those wool shirts while constantly turning our heads. That was the purpose of the scarf, not flamboyancy. You had to look backward 90 percent of the time when flying."

As the newest entry to the war, the Thunderbolt, said Johnson, confused the Germans. "We got a lot of them because the elliptical wing of a P-47 at first glance looked like a Spitfire if you didn't happen to notice that big, bulky nose. The Germans might fly under us or maybe we would catch them beneath and they'd simply roll over and dive because they could always outdive a Spitfire. We'd roll over, throttle back, slide right up their ass, and shoot them down. They were not going to get away from the P-47s straight, level, or down. Our guns narrowed around 400 yards until the eight .50s came together in a two-foot-square box."

Johnson remembered his first operational sortie. "It was simply a fighter sweep and it was a little bit unreal—you were anticipating something but you did not know what. We didn't really believe they were shooting to kill over there. We thought it was a big game. All we had done was shoot camera gunnery and then always you would come in and land with the guy you shot at. You could not believe that you were shooting to kill and you were being shot at to kill.

"That first mission, I was flying as [a wingman]. There were forty-eight of us altogether, sixteen per squadron, with three squadrons at different levels and we made a sweep at 35,000 feet back to England. We were way up at the top and I was way to the right of everyone else when they made a turn. I was following orders, 'Stay on your leader,' and I was looking around and did not realize they had turned a little bit sharper and really left me. So when I looked back and saw them leaving me, I pulled in the stick and hit my gun trigger. That scared the hell out of me; of course, there was no one around.

"I had heard about flak and seen two or three airplanes up above us quite a ways back. I wasn't worried about them because they were quite [far off]. I saw all these little white things popping all around me and thought, 'That must be the antiaircraft they are talking about. I wonder where my buddies are.' I looked to the right and out of the corner of my eyes saw something blinking at me. There were two 109s! I rolled that thing over and instinctively to the left. [I had been told] never fly a straight line. I started to split-S and then as I got halfway through it, I realized this was enemy country that I was split-S-ing into. So I straightened it up and at a good 45-degree angle—I was kicking rudders at the same time—upside down. I was really slashing that airplane all over the sky. I had the throttles bent forward; got home a good thirty minutes before anyone else."

Johnson flew a number of missions without engaging the enemy. One evening, after a day on which he saw German fighters pass apparently unobserved by flight leaders, Johnson, mindful of the requirement to maintain position, asked one of his seniors, "Suppose I am not the leader but I see an enemy and he is a perfect spot for me to bounce [attack] and there is just not time to do anything but call him in and bounce him. If I call him in and then we [the flight] try to maneuver so that the other planes are in position to bounce him, he is gone. What do you do?

"He said, 'That's a good question.' And that was his answer. But to me it was enough—go get him. Call them in and then go get 'em. The next day, [Hub] Zemke was leading the whole group. I was on [Paul] Conger's wing, sitting up there on the top and I saw about twelve Focke-Wulfs pass under us. I knew someone had to see them. I wasn't the first.

I called them in and said 'Come on, Paul.' I went right down through our guys. I pulled up behind their Vee echelon.

"I took it very slow, easy, and casual, my airplane was really coming in, overtaking them. The pipper [on the gunsight] was on the cross piece of the rudder and the elevators. I thought, nice and gentle, and then, that is not right. I remembered in our camera gunnery, you always put the pipper on the back of the pilot's head. I put it up on his head, calmly checked the needle ball. It was centered and I pulled the trigger. My whole airplane vibrated. All this smoke and fire—all this noise. I released it immediately, because I thought I am hit. Then I realized it was my own guns and I saw what was happening to the guy ahead of me. He went all to pieces. This was the leader of that German formation. If I had any experience at all, I could have gotten one or two more, but, as it was, I was rolling out through the sky, having a great time. Then suddenly I realized that it was easy and I should go back and get some more. I ended up alone over there wandering around enemy country—Belgium and that area.

"I got home thirty or forty minutes later than anyone. They weren't sure what happened to me. When I landed, flight commander Jerry Johnson right on through [Francis] Gabreskie and Zemke really reamed my butt and rightly so—I was wrong. But after they all chewed me out, they congratulated me on getting my first one."

Because of his eagerness, Johnson admitted he quickly earned the reputation of "a wild man. Everyone said, 'Don't fly with Johnson, he will kill you.'" Even when not in the cockpit, Johnson personified the stereotypical image of the swaggering fighter pilot. "We were confined to the base one time. It was cold, too cold to get up and put out the lights. I shot them out with my .45. It became a standard joke, fusillades of bullets to put out the lights. One man had a Tommy gun, another a rifle." After rain leaked through roof holes, higher echelons firmly requested less violent means to extinguish the bulbs.

Just shy of three weeks after his first victory, Johnson's career almost came to a crashing halt. "I was so badly shot up that had I been able to get out of the airplane, I would have been a prisoner, or dead, or an evadee. I couldn't get out of the airplane. My oxygen had been shot out and flash-flamed my cockpit. That singed the side of my head a little. My wrist bone was part of the damage that I did to myself trying to fight my way out of the cockpit.

"This was the one mission on which I had not worn my goggles; I had cracked them the day before, so I'd left them at home. One of the 20mms had exploded in the left-hand side of my cockpit and knocked out my hydraulic throttle or control. Hydraulic fluid was all over the floor of the airplane and flying around in the air of the open cockpit and getting into my eyes, which were starting to swell. I was flying half the time with my eyes closed and part of the time with my head sticking out of the window, getting air blown into my eyes just trying to see.

"I had dropped down to about seven or eight thousand feet and my head was beginning to clear. I was heading north, going toward England and I had to cross the Channel. I looked back to the right at about four o'clock and slightly high, and saw a beautiful, dappled, blue gray [plane] with a yellow nose coming in at me. Black crosses on it. I recognized it of course as a Focke-Wulf. I was sitting there, thinking about it as he kept coming right at me. I waited for him to move the nose of his airplane forward of my airplane but he kept his nose directly on me, which meant he was taking pictures. Then when he got about fifty yards from me, I thought, 'Now what would I do if I was in his shoes? I would stick my guns in the guy's cockpit and blow him out of the sky. That's what that bugger is going to do to me."

"I turned and went under him real quick and headed again to the north. I didn't know how badly my airplane was banged up and didn't know whether I could fight him or not—so I didn't try. As I went under him, he pulled up, pulled back around, came directly in on my tail, and emptied a lot of .30-caliber machine-gun shells into me. They all hit me. All I could do was sit back there, leaning against the armor plate and take it." As Johnson turned his head, a bullet nicked the end of his nose. Another passed through the side of the cockpit, split, and half of it pierced the upper part of his right thigh while the rest entered several inches below.

"I held my course. He overshot me and just out of anger, I stuck my head out of the window and hit hard right rudder, and skidded a little bit and fired at him. I got two bullets into his left wingtip. It didn't really hurt him, but he at least knew I still had a little fight. He came back around and got in formation with me. I could have reached out and touched his wingtip. He was sitting in there the way we flew when going through weather. He probably saved my life. We went over Dieppe at 4,000 feet, a P-47 and a Focke-Wulf in tight formation. So, no antiaircraft. He took me out over the water. He was looking at my airplane up and down. He'd just shake his head. Incidentally, he had black eyes. He shook his head and kind of waved at me, tipped his left hand like a little salute, and pulled off. I thought, 'Thank God, he's going home.' Then he pulled in behind me and emptied the rest of his .30-calibers. It sounded like a goat on a tin roof. This time he didn't make the mistake of overshooting me. He came back in formation with me, stayed with me until I was down to about 1,000 feet over the Channel, then waved his wings and went home.

"I was directed to an air base in southern England. I had kicked out my instruments trying to bail out. I had thrown my feet up on the dashboard and leaned back as I tried to yank the canopy open but it was jammed shut. I was brought over the air base in southern England, but I couldn't see the field when I looked down, partially because my eyes were swollen and partially because it was so well camouflaged. I told the controller I'd just go on up to another base where all my buddies were, at Manston. I called Manston and told them I expected to make a gear-up landing because I had no brakes, no hydraulics, no flaps, and I wasn't sure I could get the gear down. I was told if possible to bring the airplane in gear-down because there were a lot of crashed airplanes coming back. I dropped the gear. The doors popped open and the tires were okay. I landed and ground looped the airplane to stop it—I had no brakes—and backed it in between two British aircraft, just like I'd parked there.

"I crawled out of the airplane and kissed the ground, then got my chute out. I went to the flight surgeon. He doctored my nose. Later, as I was taking my trousers off for a shower, I discovered the two partial bullets in my right leg. I put iodine on the holes thinking that would cure everything." To his enormous satisfaction, Johnson heard over the radio a German flier describing how he had seen a P-47 with Johnson's number going into the water.

In January, Eaker could call on only six bomber groups, but by the end of June he commanded thirteen of these plus three fighter groups. But the statistics hide a scarcity of operational strength. The Mighty Eighth could dispatch little more than 200 of the heavyweights. The number fell short of what the strategists on the scene deemed necessary.

Eaker, eight months earlier, had written Hap Arnold that his people were "absolutely convinced that . . . 300 heavy bombers can attack any target in Germany with less than 4 percent losses." The magical figure of 300 seems to have been plucked from the air, like a .300 batting average as a magical talisman in baseball, for no evidence supported Eaker nor, as became woefully apparent later, the idea that the German defenders would be overwhelmed by 300 or more aircraft.

Furthermore, the top command clung to another deadly misperception. The battles in the early months of spring persuaded the brass that the strongest German fighter defense lay near the channel coast, a crust that once pierced opened up the heartland to a more lightly resisted attack. That theory was obliterated within a few weeks with the discovery of an intricate web of German airfields arranged in depth. Moreover, the *Luftwaffe* had also developed its own radar and early-warning apparatus, much like that which helped preserve England in 1940, and intruders found the defenders ready and waiting. To knock down bombers, the Germans, in addition to machine guns and cannons, added rockets, explosives dangling from parachutes, and even tried unsuccessfully to deploy an infantry mortar shell as part of the air-to-air ordnance.

Archie J. Old Jr., a thirty-seven-year-old Texan, brought his 96th Bomb Group to a base at Grafton Underwood that spring. Old had abandoned his career in construction and won a commission in 1929. He left the Air Corps but signed up for the reserve. Called to active duty in 1940, Old progressed up the chain of command. Following activation of the 96th in July 1942, Old became its CO within a month. He faced two major problems immediately: inexperienced pilots and a shortage of aircraft. Old instituted a rigorous regimen based on eight hours in the air, eight hours of schooling, eight hours reserved for sleep. He scheduled airmen to fly on rotating shifts that gave them experience both day and night. To avoid any downtime, recalled Old, "If the airplane didn't need any particular maintenance, we would actually change crews with the engines running to save time. We refueled with engines running. It was dangerous as hell, but never did we burn one up. We were getting the maximum amount of flying time, since we had only twelve planes and thirty-five crews who needed to fly. We were flying those damn aircraft twenty hours a day."

According to Old, common sense taught him that evasive action in the face of flak brought no real protection. It inevitably led to missing the target because the changes in airspeed and angle among the bombers in formation significantly altered the direction of ordnance. He insisted on no evasive action during bomb runs. "If you were a German fighter pilot leading a bunch of fighters out there, you would start looking for the ones split out a little bit, not in line. Every man in my outfit heard me harp all the time, 'Get that goddamn formation in there and keep it there if you are interested in a long life and doing a good job. The tighter the formation is, the better the bomb pattern. And those damn fighters looking at you, if you have a nice, tight, compact formation, they know there are a hell of a lot of guns that can start unloading on them.' The idea would be, 'Don't go for that guy. Look at the outfit yonder that is scattered all over the sky.' I didn't pass this information right on because I knew it would be unwelcome and have to be sold."

The ideas of the 96th CO meshed with the thinking of Curtis LeMay, who had ascended to the leadership of the 4th Bombardment Wing. "LeMay invited me up invariably after I led a mission," said Old. "We also had critiques on every damn mission where the lead crews would critique a half-dozen missions at a time. We would go over them in detail and discuss the mistakes. One of the things that made LeMay a great leader was that after I had just led a mission he had me up at his place for dinner. We had a drink or two and we were talking about that mission. We ate and we talked about that mission. We had an after-dinner drink; we talked about that mission. I'll guarantee you that by the time we got through, he knew as much if not more about that mission than I did. I felt like I had to keep flying missions to stay abreast. That's why I flew a lot until LeMay would ground me. He would say, 'You're flying too much. Let someone else lead a few of them for a while.' Hell, the low group, the low squadron of the low group, that was the hotspot. Everybody was always talking about it, so I would go down there and fly it. I would fly the low airplane of the low squadron of the low group. If you wanted to see a lot of fighters, that is where you saw them, particularly the head-on attack that the Germans primarily used." Old believed that he actively participated in seventy-two missions—often riding as an unofficial observer.

Billy Southworth continued to praise some and blame others in his diary as he and those who had come to the 303d and the United Kingdom with him approached their last missions. He remarked, "Just back from Kiel, where I dropped incendiaries, 4,000 pounds of them, tired as hell and glad to be alive. Fighters greeted us at sea and a continued two-hour battle ensued. Before it was ten minutes old I saw two fighters and three B-17s shot down. The fight out was fierce, ME 110s shooting from the front, side, and rear, FW 190s bursting in from head-on. What a day, Cards lost to the Dodgers 1-0. Henderson shot one down at 200 yards."

A few lines later he confided, "An interesting question

asked of me. 'Do you feel the same before each mission?'
The answer is no. It used to be a big thing like the opening
game of the season with the bases loaded, only more so. As
we taxied down it was all business. The night before it was
on one's mind, anxious to go but sleeping light as a mouse.
First time over enemy territory seemed like a new world
waiting for the big fight to follow. Once it came, I worked
harder than ever before and keen as a razor. It's all the same
now, except preceded by a sound sleep, mindful of the crew,
target position in formation, and characteristics of the ship [I
am] scheduled to fly. Mind on the new boys on my wing.
Are they new? Green? Fly close? Stick in on evasive action?
Do they understand their job and their ship? Today I heard
from Dad, the Cards beat Brooklyn. Took pictures of Clark
Gable and met him." Toward the end of June, Southworth
wrote of a number of farewells as various members of his
crew recorded their twenty-fifth mission.

Desperate as the Bomber Command was for bodies, they
could not at this point extend tours without crushing morale.
In the summer of 1943, as the number of missions piled up,
so did the bodies. The 306th Bomb Group, for example,
which had become operational on 19 October 1942 with 35
air crews consisting of 315 men, lost 27 of its crews and
only 8 completed the full 25-mission tour. KIAs added up to
93 and POWs covered another 88. More than 12 men died
in training accidents and 29 had to be relieved and reassigned. Other groups recorded similarly dire results.

Drained of men and aircraft by punishment meted out by
the foe and the need to siphon off assets for the Twelfth Air
Force operating out of North Africa, the Mighty Eighth
hardly offered the prospect of a long life to its members. On
19 May, the publicity flacks could trumpet the news of the
91st Bomb Group's *Memphis Belle* as the first bomber to

complete a twenty-five-mission tour without losing any of the crew. The feat, celebrated with a documentary film and later a fictional movie, emphasized the fragile lifeline. Many other crews had preceded the 91st to Europe ten months earlier and yet only this solitary bunch had completed a tour.

The 95th Bomb Group had the ill luck to be chosen for an experiment devised by Gen. Nathan Forrest. Instead of the box at staggered altitudes formulated by LeMay, Forrest drafted a blueprint that flattened the setup, placing the planes wing tip–to–wing tip. He was convinced that could concentrate firepower ahead, below, above, and to the rear. For two weeks the 95th practiced the new system and when the outfit headed for Kiel, the huge German naval base on the Danish peninsula, Forrest occupied the copilot's seat of the lead airplane.

Lieutenant Robert Cozens, deputy leader of the group for the mission, said, "I was instructed to keep the nose of my B-17 tucked up under the tail of the lead aircraft. The Forrest formation underwent the 'true test' when, as we completed the bomb run, the formation received a massive diving frontal attack from the German FW 190s and ME 109s. In our position in the formation, as well as that of our wingmen, we were unable to clear any of our guns on the attacking aircraft because of the line of sight through our lead echelon aircraft. Consequently, the lead aircraft was raked with enemy fire from one end to the other and immediately fell out of formation."

A total of sixty bombers from the 4th Bomb Wing, hewing to Forrest's arrangement, attacked Kiel. "Goddamn," said Old, "the fighters blew him [Forrest] out right ahead of me. They took his whole squadron out at one time." Indeed, the enemy shot down ten of the twenty-four effectives of the 95th Bomb Group with whom Forrest rode as an observer and rendered one more fit only for the salvage heap. Nor did the other raiders fare much better; the 94th Bomb Group lost nine and Old's outfit another three, a daunting 37 percent casualty rate.

The Casablanca conference of Churchill and Roosevelt set in motion around-the-clock bombing against the Third Reich's war industry. The massive British assaults upon Ruhr Valley installations hampered production sufficiently and killed enough civilians to persuade the enemy to deploy increased numbers of fighter aircraft for defenses. FW 190s and ME 109s battered the Eighth Air Force. The Allied high command decided that continued operations in the face of this formidable resistance demanded a shift in emphasis.

On 10 June 1943, RAF bomber commander Air Marshall Arthur Harris and his counterpart, the Eighth Air Force's Ira Eaker, received a directive which read, "It has become essential to check the growth and to reduce the strength of the day and night fighter forces which the enemy can concentrate against us in this theater. . . . First priority in the operation of British and American bombers based in the United Kingdom shall be accorded to the attack of German fighter forces and the industry upon which they depend." The program, known as Pointblank, delineated a series of sites for bombers to visit. Means to carry out Pointblank against enemy fighters already on the wing, however, remained unavailable because the proposed targets for bombers lay well beyond the range of Allied fighters. Furthermore, to guard the limited number of U.S. bombers, the outriders were forbidden to leave the herd in pursuit of marauders. Frustrated pilots watched packs of hostile aircraft, lurking in the distance, awaiting the moment when the P-47s or Spitfires would be forced to return to base. Once the shepherds departed, the wolves would ravage the flocks of Forts and Libs fending for themselves against the savage onslaughts.

On 24 July, the Allies opened a subset of Pointblank, Blitz Week, combined strikes by the RAF and the Eighth Air Force, upon a wide-ranging series of targets: Norway, Kiel, Hannover, Hamburg, Kassel, and Warnemünde. Hamburg indicated one exception to the concentration against aircraft. The port city held shipyards that built and assembled U-boats as well as merchant and naval vessels. As the Battle of the Atlantic, the threat to the seaborne lifeline from the U.S. to the United Kingdom, raged, submarine pens and production centers stayed on the target list.

The raid by the British upon the port of Hamburg at the beginning of Blitz Week witnessed the first use of chaff, also known as window, tens of thousands of strips of aluminum foil that confused ground and air radar into the belief of a massive 11,000 instead of the actual 740 bombers. The local radar-guided searchlights wandered futilely through the night skies, antiaircraft batteries fired aimlessly. One German night-fighter controller was heard to shout, "I cannot follow any of the hostile; they are very cunning."

The British dumped 2,400 tons of explosives upon Hamburg during the night. When the Americans came the following day, their 350 tons, a fraction of the RAF contribution, nevertheless kept the pressure on the weary firefighters. Successive waves of British planes over the next three days with incendiaries ignited a firestorm. "The last day that we went," said Southworth's erstwhile gunner, Bill Fleming, "you could see the smoke from a hundred miles away. When we flew over the city at 30,000 feet, the smoke was coming up through the formation. On July 26th I was making my fourth trip to Hamburg, flying with Lieutenant Lefevbre on the bomber known as *Flak Wolf.* At

28,000 feet over the target the plane was hit by I do not know what, either antiaircraft or a fighter plane. We went into a diving spin and the pilot rang the bail-out alarm but nobody could jump out because the centrifugal force was holding us. The experience is impossible to describe. Once I couldn't move, I knew there was no way we could come out of that dive and I was going to die. The fear I felt was unbelievable. As we came down, somehow, even the pilot couldn't say later how he did it, he pulled that plane out of the dive. We started at 28,000 feet and leveled off only at 6,000.

"Once he leveled off, everybody was very quiet. I realized I had a terrific pain in my left leg, a searing pain. I thought I'd been hit by antiaircraft. I tried to paw along my clothes to see where the hole in my clothes was but couldn't find it. Then it dawned on me. I had wet myself and shorted out my electric suit and it was burning me from my crotch down to my ankle, resulting in a solid blister all the way down. When we got back I spent two weeks grounded on that account. It wasn't that funny when it happened."

The holocaust at Hamburg reached 1,000 degrees centigrade, creating a tornado of fire that yanked trees from the ground, burned up asphalt streets, sucked human beings from buildings into its vortex, cremated alive citizens who had sought refuge in bomb shelters. Those who did not succumb to fire died of smoke inhalation or asphyxiation from carbon monoxide. The official figures counted 50,000 dead but no one really knew the count because the city held vast numbers of slave laborers, displaced persons, and foreigners. An estimated 900,000 residents were homeless. When Fleming read an account in the GI newspaper *Stars and Stripes*, he said it disturbed him. "German children and old people were there. Of all my experiences that's the one that continues to bother me, even though I never spoke to my wife about it."

Hamburg cost the RAF 2.8 percent of the dispatched aircraft, 87 of 2,592 sorties. The Mighty Eighth paid a much higher price for Blitz Week, 8.5 percent of its attacking force, or 88 aircraft from 1,720 sorties. Worse, the Eighth could not even muster 200 heavies upon conclusion of Blitz Week. For that matter, the Hamburg effort also exhausted the RAF. According to Dudley Saward, a former RAF group captain and author, who visited Albert Speer, Nazi Germany's minister of armaments production, after the war, similar sacking of a half-dozen other German cities immediately on the heels of Hamburg might have actually ended the war. Whether this would have been the case is questionable but in any account the British bombers could not return in force for another two weeks and in markedly lesser numbers.

The most notable first for the Americans during Blitz Week was the use of auxiliary fuel tanks on the Thunderbolts that had previously been restricted to about 200 miles from home bases, able only to escort as far as Amsterdam. The VIII Fighter Command contracted locally and slung a cardboard tank that could be jettisoned on the P-47s. However, these added a mere sixty miles, leaving the big planes still unprotected when they ventured any significant distance beyond the coastline. The newest B-17s installed "Tokyo" wing tanks that allowed them to travel considerably farther, eventually enabling them to reach anywhere in Germany. Overall, however, Blitz Week may have done more damage to the Eighth Air Force than to the German war effort. When the period ended, the heavyweights basically stood down for nearly two weeks.

In principle, Pointblank set a limit to the types of targets that the Allied air arms would strike; but in practice, the spectrum of targets widened, as almost any kind of industrial or manufacturing site could be related to the enemy air strength. Certainly, the huge oil refining plants located at Ploesti in the heart of Romania qualified as vital to the German fighter effort. If this source of petroleum could be eliminated the Nazi war machine would be forced to rely on costly and scarcer synthetics extracted from coal. Ploesti lay beyond the longest-range RAF bombers in England, but the Allied conquest of Rommel in North Africa that led to bases at Benghazi put the Romanian oil complex within reach of B-24s equipped with extra fuel tanks.

Strategists plotted a low-level attack that might evade early detection, conserve fuel for the extended run, and enhance bombing marksmanship. Leon Johnson, the commander of the 44th Bomb Group, said, "We went to General [Uzal] Ent [the Ninth Air Force bomber chief] and asked him if we couldn't go in at high level and were turned down. We said we thought we could hit the target from high level and wouldn't take the losses we'd have at low altitude. If there is anything as large as a bomber flying at low level, [and] someone is in a position to fire at it, they are very apt to hit it. But General [Lewis] Brereton [Ninth Air Force commander] said it would take a campaign to knock out the targets from high level and they wanted to do it in one fell swoop. They assured us that if we knocked it out adequately, the war would be over in six months. Brereton did not think up the low-level attack; that came from Washington."

In preparation, at the end of May 1943, two B-24 bomb groups in England, the 44th and 93d, halted missions for the Eighth Air Force to practice low-altitude flights and maneuvers. They were joined by the 389th, which had yet to go operational. Within a few weeks all three outfits flew to North

Africa, temporarily attached to the Ninth Air Force, for a strike at Ploesti. Ramsay Potts, now a major and squadron leader for the 93d Bomb Group, recalled, "We were told there was some sort of special mission coming but not what it was. While we were training, the higher echelons were holding their conferences, discussions, and arguments. Conditions were not very good. The food was terrible, C rations, maybe some canned fruit salad, and it was terribly hot. Sand storms, frequent high winds during the day forced us to work on the planes at night, after six o'clock, and before seven in the morning. The sand blowing in the engines was difficult to deal with. We had a large number of diarrhea cases; everyone lost weight.

"We flew a few missions up into Italy and one long one to the Messerschmitt plant at Wiener Neustadt. Then we settled down to practice low-level runs over some dummy installations in the desert. The planning, training, and briefing preparations were quite thorough. We were briefed on our approaches. We had dummy mockups for targets. Everything that we could do within limitations was done. The mission was recognized as being of utmost importance and everyone had a real keenness that it had to be accomplished at any cost.

"We had some RAF bomber pilots who had flown through barrage balloons in Germany and they briefed us on balloons surrounding Ploesti. Operations officers and the command were a little skeptical but we accepted the hazard of the balloons as one of the things you had to go through. We had been briefed on the balloon barrages, the flak defenses, the fighter units, and their locations. We had been briefed on the hazards of exploding oil tanks and distillation units. The low-level aspect didn't frighten anybody. Many of us looked forward to this because it was the only way to get the necessary range out of the airplane.

"It was to be a thirteen-hour mission. Even with an extra tank in the bomb bay, you couldn't have done it flying at a high altitude. Five groups were going and attacking seven targets. The 93d was split into two forces. The main one was to be led by Colonel Baker, the group commander, and the other by our former group commander, Colonel Timberlake, who'd just been promoted to brigadier general. He was going to fly in the copilot seat of my airplane. Just prior to the mission, General Brereton decided there were too many generals going and he told Timberlake not to go. That meant I had to act as commander of the force as well as be the pilot."

The top echelons were aware how precarious the business could be. Brereton emerged unscathed from his stint as MacArthur's Air Corps chief. This despite the fact that during his watch the Japanese caught half of the entire B-17 fleet in the Philippines on the ground and destroyed it eight or nine hours after word of the events at Pearl Harbor. Brereton said, "We expect our losses to be 50 percent but even though we should lose everything we've sent, but hit the target, it will be well worth it."

Lewis Ellis, a pilot for the 389th, temporarily transferred to the 98th because his own outfit had more crews and ships than its quota. He recalled practices at extremely low altitudes. "I guess we frightened every Arab off every hay wagon and blew down half the tents for fifty miles around. The British engineers erected a 'target' on a clear space in the desert . . . a large number of long, low wooden buildings with an occasional circular one and a few towers. We always dropped a few one-hundred-pound practice bombs, but on the last day we put in some live five-hundred-pounders and blew the whole thing sky-high. Every airplane had a *specific* building or a part of a building on which the bombs were to be placed. Our target was the *left* end of a boiler house; the ship behind us was assigned the *right* end. We had draftsmen to make drawings and sketches of every route, every target, every building. They constructed wooden models of every building and every oil storage tank. We had pictures, maps, and drawings galore. Every pilot, navigator, and bombardier knew exactly what he was supposed to do."

At 4:00 A.M. on 1 August, tower controllers fired flares into the dark skies and, to begin Operation Tidal Wave, *Wingo Wango*, the leader for the entire attack, rolled down the runway. Like the other planes it was laden with extra fuel and ammunition as well as the maximum bomb tonnage, but it also bore the lead navigator for the attack. Of the 175 Liberators that headed for Romania—one crashed on takeoff, killing most of the crew—ten aborted enroute. Potts, piloting *Duchess*, recalled, "We formed up and started over the Mediterranean, seven different task forces numbering about 175 planes. We were flying at low altitude, maybe a few thousand feet over the Mediterranean and quite a bit spread out. Looking out, I saw the lead airplane suddenly turn off to the right and then he fell into the water and burst into flames. It was a shock and my radio operator, who was pretty callous, stood up and said, 'Look at that fire.' I was so indignant that I turned around and knocked him back into his seat."

Unfortunately, the doomed *Wingo Wango* not only carried the mission lead navigator to his death, but also the wingman pilot disobeyed the rules. The wingman descended to scout for survivors and drop them rafts. He found none but the time and fuel spent in his search made it impossible for him to climb back into position. He headed back toward

Benghazi, taking with him the deputy route navigator. Other B-24s filled the empty slots but key personnel were now gone.

Undeterred, the B-24s skimmed the water until they crossed the coast where Albania and Greece meet. "We started climbing up to get over the mountains," said Potts, "and ran into a few cumulus clouds. I stayed in close on the heels of the leader of the second group and we wound our way through these clouds, finally either climbed on top of them or skirted them, over the mountains and then started to let down to the minimum altitude over the Danube Plain. But the four task forces behind us had disappeared. We didn't know what had happened to them. They vanished while we were passing through those cumulus clouds. We in the first three groups were still together but couldn't see the ones who'd been following."

In *Teggie Ann*, Col. Keith Compton, the Ploesti expedition commander, flanked by Brig. Gen. Uzal Ent, IX Bomber Command boss, anxiously studied the landmarks that delineated the last navigation keys before the final bomb run. The topography, the streams, even the villages and towns looked similar, and the leaders became confused. Believing they had reached the final marker, Compton instructed *Teggie Ann*'s pilot to bear right. "We were all getting keener and keener," recalled Potts. "My navigator and I were coordinating with each other. On the intercom he gave me the time of nine minutes to the Initial Point. Just after he said this, the leader started to turn to the right. I was behind him, a little bit higher and about the same altitude as the number two group, which was in echelon off to the left. When both turned to the right, I did also, because I couldn't do anything else. I was boxed in. I checked again with the navigator and he said that wasn't the right place. We were still short of the Initial Point. At the same time as we completed the turn, the descent to treetop level started."

Lewis Ellis, flying *Daisy Mae*, reported, "Bombardier [Guido] Gioana pointed out a Romanian festival in full swing with girls in colorful dresses. They were unaccustomed to air raids and waved. Farmers were plowing in the small square fields. Some fields were green with wheat. In others, sunflowers were growing between rows of corn. Occasionally we passed yellow haystacks that reflected the bright sunlight. It was a beautiful country and looked peaceful."

Potts was disturbed by the direction of his group. "This was part of the bomb run up to the target. The plan was to do this in line abreast with each task force assigned its own refinery. Within the task force you had elements come across in line in a sequence. The leaders, first over each target, had delayed-action bombs in the hope they wouldn't have anything blowing up in front of the planes coming behind in their attack. As we came down to the minimum altitude, seeming to have made a mistake with the turn, I broke radio silence and talked to the leader."

Norman Appold, piloting one of the B-24s, broke radio silence to shout, "Not here! Not here!" Potts reportedly exclaimed, "Mistake! Mistake!" Other aircraft now chimed in. Remembered Potts, "He [Compton] said he was aware they had made the wrong turn and now were going to turn back to the left. It was unclear to me exactly what he was going to do at this point, making almost a 180- or perhaps 165-degree turn to go back to the IP, but he did start his turn. You could see Bucharest up ahead. We had good visibility but were going along at 210 miles per hour right on the deck, with confusion everywhere. After we turned, [we saw] that the leader was coming in on his target by skirting the Ploesti area and at a heading of 180 degrees opposite the one he was supposed to follow."

The change in course shifted the Liberators to a path directly over the heaviest flak concentrations in the area. As the ground batteries opened up, gunners on the B-24s sprayed the installations with countering fire. The second result of the error on *Teggie Ann*, more fortunate for the air armada, lengthened the distance between it and the enemy fighter fields, delaying the arrival of hostile interceptors. Because of the deviation, ground spotters issued alarms not only for Ploesti but also Bucharest, thereby confusing the defenders. According to Ellis, the delay enabled the enemy to sound the alarm. "Haystacks opened up and turned into gun nests, machine guns and flak guns were on every hill. By now we were down to two hundred feet but we knew instantly that we were still much too high. Down we went to one hundred feet, fifty feet, twenty-five feet, just clearing bushes and shrubbery. As we got closer we were surprised to see B-24s from another group bombing our target."

Leon Johnson, leading the 44th Bomb Group, said, "We were quite low, about 100 feet or so. You could see about the time we got some thirty miles away, all kinds of smoke and flames down in our target areas. We didn't know what damage they had done and we didn't know how successful they had been. We started in on our course. As we got within ten to fifteen miles I could see this gun firing at us. You could see the flash of the gun; you didn't see any shells break around you because those were down low. Right ahead of us, right over our target area, was this complete flame and black smoke. It looked like a solid wall. The thought ran through my mind for a moment, 'My God, we are going to have to go into this?' There didn't seem to be much of an alternative. We all said we were going to hit our targets if we made the trip. I had briefed the crews, we don't go that far and not hit our targets. I had explained that I didn't want them to go on to the target if their planes were in bad condition and they couldn't make it. But I expected to go to the target and didn't want to look around and find myself [alone].

"As we got right over it, there was a kind of steeple, almost like a church, and it was the cracking tower, our aiming point. Went right under us. We were directly on course, still running into this wall of flames and smoke. Just as we got ahead, there was a hole big enough to get about three planes through that wall. We turned and went through and everyone else came through. It probably wasn't as large for the planes that came after us. Some got singed going through, but that was the only opening. There was not a single turnback for the whole thirty-six aircraft [of the bomb group], which is remarkable for a trip that long with all that can go wrong on an airplane. I later found that one of the planes pulled out at the last minute and didn't drop his bombs.

"I believe we got our bombs off right in the cracking plant. As we turned off the target and got through this mass of smoke and fire, we could see planes from the other group. Planes were going in all directions. It was almost as you see in a war movie. You could see planes going, some crash landing. I remember one going straight up off to my right, one from another group. Two chutes came out of the open window, then the plane went into a complete stall and went in.

"I looked over and there was a German 88 millimeter aimed right at us. We were so close and so low and I yelled at Brandon, 'Pull left fast!' We turned and went right over it. I figured it couldn't traverse as rapidly if we went over it [instead] of in front of it. Fighters came in at us from the nose and various places. It was pretty touchy as you went through but it didn't last very long, fifteen minutes was the entire operation."

Ramsey Potts said, "I was coming up and running over some refineries, and we were being shot at by a lot of small antiaircraft weapons on the ground—machine guns, 40mms, and that sort of stuff. We gradually approached our target for an attack on it. Some other planes in my outfit actually dropped their bombs on the refinery we had just passed over. I think they may have been confused, believing maybe this was the target, or else maybe they were hit because quite a few planes in my formation were shot down. They may have simply jettisoned their bombs at the earliest target of opportunity. We made our [prescribed] attack but I don't think more than three airplanes in the unit actually hit the refinery they were supposed to. We had made our drop on the primary target because I had a very good navigator and he knew at all times exactly where we were. Some others had either been hit and felt it necessary to jettison or else did not know where they were because we had come in from a totally unfamiliar direction. There had been no study or planning for a run-up from the southerly direction. I had no trouble with the barrage balloons but one plane in my group hit one, partially shearing off his wing. My airplane was hit several times."

Others fared much worse. A direct hit in the bomb bay of *Euroclydon* ignited an auxiliary tank needed for the return trip. Flames sprouted from the tail and amidship as bodies hurtled free. One chute opened; another did not. The B-24 smashed to earth and burned. *Hells Wench*, bearing Col. Addison Baker, the 93d's CO, struck a balloon cable, then absorbed four punishing blows in the nose, wing, wing root, and ultimately set the cockpit ablaze. Fire raged in the now mortally struck B-24. To remain in the air and lead to the target, *Hells Wench* dumped its ordnance a few minutes before the bomb-release point. The flaming aircraft bore on, passing up an opportunity for a crash landing in wheat fields to aim at an opening between a pair of refinery stacks. Another pilot saw a man tumble out of the nosewheel hatch, his parachute burning as he drifted by so close they could see his burned legs. By Herculean effort, the pilot at the controls held the fiery wreck on its course until it fell to earth. Even though several tried to jump at the last moment, no one survived. A third doomed B-24, both wings sheared off, careened toward the ground and another suddenly exploded into a gaseous red fireball.

"While others were dropping on different installations," said Potts, "My target lay right in the middle of the Ploesti defenses. I went through those on the southern side of the refineries and then through the main defenses, passing over the northern side batteries before we finally got through. On the way home, as we were turning at low altitude in the target area, we came abreast of what appeared to be a distillation unit, a cracking plant. My left waist, a young fellow about nineteen years old, let loose with a barrage of .50-caliber machine gun at the unit, which suddenly burst into flames. That was sort of a dividend."

Ellis also steered *Daisy Mae* to its destination. "When the smoking target was almost in the windshield, Cal [Fager, his copilot] and I both hauled back on the wheel, held it a few seconds and then pushed it forward, barely clearing the chimneys as we plunged through the smoke. I felt the bombs go and saw several balloon cables snap as they struck our wings. A ship on our left waited too long to pull up and flew directly into a storage tank. Burning pieces of it disintegrated into the air and crewmen were thrown in every direction." Appalling as the carnage from antiaircraft, the nightmare entered a new phase. Enemy fighters now arrived on the scene just as the first B-24 elements from North Africa completed their runs and fled. A substantial number of the later Americans, battered by the ground batteries, were victimized by savvy German fliers.

Said Potts, "We came out of the target area, turned left to head home. I regrouped the remaining airplanes in my formation and we started back. It seemed to me I had ten or eleven planes in my formation at that point; I think we had fifteen when we began. We had lost four or five in the target area. As we climbed over the mountains coming out of the Danube Plain, we ran into those cumulus clouds again but they seemed thicker. I gave the signal to loosen up the formation to go through them. As we came out of the clouds, my right waist gunner reported that parts of an airplane were falling down through the clouds. One of the best pilots in my squadron, flying with a very good formation pilot on his wing, but who always tried to fly a bit too close—I'd warned him about it—flew in very tight, not loosened up enough. When they went into the clouds, the two planes came together. After the war I learned that three or four of the crew survived.

"When we got home," said Potts, "I believe there were seven airplanes from my formation that landed at the base and some landed elsewhere. A couple went down in Turkey and another was lost. It was a very gloomy base that night."

*Daisy Mae*, with Ellis in the cockpit, staggered toward its home field. Over Ploesti the plane had lost its number-three engine; the nosewheel was knocked out; the hydraulic system inoperative; the top turret no longer worked, and one of the .50s in the tail had been lost. In a ragged formation with eight surviving B-24s, several hours into the return, and just as the crew felt it had escaped, a coven of ME 109s appeared. They commenced a well-organized attack with a quintet charging head-on. "We either had to shoot them down, be shot down ourselves, or wait for them to run out of gas. At one-thousand yards we started firing and at eight hundred yards everyone was firing. Tracers literally covered the sky and 20mm shells exploded all through our formation. Our gunners got the range and the two ME 109s on the right were hit hard; one exploded immediately, and the other blew up just after passing the formation. But we didn't exactly win that round. One B-24 was burning furiously, and the crew members were already bailing out. That left eight B-24s in formation for the second attack. The Jerries tried the same tactics, this time six abreast. Again they all fired together and the lead ME 109 completely disintegrated as it was caught in our deadly crossfire. Another was smoking and again a B-24 went down in flames. This time we only counted five chutes out."

The enemy fighters changed their tactics, buzzing from all directions. Holes appeared in the fuselage and a 20mm shell injured bombardier Gioana and engineer Sgt. James Ayers. A direct hit smashed the tail turret. Another 20mm ripped the left rudder, a chunk of the elevator surface disappeared, and two more shells into *Daisy Mae* sprayed Gioana with shrapnel. The damage included severed control cables and the ME 109s, now short on fuel, departed. Over the ocean, the crew jettisoned most of their machine guns and ammunition. Ellis hoped to avoid going down at sea since Gioana had lapsed into unconsciousness. *Daisy Mae* wobbled to a night landing fifteen hours after it had left the desert. Four of the crew merited Purple Hearts.

Of the 1,600-plus airmen who got off the ground for Operation Tidal Wave, more than 300 died, hundreds more were wounded or captured, seventy-nine were interned in Turkey. From the 176 Liberators assigned to the affair, only thirty-three could be listed as fit for duty the following day. It was altogether the worst day in the Air Corps' war so far. Perhaps conscious of the impact upon morale, the authorities conferred four Medals of Honor (two posthumously). No other mission during World War II brought more than a single such decoration upon the men involved. Two subsequent attacks on Ploesti added another pair of Medals of Honor (both recipients KIA on scene), a bleak testament to the ferocious defenses that surrounded the oil complex.

The fire, smoke, and destruction observed by the aircrews and shown on reconnaissance photographs taken after 1 August indicated a serious blow to enemy facilities. President Roosevelt apprised Congress of the casualties, but declared, "I am certain that the German or Japanese High Commands would cheerfully sacrifice tens of thousands of men to do the same amount of damage to us, if they could." But in fact, Ploesti prior to Tidal Wave functioned at only an estimated 60 percent of capacity. While some installations had been reduced to rubble, the production pace quickly resumed a normal rate. Ploesti registered one essential fact with the Air Corps. The surest, most awful route to disaster lay in low-level attacks by its heavyweights. Within a few weeks, an event of almost equally terrible magnitude would befall the Eighth Air Force.

To directly implement Pointblank, the Eighth embarked on twin strikes at the Messerschmitt factory in Regensburg and the ball-bearing plants at Schweinfurt, both of which lay deep inside Germany. Curtailment of enemy fighter-plane production at an installation that supplied 200 MEs a month was an obvious goal. Schweinfurt churned out 42 percent of the country's ball bearings, the antifriction mechanisms vital to aircraft, tanks, weapons, ships, subs, and other manufacturing operations. For the first time, the mission would reach the magic figure of 300 heavy bombers with 376 from 16 bomb groups assigned to the runs.

Actually, the strategists had planned a three-point attack. While the U.K.-based heavyweights slammed Regensburg and Schweinfurt, planes from North Africa, including those that attacked Ploesti, would return to England via Wiener Neustadt, site of a Focke-Wulf factory. However, the bomber groups based in England, busy pounding airfields in hopes of suppressing fighter attacks, and plagued with habitual weather problems, postponed their effort. Carl Spaatz, in charge of the Ninth, impatient with the delay, and probably prodded by Hap Arnold in the States as well as his RAF colleagues, ordered the strike against Wiener Neustadt 13 August without waiting any longer for the Eighth to dispatch its aircraft.

Ramsay Potts, flying one of the 93d's B-24s to Wiener Neustadt recalled, "It was another thirteen-hour mission, with no fighter escort like all those flown from North Africa. When you got attacked by enemy fighter planes it was just a question of trying to fight it out. Because of previous strikes at the Wiener Neustadt plant, the Germans knew it was in range of our bombers. Therefore, they increased the flak defenses as well as enemy fighters in the target area. It was very important that we compress our attack time in order to have minimum exposure to flak. I led the third group. As we flew up toward the area, the second group lagged behind and I closed in as much as I could trying to get them to move up. When we finally got to the target area and the second group still hung back, I closed the gap. Finally, we were over the target and I was now number two in sequence rather than number three.

"If you have the maximum amount of planes going through over the target at about the same time, the ground guns can only fire at the lead ones and by the time they reload, resight, and reaim, a number of planes have passed over. The gunners then must pick up someone from the rear. So the number of shots any battery can take at a formation is more limited than if you are spread out. We came off the target and there was a very severe fighter attack from the rear. It centered on the original number-two group that now occupied the third position. If I hadn't closed in, the fighters would have hit us. The other group had very heavy losses, as much as half their force. I think my group lost only two airplanes.

"We got home and the other group commander was very upset about his losses to severe antiaircraft plus aggressive fighter opposition. He and I had rather strong words about what happened. There was a board convened to analyze whether there was any fault or blame. Finally, they said I'd done the right thing closing in. But for a while that didn't relieve the tension between the other commander and me. After a while when he had thought about it, he realized it was just one of the things that happen in a war. If he had been where he should have, my groups would have caught the heaviest part of the attacks, not his."

Meanwhile, the script organized the B-17s into a single compact force that would split south of Frankfurt, with 230 ships from the 1st Air Division destined for Schweinfurt. The remainder, drawn from the 3d Air Division commanded by LeMay and all of which had the Tokyo tanks, would continue toward Regensburg, 110 miles southeast. They would then fly over Austria and Italy to bases in Algeria. The crews who attended the predawn briefing, and saw the maps with the extended ribbons into southern Germany, understood what they faced.

On 17 August, exactly one year after the very first B-17 paid a call on occupied Europe, the Eighth Air Force gave the go signal. At the scheduled takeoff times a ground fog so thick as to make it impossible even to taxi aircraft to the runways halted operations. The opaque clouds extending high above the United Kingdom obscured the skies, rendering formation assembly too susceptible to midair collisions. Bomber Command delayed the beginning of the mission to Regensburg for ninety minutes. LeMay, who had insisted that those in his 4th Bomb Wing practice instrument take-offs, advised Bomber Command he believed his outfit could get airborne if he used ground crews with flashlights to guide the aircraft as they taxied to the end of the runways. Any further wait meant the aircraft would be hunting for the unfamiliar Algerian fields as darkness came. LeMay himself scrambled aboard the lead aircraft of the 96th Bomb Group.

The assembly above the overcast skies went off relatively smoothly, but an angry LeMay demanded of Bomber Command the whereabouts of the escorts and the 1st Bomb Wing (assigned to Schweinfurt). The P-47s, socked in by the weather and without the navigational tools installed in the bombers, never connected with his 4th Bomb Wing. The Schweinfurt groups, also bowing to the restrictions on visibility, delayed departure. Disgusted, LeMay headed for Regensburg without the others. The 1st Bomb Wing took off almost four hours late, eliminating any possibility of the two forces entering Germany as a united phalanx to divide German predators and mitigate concentration upon either element. In fact, having hammered LeMay's troops bound for Regensburg, the *Luftwaffe* refueled and rearmed to savage those targeting Schweinfurt.

The 100th Bomb Group, one of the most recent additions to the Eighth Air Force, part of LeMay's contingent, took off from its base at Thorpe Abbotts, northeast of London. Operations officer Maj. Jack Kidd occupied a copilot's seat as the group filled the unenviable position of the last outfit in the formation. Harry H. Crosby, a navigator for the 100th, an outfit that had a reputation for slack discipline and sloppy formations, credited Kidd with having brought to the outfit a more disciplined attitude. "I remember once during a briefing the air crews were acting up and making smart-ass, ribald remarks. Jack pointed to one and said, 'Stand up.' Jack said, 'You're the kind of person who does not listen. Unless you shape up, you will be the kind of person who does not come back from a mission.' The man sat down and the briefing was quiet."

Like all staff officers, Kidd flew selected missions. "Somebody else was scheduled to lead that shuttle mission from the 100th [Regensburg] to Africa, but at the last minute I was put in as the command pilot to lead our group, which was the last and the lowest in the 3d Division." Some 240 P-47s sought to provide safe conduct for the B-17s as they entered enemy air space. Unfortunately, those assigned to protect the 3d Division never caught up with the bombers bound for Regensburg. "The enemy fighters," reported Kidd, "seemed to gang up on us. It took less fuel for them to get up ahead of the group and come on back in. The farther ahead they flew, the less fuel they would have. Their fire was murderous."

Harry Crosby, as navigator in Kidd's aircraft, noted the appearance of the first Focke-Wulfs over Holland as the fifteen-mile-long fleet of B-17s flitted across the foe's radar screens. "Gaggles of ME 109s and FW 190s came up behind us, paused, and then slid up and under us. Arcs of our .50-

caliber tracers and their 20mm cannon fire scorched the sky. Beams of horror threaded our formation. The tail gunner reported, 'The whole last element in the low squadron went out.' " Crosby wrote in his logbook the names of the crew commanders who were shot down and counted thirty lost friends from the three aircraft. As the opposing aircraft flailed away at one another, both sides scored kills; the ball gunner reported over the intercom that he had counted sixty parachutes in the air at one time, men leaping from bombers and fighters.

In the copilot seat of a B-17 of the 100th sat Lt. Col. Beirne Lay, a veteran of just four missions but expected to command a bomber group. He was on hand as an observer, charged with drafting a first-hand account of events along with recommendations for improvements in procedures. Lay, gifted with reportorial skills, later would coauthor with Sy Bartlett, another Eighth Air Force staff officer, the screenplay for the film *Twelve O'Clock High*, based upon what Lay saw. (Veterans of the air war over Europe consider it the best movie on the subject.)

"At 1017 hrs," said Lay in his official report, "near Woensdrecht [Holland] I saw the first flak blossom out in our vicinity, light and inaccurate. A few minutes later . . . two FW 190s appeared at 1 o'clock level and whizzed through the formation ahead of us in a frontal attack, nicking two B-17s of the 95th Group in the wings. . . . Smoke immediately trailed from both B-17s but they held their stations. As the fighters passed us at a high rate of closure, the guns of our group went into action. The pungent smell of burnt powder filled our cockpit, and the B-17 trembled to the recoil of nose and ball-turret guns. I saw pieces fly off the wing of one of the fighters. . . . For a few seconds the interphone was busy with admonitions; 'Lead 'em more' . . .

'short bursts' . . . 'don't throw rounds away' . . . 'there'll be more along in a minute.'

"A coordinated attack followed, with the head-on fighters coming in from slightly above, the 9 and 3 o'clock attackers approaching from about level, and the rear attackers from slightly below. Every gun from every B-17 in our group and the 95th was firing, crisscrossing our patch of the sky with tracers to match the time-fuse cannon-shell puffs that squirted from the wings of the Jerry single-seaters. I would estimate that 75 percent of our fire was inaccurate, falling astern of the target—particularly the fire from hand-held guns. Nevertheless, both sides got hurt in this clash, with two B-17s from our low squadron and one from the 95th Group falling out of formation on fire with crews bailing out, and several fighters heading for the deck in flames or with their pilots lingering behind under dirty yellow parachutes. Our group leader, Maj. John Kidd, pulled us nearer the 95th Group for mutual support."

The dismayed Lay looked out his window at two entire squadrons of interceptors climbing to a parallel position, and ahead of the 100th, preparing to turn and slash through the formation. Over the interphone he heard reports of a similar situation building on the other side while down below more enemy planes rose into the air. Off to one side, out of range, an ME 110 radioed information on the disposition, route, speed, and other vital information on the Americans.

"At the sight of all these fighters, I had the distinct feeling of being trapped—that the Hun was tipped off, or at least had guessed our destination and was waiting for us." Americans frequently insisted the Germans learned of missions through spies, but more likely, early-warning radar stations tipped the *Luftwaffe* to operations. "No P-47s were visible," continued Lay. "The life expectancy of the 100th Group suddenly seemed very short, since it already appeared that the fighters were passing up the preceding groups, with the exception of the 95th, to take a cut at us.

"Swinging their yellow noses around in a wide U-turn, the twelve-ship squadron of ME 109s came in from twelve to two o'clock in pairs and in fours and the main event was on. A shining silver object sailed past over our right wing. I recognized it as a main exit door. Seconds later a dark object came hurtling through the formation, barely missing several props. It was a man, clasping his knees to his head, revolving like a diver in a triple somersault. I didn't see his chute open.

"A B-17 turned gradually out of the formation to the right, maintaining altitude. In a split second, the B-17 completely disappeared in a brilliant explosion, from which the only remains were four small balls of fire, the fuel tanks, which were quickly consumed as they fell earthward.

"Our airplane was endangered by various debris. Emergency hatches, exit doors, prematurely opened parachutes, bodies, and assorted fragments of B-17s and Hun fighters breezed past us in the slip stream. . . . I watched two fighters explode not far beneath, disappearing in sheets of orange flame, B-17s dropping out in every stage of distress, from engines on fire to control surfaces shot away, friendly and enemy parachutes floating down, and on the green carpet far behind us, numerous funeral pyres of smoke from fallen fighters, marking our trail.

"I watched a B-17 turn slowly to the right with its cockpit a mass of flames. The copilot crawled out of his window, held on with one hand, reached back for his 'chute, buckled it on, let go, and was whisked back into the horizontal stabilizer. I believe the impact killed him. His 'chute didn't open. . . . Our B-17 shook steadily with the fire of its .50s and the air inside was heavy with smoke. It was cold in the cockpit, but when I looked across at Lt. Thomas Murphy, the pilot, sweat was pouring off his forehead and over his oxygen mask. He turned the controls over to me for a while. It was a blessed relief to concentrate on holding station in formation instead of watching those everlasting fighters boring in. . . . Then the top-turret gunner's twin muzzles would pound away a foot above my head, giving a realistic imitation of cannon shells exploding in the cockpit, while I gave an even better imitation of a man jumping six inches out of his seat.

"After we had been under constant attack for a solid hour," continued Lay, "it appeared certain that the 100th Group was faced with annihilation. Seven of our group had been shot down, the sky was still mottled with rising fighters, and it was only 1120 hours with target-time still thirty-five minutes away. I doubt if a man in the group visualized the possibility of our getting much farther without 100 percent loss. . . . I had long since mentally accepted the fact of death and that it was simply a question of the next second or the next minute. I learned firsthand a man can resign himself to the certainty of death without becoming panicky. Our group firepower was reduced 33 percent, ammunition was running low. Our tail guns had to be replenished from another gun station.

"Near the IP at 1150 hours, one hour and a half after the first of at least 200 individual fighter attacks," said Lay, "the pressure eased off, although hostiles were still in the vicinity. We turned at the IP at 1154 hrs with 14 B-17s left in the group, two of which were badly crippled. They dropped out soon after bombing the target and headed for Switzerland. . . . Weather over the target, as on the entire trip, was ideal. Flak was negligible. The group got its bombs away promptly on the leader. As we turned and headed for the Alps, I got a grim satisfaction out of seeing a rectangular column of smoke rising straight up from the ME 109 shops, with only one burst over the town of Regensburg." Beirne regarded the trip to Africa as anticlimactic. Only a few fighters pecked at the planes and a single burst of flak greeted them over the Brenner Pass. "At 1815 hrs, with red lights showing on all our fuel tanks in my ship, the seven B-17s of the group still in formation circled over Bertouz [a Tunisian airfield] and landed in the dust."

Kidd recalled, "We lost on that mission seven out of our twenty-one airplanes. [Official figures say nine.] One of ours belly-landed on a lake in Switzerland and they spent the rest of the year there. The flight to Africa was about twelve hours, quite a number of planes hit the water. We landed at a little dirt field that was hard and smooth. We stayed for a week. At a postmission critique, General LeMay asked me where the rest of my airplanes were. I said, 'They were shot down, sir.' That ended the conversation."

The scorecard for the 3d Division appalled everyone. Of the 127 "effectives" after 19 aborted, 24 B-17s went down and one more could not be restored. Fifty aircraft needed repairs. Aircraft could be replaced relatively quickly and painlessly as the war plants in the States accelerated into high gear. The human cost of Regensburg was another matter. The aircraft that survived brought back 4 dead or mortally wounded, and 9 men who required hospitalization. Two hundred MIA were either dead, in prison camps, or enemy hospitals.

Regensburg was only half of the savagery visited upon the Eighth Air Force on 17 August. An even bigger armada consisting of 188 B-17s (a whopping 42 from those originally dispatched chose to call off their participation for mechanical or other reasons) struck at the ball-bearing center of Schweinfurt. The long interval between the start of this mission and LeMay's enabled the enemy fighters to rearm and greet the day's second stream of B-17s with fury. For ninety minutes, from the Belgian coast to the target, the MEs and FWs battled the stolid procession of Forts.

More than 424 tons of ordnance exploded amid the ball-bearing factories. The return from the target eased only near Eupen on the German-Belgian border where squadrons of P-47s appeared to fly shotgun. When back on the ground, the 1st Bomb Wing counted 36 B-17s missing with 352 airmen. Three aircraft that crash-landed in England went on the scrap heap and another 118 required the attentions of mechanics and sheet-metal workers. The maximum effort drained so much strength from the Eighth Air Force that for the following two weeks, the magnitude of missions dropped below 100 bombers per objective.

# 4

# Avalanche, Shingle, and Defeats

AN IMMEDIATE RESULT OF THE CAPTURE OF SICILY WAS THE END
of Benito Mussolini's dictatorship over Italy. In his place
Field Marshal Pietro Badoglio assumed the mantle of premier. Although Badoglio publicly said he intended to continue the fight alongside the Germans, whose troops
pervaded the country, he secretly sought to negotiate a surrender. Cloak-and-dagger plots abounded, with representatives of the premier in clandestine meetings with Allied
officials in neutral Portugal, and Gen. Maxwell Taylor slip-
ping undercover into Rome in an attempt to set up an airborne coup that would liberate the Eternal City.

While diplomats conferred and secret agents schemed, on
3 September, from Messina, Montgomery put two divisions
ashore near Reggio Calabria, the toe of the Italian boot.
When Badoglio temporized about surrender, Eisenhower
forced the issue. With four American divisions scheduled
to strike at Salerno in the early hours of 9 September, the
supreme commander informed Badoglio he would announce

Italy out of the war shortly before the GIs landed. The Italian leader capitulated.

Operation Avalanche, the Salerno attack, united the Rangers and the British Commandos who came ashore north of the city to block enemy forces concentrated toward the Naples area. "Our landings went like clockwork," said Allen Merrill. "We had the total element of surprise. We started down the coast road while dawn's first light was in its earliest stages." Through his field glasses, Merrill saw the panorama of ships streaming toward the harbor, with the small craft filled with troops already assembling. "I heard shellfire and the loud ka-boom of our naval guns beginning the softening-up process. If they had the element of surprise, with this bombardment, they had lost it."

The sound of a vehicle alerted the Ranger scout. A motorcycle with a sidecar approached him. Merrill vaulted into its path. "I levelled my Thompson submachine gun at the driver's head and yelled in my best German, *'Alt, Ve gast!'* The motorcycle skidded to a stop within ten feet of me. I ran up to it and pushed my Tommy gun into the ribs of the driver and yelled, *'Hanz oiten!'* I saw the unmistakable look of fright in his face. Beside him sat a German officer, no helmet, his officer's dress cap at a jaunty angle, and a sneer upon his otherwise handsome face. I motioned for him, saying the same *Hanz oiten*. He did not raise his hands. I was close enough to reach out and touch him. I did, with the butt end of my Thompson. He got the message. His hand fingered the blood dripping from his bruised lip and both hands raised. A scabbard held a rifle on the motorcycle. I took it out and flung it as far as I could."

The prisoners were led off while Merrill and the second scout cautiously explored the road in search of the German officer's destination. They discovered steps leading down from the road to a building. The company commander decided it was an observation post, and a squad, with Merrill and Bob, the second scout, in the lead, carefully approached a concrete structure behind a closed gate. "Bob and I unlatched the gate and slowly entered the courtyard. We stepped to the double door and called out again to come out [in Italian and German] but got no reply. I raised my foot and smashed the doorknob with the heel of my boot. It never budged. In a matter of seconds, two objects came flying out of the open window and landed with a tremendous roar in the sheltered courtyard. The concussion deafened me. The shrapnel tore into our bodies. I don't remember seeing Bob nearby. I rose after being knocked down and ran for cover.

"I yelled for cover fire as I ran behind some of the mountain jutting into the courtyard. I would be safe here from our own guns that would be opening up on this place. My squad had orders to hit the place with everything they had, bazookas included. I could not hear a thing. But from the vibration, smoke, and debris falling around, I knew the squad were hitting them with all the firepower we had. I sat on a rock and kept my eyes on the space between the fence and the mountain. My Tommy gun was trained on that space.

"Slowly I tried to ascertain my injuries. I felt a burning sensation in my legs. It seemed to be where most of the damage was. I used my first-aid kit and sprinkled sulfa on all the wounds I could see. I gave myself a shot of morphine from the break-off vials we carried. I was not aware of time passing. Something very heavy had hit the concrete building. The vibration and rocks scattered high and far. But they were in another direction away from me. I wondered about Bob and what had happened to him. I stood and found I could move around. I decided as long as I could walk I would have to move away from here. The only way was up the side of the mountain. It was steep and boulder-strewn with outgrowths of small trees and shrubs. The pain wasn't too bad as I made my way. The sun was up fully. It may have been ten or eleven A.M. Slowly I trudged upward. After some time, I found a small flattened hollow of ground and lay down to catch my breath. When all the shooting stopped and the OP was taken, the CO sent a couple of guys to look for me. They found me asleep in the noonday sun, in the small hollow.

"They carried me topside and a medic bandaged my legs. I explained what had happened. The CO already knew. Bob had run the opposite way from me and back to the squad waiting on the stairway. They had taken him to a medic and then notified the CO, who brought the company to deal with the OP and its inhabitants. There were four Italian soldiers in it and a German officer. It was at his insistence that they fought it out. They had had a white flag ready for total surrender when we approached. The German is the one who threw the grenades out the window. After the barrage from the company, one of the Italians shot the German from behind in the head. Then the rest ran out with hands up. Only two of them made it to surrender. Mortars have no way of discriminating between the good guys and the bad."

Merrill, his legs bandaged from toe to hip, rode to a field hospital in the motorcycle that he had captured a few hours earlier. As he awaited evacuation, he saw Bob, lying on his stomach, posterior and back swathed in bandages. The following morning both boarded an LST to the British hospital vessel *St. Andrew*. "The ship was taking on wounded soldiers all through that day and most of the night. There were two air raids that night; the *Luftwaffe* was out in strength. On the second raid, around midnight, our ship took several bombs amidship and started to sink. Many were killed that night. Some who had been wounded ashore thought they were out of harm's way on this well-lighted ship, plainly marked with red crosses. The bombardment of the *St. Andrew* sent it to the bottom of Salerno Bay, along with hundreds of Allied wounded and the gallant crew that worked feverishly to take as many of us littered wounded off before it sank with a gurgling, horrible sound.

"We hovered alongside another British hospital ship for hours, each waiting his turn to be hoisted up the side and bedded down in the ship's hold. Many were treated again for shrapnel wounds from the air bombing. Some of the wounded did not make it to the new ship, the *Newfoundland*. It left the battle zone the following morning, heavily shelled but sailed under its own power to North Africa where it discharged its human cargo."

Mark Clark nominated the 36th Division, a former Texas National Guard outfit, to lead the U.S. VI Corps into Salerno. The division commander, Maj. Gen. Fred L. Walker, declined a prelanding barrage from the Navy because he expected minor opposition and wanted to spare civilians in the city. His decision exposed the first waves, crawling and cutting through barbed wire, to considerable German fire. Nevertheless, the troops overcame the defenses and gained a four-mile-deep foothold. The 45th and 3d Infantry Divisions were to follow the 36th.

The Germans quickly recovered and applied increasingly strong pressure upon the narrow foothold carved by the 36th and its Ranger attachments. At some places the beachhead shrank to only two miles, into which the enemy concentrated artillery and air raids. With his forces in danger of being divided, Clark drafted emergency plans to evacuate his command.

In Sicily, the prickly William Yarborough, executive offi-

cer for the 504th Parachute Infantry Regiment, joined Mark
Clark's staff to plan the use of airborne forces. Yarborough
visited the Salerno beachhead. "We were bombarded by
Kraut airplanes both day and night. It was a real nerve-
wracking thing and Fifth Army headquarters would be
crawling around on hands and knees in the weeds, no higher
than the waist, four stars, three stars, all of us together."
Clark requested reinforcements by the 82d Airborne. "We'd
gone through the terrible experience of Sicily, where our
planes had been shot down by our own gunners, so I picked
out a section of beach where we'd have this great cross
marked by five-gallon containers of gasoline-soaked sand
and light them.

"General [Alfred] Gruenther put out instructions urging
that no antiaircraft battery on the beachhead would fire at
anything under any circumstances during the period when
the airlift was coming in from Sicily. Didn't matter whether
we were being attacked. There was a real dramatic business
waiting for them to arrive. Everything was quiet on the
beachhead. Finally hearing the hum of the motors in the distance. Because we had no mechanical means of picking
them up from that distance we were wondering whether they
were German bombers or our planes. Finally, the first of the
C-47s came over." In at least one instance the gasoline-
impregnated signals were only ignited after the troopers
jumped, having recognized from the moonlight their target.
Two regiments dropped on 13–14 September, while the
third jumped the following evening.

Lieutenant Ed Sims, the paratrooper, after a few months
as a military governor in a Sicilian town, returned to Bizerte
as a platoon leader for Company H of the 3d Battalion of the
504th as it prepared for a special operation. "Early in September Company H loaded onto an LCI and left Bizerte for

Rome. Our mission was to enter the Tiber River, south of Rome, and then land and capture a nearby airfield so the remainder of the 82d Airborne would airdrop and seize Rome. The Italian Army in that area was to assist. As we approached the area of the Tiber, orders canceled our mission. Subsequently we received new ones to head for Salerno." Maxwell Taylor had realized he could not arrange a strong enough commitment from Italian officials for support against the Germans in the Rome area.

Sims's outfit coordinated its operations near Salerno with the Rangers in the locale. "We moved inland and went into the mountains where we seized some high ground near the Chiunzi Pass area, including a vital tunnel. My platoon occupied positions at the tunnel on the right flank of the company. Our strength at that time was about 120 men." The rugged mountain area was not difficult to defend. There were only two roads by which Germans could move heavy equipment. "During [our] ten days in this area, the Germans made a number of attempts to get through but were repulsed. For our action, the company received the Presidential Unit Citation."

Yarborough said, "I went up to see [Ruben] Tucker and his people the morning after they had gotten in. The results of combat were all over the place. There were a lot of dead lying around. They didn't have a chance to bury them. They were fighting too hard." Yarborough plotted an airborne assault upon Avellino, a town nestled in a mountain pass twenty miles inland. It was a choke point for traffic toward Salerno. The action failed to follow the plan. The pathfinders, dropped earlier to home in the main body of the C-47s, missed their marks and there was no time for an adjustment. The devices designed to guide in the aircraft either did not work or functioned only intermittently. The scattered troopers harassed the enemy but while making their way back to the Fifth Army lines, the battalion commander, Doyle Yardley, was wounded and taken prisoner. Yardley's misfortune, however, enabled Yarborough to achieve his goal, command of a battalion.

Meanwhile, the British Navy ferried that nation's 1st Airborne to the port of Taranto on the east coast. Eisenhower has argued that the move drained away opposition to Montgomery coming from Reggio Calabria, but some military historians suggest the troops and the scarce landing craft could have been more useful at Salerno. Still, although the Nazi forces in Italy considerably outnumbered the Allied troops, heavy support from the Air Corps, the fleet offshore, and the timely introduction of the 82d Airborne elements established the U.S. Fifth Army under Mark Clark as a going concern on the mainland. The Allied purchase on Italy continued to expand and by mid-December the ground forces pushed nearly 100 miles up the shin and calf of Italy. Three British divisions fought under the banner of the U.S. Fifth Army along with five American ones. Montgomery led six more divisions, including units from the British Empire as well as Englishmen. The Allies captured two vital objectives: the great port of Naples on the west coast, and the airdrome at Foggia in the east near the Adriatic.

Sims and the entire 504th Parachute Infantry Regiment attacked north to help oust the enemy from Naples. He characterizes the resistance there as sporadic, with three days of house-to-house combat against small groups of enemy soldiers who had been cut off. Behind them the Germans left numerous booby traps that brought additional casualties, particularly among civilians. The advance, however, slowed until progress was measured in yards. In place of the "soft underbelly" promised by Churchill, the soldiers fought a skilled, well-armed enemy in mountainous terrain optimally suited for defense and in increasingly wretched weather.

Bill Kunz, with a 3d Division artillery battalion, said, "We began many weeks in the miserable Italian rainy season. We got cold and stayed that way. The mountains seemed endless. Mule trains with ammo, rations, radio supplies moved up, the dead and wounded back down. Much of this was night activity. We would establish an OP on a hill, fire some missions, move down into a valley, up another hill, and repeat the operations. Mud was everywhere; sometimes the only things that could move were men and mules." After the GIs crossed the Volturno River, in mid-October, the Italian winter worsened.

While all other elements of the 82d Airborne left Italy for England, where they would ready themselves for the cross-channel invasion, the 504th PIR, with Ed Sims, pursued the enemy northeast of Naples into the rugged Apennine Mountains. "We were restricted to movement by foot," said Sims, "and had to carry our equipment and ammunition. The few mules we had were a big help, but progress was slow in these treacherous mountains. The numerous booby traps and destruction of trails made it more difficult. Near Colli Lazali, Company H was ordered to attack and seize Hill 1017. The attack started by fording a raging stream, then up the south slope of the hill. Resistance was moderate but the entire area had been heavily mined with antipersonnel devices. The first casualty was the company commander who had his heel blown off. The officer who then took command, within minutes fell from a cliff when he tried to avoid incoming artillery and broke his leg. At that point I assumed command of the company and continued to direct the attack. Due to enemy fire and the mines we had to proceed slowly and cautiously. While doing so, many S-mines were activated causing a number of casualties. Of the three mines I stepped on, the first one angled up under a mule in front of me and demolished his rear end. The second one, while I was carrying a wounded man, exploded in the ground when it failed to bounce up, and the third bounced up but failed to explode. By late afternoon, we were able to take the hill and set up a defense. I ordered everyone to stay in place until I could get our engineers to clear the mines.

In the increasingly frigid, rainy winter, fighting in the mountains, crouched in foxholes for extended periods, men developed trench foot, a World War I malady. Wet, near-frozen feet, with no opportunity to dry, developed circulatory problems that could cause gangrene, loss of toes, or even the foot itself. Harold Taylor observed, ". . . a caravan of stretchers winding its way down the side of the mountain to a clearing. These were men killed in action . . . their corpses were in white bags. In this clearing the tagged bodies were stacked like a cord of wood until they could be removed to a burial site. It brought a prayer to my lips and sadness to my heart."

Ernie Pyle, who accompanied the 36th Infantry Division as it drove north into the mountains, wrote, "Dead men had been coming down the mountain all evening lashed onto the backs of mules. They came lying belly-down across the wooden packsaddles, their heads hanging down on one side, their stiffened legs sticking awkwardly from the other, bobbing up and down as the mules walked.

"The Italian mule skinners were afraid to walk beside the men so Americans had to lead the mules down that night. Even the Americans were reluctant to unlash and lift off the bodies when they got to the bottom, so an officer had to do it himself and ask others to help." Pyle's column describing the recovery of a company commander's body and the sorrow of his troops inspired the film *The Story of GI Joe*.

In late November, Bill Kunz and his section dug in on the side of a draw looking down on the village of Mignano. "Normally, you stay out of draws because Jerry has his mortars zeroed in on them. We thought this one a little safer and there was an aid station located across from us. It had about thirty or so wounded, plus a few medics located under shelter halves [half a pup tent] spread out over the dugout area. It seemed okay until one of our fighter planes dropped a bomb short of the bomb line, a direct hit on our aid station. All wounded and medics were buried. It was raining so hard and was so muddy that a rescue attempt was useless."

Unhappy with the pace of the offense, the high command had replaced the VI Corps leader with John Lucas. Bespectacled, gray-haired, habitually chomping on a corn-cob pipe, Lucas hardly sprang from the leadership mold that formed his friend Patton. The change in command failed to generate any momentum. The Allied armies faced a series of German positions known as the Winter Line that stretched across Italy. It actually consisted of three separate defense systems, the Barbara Line, the Bernhard Line, and the most daunting Gustav Line. These barred the path to Rome, a glittering attraction because of its prestigious status, its equal importance as a hub for roads and rail lines, and as the home of the Vatican.

The strategists pondered a way to drain off the formidable forces that blocked passages through the steep ranges between the Allied soldiers and Rome. Mark Clark and his staff proposed to strike the enemy head-on and simultaneously leapfrog beyond the Winter Line with an amphibious operation that would put a minimum of two infantry divisions ashore at Anzio and Nettuno. These were Tyrrhenian

Sea towns sixty miles beyond the coastal positions occupied by British units, but only thirty-five miles from the outskirts of Rome. The theory held that the Anzio encroachment would force Field Marshal Albert Kesselring to withdraw elements preventing further advances from the south. That retreat would be cut off by the troops based at Anzio. And if Kesselring did not pull his defenders back to Rome, the GIs at Anzio could head for the Eternal City. Anzio drew the enthusiastic backing of Churchill. Eisenhower, in *Crusade in Europe*, indicates he was less sanguine, warning of shortages in means of supply and reinforcement for the beachhead.

The quickest route for the main body of the Allied armies from the south lay through the wide plain of the Liri Valley along the axis of Highway 6. But the Germans, entrenched in the hills and mountains on both sides, mounted stalwart defenses at the gates. In particular they infested Monte Cassino, crowned with a historic Roman Catholic abbey. The town of that name, at the base of the slope, bristled with enemy troops and guns. As the two sides organized themselves in front of Monte Cassino, considerations other than military ones governed their actions. Neither wanted to antagonize the Vatican by destroying a venerated piece of religious ground and its artistic treasures. Franklin D. Roosevelt, as a political animal, was always sensitive to complaints of insensitivity to ethnic voting blocs such as Roman Catholics or Americans of Italian descent.

On 29 December, Eisenhower informed all commanders, ". . . If we have to choose between destroying a famous building and sacrificing our own men, then our men's lives count infinitely more and the buildings must go. But the choice is not always so clear-cut as that. In many cases the monuments can be spared without any detriment to operational needs. Nothing can stand against the argument of military necessity. . . . But the phrase 'military necessity' is sometimes used where it would be more truthful to speak of military convenience or even of personal convenience." That proscription notwithstanding, some Roman Catholic institutions had been hit and church personnel killed.

The Germans also appeared to refrain from exploiting Monte Cassino's massive stone walls as a ready-made defensive fortress. They did remove artwork, ostensibly to protect it from damage, but some of it was consigned to Hermann Goering's private collection. In addition, livestock had been requisitioned as food for the *Wehrmacht*. Even as both sides pledged to respect the integrity of the abbey, their artillery whistled overhead, generally targeted upon each other. However, errant shells struck the monastery buildings and a steady stream of injured civilian was brought for care by the clerics.

Ernest Harmon, as CO of the 1st Armored Division, attended the conference where Fifth Army boss Mark Clark and the other senior military honchos considered possibilities for a breakthrough. Clark proposed a plan for crossing the Rapido, establishing a bridgehead, and then pushing the 1st Armored up the Liri Valley to Highway 6 which led directly to Rome. "Everyone in the meeting except Clark was opposed to the plan," remembered Harmon, "because they felt you couldn't possibly cross the river with the enemy holding both ridges and looking down your throat. We felt you had to have at least one of the ridges. We were overridden and the 36th Infantry Division was assigned to make the crossing." Clark and his staff drew up a plan in which the French Expeditionary Corps and the British would strike at the high ground while the GIs forded the Rapido River. That icy stream, thirty-five to forty feet wide, about four feet deep, coursed swiftly between six-foot banks. The heavily entrenched enemy had sown mines on both sides.

General Fred Walker of the 36th regarded the enterprise with trepidation. He told his diary, "I do not know a single case in military history where an attempt to cross a river that is incorporated into the main line of resistance has succeeded. So I am prepared for defeat." News that the attacks on either side of him by the French and British had flopped added to his gloom.

John Goode entered the ranks of the 36th Division as a replacement officer about a month after the start of Avalanche. As the executive officer for K Company, 141st Regiment, Goode had endured six weeks on the line before the outfit started a ten-day R & R as 1943 ended. "When we reentered combat about January 10th," said Goode, "we moved close to the Rapido. Our first forty-five-day combat tour had seen K Company reduced to sixty men for duty. I was the only surviving officer because of transfers and casualties. Our losses were more from weather, mud, and cold than battle casualties, although we had our share of them. We had never been used in an attack, such as our 2d Battalion at San Pietro. Forty-five days of K rations had taken its toll. I developed night blindness because of a vitamin deficiency, where my vision declined with darkness to a point and then to total blindness. Discouraging for a combat officer. It would come and go, and it didn't seem to make that much difference. Our second tour of combat saw a company filled with replacement officers and enlistment. We were no longer a team. Gone was the feeling that you could rely on your people.

"On the night of January 19 I was ordered to take a patrol across the Rapido and take prisoners or kill a Jerry and get his 'Pay Book' so that his unit could be identified. I did get to see a bit of the German sector just north of our position but didn't learn anything.

"The next night we were ordered to proceed north on a road just east of the Rapido to a point about one mile north of our position, just west of Mount Troccio. We were told that we were to cross the Rapido and take the town of Pignataro, some distance west of the river. No field order was issued. You might have thought we were off on a stroll in the park, from the mood of the occasion. We were ordered to send a detail of riflemen to guard the Battalion CP. We should have learned something from that. We were not shown a map of our crossing area, which would have revealed we were crossing an 'S' bend in the river. We were not advised that this peninsula was sealed off by a double apron, barbed-wire fence. German barbed-wire fences were usually rigged with mines and trip wires to antipersonnel mines.

"On our way from below San Angelo to the point above it we were very close to our artillery pieces, which laid down an artillery concentration of at least ten minutes. You could have read a newspaper from the muzzle blasts of light produced by these guns. The artillery seemed to always fire shells with super-quick fuses, rather than delayed-action fuses. One had only to turn a screw in the fuse to set on five-second delay. Super-quick fuses are best when firing on an attacking enemy. Against dugouts and the heavy emplacements of a German deliberate defense only delayed-action fuses could hurt them. In addition, each such shell would have dug a place for a man to hide, while advancing under fire.

"We picked up an 'assault bridge' at this point. It was made of three or four inflated rubber life rafts or boats from ten to twelve feet long, with a slatted catwalk connecting each boat, and tied to it by rope. A conventional infantry assault bridge was not available for this attack. Ropes were strung along the side of this bridge so that with about fifteen men on each side it could be moved to the river. With engineer people as guides, we moved across our access road, down a 'cleared' lane through the mine field running parallel to the river. I led the way, little knowing I was like a Judas Goat, leading the sheep to slaughter. Then Sgt. Herbert W. Caulery of Alice, Texas, stepped on a Schuh mine. I was knocked flat on my face and stunned by the half-pound blast of TNT. We withdrew in confusion, jumping on the catwalk of the bridge to avoid mines. The first of the inflatable rubber boats had been deflated by debris from the explosion. Aid men went to treat Cauley and perhaps others wounded by the first mine. Several more mines were detonated. One of these men lost both eyes. I don't know how many others were wounded.

"Whether these Schuh mines were missed by our engineers or replanted under cover of darkness by subsequent Jerry patrols, I don't know. This 'cleared' mine lane was marked by white tapes as wide as ones used to mark a tennis court and would have been visible to German positions across the river. I believe they were replanted. There ought to have been camouflaged tape for marking mine lanes. White on one side only, to be reversed at night to show that side.

"I remember standing on the catwalk and meeting a major from the 141st. I [believe] I told him that with the bridge destroyed, the attack was off and we ought to get some orders to get out of there before the alerted Germans began their artillery. About that time the Germans did begin to shell the area with mortars, artillery, and *Nebelwerfers* [multibar-relled rocket launchers]. The major told me the attack was very important, because we were landing forces at a place called Anzio, which of course I had never heard of.

"When the German fire began, I found a large culvert under the road and crawled in. We were still waiting orders to stay or withdraw. Some projectile went off near the drainage ditch leading to my culvert. The blast blew me flat against the bottom. Close explosions leave one vibrating like a tuning fork. We were finally told to return down the road to our old position."

Clark directed a second assault on the Rapido. The 36th's commander, Fred Walker, glumly scrawled in his diary, "I expect this attack to be a fizzle just as was the one last night."

Goode wrote, "The next night we were ordered to run the same 'play.' Back up the road, pick up the same type bridge, down the same mine lane. Noted a dead soldier just beside the mine lane this second night. Found the river bank; slid the 'bridge' into the river like one might launch a canoe, bow first. An engineer walked upstream with a rope attached to the bow to keep it from being swept downstream. Another engineer crossed the bridge and flopped a piece of catwalk up on the German shore and we crossed. It was nighttime. There was fog along the river. I learned later that smoke pots had also been used. Visiblity was ten feet at most. The single file of men stopped. I went forward to see if I could find 1st Lt. Robert L. Davey and learn what was holding up the column. I found him in front of the double apron, barbed-wire fence, where it joined the bank of the river on the downstream side of the river. I suggested we send a man out to see if there was a gap in the wire through which the Jerries might be going out on patrols. I didn't know I was on an 'S' bend and now fenced off from the rest of the west bank on a peninsula. There was nothing to do but start cutting the wire with our cutters. The Corps of Engineers had bangalore torpedoes. We didn't have a bangalore torpedo. Our own engineers could have improvised a similar device with a length of pipe or a thin plank and explosives. Placed under barbed wire, it could have exploded and snapped the wires.

"Some Jerry on outpost near the wire heard us. We heard him sound the alarm as he ran away from us toward the German positions. Shortly thereafter came the first, small explosion of a grenade or rifle grenade. I remember how the fragments glowed in the dark as it exploded. Then the orchestra began to tune up. Dark, foggy, no targets. There was a bit of machine-gun fire. At 100- or 150-rounds-per-minute cyclic rate of fire, you only have to hear it once to remember it! Twice as fast as our MGs. By now we were prone and started to crawl for what little cover could be found on the flat ground. I decided that to stay here and wait for daylight would be suicidal. I told Lieutenant Davey I was going back across the bridge and get permission to withdraw. I had not gone twenty feet when a lieutenant colonel I had never seen stopped me and asked where I thought I was going. He ordered me back where I came from. He said he was Lieutenant Colonel Gault of the 88th Division. He was part of an advance party of 88th officers sent to observe us 'battle-tested veterans.' I heard he was killed at the Rapido.

"I went back downstream along the dike that the Italians had erected to contain spring floods and started to dig in, into this dike directly on the bank of the river. The dike had been made from white, marble gravel, and as fast as I dug, the gravel would collapse into the hole. About this time a Jerry whose MG was sited along my bank of the river (with the fog and smoke he could not see us, but the sound of digging might have alerted him), fired a burst of rounds. They struck the river downstream, about five yards from me. The splash of those bullets in the river was spectacular. I now realized I had to get out, and must take the company with me. I went down the bank to the bridge, crossed, and bumped into Major Mehaffey. I explained the situation. He phoned regiment and I think spoke to Lieutenant Colonel Price. Price ordered him to send me back 'and set up a base of fire.' This was ridiculous. We had minutes to spare to get our people out before the Jerries realized the enormity of the 'barrel of fish' they had before them.

"I returned across the bridge," wrote Goode, "and tried to find other officers and noncoms and see what we could do about moving inland. It was then, for the first time, that I discovered this sprawling horde was not just K Company but also L, and E, and F, as well. I shall never forget shaking a man to find that he was dead. A not uncommon occurrence in such a situation.

"Now, more than ever I was convinced that when the sun rose and burned off the mist—I didn't know about the smoke pots at this time—that a minor concentration of artillery and mortars would wipe out what I now felt was about 450 people. It did, as it turned out. I returned across the bridge, by now partially deflated, and reported to Major Mehaffey that there was complete loss of 'control' among our people and I saw no hope to get them forward through that barbed-wire fence and the increasing volume of MG fire. As I had crawled and crouched my way around, across the river, I had seen bullets striking the damp sod and decided I would be safer if I jumped into the Rapido and made my way back to the bridge holding onto the stumps of brush along the bank. The water was very cold. By the time I had finished talking to Major Mehaffey my legs were locked by cold. I was now convinced that I had 'sold' Major Mehaffey and through him, the regiment, that the only practical thing was to get those men out. This was the bulk of what was left of the 141st, as A and B Companies had been largely lost the night before. Perhaps three companies of the 141st were uncommitted at this time. I asked permission to go back to an aid station and try to thaw out. It was granted. I walked through the famous 'cleared' land-mine lane and found an aid station. I walked back down the road to our previous position downstream of San Angelo. By that night, the enormity of what had happened fulfilled my prediction. Very few of our men came back to join us in our position."

Sergeant Bill Kirby, a twenty-two-year-old machine-gun section leader who was caught in the Rapido slaughter, recalled, "We were under constant fire. I saw boats being hit all around me, and guys falling out and swimming. When we got to the other side, it was the only scene that I'd seen in the war that lived up to what you see in the movies. I had never seen so many bodies—our own guys. I remember this kid being hit by a machine gun; the bullets hitting him pushed his body along like a tin can. Just about everybody was hit. I didn't have a single good friend who wasn't killed or wounded."

From the 143d Regiment, Carl Tschantz, a lieutenant with Company I, said, "When word of the attack was finally passed down to the rank and file, it was readily apparent that a deep sense of futility prevailed among the men. Everyone knew that the Germans had had months to prepare a deep belt of dugouts, concrete bunkers, and slit trenches protected by barbed wire, booby traps, and thousands of mines. No matter which way you approached the Cassino front, the Germans on the highest ground were going to be looking down your throat. To make matters worse, the division was in bad shape. The 36th had been clobbered at the invasion of Salerno and shattered at San Pietro. Reinforcements of green recruits were hastily sent to patch up [heavy losses]. A high percentage of officers were new and did not yet know their men. The final blow was to have to go it alone without any protection on our flanks by other outfits.

"The attack began at 8:00 P.M. January 20, in a heavy fog that cut visibility to only a few yards. Almost at once, while we were still a mile from the river, German shells began to fall all around us. At the same time, our men had to lug the bulky twenty-four-man rubber rafts down through safe lanes marked by tapes. In the darkness and fog, guides lost their way and stumbled into minefields. By the time our outfit was approaching the crossing site, about a third of our boats had been destroyed and we had suffered about 30 percent casualties. Foreseeing annihilation, our battalion commander requested permission to withdraw, which was granted by higher command.

"Our period of recuperation was not long," Tschantz continued, "because late [the next afternoon] under cover of a heavy smoke screen, laid down by artillery, we were attacking again. Only this time Company I of the 143d was the leading company to cross the river. After much of the same pounding from enemy shells as the night before, we somehow managed to reach the crossing site. We launched our boats and immediately came under fire from both artillery and small-arms fire. I saw boats being hit all around me, and men were falling out and trying to swim. I never knew whether they made it or not. I only knew it was impossible to swim in the rapids with a full field pack and equipment. After we got to the other side and regrouped, I was surprised that approximately half of my men had made it. Our only hope for survival was to move forward, stay dispersed, and at the same time remain coordinated. This was easier said than done. Because of the smoke and the fog, visibility was about zero. In spite of the conditions, we moved forward and overran German positions, but with heavy losses. By this time, the most I could count were about a dozen of my men, and about five or six who had strayed in from other companies. Later that night a sudden quiet developed with only an occasional burst of an artillery shell.

"Early the next morning we were joined by a couple of officers and about twenty men from various other companies. No sooner had we started to move forward again when all hell broke loose. The Germans were hitting us with everything they had and, to make matters worse, our own artillery was dropping shells in our midst. We had a couple of battery-powered radios but neither would work, so we had no way to communicate our positions to our artillery units. I know that some of our men were hit by our own artillery. The situation was now getting even more desperate. Our ammunition was running out when we heard German tanks moving to form a ring around us. We tried to break out several times but each time lost more of our men.

"I could see no way out and began to feel that maybe my number was up. I thought of only two alternatives. Either I would get killed or wounded. Somehow it never dawned on me that I might be taken as a prisoner of war. It was early afternoon on January 22 when the ranking officer and another officer crawled over to my position and advised me that, since we had no means to fight the enemy and had no chance of being liberated by our own forces, it would serve no useful purpose getting ourselves killed. He recommended we take our chances as prisoners of war. Finally an agreement was reached. Ironically, we negotiated our surrender with the Germans by using a couple of German prisoners we had captured early in the day to act as our intermediaries. In our sector, three officers and nine enlisted men became prisoners of war."

According to Goode, "The situation of the 36th Division was now so precarious that they ordered artillery and all remaining machine guns to fire into the general area of German positions to pretend that we were attacking again. A small force of Germans, as few as a company, could have pushed right through the thin, demoralized remnants of the 141st and 143d."

The German booty from the ill-fated assault included carrier pigeons. They sent one back addressed to the 36th Division, and taunted, "You poor nightwatchmen, here is your pigeon back so you won't starve. What do you plan in front of Cassino with your tin-can armour? Your captured syphilitic comrades have shown us the quality of the American soldiers. Your captains are too stupid to destroy secret orders before being captured. At the moment, your troops south of Rome are getting a kick in the nuts—you poor nosepickers."

Said Goode, "I had now gone for three nights without sleep. After the debilitation of the first forty-five-day tour of combat I found I could not get to sleep. I had a small, painful infection on the knuckle of my right hand and went to the aid station for treatment. I also asked if they had anything to help one sleep. The battalion medical officer sent me to the rest area at Caserta. There I was given barbiturates to help me get some sleep. I returned four days later to find the division had moved. I found the headquarters of the 141st and was told to report to the regimental surgeon. He asked me how I felt I would handle myself if returned to combat and how long I had spent in combat. During my rest time at Caserta, the 36th had verged on mutiny, and rightly so, in my judgment. I answered the surgeon, 'as well as I always had.' He said he was sending me back to Naples. I ended up in the 45th General Hospital and was declared a 'battle fatigue' case. Everyone but one of the officers in my room were 36th Division officers.

"During my trip back to Caserta I had begun to wonder if I had crossed the vague line between 'cowardice in the face of the enemy' and showing commendable initiative, to get those people out to fight another day. General Patton had said, 'We're not here to die for our country, but to kill some S.O.B. for his country.' I looked up Major Mehaffey in a field hospital. He was severely wounded and so narcoticized that I wonder if he knew who I was. He did show me his Purple Heart and Silver Star. I looked up First Lieutenant Davey in an evacuation hospital where he was being treated for a shell fragment wound of the lower leg. We compared notes and felt there would be no investigations. There was no one left in Battalion or Regiment who knew what had happened or gave a damn.

"The blame for the Rapido has been shoved upward to [Geoffrey] Keyes [II Corps commander], Clark, Churchill, etc. But a lot of K Company problems were right in the 141st CP. What other infantry regiment in Italy had its CP shot up by the Jerries twice?" In his critique, Goode questioned the structure of infantry divisions, the reliance upon untested replacement officers from the Naples depot instead of battlefield commissions for experienced senior noncoms, and the system that filled depleted ranks with individual replacements rather than cohesive units. The latter point was made by Stephen Ambrose in his book *Citizen Soldiers*, which detailed the American advance across Europe after the invasion of Normandy. Goode also noted that during the Italian campaign company officers became casualties before they could be promoted to the battalion or regimental level. "No number of months behind the front-line rifle companies can give an officer the 'feel' or the insights that being out on the line can give one.

"The aftermath of the battle left an awful feeling of having been betrayed by our leadership. Stupid tactics. Oversights such as those mines in the 'cleared-mine lane.' Why had the attack been launched so quickly that no adequate patrolling could be done? The double apron, barbed-wire fence. Why didn't we in K Company know about the barbed wire? Did Regiment know? Why cleared-mine lanes were not guarded at night against Germans replanting new mines. All those men, their lives, their training gone for no impact on the Germans or the war. The feeling of how utterly unprofessional we looked. How stupid. I wavered between feeling justified for leaving the scene and not returning to face my fate with the men of Company K."

Many survivors from the stricken 36th Division blamed Mark Clark for the catastrophic results. Hamilton Howze, in a position to observe the assault and to question participants, blames others. "They made this attack in an extremely awkward way. It was very badly done. We had a tank battalion a few hundred yards back in the woods and its mission was to cross over the bridges behind the infantry once they were established and exploiting the gains they made on the far side. We had three more tank companies available and they could have been used to assist the infantry in the assault. The tanks could have been brought up right against the banks of the river. They would have had most excellent defilade because they could have just hung their guns across the banks, and tank commanders with the benefit of their field glasses could have watched the hills on the far side. These were usually about 100 to

200 feet high. Germans had put wire and mines on the bottom by their side of the river and they had infantry positions in the low hills, mostly treeless. The tanks, using overwatching fire, could have done an enormous amount of good whenever they saw one of the infantry units receive fire. Tank commanders could have whomped the German position very effectively from a range of no more 600–800 yards, an ideal position to use tanks in overwatching fire support of infantry on the far side of an obstacle.

"Another example of incompetence was the assault bridges brought down by the engineers and infantry. One was named Yale and the other Harvard and they were put down on mines, which blew them up. It is an indication of how inadequately the area was swept. In my interviews of two infantry battalion commanders after they had brought back only a handful of men from each of their companies, I was told that most of their people had gotten on the other side where they were either killed, wounded, or surrendered; large numbers surrendered. The battalion commanders obviously had the most confused ideas of what they were supposed to do and what happened to them. I asked what was the artillery-fire plan and both replied in approximately these words. 'It was falling out in front of us for a while and then it lifted.' I said do you know the details of the artillery-fire plan? They both answered, no, they didn't tell us. These things present a picture of a division attack which was so inept that the fact that it failed can't be laid to the belief that the concept was improper. We watched this division come streaming back, having accomplished essentially nothing, and lost very heavily. It was a very bad show."

While the Allied armies stumbled if not fell in their first

steps of the winter offensive for Rome, Operation Shingle, the invasion at Anzio, began 22 January, the day of the final disaster at the Rapido. John Lucas commanded the VI Corps at Anzio and vacillated between dire forebodings and great optimism. At a conference shortly before Shingle's onset, Lucas met with top-echelon officers, including Gen. Sir Harold Alexander. Two of the staff had been to Marrakech where Prime Minister Churchill personally questioned them about the forthcoming action. "Sir Harold started the conference by stating that the operation would take place 22 January with the troops as scheduled and there would be no more discussion of these points," Lucas wrote. "He quoted Mr. Churchill as saying, 'It will astonish the world,' and added, 'it will certainly frighten Kesselring. Overlord would be unnecessary.' " Alexander spoke to Lucas about an advance that would seize heights known as Colli Lazali, twenty miles inland, and that he should be prepared to march on Rome. "I felt like a lamb being led to the slaughter but I thought I was entitled to one bleat so I registered a protest against the target date as it gave me too little time for rehearsal. This is vital to the success of anything as terribly complicated as this. I was ruled down." Lucas believed politics, the desire to capture Rome for nonmilitary reasons, dictated the timetable.

"I have the minimum of ships and crafts. The ones that are sunk cannot be replaced. The force that can be gotten ashore in a hurry is weak and I haven't sufficient artillery to hold me over. On the other hand, I will have more air support than any similar operation ever had before. A week of fine weather at the proper time and I will make it."

At a subsequent meeting, Lucas reported expectations scaled down. "The primary mission is to seize and hold the beachhead." Rome as an objective was not even mentioned. At a boozy dinner with Lucian Truscott, the 3d Division commander, Lucas celebrated his fifty-fourth birthday buoyed by word that "The general idea seems to be that the Germans are licked and fleeing in disorder and nothing remains but to mop up. I think we have a chance to make a killing. I have misgivings and am also optimistic."

Upon recovering from his wounds at Salerno, Allen Merrill located his old outfit, the 4th Ranger Battalion, which occupied a ridge. Merrill felt the men seemed "sullen," "morose," "listless" during the early-winter, stalemated campaign. Withdrawn from the front lines, the Rangers embarked on another training regimen for Shingle. They practiced landings, worked on endurance. Merrill relished a three-day pass in Naples, where he and several friends "got ripped, laid, and re-laid." Then back to the grind, which intensified early in January. "I got to know some of the replacements pretty well. I had sworn that I wouldn't do that anymore. That way you don't miss them if they are killed. How can you not miss a guy you served with? Replacements or not, they all mean something to you once you go into combat with them.

"The night before we boarded the boats for our fourth invasion, I could not sleep. I thought of everything I had been through, all the places I'd been, and all the people I'd seen killed or maimed. I thought too of all the soldiers I killed and thus rendered them fatherless. I wondered in that long dark night if I ever made it back in one piece would I ever be able to handle the guilt of it or be able to justify any part of my actions.

"I was as frightened on this my fourth landing as I had been on my first. I relaxed in my usual way, reading from my small volume of poetry. At 2:30 A.M. we went over the side into the small LSTs. Colonel Darby's husky voice could be heard plainly as the flare signaled onward to the landing zones, 'Rangers lead the way.' " As the first scout of F Company, the lead Ranger unit at Anzio, Merrill said, "I was the first man to step across the beach that morning. There was no opposition waiting for us. No shots were fired in either direction. Nothing moved but us. The only movement of the section of beach I landed on was an old, grizzled man pissing against a seawall. He bade us 'Buon giorno' and finished what he was doing. We knifed through the town of Anzio in the predawn hours without mishap. Farther down the beach, a momentary firefight erupted. Some German officers on leave from their units and enjoying the talents of a few of the local females were caught literally with their pants down and captured in position *indelicato*, so to speak." Merrill was one of almost 34,000 to cross the Anzio shore the first day.

He reported, "On the second day, Ranger companies had advanced to within six short kilometers of the Holy City and not a German soldier in sight. In another hour we could have been in the outskirts of Rome itself. Our captain radioed back for confirmation to begin the final advance to the city limits. That confirmation never came. Instead the commanding general of the beachhead chastised us for extending our lines too far ahead and instructed us to fall back to the factory town of Aprilia, dig in, and hold. Colonel Darby was livid but he was a West Pointer who took and gave orders without question. There was absolutely nothing of any military importance showing signs of resistance in those foothills of the Colli Lazali.

"The 82d Airborne were on our right flank and the No. 6 British Commandos under Lord Lovat were on our left. Together we could have been in Rome by nightfall of that

D plus 1 day. Instead, where we were told to dig in and hold was eight miles inland and that became the limit of the doormat-size beachhead that remained static until five months later."

Merrill mentioned the 82d Airborne on the Ranger flank; the unit was the 509th Parachute Infantry Battalion, under the command of Bill Yarborough. Like the Rangers, the troopers whored and brawled, but mostly prepared in the Naples area in the weeks before Anzio. Having expected extensive casualties, Yarborough said he had requested a large number of replacements. "When they arrived," he said, "we isolated them behind wire like they had measles and then sent a guy with the badge of the 3d Zouaves [awarded for valor in North Africa by the French] who talked to them about the history, the honor, and the integrity of the unit. It gave them pride and it would pay rich dividends when they went into combat."

Yarborough personally felt comfortable to be working alongside the Rangers. "I had known Darby and had high regard for him. But mixing paratroopers and Rangers was like oil and water. There was bad blood between our units. We went for the traditional esprit of the soldier based on the military service. Even in foxholes, every man shaved, every day, no matter what. Our people looked sharp. I required them to take pride in their parachute uniform, their barracks, the whole bit. Darby's guys looked like cutthroats. They looked like the sweepings of the bar rooms. They had stubble beards, they wore any kind of uniform; some of them tanker uniforms. Darby and I approached leadership from two points of view. When you have an extraordinary mission, there is a traditional one, which I prefer, and the other was his approach, which offers only blood, sweat, and tears. It would offer you nothing except the hardest bloody job and the smallest recognition. You would get guys who would go for that sort of approach."

At Salerno, members of the 3d Infantry Division drilled for Anzio. Bill Kunz recalled in mid-January, Operation Webfoot, a practice landing. "We were to come ashore in DUKWs [Ducks, or amphibious craft dispatched from LST ramps, capable of carrying men and heavy weapons]. Our artillery was to have one gun per Duck and to fire on the way ashore. There was an argument, Army v. Navy. 'The waves were too rough,' said the Navy. 'This is our operation,' the Army said. 'Launch them!' The Navy was right. The Ducks were too low in the water, were swamped, and sank. Men, guns, and equipment to the bottom. None of the guns were fired enroute. Our battalion lost twelve guns, 105mm [howitzers]."

At Anzio, the 3d Division batteries borrowed guns from the 45th Division to replace those lost during the Webfoot fiasco. Said Kunz, "Our artillerymen spent time 'zeroing in' and learning the quirks of the 105mms from the 45th. Guns have individual characteristics that you have to know to fire them with pinpoint accuracy."

William Rosson, shifted from a staff position at regiment to command of the 3d Battalion of the 7th Regiment, recalled no fire at all as they crossed the beaches and reached their objectives. The 3d Division struck off east to seize the seaside town of Nettuno, widening the turf controlled by the invaders. Rosson remembered he had been instructed that there would be "a rapid, sustained drive inland once we had established a beachhead." The advisory noted his unit might be forced to operate independently for periods of time. "Presumably, this landing would dislodge [the enemy] from the Gustav Line. . . . He would be forced to give combat where he found us. But no orders were received to move in a major offensive position toward the distant objectives. Several days passed. Then came information from regiment there was to be an attack carried out by the Rangers under Col. Bill Darby."

Harmon said British intelligence mistakenly advised there were no German divisions available in the north to reinforce the Italian-based garrisons. According to Corps Commander Lucas, on 29 January his 61,000 soldiers were opposed by a force of 71,000 still being reinforced. Harmon noted that a second flaw of the Shingle plan lay in the inability of air forces to destroy the bridges and rail lines from the north into Italy.

Against this largely undetected strength, the Rangers kicked off the Allied attack. As a lieutenant in C Company, 3d Ranger Battalion, platoon leader Clarence Meltesen said, "On 29 January [a week after the troops landed] orders were received and reconnaissance initiated for a night-penetration march and dawn attack on Cisterna di Latina. We were to move in a column of two battalions, entering the Mussolini Canal and then the Pontana Ditch to exit immediately southwest of Cisterna. We were to seize Cisterna and hold until linkup with attack elements of the 3d Infantry Division." Because of a shortage of ships and the start of the buildup in England for the cross-channel invasion, the 1st Armored Division only began to debark at Anzio on that day.

Initially, the Rangers advanced with no significant opposition and sentries who might have sounded an alarm were eliminated. The Americans slipped beyond German emplacements, close enough to hear conversation among the enemy. But lying in wait for them were massive forces, undetected by patrols or from the air, that had come from Austria through the Brenner Pass to seal off the small plot held by the Allies and systematically grind up the entire II Corps. When morning came, the 1st and 3d Ranger Battalions found themselves cut off and battling against far superior forces that included artillery and armor. The Germans blocked the 7th Infantry of the 3d Division from linking up with the Rangers. Nor could the 509th paratroopers gain ground. The 3d Rangers bought some protection with their machine guns that swept the ground by using a deep drainage ditch, but the enemy in houses and elevated roosts unleashed fusillades upon the Americans. Mud into which the heavy base plates of the 4.2 mortars sank limited the usually effective mortar support. A handful of the attackers actually broke through to the Cisterna railroad station but, according to Meltesen, most were caught in the open and pinned down by fire from several directions. Meltesen himself fell with a neck wound inflicted by a sniper. The 4th Ranger Battalion vainly tried to break through to the encircled troops.

Because of casualties, Jim Altieri, upon whose shoulders Mark Clark pinned lieutenant's bars on Christmas Day, now commanded Company F. Supported by a couple of half-tracks and tank destroyers, Altieri attempted to halt a counterattack. "Ground-grazing machine-gun fire covered every ditch and their mortars crashed all around us," said Altieri. "In one attack I lost one of my platoon lieutenants and four key noncoms as well as ten men badly wounded. We were desperate; we knew we had to crack through to save the 1st and 3d—but each attack in broad daylight over open ground brought frightening casualties."

Allen Merrill recalled, "The Rangers were surprised in their attack upon Cisterna by the Germans, recently reinforced by two divisions, the elite Green Devil Paratroops and the Hermann Goering Panzers, both up to full strength.

In the early morning ground fog, the first two battalions realized they had walked into the middle of a German counterattack planned for that very morning. Rangers fought valiantly in small pockets and by ones and twos until their ammunition was gone. They faced point-blank tank fire and were outnumbered four to one.

"In the village in the suburbs of Cisterna, called Femminamorta [dead woman in Italian], I was wounded [in the lower leg] and captured. I had saved one round of ammo for myself in case this happened. But a kick in the ribs deflected my weapon and two Germans carried me to a farmhouse with many other Ranger wounded and they dumped me on the floor with the others."

Platoon leader Clarence Meltesen, with C Company in the 3d Battalion, still dazed from a morphine injection after being wounded, said, "I had decided that with my right lung affected by my rifle-shot wound I should not try leading my platoon back. I prepared to surrender and after two minutes of absolute quiet, I saw a German three-man patrol headed my way. I had been informed that the large shed [nearby] contained a fair number of our wounded. I waited and tried to surrender at a distance of fifty yards. I could only raise my left arm and was given an overhead machine-pistol burst. I dodged behind the medical collecting point and pulled out my new Red Cross handkerchief, took my helmet off, and wiggled a white flag on a tattered end of a piece of cane. I made another appearance and was allowed this time to surrender. In my schoolbook German I tried to tell my captors my condition and that there were wounded in the shed. My captors were very happy capturing Rangers. One did a little jig and said he had been in Sicily when the 1st Battalion had shellacked them. They told me to go 'thataway' and they went on."

Other Rangers recalled the sight of their comrades being used as hostages, hands held high in front of armed Germans who called on the GIs to surrender. Bing Evans, as CO for F Company of the 3d Battalion, prepared to order his troops to shoot the guards when suddenly an artillery shell burst nearby. "I remember my face in the dirt," said Evans, "but nothing else for the next two months until I was in a prison camp."

Enemy barrages bracketed the command post occupied by Darby. The blasts killed a staff officer and Darby's runner. German armor relentlessly attacked and counterattacked. Darby briefly lost his composure at the realization that nothing could save the more than 750 men from his two trapped battalions. Fewer than 20 Rangers from the 1st and 3d Battalions evaded capture. Statistics of the Ranger Association list only 12 from the two battalions killed, 36 wounded, and 743 captured. The figures seem low. The 4th Ranger Battalion itself had 30 KIA and 58 WIA.

Post-mortems blamed the failings on the strategy, the poor intelligence, and the use of Rangers for such a mission. Mark Clark stated, "Neither Truscott [3d Division commander] nor I knew of the organized defensive position they would run into." Lucas absolved himself for the destruction of the Rangers. "Instead of performing their assigned mission, [they] seem to have advanced without proper security and were surrounded and captured by hostile forces outside the town." However, he admitted he approved the plan of attack.

Absent was coordinated tactical support from the air and sufficient artillery. Harmon, whose armor had only bivouacked for the first night on 29 January, later said, "I always felt that if the 1st Armored strength had been assigned to the Cisterna sector, instead of the British one, my tanks could have supported the Rangers. It would have made the sacrifice of these crack troops unnecessary. We certainly could have gone in and got them out." The Cisterna attack failed but the furious fighting prevented the enemy from eradicating the beachhead.

# 5

# Solomon Finales, Galvanic, and Flintlock

FARTHER UP THE NORTHWEST TRAJECTORY FROM GUADALCANAL lay more stepping-stones toward the expanded Japanese Empire. The Solomons' Bougainville was the northernmost footprint at the head of the Slot and New Britain and New Ireland stood off the coast of New Guinea. Bougainville attracted Allied strategists as an excellent site from which to batter the massive enemy concentration at Rabaul. Aware of such a prospect, the Japanese had already begun a buildup on the southern end of this replica of Guadalcanal. To retain control of Bougainville, the Imperial Army gathered 45,000 soldiers with all of the arsenal necessary for a protracted struggle.

Instead of directly confronting the foe at the southern tip, the 3d Marine Division on 1 November 1943 scrambled ashore in midisland at Cape Torokina on Empress Augusta Bay. To divert the enemy the 2d Marine Parachute Battalion attacked neighboring Choiseul Island. [They came by sea and the outfit never performed as airborne during the entire war.] At Cape Torokina, only a single infantry company, albeit with well over a dozen pillboxes, defended the beach. The prelanding naval bombardment missed its mark and the Japanese gunners shot up many of the landing craft. Marine airplanes helped quell the resistance but hard fighting occurred before Cape Torokina could be declared secure.

The enemy, determined to hold Bougainville, countered with naval and air assaults as well as bringing in a battalion of soldiers from Rabaul. In swamps so deep with ooze they could completely swallow a bulldozer, the two sides fought it out. The 3d Marine Divison expanded its grasp of territory, aided by the insertion of U.S. Army forces from the 37th Division in early December. With tanks, flamethrowers, heavy artillery, and control of the air, the Americans hammered a stubborn foe. Months of dogged fighting slowly whittled away the Japanese defenders, who, as at Guadalcanal, could not count upon reinforcements or resupply. The struggle for Bougainville would drag on for a year.

As part of the further isolation of Rabaul, the strategists focused on two more former pieces of the British Empire, New Britain and New Ireland. Ed Andrusko, bloodied with the 1st Marine Divsion on Guadalcanal, recalled Christmas Day 1943, as his company sailed toward New Britain. The public-address system summoned the leathernecks to an assembly on the fantail for some last-minute instruction. There an intelligence lieutenant with a background in biology, a Navy doctor, and a coast watcher instructed them on some of the perils that awaited them.

The lieutenant began, "Men, you will be in the first wave of the invasion tomorrow. When your attack boats drop you near the shore be careful *not* to stay in the water too long.

The sharp coral can cut you badly, and this will attract sand sharks, barracuda, and poisonous large eels. Watch out for giant clams; if you step into one, it will close and lock on your foot with a vicelike grip, breaking your leg, causing excruciating pain." He continued with warnings about large biting ants, scorpions, and small scrub typhus–bearing fleas. He spoke of a variety of poisonous snakes, spiders, and centipedes hidden in the thick jungle.

According to Andrusko, the doctor added, "Remember, if you're bitten, we don't have antidotes, so try to recall the color of the snake or spider; it might be a helpful warning to the next person. There are giant wasps and thousands of other insects that can bite or sting you day or night. The anopheles mosquito can give you one of four types of malaria. All types will make you very sick; two will make you sick for a long time; the other types will kill you in a few weeks. We have some medication called atabrine but it has limited use—mainly because the men won't take it. It has a tendency to turn your skin, eyes, and clothing a bright yellow color and rumor has it that it will make you permanently sterile."

The Australian coast watcher added his comments about massive, dangerous, almost impassable swamps. "These swamps contain the large sea-going crocodiles. Please be sure of where you step! I can assure you that there are also alligators that will attack a person with deadly results. Be on the lookout for sink holes and quicksand under the dark brackish swamp water. You'll need help pulling each other out of the mud and removing the blood-sucking leeches off your bodies. Unfortunately, it is the monsoon season and you are five degrees south of the equator so you will be constantly hot and wet. The continued torrential rain and the high sweat-producing humidity will cause mold and you will soon acquire the infamous jungle rot, a skin condition that will be ulcerated, painful, and itchy. It will never heal until after you leave here. And large blowflies will constantly try to get at your sores. These same swarms of biting flies will bring amoebic dysentery."

The briefing noted, "Not too many natives live [here] due to dengue fever, scurvy, beri beri, leprosy, and many other diseases we have never heard of. Plus the large, smoking, rumbling volcanoes and daily earthquakes frighten them off. They feel it will erupt any day."

The Marine lieutenant then called for questions from the troops—"[they] sat stunned by what they had just heard," recalled Andrusko. "A young Marine raised his hand. 'If all you say is true about this place, why don't we just let the enemy have this horrible island—the enemy will be dead in no time. All we have to do is sit out here on the ships and wait, or go back to Australia.'

"A chorus of agreement and obscenities filled the air. Voices yelled, 'Who needs this God-forsaken place. Let them have it. It is Christmas time. Let's give it to them as a Christmas present.'" But on the morrow, Andrusko and his comrades went over the side. To their delight they met almost no opposition when they touched down at Cape Gloucester. They headed inland to find the "Damp flats" about as advertised. On their third day, sixteen inches of rain pelted down. Bolstered by Sherman tanks, the Marines steadily drove the enemy ever deeper into the jungle.

"On the seventeenth day of the battle for Cape Gloucester," said Andrusko, "our battalion had fought through the thick jungle and monsoon rain since landing. Our destination was a hill called '660.' As our company advanced, enemy shells rained down and we sustained heavy casualties. A large enemy shell exploded nearby and I was wounded, then evacuated." Through amphibious operations, the Marines enveloped the enemy on New Britain, controlling the perimeter while enemy soldiers remained at large in the interior.

High on the American agenda stood the necklaces of coral atolls known as Micronesia that lay athwart the sea-lanes from the U.S. to the major Pacific objectives. Operation Galvanic proposed to conquer within five days the atolls of Makin and Tarawa, in the Gilbert colony. Flat and sandy over coral bases, unlike the densely vegetated and mountainous terrain of Guadalcanal and New Guinea, these islets provided surface cover for neither defenders nor invaders. But the Japanese had tunneled deep in the coral to provide excellent protection against bombs, shells, and small arms. The timetable called for landings to start on 20 November.

The traditional inter- and intra-service rivalries sorely afflicted Galvanic. Naval airmen complained of exclusion from key planning sessions, even as more carriers with improved airplanes and radar-control systems bolstered the fleet. Admiral Richmond Kelly Turner and Gen. Holland M. Smith squabbled over the precise point at which authority over the operations shifted from the Navy to the Marines. In a bizarre twist, an Army Air Corps officer, aboard a Navy ship, was to direct the naval and marine aircraft supporting the leathernecks on land. Evans Carlson's ill-fated 1942 Marine Raider sortie against Makin had triggered an intensive effort to create excellent defenses with interlocking fire to sweep every inch of terrain. The intelligence on Makin estimated a relatively small garrison and the American strategists figured a massive strike from the sea and air would soften up the inhabitants sufficiently for a quick victory. Instead, when the 6,500 soldiers drawn from the Army's 27th Division reached the Makin strand, 500 resolute Japanese soldiers and 300 laborers staunchly fought from almost impregnable bunkers. They pinned the invaders on the beaches and a battle dragged on for four days, to the dismay of the two overall commanders, the Navy's Admiral Turner and the Marines' "Howlin Mad" Smith. From this point on, Smith regarded the 27th Division as unreliable.

The Americans expected a much tougher fight at Tarawa. There the enemy numbered 5,000 and they brought to bear everything from 8-inch naval rifles, prizes taken from the British at Singapore, to infestations of machine guns. The most important item in the atoll was Betio, a 291-acre fortress with an airstrip, girdled by a three-to-five-foot-high seawall, and stuffed with concrete and coral emplacements that housed numerous artillery pieces and troops. The approaches from the sea bristled with concrete tetrahedrons festooned with mines and wire. As troubling as the man-made defenses was the coral reef that entirely ringed Betio. The hard, jagged, natural obstacle could hang up landing craft, even rip open bottoms, forcing leathernecks to wade through deep water to gain the shore. The experts who had guided ships in the Gilberts predicted five feet of water over the reef at high tide, adequate for the Higgins LCVP [landing craft, vehicles and personnel] that ordinarily drew four feet. However one aged British civil servant, who had lived on the atoll for fifteen years, warned that in November, tides frequently fell below the norm. The Pacific fleet had begun to deploy Alligators, or LVTs, new amphibious tractors that could crawl across a reef if necessary; but a limited stock was available for Tarawa. Nimitz and the staff delegated to carry out Galvanic fretted over the problem. They were urged not to postpone operations until more favorable tidal conditions. Allied momentum in the Pacific was quickening.

Delay might allow the enemy to regroup and reinforce the objectives.

Questions about tactics stirred debate, particularly in the matter of air and naval bombardment. General Julian Smith, whose 2d Marine Division would ride the Alligators and LCVPs, wanted a lengthy preparation from the big guns off-shore and in the air. Navy brass worried that this would alert the Japanese to the intentions of Galvanic and bring ships and planes down upon the fleet. In this concern, U.S. intelligence had failed to discover that the enemy, hard hit by previous engagements, could not react with any substantial force.

Reports from Air Corps bombers that struck Betio and met weak antiaircraft opposition elicited hopes that most of the Japanese had been evacuated. About 4:00 A.M. the am-tracs, loaded with leathernecks, chugged toward the line of departure, the rendezvous point from which the first wave would frantically jounce toward the beach. Overhead, shells from some Japanese shore batteries testified to life and fight on the island. The battleship *Maryland* answered with the full-throated roars of its 16-inch cannons. Two other dread-noughts, four cruisers, and some twenty destroyers cascaded 3,000 tons of ordnance upon the target, pausing only to allow carrier planes to swoop in and deliver their own ex-plosives. It was the heaviest bombardment of any invasion beach to date.

Correspondent Robert Sherrod watched the overtures to the Tarawa venture aboard the transport *Zeilin*. "At 0505, we heard a great thud in the southwest. We knew what that meant. The first battleship had fired the first shot. . . . The curtain was up in the theatre of death. We were watching when the battleship's second shell left the muzzle of its great gun, headed for Betio. There was a brilliant flash in the darkness of the half-moonlit night. Then a flaming torch arched high into the air and sailed far away, slowly, very slowly, like an easily lobbed tennis ball. The red cinder was nearly halfway to its mark before we heard the thud, a dull roar as if some mythological giant had struck a drum as big as Mount Olympus. There was no sign of an explosion on the unseen island—the second shot had apparently fallen into the water, like the first.

"Within three minutes the sky was filled again with the orange-red flash of the big gun, and Olympus boomed again. The red ball of fire that was the high-explosive shell was again dropping toward the horizon. But this time there was a tremendous burst on that land that was Betio. A wall of flame shot five hundred feet into the air, and there was another terrifying explosion as the shell found its mark. Hundreds of the awestruck Marines on the deck of the [*Zeilin*] cheered in uncontrollable joy. Our guns had found the enemy. Probably the enemy's big eight-inch guns and their powder magazine on the southwest corner of the island.

". . . This was only the beginning. Another battleship took up the firing—four mighty shells poured from its big guns onto another part of the island. Then another battleship breathed its brilliant breath of death. Now a heavy cruiser let go with its eight-inch guns and several light cruisers opened with their fast-firing six-inch guns. They were followed by destroyers, many destroyers with many five-inch guns on each, firing almost as fast as machine guns. The sky at times was brighter than noontime on the equator. The arching, glowing cinders that were high-explosive shells sailed through the air as though buckshot were being fired out of many shotguns from all sides of the island . . . the whole island of Betio seemed to erupt with bright fires that were burning everywhere. They blazed even through the thick wall of smoke that curtained the island.

"The first streaks of dawn crept through the sky. The warships continued to fire. All of a sudden they stopped. But here came the planes—not just a few planes: a dozen, a score, a hundred. The first torpedo bombers raced across the smoking conflagration and loosed their big bombs on an island that must have been dead a half hour ago. They were followed by the dive bombers, the old workhorse SBDs and the new Helldivers, the fast SB2Cs that had been more than two years a-borning. The dive bombers lined up many thousands of feet over Betio, then they pointed their noses down and dived singly, or in pairs or in threes. Near the end of their dives they hatched the bombs from beneath their bellies; they pulled out gracefully and sailed back to their carriers to get more bombs. Now came the fast, new Grumman Hellcats, the best planes ever to squat on a carrier. They made their runs just above the awful gushing pall of smoke, their machine guns spitting hundreds of fifty-caliber bullets a minute.

"Surely, we thought, no mortal men could live through such destroying power. Surely, I thought, if there were actually any Japs left on the island (which I doubted strongly), they would all be dead by now." Sherrod forgot the warning from the former Raider leader, Merritt Edson, now chief of staff for the 2d Marine Division. "We cannot count on heavy naval and air bombardment to kill all the Japs on Tarawa, or even a large proportion of them."

The gigantic blasts flung smoke, sand, coral, chunks of wood, concrete, and steel into the air. Concussive effects momentarily stunned the well-shielded defenders. Unfortunately, the Marines could not exploit the brief period when the enemy was dazed because the first waves required longer than expected to make it to shore. Smoke and haze from the preinvasion barrage prevented the naval observers from using their heavy guns to the best advantage of those in the landing craft. Likewise, the strafers from the air quit too soon. Only the first group of the assault teams reached the beach before the Japanese recovered and commenced to fight.

The timetable scheduled the first wave to hit the beaches at 0830 but miscalculations on the distances and the rate of speed through the choppy waters delayed the arrival until 0913. Aware of the tardiness, the naval commander revived the offshore bombardment for a few minutes but, nevertheless, the defenders had almost twenty minutes to recover their wits and man their weapons. Some groups of amtracs met relatively minor opposition but at Beach Red 1 devastating fire greeted the Marines. Private N. M. Baird remembered, "Bullets pinged off that tractor like hailstones off a tin roof. Two shells hit the water twenty yards off the port side and sent up regular geysers. I swept the beach [Baird had a machine gun], just to keep the bastards down as much as possible. Can't figure how I didn't get it in the head or something.

"We were 100 yards in now and the enemy fire was awful damn intense and gettin' worse. They were knockin' boats out left and right. A tractor'd get hit, stop, and burst into flames, with men jumping out like torches. The water here was only about three feet deep, just covering the coral reefs that the tractor'd bounce onto and over. Bullets ricocheted off the coral and up under the tractor. It must've been one of these bullets that got the driver. The boat lurched and I looked in the cab and saw him slumped over, dead. The lieutenant jumped in and pulled the driver out, and drove, himself, till he got hit.

"That happened about thirty yards offshore. A shell struck the boat. The concussion felt like a big fist—Joe Louis maybe—had smacked me right in the face. Seemed to make my face swell up. Knocked me down and sort of stunned me for a moment. I shook my head. Shrapnel was pinging all around. Nicked the hell out of my face and hands. One piece, about an inch long, tore into my back. A fella later pulled it out onshore. I looked around. My assistant, a private with a Mexican name, who was feeding my gun, had his pack and helmet blown right off. He was crumpled up beside me, with his head forward and in the back of it was a hole I could put my fist in. I started to shake him and he fell right on over.

"Guys were sprawled all over the place," said Baird. "I looked across at my buddy who was only five feet from me. He was on his back and his face was all bloody and he was holding his hand over his face and mumbling something. Our boat was stopped, and they were laying lead to us from a pillbox like holy hell. Everybody seemed stunned, so I yelled, 'Let's get the hell outa here!' I grabbed my carbine and an ammunition box and stepped over a couple of fellas laying there and put my hand on the side so's to roll over into the water. I didn't want to put my head up. The bullets were pouring at us like a sheet of rain. . . . Only about a dozen of the twenty-five went over the side with me, and only about four of us ever got evacuated."

The first three waves, riding Alligators, could not move off the narrow beach. Pinned down, they lay at the base of the coconut-log and coral-block seawall unable to advance or retreat. A murderous storm of bullets and shrapnel pelted across the strip and out to the reef where the carcasses of twenty disabled amtracs and a pair of LCVPs loaded with dead and wounded piled up. The tide stubbornly refused to rise sufficiently for LCVPs with tanks and artillery to navigate the coral ridge. The Marines ashore could attack pillboxes only with their small arms, a few flamethrowers, grenades, and blocks of TNT fashioned into pole charges. One Marine special outfit, an elite Scout-Sniper Platoon led by Lt. William Deane Hawkins, somehow went on the offensive. The thirty-four leathernecks, sharpshooters, and experts in close combat, shot numerous snipers from their perches in trees and blasted those concealed in foxholes.

Deane Hawkins, as Sherrod knew him, had attended the Texas College of Mines before the war, married, and divorced before he enlisted as a private around Christmas of 1941. "Hawk" to the troops, he won a battlefield commission in the Solomons and at twenty-nine was among the oldest of the junior officers. He had told Sherrod, "We're going in first. We are going to wipe every last one of the bastards off that pier and out from under that pier before they have a chance to pick off the first wave." But although the Scout-Sniper Platoon eliminated defenders far beyond their own limited number, they could not prevent the carnage inflicted upon the first waves. The Hawk continued to fight even after being wounded by shrapnel. He reportedly shrugged off medical treatments: "I came here to kill Japs: I didn't come here to be evacuated."

The LCVPs bearing 37mm cannons could not pass the reef and were forced to wait until nightfall to make their approach. Sherman tanks, disgorged at the outcrop, climbed over that natural barrier and through three or four feet of water. Eleven of them rattled onto the beach and added their firepower to that of the beleaguered invaders.

Sherrod, scheduled to accompany the fifth wave, climbed into an LCVP. He peeked over the ramp even as water splashed over the bow and to his dismay saw very few boats on the beach. A naval officer came alongside and announced they would transfer to an amtrac in order to get through the shallows. Combat soldiers boarded the first Alligator before a second craft took the remainder of the men and Sherrod close enough to hike the last several hundred yards.

"We started wading," said Sherrod. "No sooner had we hit the water than the Japanese really opened up on us. There must have been five or six of these machine guns concentrating their fire on us—there was no nearer target in the water at the time—which meant several hundred bullets per man. I don't believe there was one of the fifteen [in his group] who wouldn't have sold his chances for an additional twenty-five dollars added to his life-insurance policy. It was painfully slow, wading in such deep water. We had seven hundred yards to walk slowly into that machine-gun fire, looming into larger targets as we rose onto higher ground. I was scared, as I had never been scared before. But my head was clear . . . I recalled that psychologists say fear in battle is a good thing; it stimulates the adrenal glands and heavily loads the blood supply with oxygen."

Sherrod and a few companions crept to comparative safety beneath a pier that jutted out into the sea, then scrambled the final distance over an expanse of twenty feet of sand and brown-and-green coral, the width of the beach-head. Nearby lay the dead driver of an Alligator, a Marine whom Sherrod learned had only recently married a girl in New Zealand. From behind a beached amtrac he watched as "a Jap shell hit directly on an LCV that was bringing many Marines ashore. The explosion was terrific and parts of the boat flew in all directions. Then there were many Marines swimming in the water. Two pairs of corspmen brought two more dead men and placed them beside the dead boy who had been married to a girl from Wellington."

He saw a sniper's bullet go through the helmet of a nearby leatherneck but the only wound was a scratch where the helmet was torn off the Marine's head. "Another Marine walked briskly along the beach. Again there was a shot. The Marine spun all the way around and fell to the ground, dead. From where he lay, a few feet away, he looked up at us. Because he had been shot squarely through the temple his eyes bulged out in horrific surprise at what had happened to him, although it was impossible that he could ever have known what hit him."

Sherrod labeled this the most gruesome sight he had yet seen. Many good reporters like Ernie Pyle, out of delicacy or regard for the censors, ordinarily never detailed the agonizing nature of the wounds made by white-hot, jagged pieces of shrapnel traveling at tremendous speed when they ripped into bodies; nor the excruciating pain of burns from napalm, oil, and gasoline fires aboard ships; nor the terrible trauma to human organs from a stream of machine-gun bullets.

At Tarawa Sherrod recorded only an inkling of the horrors. "The number of dead lined up beside the stalled headquarters amtrac grew steadily. But the procession of the wounded seemed many times greater. There went a stretcher with a Marine whose leg had been nearly torn off; another had been hit in the buttocks by a 13mm bullet or a 20mm shell—a man's fist could have been thrust into the jagged hole; another was pale as death from the loss of much blood—his face seemed to be all bones and yellowish-white skin and he was in great pain."

The delicacy in describing the killing extended only partially to enemy casualties. Sherrod reported that immediately after the sniper felled the grinning Marine, the Japanese soldier was flushed from his dugout by TNT and then, as he ran, a flamethrower caught him: ". . . the Jap flared up like a piece of celluloid. He was dead instantly but the bullets in his cartridge belt exploded for a full sixty seconds after he had been charred almost to nothingness."

In a huge shell hole that served as a command post, Sherrod heard the senior officer order the Marines crouched around them, "You men, get on up front. They need you out there." The correspondent watched a few men pick up their weapons and go over the seawall, "singly and in two and threes, but many were reluctant to move."

By the end of the first day, 5,000 Marines were on the island with an estimated 1,500 killed or wounded. The Navy warships had continued to fire missions, and carrier aircraft also struck at the defenders. While the Marines held their positions, the first 75mm pack artillery began to land during the night along with medical supplies, water, and ammunition. Reinforcements straggled in. The Japanese, notoriously skilled in night attacks, might have tried to eliminate the beachhead, only 300 yards wide at most places. However, the constant barrages from the battleships, cruisers, and destroyers, plus what the planes unleashed, and the small arms and explosives of the ground forces, had destroyed the communications links between the Nipponese commander and his units. Half of his force was now dead or wounded.

To Col. David Shoup, in his sand shell-hole CP, the issue remained in doubt as the sun rose. He radioed a number of "imperative" messages calling for ammunition, water, rations, medical supplies, and evacuation of the wounded. Sherrod, on the scene, reported, "Colonel Shoup is nervous. The telephone shakes in his hand. 'We are in a mighty tight spot,' he is saying. Then he lays down the phone and turns to me, 'Division has just asked me whether we've got enough troops to do the job. I told them no. They are sending the 6th Marines, who will be landing right away.' "

Word circulated about Deane Hawkins. A lieutenant recounted to Sherrod, "He is a madman. He cleaned out six machine-gun nests with two to six Japs in each nest. I'll never forget the picture of him standing on that amtrac, riding around with a million bullets a minute whistling by his ears, just shooting Japs." But in addition to the shrapnel of the previous day, he was hit twice by bullets, and loss of blood from the three wounds would eventually kill him.

The 6th Marine Regiment, building on the gains achieved by their predecessors, forged ahead. By four o'clock in the afternoon, Shoup's spirits had lifted and he announced, "We are winning." Terrible as the losses to the invaders, the defenders could not match the manpower and firepower thrown at them. "On the third day," said Sherrod, "the question was not, 'How long will it take to kill them all?' but 'How few men can we expect to lose before killing the rest of the Japs?' " Without letup, the deluge of shot, shell, and fire ravished the dwindling enemy.

Aware of impending doom, the last radio message from the garrison said, "Our weapons have been destroyed and from now on everyone is attempting a final charge. . . . May Japan exist for ten thousand years!" On that third night, bands of survivors staged suicidal attacks that were repulsed with everything from artillery to bayonets. Seventy-five hours after the first leathernecks waded and crawled onto the thin strip of beach, Betio was declared "secured." Some killing continued; holdouts, hidden in bunkers or bypassed, potshotted unwary leathernecks before they were eliminated. A number blew themselves up rather than surrender. The official totals for Americans were 685 killed, 77 who died of wounds, 169 missing, and about 2,100 wounded.

Conquest of the remaining bits and pieces of coral that composed the Tarawa atoll brought additional casualties, albeit on a much lesser scale than Betio.

The bittersweet taste of victory turned to ashes less than twenty-four hours after Betio became "secure." Because the conquest of Makin lasted four days instead of one, the naval task force had remained on station in the nearby waters, rather than steaming away from any Japanese submarines that might lurk in the area. In the early-morning hours of 24 November, the escort carrier *Liscome Bay*, in the company of some other vessels, prowled the area. The thin, four-ship screen around the *Liscome Bay* included the new destroyer *Franks*. Radar detected bogeys, unidentified aircraft, and the admiral in charge dispatched the *Franks* to investigate, punching a hole in the protection for the task force's three carriers.

Another radar contact registered a surface vessel but that blip vanished, indicating either the presence of a submarine that had just dived or perhaps a false image. The convoy started to execute a planned maneuver just as the *Franks* spotted a light on the water. Later investigation revealed that an enemy airplane had dropped a floating flare to advise a Japanese sub of nearby targets. At 0513 a torpedo ripped the *Liscome Bay* midships. From a distance of some two or three miles, Michael Bak, on the bridge of the *Franks*, saw a gigantic explosion of fire soar into the sky as the initial detonation of the torpedo ignited the aircraft bombs stowed in the carrier's hold. Fragments of steel, clothing, and human flesh showered the deck of the battleship *New Mexico* almost a mile away. Little more than twenty minutes later, the shattered hulk sank. "It was just like putting a candle out," said Bak. "The ball of fire was snuffed out as the ship sank. We were just dumbfounded. That's the first time we experienced the horrors of war. I think it sort of scared everybody. They just sort of felt, 'My gosh, this is for real.' We knew it was a lot of men lost because of the way the ship blew up and looked like a ball of fire. It happened so fast."

In fact, 642 officers and men went down with the carrier; only a hundred or so fewer than died wresting Betio from the determined Japanese. Among those who perished was Dorie Miller, the African-American steward who shot down a pair of enemy planes at Pearl Harbor. In the segregated Navy, he died still a food handler.

For all the bloodshed in the Gilberts, the Nimitz braintrust coveted much more highly the Marshall Islands, in particular Kwajalein and Enewetak. The ultimate plan went under the heading of Operation Flintlock. Mindful of the experiences at Tarawa, Richmond K. Turner issued a paper that prescribed considerably heavier advance bombardment from the sea and air. He also demanded increased training to ensure getting one's shells' and bombs' worth. Submarines, which had been invaluable in collecting intelligence for the invasion of the Gilberts, performed the same service in the Marshalls. Reconnaissance flights from the new U.S. air base on Betio, named for Deane Hawkins, brought detailed photographs enabling the strategists to plot the attack more precisely; a small return for the high investment of life at Tarawa. Underwater demolition teams made their debut, swimming in to check out the shoreline defense systems. Flintlock mounted an assault force of 54,000 as against half that number in Galvanic. Amtracs, without which Galvanic might have totally flopped, became a top production priority. The latest models added armor plate to protect drivers and machine guns for inshore fire support. One version carried no troops, but its turret, equipped with a 37mm cannon and machine guns, acted as a kind of seagoing light tank.

Following the lead of the RAF and the Atlantic air arm, the Pacific fleet laced its fighters with rockets to strafe beach emplacements.

The shipyards in the States had been busy; Task Force 58, commanded by VAdm. Marc A. Mitscher, boasted twelve carriers, eight new battleships, and a host of cruisers, destroyers, and lesser vessels. From the flight decks, 650 planes were available for Flintlock. The attack on Kwajalein actually involved not only that coral atoll, but also two smaller ones in the vicinity, Roi and Namur. The 4th Marine Division drew Roi and Namur while the Army's 7th Division, bloodied during the Aleutian campaign, swapping its parkas for lighter-weight khaki, struck at Kwajalein.

The hapless garrison on Kwajalein could do nothing to prevent the enemy from occupying islands that flanked the main objective. On Enubuj, the 7th Division installed forty-eight pieces of artillery that quickly zeroed in on Kwajalein. Simultaneously, missiles delivered from the battleship-stuffed fleet rocked boomerang-shaped Kwajalein for two days. Unlike many other amphibious operations, Flintlock proceeded with almost paradelike precision. The Navy and Army smoothly coordinated supply and troop buildup.

Samuel Eliot Morison, commissioned by Navy buff President Roosevelt for the purpose of providing an eyewitness history of seagoing operations, frequently displayed prejudice toward the brother service. He had been acutely critical of the 27th Division at Makin and only slightly less so in recounting the Aleutian campaign of the 7th Division. Describing Kwajalein operations, he credited the 7th Division with professional skill but nevertheless held to his bias. He noted that by the afternoon, while the Japanese were admittedly putting up well-organized resistance, "the troops had advanced only 950 yards. . . . The 11,000 men ashore by

1600 might have rushed the enemy lines, but that was not Army technique. In contrast to the Marines, the Army was taught not to advance until all possible fire had been brought to bear on the path ahead of the troops."

Throughout the war, the "experts" debated the philosophies behind the operations of the Marines and the Army. Leatherneck tacticians insisted that plunging head-on against the foe, which, while the approach piled up dead and wounded initially, resulted in fewer men lost over time than the more gradual approach of the Army.

Bob MacArthur, as a 7th Division engineer officer, participated at Kwajalein. "The assault was a classic one on fortified positions. I went in on the third wave and there was no opposition at first [testifying to the improved preinvasion barrage]. We worked with small teams of infantry. They kept the ports [for pillboxes] covered with small-arms fire and we had these seven-second fuses on the fifty-pound satchel charges—dynamite [another improvement over the improvised means at Tarawa]. We'd blow doors open and then the flamethrowers would come in through the smoke and dust. It was all over in six days."

While this part of Flintlock required less than a week, only 265 enemy soldiers were taken prisoner; the remainder of the roughly 4,000 fought to their death. American casualties numbered nearly 2,000, with 372 KIA.

A truly intensive bombardment by battleships and aviation, almost triple in tonnage to what fell upon Betio, blasted Roi and Namur, devastating the defenders. The first Marines ashore met enemy soldiers still disoriented from the concussions. On Namur, a Marine platoon led by Lt. Saul Stein crept up to a large blockhouse. One leatherneck placed a shaped explosive against a wall, blowing a sizeable hole. Suddenly, Japanese soldiers rushed out of the place. Stein ordered satchel charges thrown into the inside. The concrete building erupted, with enough force to hurl a fighter plane overhead a thousand feet higher. The Marines had detonated a warehouse of torpedo warheads. The explosion killed forty Marines, including Stein and most of his men, while flying debris wounded another sixty.

On Roi and Namur, the Japanese soldiers stubbornly fought back from their wrecked blockhouses and rubble. TNT, flamethrowers, and other assorted weapons vanquished them. The entire operation required little more than a day. During the brief but deadly twenty-six and one-half hours, three Marines won the Medal of Honor, posthumously.

The greatest prize in the Marshalls was Enewetak, a rough circle of some forty islets that surrounded a lagoon twenty-one by seventeen miles. It was capable of serving as a staging area for assaults on two major enemy strongholds, Truk and Saipan. A joint Marine-Army assemblage of 10,000 sailed to the atoll and again the outnumbered, outgunned Japanese succumbed to a coordinated assault by ships, planes, tanks, and troops with massive firepower.

During this period, the 37th Division on Bougainville carved out a fifteen-mile-long, seven-mile-wide stretch as a safe haven for supplies, a hospital, radio station, and large airfield. Once the Americans established strong perimeters with open fields of fire and barbed-wire barriers, they assumed a defensive stance. "It became a waiting game," said Cletus Schwab, a lieutenant in the 37th, "because we knew the Japanese forces would try to drive us into the ocean."

Around Empress Augusta Bay, the Americal Division similarly fortified its perimeter. Matters reached a crescendo in March. Bill McLaughlin, as a private with the Americal Division's 21st Recon Company, recalled, "They attacked and we had a grand fight as they piled up some thousands of bodies on the wire, penetrating to within a half mile of the sea. Every man in the Army was fighting them that day and they buried them with bulldozers when it finally ended."

In a two-day battle, the enemy lost as many as 4,000. Henceforth, those Japanese still on Bougainville could only mount small-scale operations while a combination of Americans, Australians, Fiji Scouts, and the New Guinea "Police Boys" gradually wore them down. For the first time in World War II, African Americans who had been trained as combat soldiers but shunted to labor and service duties confronted the enemy. Private First Class Thomas E. Lewis left the safety of a tank to rescue three wounded GIs; he was hit by a mortar burst. He received a Purple Heart and a Silver Star. Subsequently, the black soldiers from the segregated 93d Division and the 24th Infantry Regiment, except for a few more encounters, returned to menial tasks.

The Army Air Corps, in its efforts to support the ground troops, however, still labored with substandard weapons. The P-40 had always been at a disadvantage against the Japanese fighters, and while the P-38 provided a powerful tool, the debut of the P-39 Airacobra added nothing useful to the arsenal. William Turner, who flew one for the 36th Fighter Squadron, called it a decent enough strafing plane with its four .30-caliber machine guns in the wings, two .50s firing through the propeller, and a 37mm cannon that shot through the propeller hub. "You could fire the wings, the .50-calibers, or the cannon, or any combination, or all of them at once," said Turner. "It was awesome firepower but the .30s were too light.

"The Allison 1150-horsepower engine sat behind the pilot with a ten-inch drive shaft running from the engine to the gear box in the nose." Some said that made an uncomfortable cockpit. "The engine had no supercharger, making poor performance at high altitudes. The engine in the back made flying at stalling speeds tricky—controls were very sensitive. It was not suited for the Pacific but was the tool at hand and used."

Turner's tour of 250 combat missions illustrates the changeover to more effective weapons. He did his first 61 in the Airacobra; then progressed to the P-47, in which he completed another 54, before finishing with 135 in P-38s, with which he knocked down 3 enemy planes. By 1944, the Japanese ability to trade punches with Americans on an equal basis in the sky was over.

# 6

# Burmese Days and Skip Bombing

THE CHINA-BURMA-INDIA THEATER WAS A BACKWATER FOR THE American war effort, particularly in terms of ground forces. Operating on the theory that the Chinese had abundant if untrained and ill-equipped manpower, the U.S. supplied advisors, weapons, and direction. From the beginning, overall Allied command dealt with a roily stew of factions—the forces of Chiang Kai-shek, internally wracked by corruption and a war-lord philosophy; the Chinese Communists with their own agenda; the American Army and its rambunctious junior partner, the Air Corps; and the British with their interests of empire. The highest-ranking American, Gen. Joseph Stilwell, nominal commander, as chief of staff to Chiang Kai-shek, thought poorly of his patron and seldom spoke favorably about anyone.

Running the British units in Burma was a highly unorthodox soldier, Gen. Orde Wingate. His prewar background of counterinsurgency against Arabs seeking to oust the English from Palestine, his open support for undercover Zionists, and a brief covert job rallying Ethiopians against Mussolini's armies, apparently qualified him as the man to direct guerrilla-style operations in Burma against the Japanese. Bearded, careless of uniform, and with a corruscating tongue toward even his superiors, Wingate had developed the "Chindits" into an effective fighting force. The U.S. Joint Chiefs of Staff met Wingate at a Quebec Conference in 1943 and he impressed them sufficiently for Hap Arnold to offer air support to the Chindits, to the chagrin of Stilwell.

The specially trained Chindit Brigade of 9,000, drawn from a variety of units including native Britons, Ghurkas from India, and Burmese, had spent many months in action. They hiked deep into the jungles of Burma where they conducted hit-and-run raids and fought off the Japanese columns seeking to block passage between India and China, the lifeline for the Chinese armies.

Flip Cochran, rotated back to the States from teaching aerial combat to newcomers in the Mediterranean theater, visited Hap Arnold, the Air Force chief, to correct an error about the newest fighter plane, the P-47, just being introduced in Europe. He said he told him, "There's a misconception. I hear from England that the P-47 will only fight at high altitude. These kids are being told and believe they won't ever fight down near the ground . . . below 12,000 feet, because they have this wonderful supercharger. I said any airplane with eight .50-caliber machine guns in it is going to be used on the ground." Cochran lectured Arnold on the need for instruction on how to properly school new fliers in the virtues and capabilities of the P-47.

Arnold listened politely but then proposed that Cochran take command of the air group that would work with the Chindits and Merrill's Marauders. Cochran balked; he preferred to go to Europe to work with the first squadrons fly-

ing P-47s, including his good friend Hubert Zemke, already
an ace. He called the other assignment "some doggone off-
shoot, side-alley fight over in some jungle in Burma that
doesn't mean a damn thing." When Cochran argued further
and remarked, "It's my destiny and I think it's my life," an
exasperated Arnold became "a little irked." According to
Cochran, he growled, "I don't know what kind of an Air
Force office I'm running here when guys come in and tell
me they are not going to do something. . . . You are going."

Arnold made it plain that Cochran had no choice and the
pilot yielded: "Where and when?" The Air Corps boss answered, "That will come later. I want to get that other mon-
key in here." The "simian" in question was John Alison, as
outspoken as Cochran. The pair received orders to lead the
1st Air Commando Task Force, designed to support
Wingate's operation.

Cochran explained, "He [Wingate] would effect long-
range forays into enemy territory. He used mules as transport and the jungle as protection. They would get in, disrupt
the enemy, and take over whole territories. He called it
'long-range penetration.' He felt that if he had some air support, it would make him more effective. We were told by
General Arnold to study General Wingate, find out all we
could, his ideas, his plans, how we could support him. Originally the idea was light airplanes, because Wingate had
brought that up with Churchill, Arnold, and Lord Louis
Mountbatten at the Quebec meeting.

"Wingate had said, 'if you could pull out my wounded;
because when we get a man wounded, we can't carry him,
because he becomes a burden. We have to prop him up
against a tree, give him a gun, or let him stay there and give
him money and stuff, hoping that the natives would take
care of him. Our attrition rate is terrible. When a man gets

wounded, his chances with this kind of warfare aren't very good.' " Operations were also hampered by the requirement that the Chindits carry on their bodies, or their mules, supplies and equipment which, when expended, forced the troops to withdraw for refurbishing.

Alison remembered Arnold's instructions slightly differently on two occasions. "He gave us a free hand in choosing our equipment, and his only directive to us was, 'I want to see the United States Army Air Forces play a large part in Wingate's coming operations.' " In another official interview, Alison reported Arnold as saying, "I am giving you 200 L-5 and L-1-type aircraft [single-engine planes ordinarily used for liaison and observation]. I want you to go in there and take out General Wingate's wounded." Alison added, "Then with a twinkle in his eye he said, 'I not only want you to do that . . . but I want the USAAF to spearhead General Wingate's operations.' "

After conferring with Wingate, and having personally seen the mountainous terrain, the absence of roads, and the streams from the air, the Americans identified movement on the ground as the principal difficulty. "The obvious answer was to move the troops by air," said Alison. "We asked for gliders and transports and light planes. We knew there was not enough fighter aviation in that theater, nor bomber aviation, to take care of the present commitments and also to give our force the protection we wanted them to have." The fledgling 1st Air Commando Task Force eventually included a squadron of P-51s, another of B-25s, along with roughly 100 gliders with seventy-five pilots, plus a squadron of troop carriers (C-47s) capable of parachuting men and supplies or towing the gliders, and about 100 of the L-1s and L-5s.

Wingate still thought in terms of trekking to the interior

but at a meeting with Mountbatten and him, Cochran boldly announced that the U.S. airmen would fly the brigade into Burma. Alison, present at the conference, remarked later that Cochran had nothing to back up his word other than his reputation. An operation of this nature had never been attempted and the assembled strategists seriously doubted him. However, the Americans worked out the details and conducted a large-scale maneuver that convinced the British leaders.

"General Wingate was an officer with vision," said Alison. "We had no sooner sold him on the idea of moving the troops by air than he immediately began to expand upon our operation and press us to do more. Instead of flying in a small percentage of his troops as first planned, General Wingate called on the Troop Carrier Command to carry almost his entire force after the troops of the Air Commando Force landed and built airdromes.

"On the night of 5 March 1944, we started out from India with our force of gliders. These gliders were loaded with bulldozers, tractors, jeeps, mules, soldiers of General Wingate's forces to guard the area in which we were to land, and members of the Air Commando Force to direct the building of airdromes."

Cochran recalled one unusual problem. "How were these animals [the mules] going to ride? They [the Chindits] depended a great deal on them. [The mule] was their mobility in the jungle. Going along in the jungle, you'd be within a hundred yards of the enemy and the enemy wouldn't quite know exactly where you were. The soldiers were trained to strap all their military utensils, everything so they didn't clank. If the mule brayed or hee-hawed, he would give you away. The poor fellows had to be 'debrayed.' [Severance of their vocal cords. Merrill's second in command, Charles

Hunter, flat-out refused to silence the animals used for the American operation Galahad, insisting the only pleasure the sexless mules enjoyed was braying.] We had these mute mules to put in gliders and aircraft and we didn't know how they were going to take to that sort of thing. We knew something of the nature of the mule and we were a little apprehensive. We had all manner of wild schemes of how we would do this. We searched the outfit to find any farm boy that had any experience or knew anything about mules. We found a couple of our guys who had mules on a farm. We had attacked the problem as though it were something you would have to sit down from square one and design something, as though it were one of these terrible, insurmountable things. This kid just cut that all out and said, 'Why don't we just try walking them in and see what they do.' Lo and behold, the mule took to it just like they take to everything else. It didn't concern them one bit. We asked the mule to go in the glider. He walked in and he stood there. We did take some precautions. We had a mule tender to go along and he had a ready revolver to clunk the guy between the eyes if he started tearing the glider apart. It wasn't necessary at all. The mules took off and enjoyed the ride, landed and did nothing. As the guys in the glider said, 'They even banked on the turns.' "

Alison noted, "We were to land in areas far in the enemy's rear which had been previously selected and carefully photographed and mapped. Elaborate plans had been made so that nothing would go wrong. The gliders took off just at dusk so as to cross enemy lines after dark. We had selected two sites; half our gliders to go into each and build an airport for transport planes at each site. Just prior to takeoff, photoreconnaissance showed that the Japanese had gotten wind of our plan and completely blocked with logs and trees one of the jungle clearings. Plans were immediately changed, and all gliders were [routed to] the other area [code-named Broadway] and if the enemy really had gotten hold of our plans to land in such force we would be able to overwhelm him." Cochran said the enemy action at one place suggested the possibility of an ambush at the second.

In sharing the command of the American air unit, Cochran grounded himself and assumed the administrative duties while Alison, as the hands-on operations chief, flew missions. He described the first insertion of Chindits into Burma by air, probably the most difficult glider tow ever tried. "There was a three-quarter moon shining, and although this was good light for night flying, the haze was bad over the mountains and over Burma, which made it difficult to see the planes from the gliders that they were towing. The DC-3 [C-47] had to climb 8,500 feet to cross the mountains through turbulent air on a flight into enemy territory that lasted three hours and fifteen minutes." Back at Wingate's headquarters ground observers flashed word of red flares, the distress signal for downed gliders. Three tow ships returned to base with the disconsolate news that the ropes to their birds had snapped, meaning a total of six gliders lost even before passing over the border into Burma. Alerted to the broken lines, the home base messaged the convoy of transports and gliders to fly "high tow," a maneuver that stationed the gliders above the towship and less likely to break off.

Alison said, "The gliders were overloaded with men and machinery; parachutes were not worn. Every pilot left our home base knowing that once he was committed to this flight the airplane that was towing him did not have enough gasoline to turn around and tug his glider all the way back home. Every pilot knew that no matter what the outcome of this venture, he was going to be deposited 200 miles [officially the distance was 165] behind the enemy lines and if everything did not go right, 200 miles is an awfully long way to walk through jungle country. The glider flight was led by Capt. William H. Taylor, who trained our pilots for many months for this operation. His was the first glider to hit the ground; two gliders were towed behind each airplane. I flew behind the second airplane to reach the landing ground.

"From the photographs we had estimated two logical places on the field where the Japanese might have machine guns. The first two gliders were down and their crews out immediately and on the dead run for these two points. Fortunately, the enemy machine guns were not there, and as my glider came over the field I saw the green flare which meant that the first two gliders were not being fired upon and my landing could be accomplished without that harassing thought. The pilot on the end of the other rope from the airplane cut, and I followed right behind him. He came into the field and had to purposely crash his glider to keep from running into the first one [there]. My landing was uneventful. I have the solution for successful glider landing at night; I use the close-your-eyes-and-pray method."

The pathfinder gliders, first to touch down, set out flare pots to facilitate succeeding waves of gliders. However, the field proved far less accessible than expected. For many years, the local people had logged teak and during the wet season, slid the huge logs across the ground down to a river. Over time the technique gouged deep ruts that elephant grass covered, making the trenches invisible in aerial photographs or reconnaissance. "They formed perfect glider traps," said Alison, "and there was no way to avoid them. The gliders arrived overhead in large numbers and when a glider starts down there is no way to stop it. As each one hit the trenches the landing gears would come off and the gliders would go in a heap. We tried to arrange the lights to spread the gliders all over the field to avoid collisions, but this was impossible—they were coming in too fast to change directions and glider after glider piled into one another in the landing area.

"It was dark, and standing on the field you would try to shout to the gliders as they whizzed by at 80 to 90 miles an hour to give the pilot some directions after he hit the ground. You would try to get the injured out of the wrecked gliders, but there just wasn't any way to stop it. You had to be on the alert at all times for gliders rushing down the field and be mighty quick to get out of the way. You don't hear a glider coming toward you—it doesn't make any noise; then all of a sudden it's on the ground and you hear the rumble of its wheels and you look out into the darkness and try to tell where it is going to go. There is not much use starting to run until you know that. It was a dramatic evening but we lived through it, got our equipment down, and got our men down without too many casualties." Actually, 31 men were killed at Broadway, including Capt. Patrick Casey, the engineering officer expected to clear debris and construct the airstrip. Another 30 individuals suffered serious injuries. Only 31 of the original 68 gliders launched actually reached Broadway and virtually every one was beyond salvage. A handful went down in enemy territory. But there were more than 500 men, 3 mules, and 30 tons of equipment on hand.

Realization of the hazards at Broadway forced those already there to send a radio message using the prearranged code to halt all flights, "Soya Link, Soya Link, Soya Link!" [The British hated an ersatz sausage manufactured from soy beans.] "The entire second wave of gliders was stopped by radio and returned to base," said Alison. "In the first wave we had enough equipment to build an airfield and it wasn't necessary to jeopardize other mens' lives as our patrols reported no Japanese nearby. The next morning, the field was a mass of wreckage. Looking at it, it was impossible to believe we could put an airfield there. I talked to our engineer [Casey's deputy], Lt. Robert Brackett, and said, 'Can you make an airfield in this place?' He replied, 'Yes, sir, I think I can,' and I said, 'Well, how long will it take?' He replied, 'If I have it done by this afternoon, will that be too late?' He wasn't just kidding—that night the first DC-3 landed at Broadway at 7:20, and altogether sixty-five sorties arrived that night bringing in fighting troops, mules, machine guns, and equipment. From then on it was just another operation—taking transports off from India at night and landing them 200 miles behind enemy lines at night. Before long we had quite a sizable army."

Indeed, less than one week after the first glider bounced to a halt at Broadway, more than 9,000 Chindits had flown in and then moved out to hit the Japanese. Eight days after the Air Commandos first arrived, the Japanese struck at Broadway with fighters. Fortunately, a flight of Spitfires happened to be on hand and they shot down half of the attackers and drove off the others. The success at Broadway inspired the creation of two similar installations behind the enemy lines, Piccadilly and Chowringhee, employing the same technique of gliderborne men and equipment.

The Japanese quickly recognized the threat of these air bases. Not only had they magnified the capabilities of the Chindits to disrupt supply lines and mount guerrilla attacks upon the Imperial Army, but also they enabled aircraft to fly offensive missions deep in Japanese-controlled territory. Said Cochran, "They had to come in and try to get them out. There was hand-to-hand fighting to protect these bases.

Both sides knew how to jungle fight. Many a time we would land airplanes in there and the Japs would be right on the end of the strips. There would be a gun or two, a party of Japanese the British hadn't been able to get out of there. You'd be taking an airplane off and someone would say to you, 'Hey, Colonel, when you go out, don't turn left, because if you do, they'll get you.' It was that close, that kind of warfare. It surprised our guys but you got so used to it that it became a way of life. At night you didn't sleep too well, because you knew there were crawly things running around and that there were Japs who could crawl right into your place, throw grenades, and start shooting up the place.

"One night we had a DC-3 run a little too long on the strip and in trying to turn around, he got stuck. He and his crew got out and started to walk back to get help. They hadn't walked very far until their whole airplane blew up. The enemy was that close they sneaked in and planted explosives."

Alison also introduced the helicopter to combat. Having heard that the first few of these machines had come off the production line, Alison plotted to add them to the 1st Air Commando Task Force. While engaged in England, and then in the Soviet Union on the Lend-Lease program, he had met Harry Hopkins, the confidant and aide to the president. Hearing of Alison's assignment to the China-Burma-India theater, Hopkins invited him for a chat. Alison seized the opportunity to ask for the helicopters, even as the Air Force brass tried to figure how best to deploy them. When Hap Arnold demanded of a bemused Cochran how these suddenly became part of his command, Cochran said he responded, "General, you just have to know the right people!"

Cochran said, "We didn't use them as tricks. We used them in the jungle for serious business. They were terribly underpowered. But they were effective for what we used them for. If you got a pilot in them, that was about their capable load. Then you would add another person. A couple of times we were able to get two wounded out at a time by using a stretcher on a sling attached on the side. We pulled out and documented the saving of eighteen lives that we couldn't have gotten out in any other manner."

Perhaps nowhere during World War II was there more internal strife than in the China-Burma-India theater. At Quebec, in an effort to establish a firm chain of command, Mountbatten had been named Supreme Allied Commander Southeast Asia. The highest-ranking American on the scene, Lt. Gen. Joseph Stilwell had a pathological dislike for those he continually called "Limeys." He was equally disdainful of most other racial and ethnic groups; his diary is sprinkled with references to "frogs," "niggers," "coons," "wops," "gooks," and "chinks." He considered the British effete, snobbish, and reluctant warriors. Mountbatten professed his dismay when Stilwell, said to him, "Gee, Admiral. I like working with you! You are the only Limey I have met who wants to fight." When Lord Louis praised Gen. Sir Harold Alexander as a model soldier, "[Stilwell] staggered me by saying, 'General Alexander was a coward and retreated all the way and never stood and fought.' I pointed out that Stilwell had retreated all the way and that nobody so far had called him a coward." Mountbatten was referring to the 1942 defeat of Stilwell in Burma, a campaign in which the Japanese forces chased the Americans and their Chinese soldiers out of the country, shutting off the supply route from India. The only way to get vital materials to the armies of Chiang Kai-shek was through the perilous airlift over the Himalayas, the fabled "hump."

Stilwell sniped at and criticized not only the British but

also Chiang. He showed little interest in Chennault's Fourteenth Air Force or the potential of the outfit led by Cochran and Alison. For the most part, Cochran and Alison got along famously with Mountbatten and Wingate. However, on one occasion, Cochran lost his temper with the leader of the Chindits. Unknown to the American, Wingate arranged for some RAF Spitfires to set down at one of the airfields during daylight hours. "The worst thing to do would be to land fighters on that field in the daytime and have the Japs see them. You're just waving a red flag at a bull. He did it and don't you know the Japs came in and got them and just about wiped them out. They got one guy who was just taking off. They got one on the ground. They had to come in and beat that place up and those airplanes were just like drawing flies. This incensed me probably more than anything ever had in my life. I felt Wingate had betrayed me. I said, 'you do that anymore and we're off you. You did a thing you shouldn't have and you doublecrossed us. You undercut us.' He looked me straight in the eye and said, 'I did, didn't I.'

"That just about cut me off. Naturally I was fuming and I imagine my language wasn't that good. I learned later that the office was not soundproof. The walls had ears, and I was told later that his whole staff and all the soldiers, everybody in the place, heard my tirade. I was accused of very bad manners by those who didn't know the seriousness of it. I can see I did sound like an arrogant Yank. We had a little bit of a different relationship after that, but still a solid one, because we had it out.

"Wingate was man enough to [take criticism. He] brought in an aide and he used his peculiar archaic words to the man who had a poised pad and pencil, 'Take a screed to the Prime Minister of Great Britain . . .' Then he started out . . . to the

Prime Minister, to Lord Louis Mountbatten, to General [J. W.] Slim [the British Army head in the CBI theater] to General Marshall, to General Arnold, and went all down the list. He read off a very concise signal of admission that he had done it, that he had been wrong and he apologized. Whether that ever got to the Prime Minister, Lord Louis, or General Arnold, I don't know, but it sure was a good show. It satisfied me, and I stormed out a little bit placated. I got those Spitfires the hell off that landing strip. We had been planning to put our P-51s there but we were going to fly them in late in the evening so the Japs wouldn't see them. During the night [we would] load them with bombs and do close support in the early morning, fly on back to the bases, stay out in the daytime so they would not be seen."

Ideally, the 3,000 in Merrill's Marauders would have been mated with Wingate's brigades, but Stilwell refused to allow the GIs to serve under the Briton. When that news reached Wingate he reacted in fine American style: ". . . tell General Stilwell he can take his Americans and stick 'em up his ass." The bitter relationships spilled over into crucial matters affecting the lives of those engaged in the fighting. Stilwell, rather than seek transport by air, marched Merrill's people deep into Burma in a flanking maneuver aimed at cutting off the Japanese long enough for slower-moving Chinese infantry and tanks to trap them. Aided by some native Kachin tribesmen, recruited by American officers of the Office of Strategic Services, and who provided excellent intelligence on the enemy, Galahad fought a sizable battle near the village of Walawabum, repulsing an attempt by superior forces to break through.

Unfortunately, the main body of Chinese soldiers under Stilwell, only ten miles off, failed to exploit the momentary success of the Marauders. Hindered by poor communications, he exercised the same excessive caution he so often denounced in others, delaying marching orders until the enemy escaped the trap. A pattern developed in which the men of Galahad thrust themselves behind the now-withdrawing enemy but, on each occasion, there was no follow-up of the opportunities to crush the Japanese. Using the few 81mm mortars they packed, along with small arms and bayonets, the Americans inflicted severe losses, far above their own. Still, the campaign under wretched climactic conditions, the usual hostile microbes, and enemy fire exacted a heavy toll upon the Americans.

"Those fellows took an awful beating," said Cochran. "The jungle got them and the Japs got them. In one of their early contacts with the enemy, they had a lot of guys hurt. They said, '[there's] Cochran's outfit. He has got some L-1s and L-5s. We'll just send him down here and he can start working for us. I said, 'No, I can't do that.'

"They said, what the hell, you're American Air Force guys and here our American guys are in there suffering and you're withholding a capability. I said, as I know my instructions, I am sent here as a project to support Wingate's penetration into Burma. That is my job. If I start using my airplanes and start losing them down there . . . by the time Wingate gets in position and I am needed there, I won't have the aircraft. I went back to the rule that I was a one-purpose outfit and was to hold my capability until the time it was to be used. Certainly those kids needed it. Hell, I wanted to do it as badly as anybody, but I also didn't want to break the orders given to me . . . Stratemeyer [Maj. Gen. George, head of the Eastern Air Command] said Cochran is right and he doesn't have to do that." In fact, the Galahad battle at Walawabum happened during the period when the Broadway field was being created.

With the big airfields in business, Wingate's people created small simple airstrips close to where the Chindits were warring. According to Cochran, "You would fly airplanes [the L-1s and L-5s] in and out of the strips. They would collect the wounded at the immediate site, come into the big bases of Chowringhee or Broadway, off-load, and go back with a replacement and some ammunition, and bring out another wounded. Then when the DC-3s came in at night with supplies or personnel or equipment, the wounded would go into the DC-3s and be taken to hospitals in the rear. Wingate's first request was more than adequately supplied. The wounded not only didn't lie in the jungle anymore to die, they were the best cared-for guys in the business. They would get out the same day and they'd be in hospitals.

"This was the very necessary and very proud work of those liaison guys. They were the beloved of the British soldier. I remember when I would go in, you had a load to take in and a load to take out. I remember bringing one kid whose leg was all shot up. I got him out and I've never seen such appreciation from that boy. There were many instances where the kids on stretchers, pretty well shot up, would kiss the hands of the pilot. We not only amazed them, but they were mighty proud to be associated with us, and a great camaraderie was set up between the forces. We admired each other."

The Americans had very little time to savor the successful combined operations with Wingate. His B-25 crashed, killing all aboard, only three weeks after the establishment of Broadway. Within a few months Stilwell added the remnants of the Chindits to his command.

At the time of the campaign in Burma, the Air Corps was also assuming a more prominent role in the island campaigns of the South Pacific. Robert Smith, the offspring of

Norwegian immigrants, a graduate of Bowdoin College, Maine, graduated as a pilot a few days after Pearl Harbor. Early in 1942 he sailed to Sydney, Australia, as a member of the 43d Bomb Group. "They had no aircraft for us. Most of the other pilots were in the ferry command." Smith expected to fly B-17s but upon transfer to the 22d Bomb Group climbed into the cockpit of a B-26, the Martin Marauder, a plane with a somewhat dubious reputation. Crashes at the Florida training site led to the motto, "One a day in Tampa Bay." A two-engine, medium-range aircraft, the B-26 was characterized by a relatively small wing area. It became known as "the flying prostitute"—no visible means of support [lift].

Smith defended the B-26. "Limited support was given to our area of the war. Everything had to go to Europe. We had good mechanics and our B-26s were well maintained. We had excellent pilots. Unfortunately, the attrition rate was quite high, mostly due to combat losses. We flew B-26s for about nine months but then stood down because we had lost roughly over half our force. We were retrained and picked up B-25s. I had flown the short-wing model, the A. New B-26 B and C models were going to North Africa and Europe. I have a lot of respect for the B-26 because it was a very, very fine airplane but it was a tricky airplane to fly. I have flown the B-26 on one engine very successfully but on take-off, if you lost an engine you had a problem."

Smith's early combat days illustrate the primitive state of tactical support in New Guinea. "The idea of a forward air controller [FAC], which we developed to a high degree during the Vietnam War, did not occur. We were never FACd. We had preplanned targets. Usually, it would be a section of the jungle marked out in grease pencil. We would bomb the target area from an initial point [IP]. We would usually come in off the coast and would have our IP and our course well identified. If we were supporting the military, they would fire mortar shells to identify by smoke flares the precise target."

Smith's group flew out of Australia and Port Moresby for its runs. "We would strike targets from one to three days, but we were bombed quite often by the Japanese. I recall one raid where there were something like eighty Betty bombers overhead. Unfortunately we had the P-40s and the P-39s and of course the Zeros knocked them off like flies because they couldn't get up high enough. We were escorted a few times but not very often because the B-26 was a little bit too fast for the fighters and, as a result, they had to burn too much fuel. We went more or less on our own.

"In the Bismarck Sea battle against Japanese, we bombed on several occasions Japanese destroyers, which were very difficult to hit because they were doing figure eights usually. [My squadron] had originally been a recon. We bombed airfields because you could see them and then see the results. There were some excellent missions flown. I think they got fifty-two aircraft at Wewak [a Japanese base] one day." Promoted to a staff position with the Fifth Air Force Bomber Command, Smith put in time as a pilot for both B-17s and B-24s.

Richard Ellis, like Smith a 1930s college graduate [Dickinson], was drafted and immediately applied for flight training. Ellis flew B-25 submarine patrol out of Massachusetts after earning his wings, but then shipped out to the South Pacific and participated in the New Guinea campaign. "We were flying against the supply lines of the Japanese. There was a target, Wairopi Bridge, a rope bridge that swung over a gorge. Here we were trying to bomb something that was maybe three feet wide from 18,000 or 20,000 feet. We dumped I don't know how many tons on that thing day after day."

He was amazed by the feat of the Australian 9th Division crossing the Owen Stanley Range, over which he flew on numerous occasions. "I had never seen any place quite like that, high mountains and deep, deep rain forests. I know it was so bad because I can remember some of them [the Aussies] coming back. When they left they were guys that were normal and healthy, but when they came back they were walking dead."

Ellis, like Smith, recalled the frustration because the American fighter planes could not compete with the enemy. "One day there was a big raid. There were P-39 fighters stationed on our strip. We could see the P-39s taking off and we headed for the slit trenches. They banged the hell out of us. We lost all of our aircraft except one or two of them. The P-39s were up against the Zeros and the P-39 was not an aircraft that could be used very well against the Zero. It wasn't an airplane that gave a lot of confidence against the Zero. I remember some of these fighter pilots coming back, and the tapes would still be on their guns. [They never could maneuver into position to fire.]

"We used to think of those enemy fighters as having first-class pilots, usually navy pilots. They were flying out of two bases on the north side, Lae and Salamaua. Once in a while we would get mixed up with them. One day, by ourselves we had just gotten over the other side of the mountains and were headed out to sea to do a little ocean surveillance and we got jumped by four Zeros. I saw the fanciest flying and the poorest gunnery I saw during the whole war.

"The first time we saw them, there was a flight of B-26s, about nine airplanes, headed up to Lae to bomb their base. These four fighters had a go at the B-26s and decided they were too tough and too many. They saw us sitting out there and said, 'Here's our meat for today.' Captain Klein [Ellis was copilot] put the aircraft into a fairly sharp descent altitude and those Zeros were all over us, coming in and rolling all the way through. I could see them out of the side and they would come up underneath us with their bellies up. We had a top and lower turret, a gunner in the top and the bottom turrets. How we didn't get the hell shot out of us, I don't know. I could see this guy come up underneath us and he was right on us. Our lower gunner just stitched him right down the belly. We nailed him. The other three sort of moved off, made a few feints at us like they were coming in again but never did. When we got down, we had been hit in only one place, one hole."

Dismayed by the poor results against enemy ships, the Air Corps, under the direction of Gen. George Kenney, revised its tactics and equipment. Ellis remembered, "One squadron of B-25s had been converted to the low-level B-25, where we had eight machine guns in the nose, two on each side, for a total of twelve .50-caliber machine guns. We flew those right down on the deck, ten or fifteen feet above the water. We would fly into the target, firing our guns and then would drop our bombs, which would have a four-to-five-second-delay fuse. You would drop the bomb and then before it went off you would have four seconds to get away. We used the technique for the first time at the Bismarck Sea battle."

Along with the increased gun power, the B-25s added racks to carry as many as six 100-pound bombs and smaller fragmentation explosives, all with delayed fuses, for what became known as "skip bombing." According to Ellis, "You would go in usually broadside to the ship. When you got within machine-gun range, you would strafe, which would help contain the flak from the ship. When you got close enough—this was all a matter of judgment; there wasn't any bombsight—you would drop the bomb, pull up over the ship and hope the bomb hit the water and skipped into the side of the boat. If you got close enough, you couldn't miss the boat. But you had to get really close. When you pulled up over the ship, there was a wrenching, you just heaved back on the controls. When you went over the ship, you immediately got down on the water again. You didn't have a lower gunner. You had a top gunner and he would strafe to the rear as you departed. It was very successful and great against merchant ships because they usually weren't very heavily armed. From then on we did everything at low level, including attacking airfields, regardless of the type target."

Piloting his own B-25 on 2 November 1943, Ellis went on a highly successful skip-bombing operation against Rabaul. An elaborately planned affair, the mission dispatched several squadrons to dump smoke and fragmentation bombs that would provide concealment for Ellis's group. "We were the first that went down into the harbor," said Ellis. "As we came between these two volcanoes, there was the harbor in front of us. I was credited with sinking two ships. We got jumped pretty heavy by Zeros as we were coming out of the harbor. Our top gunner got another confirmed kill on that mission." For his performance Ellis earned a Silver Star.

The new low-level approach surprised the Japanese at their big Wewak complex. Ellis recalled, "They were just about to launch a big mission of their own because, as we came over the hill, we could see the airplanes lined up wingtip-to-wingtip along the runway. It was a dream target. We had 23-pound fragmentation bombs with a little parachute on them. We had somewhere between thirty and forty of those on a B-25 and you would just string them out as you flew over. It took long enough for the bomb to float down,

even though you were at low level, for you to get away."
The growing achievements of the Air Corps under Kenney's
command won the respect of MacArthur, who had previously regarded aircraft as a minor component in his arsenal.

# 7

# Big Week, Berlin, and Assaults and Batterings in Italy

THE NEW YEAR BROUGHT PROFOUND CHANGES TO THE EIGHTH Air Force in England as Lt. Gen. Jimmy Doolittle replaced Ira Eaker on 6 January. For months Hap Arnold had grumbled about the progress and achievements of the biggest of his commands and the one charged with bearing the heaviest burdens of strategic bombing in Europe. Arnold brushed aside excuses, largely legitimate, for the many aircraft grounded because of mechanical defects. He chafed at constant demands for more of everything from Eighth Air Force headquarters. Instead of lessening enemy opposition through Pointblank, the *Luftwaffe* seemed stronger. For all of the devastation supposedly visited upon the manufacturing sources, the Germans actually rolled out more planes per month than they lost during 1943. Although during the final weeks of that year the bomber fleets of more than 500 B-17s and B-24s—far in excess of the original magic figure of

300—struck several times, the appalling tolls for the final six months of 1943 demanded a scapegoat.

Doolittle's first vital policy decision reversed Eaker's dictum that fighters could never leave the bombers. Even when the enemy appeared vulnerable because of numbers and position, standing orders dictated that the Little Friends maintain their place as escorts. Doolittle announced that the P-38, P-47, and P-51 groups could engage the *Luftwaffe* on sight. When he visited the office of Maj. Gen. William Kepner, boss of the Eighth's fighter command, and saw on the wall the motto, "Our mission is to bring the bombers back," he ordered it removed. "From now on," Doolittle declared, "that no longer holds. Your mission is to destroy the German Air Force."

While the fighter groups heartily endorsed the new directions, the bomber people naturally reacted negatively to what they perceived as a policy that would leave them naked to enemy onslaughts. Their fears were not allayed by initial explanations that offensive action by fighters was conditional upon having enough aircraft to remain with the bombers in the event interceptors showed. But as the flow of planes and pilots from the U.S. swelled, the Mighty Eighth would enjoy increasing luxury to go after the foe whenever he appeared.

Doolittle demonstrated his command at the end of January in the form of an 806-bomber assault upon Frankfurt, the most massive strike by the Eighth yet. More than 630 fighters roamed the skies in support. Encouraged to seek and destroy, the Americans punished the *Luftwaffe* severely and gun cameras from both bombers and fighters confirmed more than 120 enemy planes destroyed and an additional 90 or so probables or damaged.

Frankfurt seemed merely the flexing of muscle when in

the third week of February, the four-engine bombers dominated what was called "Big Week." Meteorologists had forecast several days of clear weather over Germany. The Eighth and Ninth Air Forces, working with British Bomber Command and the Fifteenth Air Force in Italy, drubbed the Continent in a six-day cycle of round-the-clock destruction that emphasized aircraft factories. On opening day, 880 heavyweights with an almost equal number of fighters visited the targets. Thick cloud cover, in spite of the predictions of the weather specialists, obscured some objectives. Poor visibility may have also limited the defensive effort but thick swarms of U.S. fighters covered the Big Friends. The enemy knocked down twenty-one aircraft, a ratio of 2.2 percent, compared to the horrendous 29 percent downed on Black Thursday. Unlike earlier days, when a maximum effort left the bomber command supine for days, the combined air forces mustered intensive operations in the following days, including massive tonnage dropped on two notorious sites, Regensburg and Schweinfurt.

Doolittle displayed no hesitation because of bad weather. Ralph Golubock, a replacement pilot with the 44th Bomb Group, after his briefing for one of the missions, looked at the forbidding skies, thick black clouds, low ceilings, and heavy rain, mandating a tricky instrument takeoff and the always dangerous jockeying into formation. He and his colleagues believed the brass would scrub the affair, even as they taxied out to their assigned positions.

"The first two planes took the runway and awaited a takeoff flare that we were sure would never come. But it did! Right on time. The lead bomber raced down the runway and took off and was almost immediately enveloped in clouds and disappeared from sight. We all followed in turn, the planes spaced apart by thirty seconds. When my turn came I advanced the throttles and immediately went on instruments. The copilot tried to watch the runway to prevent accidentally drifting off and onto the grass. The engineer stood between the pilot and copilot to carefully monitor the engine instruments. He also called out our airspeeds so I could concentrate on taking a whole lot of airplane off the ground safely.

"Upon leaving the ground we were immediately immersed in rain and clouds. The tail gunner was back in his position with an Aldis lamp that he blinked on and off so that following planes would see the light and keep their distance. The climb was long and grinding, and to our horror, we saw a huge flash of light in the sky. We all knew that two planes had collided and exploded." His Liberator broke through the clouds at 17,000 feet to a deep blue sky and a sun bright as a ball of fire. "I drank in the beauty surrounding me and wondered why I was carrying a load of death to be dropped on people I didn't even know. My meditations were shortlived. There were hundreds of airplanes around us and this was not the time for daydreaming. We had to find our proper spot in formation. The procedure was to fly a racetrack course around a radio signal called a buncher. The lead plane was constantly firing flares so we could identify him. Each group had their own buncher. Out of all of this confusion, we began to form up. First as elements, then as squadrons and groups, finally as wings and divisions.

"The outside air-temperature gauge on the instrument panel was against a peg at -50° Fahrenheit. The biting cold was almost unbearable. We did not have heated flying suits or heaters that worked. We only had sheepskins that just could not keep the cold out. It was a numbing and strength-sapping cold that made concentration on flying and staying in proper formation difficult." Over the primary target, the bomb guidance–equipment system aboard the lead plane malfunctioned. Golubock's flight sought out a secondary site and dropped its ordnance. For all of the massive numbers and airmen involved, Golubock counted that Big Week expedition a "screwed-up mess. Three aircraft and crews lost. We bombed a secondary target and probably achieved nothing. All to fly a mission that should have been scrubbed in the first place."

Nevertheless, Big Week demonstrated that strategic bombing now meant sustained campaigns. The mounting production of bombers on U.S. assembly lines and the thousands of airmen completing their training was vital to Big Week's success. But the numbers were only part of the story. Technological advances that allowed the Little Friends to come along on even the most distant excursions made a substantial difference.

The P-51 Mustang, endowed with a Rolls-Royce Merlin engine that had a supercharger, was transformed from a mediocre, low-level, ground-support ship into a superb, high-altitude fighter with enough speed and maneuverability to outfly anything the Germans offered until the advent of the first jet fighter. External wing tanks extended the original scant 200-mile combat radius. In mid-December, P-51s chaperoned bombers to Kiel and back, a distance of nearly 1,000 miles. Engineers then crammed an extra fuel-supply tank in behind the pilot's armor plate, enabling P-51s to go the distance of the bombers throughout the Continent.

Tommy Hayes, after his tour in the South Pacific, where he knocked down a pair of enemy planes but suffered through a period of flying the P-39, had earned a month of R&R back in the States. He was reassigned to the 357th Fighter Group, again committed to P-39s. "The P-39 was an aircraft you flew with a cerebral sense. It did not warn you how close the P-39 was to the edge. Zap! and you're in trouble. We had too many crashes in a short time, evenly spread among the squadron. Maybe we commanders and flight leaders were pressing too hard. It was usually the newer pilots who bought the farm."

To Hayes's amazement, after his group sailed on the *Queen Elizabeth* for England, instead of the P-39, they were ticketed for Mustangs. The outfit, on its fourth mission, scored its first kills during the first day of Big Week. Colonel Henry Russell Spicer, a new group commander, known as "Hank," "Russ," or "Pappy," quickly endeared himself. "He was a natural leader, a Pied Piper," said Hayes, "having the qualities absent in his predecessor. Appearance, posture, caring, respect, voice, eyes. His arrival was an example. We were called to a personnel meeting. Spicer took the stage, introduced himself, related that he was familiar with our past, said we were a great group and, weather permitting, our mission tomorrow would show just how great the 357th is. He had physical presence and personality. After seven months, we had a commander again."

Beginning with Big Week, the air war visited the Third Reich with an intensity previously unseen. Whereas the sacking of cities and factories had earlier been spaced by intervals of days, even weeks, the Forts and Liberators showed almost daily and with them came hordes of fighters prepared not only to protect their Big Friends, but also to seek, pursue, and destroy any enemy planes that ventured aloft. For the first time in the war, the German aircraft industry could not match or surpass their losses of fighters. That deficiency was temporary as manufacturing installations pushed up their pace of production. But the *Luftwaffe* could not churn out capable pilots fast enough to offset the loss of experienced and skilled hands in the cockpits. Bob

Johnson, the veteran fighter pilot from the 56th, said, "As time went on, we were knocking the best boys the Germans had out of the air. We were knocking off some of the best German pilots, primarily because we didn't know any better. We didn't know we were supposed to be afraid of these guys and that they were so much better than we were. We went after them and we got them."

At the same time, a number of American fighter pilots using P-38s and P-47s quickly saw the virtues of the latest entry, the P-51. "We all wanted the P-51," said Jim Goodson. "It was the most remarkable plane of the war. It had as much range as a B-17, was about the size of a Hurricane and only slightly larger than a Spit." His boss, Col. Don Blakeslee, commander of the 4th Fighter Group, which had started out with Spitfires and then Thunderbolts, pleaded with Kepner for Mustangs. Kepner balked, noting that the Eighth in the midst of its huge offensive could not afford to stand down a fighter group while the pilots accustomed themselves to the new ships. Blakeslee supposedly pledged, "Give me those Mustangs and I give you my word—I'll have them in combat in twenty-four hours. I promise—twenty-four hours." His guarantee persuaded Kepner.

When the first P-51s arrived at the Debden airdrome, Blakeslee informed his subordinates of his promise to Kepner. "You can learn to fly them on the way to the target." In fact, the 4th's pilots squeezed in about forty minutes of flight time to familiarize themselves with their new equipment before heading out on a mission at the end of Big Week. Within a matter of weeks, group after group converted from P-38s, which continued to develop problems in the frigid climes of upper altitudes over Europe, and from the dependable but less agile P-47. Only the 56th Fighter Group in the Eighth Air Force, led by Hub Zemke, retained the Jugs. All fourteen other groups in the Eighth eventually manned Mustangs, although the Ninth Air Force, with heavier tactical responsibilities, continued to operate a number of P-47 outfits.

Little more than a week after Blakeslee's outfit adopted the P-51, the 352d Fighter Group, with Punchy Powell, switched. "I flew the P-47," says Powell, "for about half my eighty-three missions—all with the Thunderbolt were shorter than those in P-51s. I loved both airplanes for different reasons. The 47 was a flying tank, most durable, more firepower, and absolutely the greatest for strafing attacks and excellent at the higher altitudes for air-to-air combat. However, it lost a lot in aerial combat at lower altitudes. Its number-one weakness was its limited range. It was a big sweat returning from almost any penetration of the Continent because of lack of fuel, particularly if you got into a fight or misjudged your time over the Continent. The Mustang doubled our range and eliminated this problem, except on a few extralong missions to which we were assigned. It had range and firepower, particularly the D models with six guns instead of the four in the Bs and Cs." Actually, the ability of the P-51 to travel greater distances stimulated the devotees of the P-47 to enlarge its combat radius, and while never quite the marathon performer of the Mustang, Thunderbolts eventually journeyed ever deeper into enemy territory.

The 357th, which went into combat flying P-51s on 11 February, was jolted by the loss of their commander less than three weeks later. Even as the *Luftwaffe* tottered under the weight of firepower poured out by the near tidal wave of bombers and fighters, and the Third Reich earth shook from the thunderous rain of explosives, the Germans continued to draw blood. Henry Spicer, who in the eyes of Tommy Hayes transformed the 357th Fighter Group into an effective instrument, had led fourteen missions and been credited with three enemy aircraft destroyed when a burst of flak struck his P-51 on 3 March. He bailed out over the English Channel, hauled himself from the frigid waters and into his inflatable dinghy. But search-and-rescue units failed to find him before he drifted onto the beach near Cherbourg. There he lay on the sand, with frostbite of hands and feet, until German soldiers discovered him. After medical treatment and interrogation, the Germans lodged him in Stalag Luft 1, an encampment of downed aviators.

The pressure for fewer drop-outs because of mechanical difficulties was reflected in an experience of Golubock. "During one assembly over England, we developed a problem with one of our props malfunctioning. We left the formation and radioed the base that we were returning and explained our problem. We were ordered to land and to taxi over to one of the maintenance hangars. It was still very early in the morning and I was looking forward to returning to my room and hitting the sack. The engineering officer told us to stay in the airplane. They wheeled out a new prop and within fifteen minutes they removed the unserviceable one and replaced it with a new prop. We were told to take off and try to catch the group at Beachy Head. That's what we did. My record for no abortions remained intact. I would much rather have been in the sack."

On 4 March, the VIII Bomber Command dispatched 238 B-17s for a run at Berlin, the first strike by the Air Corps at the German capital. As the navigator for *Spirit of New Mexico*, 95th Bomb Group, housed at Horham, Lt. Vincent Fox remembered, "If Berlin could be attacked in daylight, then all of Germany would become accessible to the full weight of American bombs. For us, the bomber crews who were assigned the mission, Berlin was a giant mental hazard, the toughest of all missions, for which we had little genuine enthusiasm. However, the briefing officer, Maj. Jiggs Donohue, the silver-tongued lawyer from Washington, D.C., had the ability to make it sound like a gallant adventure into the wild blue yonder to be cherished.

"But the procedure wasn't new to us. We were on our twenty-fourth mission. We'd been briefed for Berlin on five previous occasions, but each time the adverse European winter weather had forced us to abandon the mission short of 'Big B.' The previous day we'd climbed to 30,000 feet over the Danish peninsula only to be confronted by a solid bank of swirling, turbulent clouds. The meteorology officer glibly promised better weather for today's mission but our faith in his predictions had suffered numerous setbacks before. At our takeoff time of 0730 hours, scattered snow squalls limited visibility down to a scant 300 yards as we peered apprehensively into the eerie predawn light while we spiraled up to group-assembly altitude. During the tension-filled climb, the English countryside was visible only momentarily through multilayered clouds."

The 95th formed up successfully but other groups were defeated early on by the towering overcast in their assembly areas. Shortly after Fox and associates crossed into Germany, Eighth Air Force supposedly sent out a recall signal. However, the mission commander of the 95th, Col. H. Griffin Mumford, leading a wing, resolutely slogged toward Berlin. Puzzled by the failure to turn back, one pilot broke radio silence to advise Mumford there had been a recall. Still the 95th's B-17s continued on the pathway that carried them over the Rhine River. Unhappy crewmen watched other groups turn back and radio to the 95th, "You'll be sorry."

Grif Mumford, however, advised by his superiors that combat wing leaders could use their own discretion, continued toward the target. Subsequently, it appeared that the recall attributed to the Eighth Air Force headquarters came from an enemy transmitter. The colonel, relying on the word from Curtis LeMay's 3d Bomb Division, decided he and his aircraft were already in too deep to simply reverse course and escape enemy fighters lurking along the pathway. Instead, he reasoned that the poor visibility might hide them until they struck Berlin. Then if they flew a different course back to England they might escape unhurt. He was obviously aware of the morale and propaganda value of a hit upon Big B.

Navigator Fox said, "We soon had the chilling realization that we were alone in our undertaking. Our ball-turret gunner could identify squadrons with the 95th 'Square B' tail markings and elements with the 'Square D' of the 100th Group [part of the wing led by Mumford] still maintaining the integrity of the formation. It seemed incredible that our token force was still bearing east toward the German capital. We got a brief glimpse of the ground near the city of Brunswick and were greeted by a barrage of enemy flak bursts."

Indeed, the ground fire began to exact a toll. Lieutenant "Doc" Thayer, a copilot said, "I could see the vivid red flashes of flame from the gun barrels and then, for the first time ever, I saw the 88mm flak shells themselves, distinct against the white snowing background, coming all the way up as if in slow motion, then rapidly accelerating the closer they got. Fortunately the flak barrage burst above us. Then another flak shell came up through the bomb-bay doors, knocked the fuse off one of our bombs, and kept on going, completely through the top of the fuselage.

"Our bomb ended up on the catwalk between the two bomb bays, making a noise like a volcano-type sparkler and spewing out what looked like small shiny pieces of aluminum. How we got the bomb-bay doors open and that smoldering bomb out of our aircraft in less than ten seconds, I will never really understand. Apparently, there was another B-17 almost directly below us that the falling bomb missed by a matter of inches." A further hit from antiaircraft punched a hole in the wing of Thayer's B-17 and damaged the engines.

Grif Mumford, in a stream of consciousness after the fact, noted, "4 March 1944, 28,000 feet over Berlin. The first of many. God, it's cold at that outside air-temperature gauge—minus sixty-five degrees, and it isn't designed to indicate anything lower. [On at least one B-17, the bomb doors froze.] Forget the temperature. Look at that flak. The bastards must have all 2,500 guns operational today. This has to be the longest bomb run yet. Krumph . . . boy that was close and listen to the spent shrapnel hitting the airplane. Look at the gaping hole in the left wing of number-three low element . . . an 88 must have gone right through without detonating.

"Wow, look at our Little Friends. Love those long-range drop tanks! That old 'escort you across the Channel' crap just wouldn't get the job done. Not to worry in the target area today about the ME 109s and FW 190s. [Others on the scene counted a dozen P-51s that apparently drove off the enemy fighters.] I wonder if they realize the significance of this mission, that it could be the turning point of the war. Stinking weather, fighter attacks and flak over Berlin so heavy it could be walked upon is enough to make one anxious to get out of this wieners-and-krautland and back to Jolly Old. . . . We made it. Wonder what old 'Iron Ass' LeMay will think of the show his boys put on today."

At the end of the month, LeMay issued a commendation to the 95th that paid tribute for completion of 100 heavy-bombardment missions and specifically stated, "On 4 March 1944, this intrepid group led the first daylight bombardment of Berlin by American heavy bombers, a feat for which it has already won world renown." While perhaps scoring a propaganda victory for the folks in the States, the raid barely laid a glove on the city. Only thirty aircraft from the 95th and 100th reached the objective as the remainder of the 502 planes assigned, thwarted by the weather or mechanical breakdowns, toted their ordnance back to base. Actually, British heavyweights had been hammering Berlin for months, but from this day on the Americans also called upon Berlin regularly and with far more weight. What's more, to the dismay of the *Luftwaffe*, they came accompanied by fighters. Hitler allegedly scoffed that they must have bene-fitted from favorable wind currents but Goering later admit-ted that when he saw American fighters in the skies over Berlin he realized the air war was lost.

"As of March 6," says Tommy Hayes, "we [his fighter group] were not experienced veterans. We were still learn-ing. Up to that date we had thirty victories with seven our high for a mission. The weather enroute to Berlin on that day was bad. The bombers flew a dogleg north of us while we flew a straight line to our rendezvous point west of Berlin. Colonel [Donald] Graham [elevated to group com-mander upon the downing of Spicer] had to abort over the North Sea and passed the baton to me. We were flying time and distance [a navigational technique] because of a solid overcast below. A cloud obscured our left as we passed the rendezvous time. Were we early or the bombers late? Or was I south of the rendezvous point? Geez, I screwed up. A little later, someone called out, 'Bombers, nine o'clock.' There they were, B-17s coming out of the poor visibility. *But* we were to escort B-24s, the 2d Bomb Division. It entered my mind to look for our 24s but then someone called out, 'Bogeys at two o'clock.' When they appeared, it was fight now.

"I called, 'Let's fight. Drop tanks.' The 109s, 110s, 410s, and FW 190s were estimated at 120–150. They were going head-on for the bombers. We turned left onto their rear. Some turned into us. Some continued for the bombers. Then a top cover of thirty or so 109s entered the fight. My high squadron, up-sun, engaged the top cover. The score was twenty kills and no losses. It was important for us because it was our first big fight against a large force. And we kicked ass. We were still learning. It was good timing, good for morale. But it wasn't the best work. We didn't escort our assigned bombers. We lucked out, getting a distinguished unit citation."

"I was on three of the first Berlin raids," remembered Bob Johnson of the 56th Fighter Group. "I was the lead airplane on March 6. I had only eight airplanes to protect 180 bombers; the 62d Squadron had dropped off to take up battle over the Zuider Zee. Gabreski had moved off the top and south to try to find some enemy. [A freelance hunt not permitted under the pre-Doolittle regime.] I was circling overhead. As I got to the front of the bomber line and made my orbit to turn left, I saw a gaggle, not any particular formation, just a group of airplanes, coming in from the north. At first I thought they were P-47s, a new group had just gotten over there and was flying all over the sky. As I came up, I said, 'Christ, they're Focke-Wulf 190s.'

"We were in line abreast, all eight of us, and we just opened fire and went right through some sixty or so 190s and 109s. As we turned to get on their tails, we saw another sixty or so above and another sixty or so to their left. Probably 175–180 German aircraft. Eight of us. We followed the first gaggle through our bombers, head on. We had no idea how many we hit. We were firing, airplanes were falling out of the sky all over, from bomber gunfire, from their gunfire to our bombers, from them ramming into our bombers. Burning bombers and fighters and parachutes filled the sky. There was no space; they weren't ramming purposely. You never saw such a sight in your life. Bombers falling, parachutes falling, fighters falling.

"I didn't have to think about the situation. It was there. I thought only of survival, and hitting the enemy. If there are crosses, shoot at them. So much damage was being done in the air there, at that moment; it took place in seconds. We lost sixty-nine bombers, and I was right in the middle of it. How many of the bombers were shooting at me and my buddies, I don't know. But they were shooting at airplanes. That's all they cared about. And I don't blame them.

"A heck of a lot of those [bomber crewmen] were out in parachutes and in burning airplanes that were falling with flames two thousand feet deep. The bombers scattered all over the sky trying to get home. We went after the 109s and 190s who were still attacking. We did not have radio contact with the bombers but we got a lot of waves from waist windows as we crossed the North Sea and a lot of free drinks in London from some of the bomber crews. I lost one guy of the eight. I think our boy ended up a POW. We got sixteen or seventeen Germans."

Two days later, Johnson immersed himself in what started out as a replica of his first trip to Berlin. But this time, as he headed into the enemy fighters with his eight planes in a line-abreast formation, he said, "All the time I was calling over various buttons [frequencies], slowly and distinctly calling our exact location on all the different channels, even the bomber channels, so they could call other fighters and get them there. When we hit them, our eight little guys scattered their fighters all over the sky. Other batches of our fighters came down to help and there was a bunch of confused Germans. Just that few minutes that it took me to get out and hit them, then brought in P-38s and P-47s all over the sky. That was one hell of a battle. We stopped the Germans at least two miles away from the bombers."

Although the loss ratio of heavyweights fell from about 10 percent during the previous attack on Berlin to less than 7 percent, that still meant close to 400 Americans were MIA, KIA, or WIA. The Eighth insisted it had destroyed or damaged as many as 400 enemy fighters in these two encounters. During the 4 March foray against Big B, assembly problems thwarted a number of groups including the 388th. Larry Goldstein's crew already had finished twenty-four raids and had hoped for a milk run. Berlin hardly seemed like a soft touch, but now that they were on the verge of ending their time in combat, the men were willing to take dangerous chances. "Our crew elected to fall out of formation, pick out a target in Germany, drop our bombs, climb back into the formation, and all would be okay.

"We did drop out, we did bomb a railroad yard, and when we attempted to climb back to the group, we were attacked by a FW 190 who hit us several times with 20mm shells. We were able to escape by diving into the clouds. My pilot asked me for an emergency radio fix from the British rescue net. Despite German jamming, I was able to get a position report, pass it on to the navigator. He plotted a course for England and when we broke out of the clouds, we were over the English Channel. When we landed we had no brakes and went off the end of the runway, ending up in a plowed field. When we left the plane, we saw the extensive damage and realized how lucky we had been to escape disaster, especially when I saw a hole in the radio room just above where my head had been. This was twenty-five and we all kissed the ground when we realized that our flying combat was over."

Even as the P-51 forged ahead as the weapon of choice, the 364th Fighter Group continued to operate P-38s. Among those in Lightning cockpits was Montana-born Max J. Woolley, who said, "I chose the P-38. I liked the two engines, probably for safety, the speed of the aircraft, and I red-lined [pushed to or past the manufacturer's limit] a number of times, and the firepower. With four fifties and a 20mm cannon up front, the Jerries knew that you could hurt them."

Placed in the 384th Fighter Squadron, one of the three operational units that composed the 364th Fighter Group, Woolley said, "I had about four or five hours of training in England before I went 'active.' A pilot learns combat by being in combat," he noted. "None of my flight instructors had been in combat so they had no firsthand experience to pass on. No one can tell you about the feeling, the tenseness, and your grinding guts. You have to have been there and felt it firsthand. Although I had quite a bit of target shooting in State-side training, nothing takes the place of shooting at an ME 109 or FW 190 while it's moving better than 400 miles per hour for a split second across your gunsight.

"My first encounter with the enemy was on my first mission [15 March]. From the Allied viewpoint, historians have classified this particular battle as one of the five greatest air battles of the European war over Germany. It wasn't great because I happened to be over Europe that day, but because of the great effort that Hermann Goering put forth with his air force to break the back of the Allied fighters. Our group was near Hannover, Germany, around 23,000 feet and heading east. A gaggle of German fighters were below us around 18,000 to 19,000 feet, set there as a decoy. Several thousand feet above us was a much larger group. Undoubtedly, this was the main strike force intent on reclaiming the skies for the Fatherland.

"The signal was given to drop belly tanks, close flight to our tactical position, increase rpms and manifold pressure as we headed down to intercept the Jerries below. This being my first mission, I was assigned the flight's most protected position—number two on my flight leader's wing. The enemy above us came down for the attack as we knew they would. Within seconds there was one massive hornet's nest stirred up in the German skies. I immediately knew that I was in a battle for my life. Planes were going everywhere, red flashes streaked the sky, puffs of black smoke started to curl upward as Orville Myers, my flight leader, called, 'Red Two. Tighten your turn. Jerry on your tail.' At that moment, streaks shot past my canopy. In my mirror I saw a 109 that appeared inches behind me tighten his turn to put me in the 'has-been column.' I had everything forward exceeding the red line, hit the flap handle again, and stood her on a point, desperately trying to save my skin. A 109 slid in front of me, intent on taking Myers. He crossed my gunsight. I hit the trigger button as four fifties and a 20mm cannon belched their hate for a fair-haired Superman. Part of his tail swished past my wing, only a superfical nick but enough for him to wing over and head below.

"P-47s in the area heard the chatter and came rushing to the fray. Friend and foe now were desperately trying to annihilate one another. 'Red Two. Tighten your turn.' Again I hit the flap handle, kicked left rudder, fought the control wheel to shake him with all needles vibrating beyond their safety zone. Soon it was over. What seemed like an hour lasted only minutes. They saw, they came, but they didn't conquer. The sky was now void of the Reich defenders. Only white-streaked contrails left by the angry hornets seeking their adversaries fluttered in the brilliant blue. Down below, a few broken machines jabbed back and forth amid the rising acrid smoke, soon to take their place in the graveyard of broken dreams. Both friend and foe paid dearly for this exercise in self-determination. The fight was a great lesson. Classroom instruction can never take the place of flak and live ammunition trying to separate a man from his inner soul."

Woolley attempted to shield himself against the impact of losses. "I tried not to become emotionally attached to any one person, as a pilot never knew when his name would be called by his maker. It was tough seeing your friends taking the worst of things, but so much harder if you were extremely close to them. Most of the pilots from our original group in California were outstanding fliers. Some had personalities I didn't care for but I never questioned any of their technical flying ability."

Joseph Bennett, in a P-47 for the 56th Fighter Group, through an accident, splashed down in the Channel. On 15 April he was briefed for a mission that might last six hours. "I had always flown with my seat belt tight and on one long mission, the bottle for inflating the rubber dinghy that was packed with our parachute cut off blood circulation, causing numbness from the knees down. To prevent this, I loosened my safety belt, giving me room to change my position and be more comfortable. We took off with a man flying his first mission on my right wing; the other two of the flight were on my left wing. We went into a cloud soon after takeoff and flew on instruments. At 21,000 feet, my supercharger cut in and I pulled the throttle back to maintain a constant airspeed. The wingman's wing made light contact with my canopy and it popped off.

"I jammed the stick forward unconsciously and in seconds I was vertical. The loose seat belt allowed me to slip up until my head was sticking out of the plane. My little and second fingers were still on the stick at the last knuckle but when they slipped off, I was sucked out through the harness or else the belt broke. When I left the plane I was falling so fast I could not breathe so I pulled on the rip cord and it slipped out of my hand. I grabbed it again and pulled so hard that when my arm extended past my body, the wind jerked it straight upward. The chute opened with quite a jerk and I was sitting on air.

"It suddenly came to my attention that I could not see. I put my hand to my face and couldn't see it. It was quite unlike anything I had ever known. Something warned me to prepare for landing. I uncoupled one leg strap and twisted the connector on the other when I hit the water. When my head came out of the water, my eyesight had returned and the parachute was folding up on the water beside me. I unbuckled the chute waist connector and reached for the dinghy but it wasn't in the pack. Part of the plane was floating about fifty yards away so I started swimming toward it. My left shoulder was hurting, the water was cold, and the swimming pretty slow.

"After about thirty feet I found the dinghy, less than a foot under the surface. I got it in position and pulled the pin for inflation, then tried to roll it under my body but it slipped out of my cold hands as it was inflating, which would make it more difficult to mount. Grabbing the dinghy I gave another roll with all the strength I had and got a part of it under my back but didn't make it to the center. Finally, I could feel it inflating where my hand was gripping and I began to rise out of the water. I slid to the center and began to put the hood on and fasten the windbreaker. I was so cold I began to shake and my teeth were clattering so hard I though they might break. I was having trouble breathing and started to blow my nose only to discover that more than half of it was almost severed. My upper body began to warm up, but my butt and feet ached and were cold.

"Opening the windbreaker, I discovered about four inches of water in the bottom of the dinghy. I took off one of my GI shoes and bailed until it was almost dry, then fastened the windbreaker. I had been there about an hour when I heard a plane go by. The clouds had lifted to another 300 feet. On the third or fourth circle he spotted me and stayed around for about an hour. It was McKennon, from another squadron in our group. That perked me up. However, I knew chances of being picked up by air-sea rescue were slim. A slight breeze had started and if I could live through the night, I'd possibly drift to Belgium.

"I fell asleep to be awakened by a sea gull standing on my head with my nose in his beak, shaking his head from side to side quite violently. I don't know how long before I fell asleep again, but the noise from a rescue-boat engine woke me. It was about seventy-five yards away, headed toward me. A native of Norway was in command of the vessel in the service of British Air Sea Rescue. I never did know how they got me aboard but they wrapped me in blankets, gave me two cups of hot buttered rum and I drifted off into a sound sleep. I awakened hours later as I was carried up a gangplank on a litter. I learned later that the boy on my right wing had called in a distress May Day." Bennett, unlike the unfortunate Henry Spicer, would fly again.

Some three weeks after Spicer went down, another squadron commander in the 357th was KIA and the musical chairs of replacement elevated Tommy Hayes, who says he now perceived the effects of the incessant pummeling of the enemy. "The all-out air war in February and March paid dividends by April. Hitting their oil was serious enough so that pilot training was reduced drastically. At the same time they were losing their most experienced people. During the period of March 2 to May 29 I shot down several who were still green. I also had engagement with the 109 and 190 where it was a toss-up. Some flew the 109 like it was a P-51. Then there was an FW 190 that outran my flight of four, all of us with the throttle against the wall gave up after five minutes. This pilot outflew me from 22,000 feet to the deck as he slipped, and skidded, power off, power on. Sometimes our pilots on the tail of a 109 or 190 saw them release the canopy and bail out, some without ever firing a burst. A victory is a victory. Some 190 pilots couldn't really handle their fighter. The 190 had a high wing loading, but when on the deck, if they pulled it too tight, they stalled and went in. Again, a victory without firing the guns."

In Italy, Shingle, rather than draining away German strength from the Winter Line, had instead become almost a liability for the Allied forces. Maintenance of a small tract required a regular infusion of replacements, reinforcements, and scarce equipment. Additional GIs and armor that might have been deployed for the Liri Valley effort went to Anzio. To abandon that beachhead would have been a propaganda as well as a strategic defeat.

The victors at Cisterna had paraded the captured Rangers through the streets of Rome by way of proclaiming to the local people that the Reich ruled. (German medics treated seriously wounded Americans before they were shipped to POW camps in Germany.) The 1 February POW show, according to some participants, was not quite what the producers expected. Captain Chuck Shunstrom, who had been leader of an antitank platoon for the Rangers, said, "The Italians were supposed to boo us and cheer the master race as we marched five abreast through the streets. Instead, the Italian women cried and the men flashed us surreptitious Vee-for-Victory signs. They would stroke their hair or brush off a sleeve with fingers shaped to a Vee. When a dumb German guard wanted to know what the Vee sign meant, none of us knew a thing about it. We marched along singing 'God Bless America.' "

Some of the local citizens, provided with garbage or rotten vegetables, however, threw them at the Americans and one prisoner recalled being spat upon. But for the most part, the Rangers under heavy guard felt the Italian people radiated good will toward them. The march through Rome began a long journey on foot, by truck, and by rail to the POW camps. (A number managed to break away while in Italy and hide long enough to be freed by the Allied advance.)

Allen Merrill missed the humiliation in Rome. Dumped by German soldiers on the floor of a farmhouse with other wounded, Merrill bandaged his leg wound and stopped the bleeding. "The first night I was alert enough to realize that only one fat Kraut soldier sat, back against the door, guarding us as if the men couldn't go anyplace anyhow. They fed us once with some kind of crackers and a broth that was mostly water. I had two D-ration bars [a high-calorie chocolate] for emergency. The next morning I raised to the window and saw the lay of the land, some trees, shrubs, and a woods about a hundred yards back of the house. Overnight, two men died in that room. We pounded on the door and told the German about it. He just said, '*Ja wohl*' [Yes, sir] and went back to his chair against the front door.

"I made up my mind I was going to try to escape after dark. I told Frank [a seriously wounded soldier] and some of the others. A sergeant said I'd better not try it. They could shoot you on sight. I said it didn't matter. I was still going to try. These Germans had no record of how many of us were there, so what the hell I had to give it a shot. I went through one of the dead guys' pockets and found another D bar. He wouldn't be needing nourishment anymore. Frank asked if I would help him and we could escape together. He was hit in both legs and there was no way I could manage the two of us. He felt bad and so did I. But what the hell, it was every man for himself in a situation like this."

Merrill did not know which direction to take but believed that with his compass and by moving only at nightfall he could avoid a sojourn in an enemy hospital and a prolonged stay in a POW camp. In his pockets he packed his D bars, several cheese tins from K rations, and a tiny can opener. He practiced crawling around the farmhouse room and found the pain tolerable. He downed the last of the sulfa drugs to ward off infection, said goodbyes, and shook a few hands.

After dark, Merrill felt his way through back rooms in search of a rear entrance. "I was aware of a steady draft from one wall. Sure enough, there was an opening to the outside of what appeared to be a kitchen. It was a potato bin where canvas covered the opening from the weather. If I could squeeze through I could crawl to the woods and be on my way. After three tries and repiling the potatoes I made it through by removing my jacket and pushing it ahead of me. Once I was free of the house I crawled in the direction of the woods. It was so dark I couldn't see my hand in front of my face. [I heard] heavy vehicles moving, tanks, probably, or large trucks. Occasionally there were voices, the low guttural sounds of German spoken nearby."

Merrill paused to rest. "Two sharp sounds made me hold my breath. They were unmistakable, from a bolt-action rifle reloading. I held my breath for as long as I could, then let it out in short, irregular exhales. Then gulped air and held that as long as possible. Not ten feet to the right of me a figure sat on a small shed roof. By the outline of his helmet I could see he was a Kraut. I felt the urgent need to urinate. I held that, too. I could smell the faint odor of cigarette smoke. The Kraut was stealing a puff or two while on guard duty. Then I heard him crush the butt out with the toe of his boot and his outline disappeared. I could hear his footsteps fade away."

Merrill resumed his slow passage toward the forest. At 2:00 A.M., when he checked the luminous dial of his watch, he saw the roof of the farmhouse some distance off. Doggedly he crawled on, his pace reduced as the underbrush became thicker. By four o'clock, shortly before the first streaks of dawn began to illuminate the area, he was deep enough into the trees to seek a hiding place. He fell asleep in some thick brush cover. When he awoke in midmorning he discovered himself covered with ants. "I must have crawled over an anthill. As slowly as possible I brushed them off my exposed skin. I felt crawly all over. But any sudden moves might make me a sitting duck. I was bleeding in several places. I gazed slowly around; the bushes had thorns the size of straight pins. There were no human sounds anywhere in the vicinity. My numb left leg ached but it wasn't unbearable. I shivered; my clothes were damp and my hands and fingers were coated with caked mud, and sore. I retrieved a D bar from my jacket and munched on it as I slowly made a 360-degree turn. Somewhere behind me vehicles moved in the distance but I couldn't tell if they were theirs or ours. Nothing else was moving anywhere I could see."

In a grove of olive trees amid oozing mud Merrill settled down for another day of concealment. "I slept soundly until my bowels again exploded in another siege of the running shits. My stomach churned in discomfort and I shivered under a gray, cold, sunless day. I would have loved to just stand up straight and stretch my limbs but I dared not. In the late afternoon I gnawed on my D bar and had two sips of tepid, stale water. My bowels rustled and ached and only liquid came out in dribbles.

"After about an hour of crawling I thought I would try hobbling. This meant double work on the right, unwounded leg. That was both good and bad. Good because I hopped faster than I crawled, but bad because the ground was uneven. After two falls the left one started to bleed again. I could feel the warm, oozing blood. I had to stop and reapply my belt tourniquet until the bleeding stopped. I lost precious time in my advance up the gully beside the road. Before dawn I crawled to a small stream crossing the road. There was a culvert and I decided to stay there. For the first time in three days I slept the daylight hours away in a flat position."

As Merrill continued his travels, a hard rain pelted down, soaking him and reducing his passage through cold, slippery mud. The pain in his left leg reached a point where he sought refuge in a farmhouse that was unoccupied. Although aware his building might become a target, Merrill decided he would have to take his chances and rest there. When he awoke, there was light outside. To protect his wounded leg against the hard floor of the house, he tried to wrap a small blanket about it. "I saw into the wound for the first time in three days. There was a white moving mass in that wound. It was maggots. I gagged once and threw up. I would have screamed and don't know why I didn't. In training they don't tell you about things like this. I used a long-handled wood spoon to scrape them out of that wound. I retched each time I pushed them off my leg. The knee had started to bleed again. I found a towel and pulled it tight around the area. When I pulled the towel away, many maggots fell away also. I had nothing inside to vomit but bile. There was some blood in it. My lungs and stomach ached with a fury I could not control. I lay on the floor of that farmhouse kitchen and cried until I must have fallen asleep."

When he awoke again, Merrill rediscovered his resolve and started out again. As on earlier nights he passed or bumped into fallen soldiers from the battle for Cisterna. "Several times I felt for the patch on their shoulder. It was there, with the Fifth Army patch just below it. The Rangers had left a trail of dead wherever they went. This time, however, they were the trail. The cold, near-freezing temperatures of late January had almost preserved these bodies. But now rain and warmer weather had started the rotting process and the smell was something you never forget. The consoling factor was that it had to be the road we came on."

Toward dawn he hid himself in a shed beside another farmhouse. That night, in spite of almost unbearable pain and in a steady rain, he started to pull himself along. "Several times I thought about crawling out of the gully onto the road and giving up. Something kept me going. Whatever it was, it is not part of Army training. It comes from a higher source, perhaps from the Creator Himself. As I crawled and thought about these things I was not aware it was growing light. I was oblivious. When I opened my eyes it was bright daylight. Two pairs of eyes were looking down at me, as though I was an illusion. Then a voice, distinctly American, yelled to others in the vicinity. 'Hey, guys, lookit what crept into our area.' Then another one said, 'Jesus H. Christ, it's a Ranger and he's hurt bad.' More GIs came running. One carried a litter and before I knew it an ambulance was pulling up. The last thing I recall before dreamland was the medic saying, 'Son, your Colonel Darby is over at our battalion headquarters right now and he'll sure be glad to see you.'

"Then I slept. An hour or so later I was aware some guy was shaking my hand and hugging my shoulder. Either I was dreaming or it was Col. Bill Darby. I was amazed to learn it was him. Hatless, jacketless, with those sawed-off leggings." Shipped to Naples for hospital care, Merrill received a Silver Star recommended by Darby.

Despite the negative results of the Ranger-led assault, Gen. John Lucas advised his diary a day or so later, "I was sent on a desperate mission, one where the odds were greatly against success and I went without saying anything because I was given an order and my opinion was not asked. The condition in which I find myself is much better than I ever anticipated or had any right to expect."

That roseate view could hardly be justified by the situation as February began. At Anzio, as elsewhere, the rain-soaked dirt mired American armor. Ernest Harmon recalled, "When tank commanders attempted to skirt gullies, they found themselves bogged down in the mud. January rains made the place a gooey mess. Four tanks became stuck in the mud and I ordered an armored wrecker to pull 'em out. The wrecker was ambushed by the Germans. I sent four more tanks to rescue the wrecker; then I sent more tanks after them. I finally learned the Anzio lesson the hard way, not to spend good money after bad. I lost twenty-four tanks while I was trying to succor and rescue four." Harmon said he visited one of the British units, the Sherwood Foresters, who had captured a bluff overlooking the enemy positions. "They'd gone up there with 116 men and there were 16 left, the highest-ranking man was a corporal. I had never seen so many dead men in one place."

The Allied forces settled in for a prolonged defensive siege. Men awaiting evacuation for treatment of their wounds crammed the tents packed around the beach while aerial predators and long-range guns worked the area over. It became known as "Hell's Half Acre." Said Harmon, "Some men hid their minor wounds so they would not have to be sent to that plague spot. At Anzio there were no goldbricks, no wooden Indians. Truck drivers, stevedores, ammunition passers, ordnance men, quartermasters, medics, engineers were shoved forward into the front line to fight as infantrymen. Ski troops fought in swamps; cooks dropped their skillets and picked up their guns. Officers were in the same boat. I never saw anything like it in the two world wars of my experience. There was an Anzio community of selflessness, a willingness of troops to help one another that I never saw again. We were there to stand or die."

The remnants of the Rangers had been integrated into a new organization, the Special Services, under Gen. Robert Frederick, leading to reassignment of Ranger head Darby as commander of the 179th Regiment of the 45th Division. The losses at Anzio also gave Michael Davison, the West Pointer on the division staff, an opportunity to enhance his career under the former Ranger boss. Darby named him exec for the 1st Battalion, telling him to report the following morning. "That night," said Davison, "the CP of the 1st Battalion got the hell shelled out of it and the commanding officer was seriously wounded and evacuated. When I arrived at the regimental CP the next morning, Darby was going out and he stopped his Jeep long enough to say, 'Johnson got wounded last night and you are now the battalion commander.'

"At Anzio we slept during the daytime and did all our fighting at night because the Germans were looking right down our throats. You couldn't move in the daytime because of their observation. We were all dug in; everything was underground. We would sleep until about four in the afternoon and then as soon as it got dark we would send hot cereal, oatmeal, or Cream of Wheat and coffee and bread up to the front-line companies. You couldn't [bring that up] during the daytime. After that we would send out our patrols for the night. Usually they would come in, three or four in the morning. You would feed them a hot meal and everybody would go to sleep."

Ed Sims, acting CO of Company H, 504th Parachute Infantry Regiment, hung in despite reversals of fortune. His battalion moved to the British sector along with the U.S. 1st Armored Division where mud, terrain, and heavy enemy fire bogged down the attack. Subsequently, he was much discomfited to find that the Britons supposed to anchor his flanks had pulled back several hundred yards, leaving the Americans overexposed. While he was reorganizing his lines, a shrapnel fragment struck his lower right leg.

In their new positions on 5 February, the company rocked from German fire. "Numerous rounds landed in my command-post area causing everyone to seek shelter. I jumped into a large open slit trench next to a building, and two men came in behind me just as an explosion took place directly above the hole. The fragments came into the hole, killing the two men, and I was hit in the right shoulder. The trench caved in on us and after [they dug us out] I was taken to the hospital near Anzio. That evening the hospital was shelled by German artillery, so I located my clothes and equipment, got dressed, and hitched a ride in an ambulance back to the front line and my company. Medical installations were bombed and shelled frequently. On one occasion, a German fighter bomber dropped a load of antipersonnel bombs on the 95th Evacuation Hospital, killing twenty-eight patients and hospital workers, including three nurses."

According to Lucas, his II Corps was losing a fearful 768 men per day while replacements averaged only 462. The GIs of the 3d and 45th Divisions, who had previously engaged only in offensive operations, assumed the unfamiliar stance of defensive warfare. By 12 February, three weeks after the start of Shingle, Harmon said there were 120,000 crack German soldiers squeezing the ten-mile-deep pocket around Anzio. On 16 February, said Harmon, the Germans at dawn opened up a massive attack against the beachhead. "These were the finest combat units in the Reich Army. Captured prisoners told us they went around and even the sick were routed out of their beds and thrown into the line, those who could fight. We had about 50,000 Americans and more than 400 pieces of artillery and it was artillery fire that saved the beachhead. I had one of the toughest decisions a commander can make. My chief of artillery reported that a battalion of the 45th Division for reasons unknown was in front of what we called the 'no-fire line.' If we laid down a barrage we'd kill our own troops. There are times when the responsibilities of a military commander involve the true meaning of the word 'awful' and this was one of them. The artillery attack might mean the death of many fine, brave American soldiers. To abandon it might mean abandoning an effort to save the beachhead. To me the choice was between the losses of some hundreds of men against the possible loss of many thousands. I ordered them to fire." Subsequently, he learned the soldiers were never where communications had placed them.

According to Harmon, the hard fighting around Anzio ended by 8 March. "Both sides lay down, you might say, panting and with their tongues out." For the next two months the opposing forces were content with raids, skirmishes, artillery, and air attacks.

Hamilton Howze analyzed Shingle as largely mistakes in both strategy and logistics. He noted the Germans were able to concentrate large forces against Anzio more rapidly than was thought possible and that the Allied troops halted before the defensive strength was sufficient to block them. "We stopped simply because the troops available couldn't man any [greater] perimeter and maintain proper tactical strength. The Lord granted the operation total initial success. Yet the planning was such that there were not enough forces to exploit the beachhead and push sufficiently far inland to cut the lines of communications to the south. I won't say the Anzio beach forces did not contribute a lot to the breaking of what was called the Gustav Line in the Cassino peninsula. Primarily the Anzio beachhead occupied a lot of German forces."

The unhappy results of Shingle, as is usual in military campaigns, mandated a change of command. Mark Clark had initially urged his VI Corps commander, Lucas, to be aggressive. "He must take chances," Clark informed his diary three days after the arrival at Anzio. He believed Lucas possessed sufficient forces to "advance on the the Alban Hills." The fuzzy instruction at the time of the invasion did not specify whether the VI Corps should seize the heights or merely reach them. The Fifth Army commander later remarked that he had never believed Anzio was a potential springboard to Rome. "They said you could have driven in your jeep to Rome. You might have but it would be the end of the war for you. There was no possibility of capturing the Alban Hills. I didn't have many reinforcements, the fighting was so hard down on the southern front. The assault at Anzio occupied many German soldiers. Nobody met us with any force at the landing and you could advance as far as you wanted to until you met opposition. The resistance amounted to eight divisions that were ordered by Hitler."

William Rosson, as a battalion commander of the 3d Division, felt that a more aggressive effort during the first few days could have secured an additional five to ten miles of defensible turf. "We failed to produce the impact on the German situation that I think the operation was intended to produce and could have done."

Below the besieged VI Corps, the gunnery between the Allied and German forces around Monte Cassino intensified. Shells struck the monastery with increasing frequency and except for a handful of monks and people too badly hurt to be moved, all residents had left. American soldiers tentatively advanced up the ridge, capturing some Germans, coming under fire from others closer to the monastery. But the GIs, too weak to extend their real estate all the way up to Monte Cassino, retreated. The monastery now occupied a no-man's-land and became exposed to the kind of treatment normally accorded such territory from both sides. As casualties accumulated, conviction that the Germans were using the monastery as an observation post, a sight for homing in artillery on them, grew stronger. To relieve the exhausted and depleted American forces, the Allies had inserted New Zealand and Indian divisions. Again a frontal assault produced only casualties. The commander of the Indian outfit, with the concurrence of the New Zealander in charge of both units, Gen. Bernard Freyberg, requested intense bombing of the monastery.

Under the chain of command for the polyglot forces in Italy, although Alexander was Clark's superior, the final decision lay with Clark, who was mindful of Eisenhower's strictures on "military necessities." Clark remarked that his allies called for bombing and shelling of Monte Cassino because "they just looked at it so long." Clark claimed he protested that all his intelligence sources agreed there were no Germans in the abbey. Field Marshal Kesselring wrote that all of his people were strictly forbidden to enter the monastery. After the war Clark spoke to the abbot, who reiterated there were never any soldiers in the monastery except for an army doctor who treated the civilian wounded seeking refuge there. Furthermore, the American general claimed he perceived that the ruins would make even better defensive positions for the enemy. Nevertheless, after Alexander approved Freyburg's request, Clark acquiesced. The bombardment of Monte Cassino began on 15 February with an air raid that dumped 442 tons of explosives and incendiaries.

In a colossal mistake in timing, the aerial effort was not coordinated with the ground forces. Instead of immediately charging up the last few hundred yards of mountain slope to occupy the monastery, the assorted New Zealanders, Ghurkas from India, and Britons, already discomfited by some bombs that fell within their precincts, crouched in their positions to await their H hour several days later. The massive air raid killed and injured many civilians taking refuge around the monastery, destroyed roofs, started fires that blazed up, and transformed walls into jumbles of rock, perfect nests for would-be defenders. After repulsing attempts by the New Zealand Corps to gain a firm purchase on its way to occupying the high ground, the enemy seized the advantage of the delay to fully invest themselves within the shattered complex. The siege of Monte Cassino would last nearly three months.

# 8

# Galahad's Joust, New Ventures, Minor Gains, and Overlord

TO PRESERVE THE CORRIDOR THROUGH BURMA TO CHINA, THE Chindits and Merrill's Marauders plotted maneuvers that would enable a large Chinese army to crush the main body of Japanese troops. The American objective was an airdrome at Myitkyina. The men of Galahad had now endured two arduous campaigns in the debilitating jungle struggles. Casualties from enemy action, disease, and an inadequate number of replacements had reduced the brigade to less than half, with Merrill himself on a curtailed regimen after a heart attack.

As disorganized as the Japanese appeared, they still outnumbered the forces available for Galahad as well as the Chindits. Stilwell, always anxious to disparage the British, crowed in his diary after the Americans grabbed the Myitkyina airfield, "Will this burn up the Limeys." The British hierarchy, up through Churchill, questioned how the small

American brigade had pulled off such a prodigious feat. Unfortunately, Stilwell and his staff gravely underestimated the enemy troops available to defend the town of Myitkyina. There was a series of bloody encounters in the vicinity. Stilwell demanded that the Chindits in their sector, in terrible shape from disease, fatigue, and wounds, fight on, and he constantly harangued Chiang Kai-shek to commit more of his soldiers. Under these circumstances he could ill afford to spare the remnants of Galahad. To maintain Galahad, Stilwell transferred engineers, untutored in jungle warfare, to fill the ranks, and ordered Marauders from their hospital sickbeds to the front. Dysentery afflicted some men so severely they cut away the seats of their pants to enable them to function in combat. Those engaged in the actual fighting lived on short rations and husbanded their ammunition and other vital needs. The capture and full occupation of Myitkyina and its environs dragged on for another three months.

As in Italy and the CBI, there were no easy victories in much of the Pacific. The jungles of tropical islands soaked up troops like a blotter. MacArthur hatched a scheme to bypass a number of enemy bases with a 580-mile leap to Hollandia, on the north coast of Dutch New Guinea. The giant step avoided confrontation with a string of Japanese installations, but it also stretched the air cover to the edge. Nimitz and his people fretted about exposure of their carriers but the Air Corps eliminated the danger of torpedo bombers by intensive air raids upon enemy bases on Dutch New Guinea. The Army's 41st Division, blooded in the Buna campaign, and the 24th Division, a newcomer to battle, boarded ships destined for Hollandia, Dutch New Guinea. Also on the menu was Aitape, a locale in Papua New Guinea, about 125 miles east of Hollandia.

Han Rants, a wireman for the 34th Regiment of the 24th, said, "My greatest concern was that I would freeze or lose control when faced with extreme fear. Publicly, no one would discuss having fear. Some who boasted the most courage and told what they would do, turned into jelly as we started to climb over the side of the ship into landing barges. Others lost control of bowels and bladders as we hit the beach. Without really knowing Christ in a true sense, I considered myself a Christian and I prayed in my way that I would not show fear or be a coward when facing death. Some of the sailors told how in earlier campaigns the officers had to hold a gun on some of the marines to get them to go over the side into the landing barges. I believe this helped our green outfit because we had to tell them to watch our smoke and generally smothered any sign of fear that might otherwise have been shown."

The 34th's Hollandia venture began, however, without any sign of resistance. The 24th Division advanced about five miles before nightfall and then, while the riflemen dug foxholes, wiremen like Rants set up field telephone lines between battalions. "The first night of combat for a green outfit is a nightmare for everyone within rifle range," said Rants. "Knowing that the enemy preferred to sneak in at night, we were all overly alert to any movement or noise. Although our training taught us to hold fire unless absolutely certain, thus not giving away our position, we threw hand grenades and fired rifles all night long. Dogs, monkeys, water buffalo, birds, snakes, land crabs, and everything imaginable except the enemy were fired upon that night."

Bruce Pierce, a South Carolinian and graduate of his home state's National Guard, had graduated from the Fort Benning OCS academy and become a platoon leader with the 19th Infantry, 24th Division. "There was no problem with the sense of responsibility for men under me and decisions that would mean life or death to them. Being an enlisted man for more than two years and an officer for two and a half helped me know how the enlisted men thought and established a rapport with them. They knew I was subject to the same results of my decisions that they were and knew I would not act foolishly.

"I was not in the invasion at Tanahmerah Bay [Hollandia] as I was in the hospital on Goodenough Island. I rejoined the regiment a week or so later. There was no heavy fighting as there was not much opposition. Most of our time was spent on patrols around Lake Sentani and mountain trails leading toward Finchhaven. The Japs' 18th Army had been cut off and a lot of them tried to come up the trail thinking they still held Hollandia. Most of the ones we found were dead of starvation or killed by the natives because the Japs were raping their women."

Among those introduced to combat in Dutch New Guinea was a former refugee from Germany, Eric Diller. Denied an opportunity to enlist because his parents' attempts to obtain U.S. citizenship were delayed by investigation of German, Italian, and Japanese aliens, Diller nevertheless was drafted in June 1943. "When processed at the Camp Upton, New York, induction center, an 'Enemy Alien' stamp in bold letters was printed on the cover of my papers, causing some unfriendly glances." Assigned as an ammunition bearer for a .30-caliber machine-gun section in the heavy-weapons unit, Company H of the 34th Infantry, Diller said, "Most GIs with the outfit had spent nineteen months protecting Waikiki Beach against an invasion which never came. Then they trained for seven months in Australia, preparing for jungle combat, all without seeing a single day of combat. They must have been waiting for me." The waiting ended as the battalion embarked for the Hollandia campaign.

Pennsylvania draftee Cpl. Joe Hofrichter went ashore with the 1st Battalion of the 339th Engineers near Hollandia. He recalled the scene during the invasion of the New Guinea beach overlooked by a site dubbed Pancake Hill. "An hour of shelling from our ships was followed by aerial bombardment. Going over the rail of the troop transport, we descended into LCVs (Landing Craft, Vehicles). About halfway down the rope ladder, a man froze. He had things tied up, at a standstill. The poor man was so frightened, he couldn't even speak. Two men were sent down to pry his locked fingers from the rope in spite of his pleas to stop. When his fingers were freed, he fell backward. He landed on the eighty-pound jungle pack we carried. While this cushioned his fall, his helmeted head hit the steel deck with such force, the back of his helmet caved in. He lay unconscious. Resistance was relatively light. But [if there had been] a few artillery pieces, some mortars, and well-placed Japanese machine guns . . . we would still be trying to land and secure Pancake Hill."

Kansan Phil Hostetter, immediately after medical school in 1942, qualified for a commission as a first lieutenant in the Army Medical Corps. He spent a year interning in Wichita before he reported to the Medical Field Service School at Carlisle Barracks, Pennsylvania. "Medical schools," says Hostetter, "had taught us very little about the actual practice of medicine in civilian surroundings and nothing in the military. Our teachers at Carlisle, talented and hard working as they were, had no knowledge of combat conditions." Assigned to the 407th Medical Collecting Company upon completion of the Carlisle course, Hostetter's duties mainly involved physical exams for men scheduled to go overseas.

Just before the 407th itself embarked for the Pacific, the medics went through the standard infiltration course, climbing obstacles, crawling under barbed wire, and live machine-gun fire at night. They also practiced climbing cargo nets.

In February 1944, the outfit docked at Milne Bay, New Guinea. They lived fairly comfortably in a tent city; gawked at the indigenous Micronesians; dined on Spam, dehydrated potatoes, and eggs; listened to the Armed Forces Radio; and awaited the opportunity to treat casualties. While staging for the Hollandia invasion, personnel like Hostetter learned to use the .30-caliber carbine, an indication of the status of medics in the eyes of the enemy.

Behind the infantrymen of the 24th Division and the engineers attached to it, amphibious vehicles, "Ducks," brought Hostetter to the beach. "We stood around wondering what to do next. The first casualty we saw was a man crushed to death by a boulder. He was bathing at the water's edge when the boulder rolled down the cliff from high above where a soldier was building a road with a bulldozer. We sent a litter squad to get the body. 'Lay him on the grass,' I said. 'The Quartermaster Department will take care of the body.' We were not responsible for the dead, only the disabled. Inland, a little farther, an enemy soldier lay on the ground. He was mortally wounded, unconscious and gasping for breath. I knew he would soon die. We felt no sense of exhilaration over the small victory. It was not small to him."

Hostetter continued to see few U.S. casualties. Detached to an evacuation hospital, he began treating patients in two large tents. "All had a psychiatric condition. It was up to me to determine what their condition was, treat them if feasible and evacuate them to other hospitals if necessary. Those who had broken down under exceptional stress and exhaustion we called 'battle fatigue' cases. In a state of chronic anxiety, exhausted, they could not relax. They were so jumpy you could practically see daylight between them and their cots when a truck backfired. They had little appetite and when they did eat they were apt to have stomach cramps and perhaps vomit. Their sleep was fitful, marred by vivid nightmares of battle experiences and friends being mutilated. Some told of 'fugues' when they would become conscious after running for miles and not knowing where they were.

"Battle fatigue cases constantly asked when they could return to duty. They would hear reports of their units on the radio and feel required to return as quickly as possible. They felt obligated to help their buddies and guilty because they had failed when needed most. To help my patients rest I prescribed huge doses of the sedatives, Nembutal and phenobarbital. The other doctors thought my doses excessive but I had seen these amounts used in mental hospitals for the severely disturbed and knew they were suitable. Before long, the other doctors agreed with me.

"We would assess their fitness for combat by estimating the severity of the stress that put them in the hospital. If it had been great, as often it was, they recovered in about two weeks and returned to their outfits. The Army had a wise policy of keeping the men as close as possible to the combat zone. They still had high motivation to return to duty. The farther away they got, the less they cared about recovery and the poorer they did."

The Japanese expected invasions closer to the major U.S. bases and most of the garrisons at Aitape and Hollandia consisted of service troops rather than combat soldiers. When the fleets showed up offshore and commenced their prelanding bombardments the third week of April, the surprised defenders mostly fled the scene. Their departure left the Hollandia area secure but the Japanese in the jungles surrounding Aitape organized for an attack upon the Americans.

Early in 1944, halfway around the world in Italy, a standoff characterized both the Allies' Anzio beachhead and the situation at the German Winter Line throughout the first months of spring. With the enemy burrowed in the rubble there was nothing to restrain air attacks upon Monte Cassino. On 2 March, Dick Gangel, a replacement pilot in a P-38, *Chattanooga Choo Choo*, for the 82d Fighter Group stationed at Foggia, flew his first combat mission patrolling the sky over Anzio. Gangel flew another one covering B-24 bombers hitting the marshaling yards at Florence and then he and his group shepherded B-17s in a heavy raid upon Cassino. His diary noted this was supposed to be the "largest on record for any small target. It spearheaded a ground attack by American infantry and tanks."

As a fighter pilot, Gangel at Foggia shared a four-man tent with wooden floors and jerry-built gasoline heaters. "Everytime a plane crashed at the field, the first thing would be to make sure the pilot or crew were okay and then try to get the copper tubing from the wreck either to improve the heater or to make whiskey." Unlike those airmen in either North Africa or the Pacific, flyers like Gangel rarely saw what was happening on earth. Operating at great altitudes and frequently with thick clouds below, there was little opportunity to gauge the effect of the air war. "You didn't want to spend your time looking down anyway," said Gangel, "because you were always watching for German fighters. They could hear us coming and get to their top altitude and pop down on us." During his first five missions, however,

Gangel never saw an enemy plane and in several succeeding ones the Germans declined to engage.

Eli Setencich, a Sacramento native and son of Yugoslavian immigrants, chose to fly rather than "being an infantryman slogging around." Graduated as a fighter pilot, he reached Italy as a replacement where he put in a few weeks in a night-fighter outfit. "I couldn't wait to get out of that because I didn't want to fly at nighttime. I had a hard enough time *driving* at night. I got into A-36s [a P-51 without a supercharger, designed as a dive bomber]. The dive brakes enabled you to go straight down. We were strafing and diving, going after trains, trucks, and resupply—anything we saw on the ground. Also repple-depples [replacement depots], railroad terminals, ships in harbors, like Genoa. Mostly it was railroads, tanks. We usually had a target when we took off but they would also say targets of opportunity. We'd go out in a flight of four and see what we could find. We'd look for trains, marshaling yards near the bigger cities. If we were supporting troops, we did a lot of close-order support; they'd say there were tanks in the woods holding our troops from going farther north. We'd circle around, see if we could find the tanks, go down and drop bombs on them if we could find them. Or if it was a bridge, it would be farther inland, that might be used for supplying their troops. Four of us would dive down and try to hit the bridge, knock it out. Generally, we had a pair of 500-pound bombs. It was all low, dirty work. We had .50-caliber machine guns with tracers every five rounds that helped our aim. You could see trains blowing up with all the steam coming out. Sometimes you hit an ammo train and that would really blow up." Unlike the Navy and Marines in the Pacific, the Air Corps in Europe did not use trained ground observers to direct and control their tactical operations.

Setencich recalled, "I crash-landed twice. My airplane was shot up near Pisa by ground fire. I didn't 'jink.' I remember my first flight. Jackson Saunders was leading it. We flew over Cassino and I could see these black puffs in the air, and no one told me what the hell they were. It was flak, bouncing around the sky. All I could hear was Jackson yelling at me over the earphones. 'Jink, for chrissakes, jink!' I didn't know what the hell he meant but I could see him jumping all over the sky. You were supposed to get your airplane going every which way so they couldn't track you with those 88s." From his testimony, it would appear that the precombat instruction he received did not include some vital advisories.

The efforts at air-to-ground support were not enough to protect the embattled forces at Anzio. Bill Kunz, as a member of the communications section with the 39th Artillery Battalion, had come off the line and was in reserve, about midway from the Anzio harbor and the front. "Gene Baron and I had dug in a fairly comfortable foxhole, almost a dugout, complete with sandbagged top, but what happened next illustrates what can happen if you relax and get a bit careless. I took one of our radios outside our 'home' to check transmission, etc. There were about half a dozen infantry in the area—enough to bring us to the Krauts' attention. They say you never hear the one that gets you! It was true in my case. While standing, I felt a hard blow in front of my right hip, like being hit with a baseball bat! Knocked flat on the ground, I heard the shell hit a dozen feet away. Instinctively I listened for the sound of the gun and heard it—at a distance, not close. The round had landed on our far side, between us and some infantry, killing two and injuring three more. I was the only one hit on our side of the shrapnel spread—usually in a V-shaped cone from the ground up.

Since we were in reserve, there were medics nearby and in a few minutes one got to me. He bandaged the torn hip, gave me a shot of morphine and said I had a 'million-dollar wound,' serious enough for a possible trip home but not totally disabling. Had I been standing or turned a fraction to my right, I would have received the dreaded 'lower-gut shot.' Four of us were loaded in an ambulance and we began a rough ride to the 95th Evacuation Hospital. The ambulance was peppered with shrapnel; enroute I saw the arm of the man in the stretcher above me fall limp. He may have taken another hit."

Kunz arrived at the medical center in midafternoon and by midnight he was on an operating table while the surgeons temporarily repaired the damage. "The next morning, an orderly went between the two rows of cots in our tent, tossing Purple Heart medals (in boxes) on the foot of each cot. About two days later we were taken out, stacked up on the pier awaiting transfer to a hospital ship. It was a British ship, clean, and we received excellent attention."

Allied political and military leaders grew increasingly impatient with the status in Italy. More than three months after the first soldiers stepped onto the Anzio beaches, 70,000 men were still tied down and the highway from Rome to the Winter Line remained securely in enemy hands. Freyberg's attempts to break through at Cassino had stalled despite the enormous effort mounted by the Air Corps. The countdown to Overlord, the invasion of France from England, had begun and the overall strategy included capture of Rome and release of the VI Corps for Anvil, landings in southern France coordinated with the cross-channel assault.

Under General Alexander, the British-dominated Eighth Army had regrouped and now prepared to take on the defenders in the Liri Valley. Alexander drafted Diadem, in which the VI Corps, instead of banging its head against the stalwart positions that blocked access to Rome, advanced east toward Valmontone to meet the Eighth Army. Diadem kicked off on 11 May with a massive artillery barrage along the fronts of the Allied Fifth and Eighth Armies. Again the Rapido River crossing cost many lives. The victims belonged to Indian, British, and Canadian units. However, the attacks persevered until the Eighth Army established a bridgehead enabling it to muster sufficient forces to drive the Germans backward. Meanwhile, on the right flank at Monte Cassino, the Polish II Corps, an army of exiles, at great cost in lives, captured the ruins.

Mark Clark's Fifth Army, spearheaded by a French Expeditionary Corps on the left flank of the Eighth Army, penetrated the German defenses and pushed deep enough to require the enemy to withdraw in an effort to straighten its front. The American 85th and 88th Divisions drove up the coast against considerable opposition. The Fifth Army in very difficult circumstances broke down the formidable Gustav Line but the British Eighth Army lost momentum. After more than four years of war, the British could not keep up with the rate of attrition. Clark directed Truscott's VI Corps to advance toward Valmontone through Cisterna. Unfortunately, that nemesis of the Ranger battalions was if anything an even harder nut to crack, because the *Wehrmacht*, in falling back from the Allies to the south, settled in that area. The first blows at Cisterna by elements of the 3d Infantry Division, 1st Armored Division, and 1st Special Service Force [created from the remnants of the Rangers and Canadian troops organized into three 750-man regiments] were repulsed. The stymie continued.

From the onset of the American entry into World War II, the two prime leaders, Roosevelt and Churchill, had agreed that the first priority for peace required a tramp through Germany itself. The boasts of both British and American airmen that their day and night bombing might crush the enemy, or at least knock him to his knees, did not pan out. While the British prime minister spoke of the "soft underbelly," the brutal campaign in Italy had not provided easy access to Germany. Nor did the struggle that had begun in North Africa, proceeded to Sicily, and then onto the mainland, and which occupied a considerable amount of the Third Reich's resources, qualify in Joseph Stalin's mind as a second front that would alleviate the awesome pressure on his country. It was clear that a cross-channel attack, which the Americans always believed in, must go forward.

Churchill, whose attitude toward an invasion of France seesawed between wild enthusiasm and brooding despair, initially had thought a 1943 operation feasible. The American generals, with the enthusiasm of ignorance, had even talked in terms of 1942. But, as the dimensions of the problems and the resources available revealed themselves, a more realistic timetable evolved. Eisenhower, in fact, was not even named as supreme commander for what was dubbed Overlord until December 1943. And by the spring of 1944, the blueprints for the operation had gone back to the drawing boards and conference rooms innumerable times.

Where to actually strike turned on a number of factors. The beaches needed to be large enough to accommodate masses of men and materials. The distance from British airfields had to be within the radius of land-based aircraft—all operational aircraft carriers were committed to dealing with the Japanese in the Pacific. Ideally, the location would be the one with the fewest numbers of enemy soldiers in the weakest defensive positions. Into the decision-making mix poured a welter of information—intelligence from aerial surveillance, tidbits supplied by Resistance fighters and spies, intercepts of telephone and radio communications on the Continent, and even what could be gleaned from post-cards, snapshots, and prewar vacationers' memories of the prospective beaches.

Theoretically, the most inviting target was Pas de Calais, the portion of France directly across the English Channel from Dover. It was the shortest distance from Germany itself and highly suitable for the swift deployment of armor. But the Germans would be expected to know all this. Allied observers detected extremely strong defenses in that sector. The extreme west coast of France, at Brittany, while shortening the sailing distance for supplies from the United States, lay beyond the range of some fighter planes based in Britain. The Cotentin Peninsula could fall under an umbrella of air cover and boasted the prize harbor of Cherbourg. However, it would be relatively easy to pinch off that neck of land, trapping the troops. The ultimate compromise choice was Normandy, whose beaches lay between the Pas de Calais and the Cotentin Peninsula. The major drawback lay in the absence of a port suitable for reinforcements and supplies.

To hide the target from the defenders, Eisenhower named Patton to command a paper organization listed as the 1st U.S. Army Group whose location in England indicated a Pas de Calais approach. To lend credence to the Patton figment, tent camps without soldiers were erected; trucks drove through the deserted area to make it seem populated; dummy tanks and landing craft added to the deception. German intelligence, which often astounded the Allies with knowledge of such intimate details as when troops turned in their winter blankets, bought the package, and nineteen enemy divisions battened down to defend Pas de Calais. Almost alone in his hierarchy, Adolf Hitler intuited Normandy as the bullseye, but military logic, for once, overcame his imagination. German knowledge was severely handicapped by the defensive posture forced upon the *Luftwaffe*. Aerial reconnaissance could not pierce the curtain drawn by Allied fighters around England.

Had the Anzio operation and the drive of the American Fifth and the British Eighth Armies achieved their scheduled advances, Overlord would also have been accompanied by Anvil, a thrust into southern France. But the latter invasion, which would become known as Dragoon, was postponed because the units designated for it remained tied down in Italy. Originally, the strategy for Overlord plotted a twenty-mile front, but that was expanded to fifty miles. The British assumed responsibility for the three easternmost beaches, designated in code as Gold, Juno, and Sword, at the extreme left of the Allied line. The Americans would come ashore west of the British at two beaches, code-named Omaha and Utah. Committed to Omaha were GIs like Bill Behlmer and George Zenie from the veteran 1st Division, the unblooded onetime Virginia National Guard 29th Division, and Rangers from the 2d and 5th Battalions. The pair of Ranger units, formed in the United States under Col. James Earl Rudder, a Texas A&M football star, college coach, and teacher, then further schooled in England, recruited officers and enlisted men while in the United Kingdom. Utah Beach would receive the 4th Division, a regular-army organization, but, like the 29th, without combat experience.

To forestall efforts to reinforce the beaches once the attack began, both the British and the Americans plotted roles for paratroopers and glidermen who would precede the seaborne soldiers, seize highways, choke points, and destroy communications. Sir Trafford Leigh-Mallory, the Briton in command of the Allied Expeditionary Air Force, argued vehemently against the scheme, prophesying a minimum of 50 percent casualties and perhaps as high as 90 percent for the airborne. The trooper generals persuaded Eisenhower they were vital to success. The American contingent included the 82d Airborne, with combat-experienced people like Bill Dunfee and Jim Gavin, as well as the virgin 101st Airborne and the 508th Parachute Regiment Combat Team. Glidermen would also be heavily committed.

The enemy, although expecting the Allies in the vicinity of Pas de Calais, attempted to make the entire coast impregnable. Field Marshal Erwin Rommel, named by Adolf Hitler as commander of the Army Group for Special Employment, held primary responsibility for the coastal defenses. But Field Marshal Gerd von Rundstedt, as commander in chief in the West, controlled dispositions of the troops. To complicate planning, command, and control further, Gen. Geyr von Schweppenburg oversaw panzer forces with their tanks and mobile armored infantry.

Rommel and von Rundstedt differed on a basic principle of the defense. The former believed it imperative to prevent the Allies from gaining a foothold on the Continent. His strategy, based on mines, beach obstacles, and gun emplacements, proposed a defense four or five miles in depth. Von Rundstedt considered the coastline far too long to fend off invaders before they established a beachhead. Instead, he posited an approach that would deploy massive, mobile forces that could be rushed to any area under attack. But the panzer boss von Schweppenburg, acutely aware of the damage done to his armor by offshore naval guns at Gela in Sicily (where the cruiser *Savannah* saved the hides of Bill Behlmer and his associates), insisted on keeping his forces beyond warship range. Because Allied bombers and fighter planes ruled the air, anything that traveled by daylight, particularly over roads, was at risk. Swift reaction by German reserves was questionable. Hitler also decreed that some armored units could move only on his direct orders.

The differences between Rommel and von Rundstedt were never resolved. Both commanders received some of what they wanted but less than they believed essential to carrying out their strategies. The most important asset acquired by Rommel was the shift of some reserves, particularly elements of the veteran 352d Division, closer to the Normandy beaches. Their presence escaped the notice of Allied intelligence, which referred to many of the defenders as raw youngsters, overage, or wounded vets from the eastern front, and unenthusiastic conscripts from occupied territories.

Deprived of all he felt necessary, Rommel still invested his considerable energy and tactical brilliance to deterrence of seaborne assault. He arranged a series of deadly barriers in front of the beaches. Metal stakes driven into the Channel floor could rip the hull of a landing craft bouncing through the water. He installed iron bars welded into the shapes of giant jackstraws to block access to land. Huge metal gates—"Belgian doors"—anchored offshore, guarded the approaches. Engineers festooned all of these obstacles with mines.

Behind the shoreline, in spite of a shortage of materials, the defenders labored to casemate large-caliber guns overlooking the beaches. Inland, Rommel directed the implantation of *Rommelspargel* ("Rommel's asparagus"), poles garnished with explosives and embedded in open fields to deny gliders a place to set down.

The extent and type of defenses were largely known by the Overlord planners. Navy reconnaissance patrols put small teams ashore, where they examined the obstacles and pinpointed some of the emplacements. Navy people argued for an invasion at low tide when the landing craft would ground before encountering the obstacles and traps lurking in the water. However, the Army strategists pointed out that would increase the stretch of open land necessary to cross while under heavy fire. A compromise set H hour for one to three hours after extreme low water. To facilitate the night-time airborne operations, full moonlight was desirable. The astronomers could specify those days precisely, but much less certain was weather prediction. High winds could endanger those on the water as well as men in gliders and para-chutes. Thick cloud cover could blot out drop zones and bombing targets. Based on the readiness of the forces and the conditions required, the high command named the period of 5–7 June as the primary target dates. The next favorable tidal time would be 18–20 June, and no one cared to give Rommel any extra time to strengthen his defenses.

Furious debate marked the discussions on the magnitude of naval power. Appalled by the preliminary order of battle, Adm. John L. Hall Jr., who had responsibility for the transport and support of Omaha Beach, met with Adm. Charles M. Cooke, the chief planning officer for Ernest J. King. Hall remembered, "I banged my fist on the table and said, 'It's a crime to send me on the biggest amphibious attack in history with such inadequate gunfire support.' Roosevelt and Churchill had agreed that the English would furnish the naval gunfire support for the Normandy landings. I didn't give a damn what they'd agreed on in conference. I wanted to give my troops the proper support."

Cooke scolded Hall for his impertinence but Hall refused to back off. He recalled his reply: "All I am asking you to do is detach a couple of squadrons of destroyers from transoceanic convoy, give them to me, [and] give me a chance to train them in gunfire support for the American Army on the Omaha beaches." Hall obtained his destroyers, as well as other warships including the battleships *Nevada*, *Texas*, and *Arkansas*. Hall's account was somewhat contested by Harvey Bennett, a Yale graduate whose specialty was shore fire control and served on the staff of RAdm. Alan G. Kirk, the senior U.S. planner for the Normandy landings. Bennett said that, on his advice, Admiral Kirk specified a quantity of ships with certain capabilities and received almost as many vessels as requested. Bennett agreed that Hall was correct in noting that compared with operations in the Pacific, the allocation of firepower for Overlord "was pretty puny."

To boost the firepower ahead of the GIs, the U.S. Navy converted British-made LCTs to rocket launching platforms. The Royal Navy, which employed these in Sicily, reported, "Prisoners taken during the Sicilian operation were awed by the effectiveness of the projectiles and told Allied military leaders that they had been able to stand up under ordinary shellfire but were not able to bear the fire, explosions, and destruction of the rockets. Nine such LCT (R)s were to blast away at Omaha Beach and five would hammer Utah.

Lieutenant (jg) Larry Carr, a reservist called up by the Navy in July 1941, was appointed commander of the rocketeers, and in December 1943 began to train crews on the missiles. Said Carr, "Each rocket weighed sixty pounds, was five inches in diameter and thirty-six inches in length. They were mounted in racks at a fixed, forty-five degree angle with a fixed range of 3,500 yards [slightly less than two miles]. Every ship mounted 1,440 rockets, fired in banks of forty. All were to fire in about two minutes. There were no specific targets; the mission was to blanket the beach areas, destroying barbed-wire defenses, pillboxes, etc." The sound, fury, and sight of the rockets would supposedly pile terror upon physical destruction.

To compensate for the absence of port facilities, engineers designed artificial replacements known as Mulberries. Hollow, floating concrete caissons, six stories tall, towed across the Channel, then submerged, would form piers extending out into the water. To provide a breakwater, the Allied navies scuttled obsolete ships labeled Gooseberries. To ensure a steady flow of fuel, the innovators prepared PLUTO—Pipeline Under the Ocean.

At Slapton Sands, on the southwest coast of England, a major area for amphibious training, the armored units learned of a secret weapon, the DD (duplex drive) tank, which was covered with canvas and an inflated rubber wrapper that enabled it to float. Aside from those devised to be fully amphibious, a second type of tank was waterproofed to the extent that the vehicle could be launched in shallow enough water for it to track across the sea bottom until able to climb up onto the beach.

The threats atop the cliffs that overhung Omaha Beach generated another ingenious scheme. In particular, two sites attracted the attention of the strategists. Near the hinge between Omaha and Utah stood a 100-foot-high precipice, Pointe du Hoc (erroneously named Pointe du Hoe on maps). A reported emplacement there of a six-gun battery of 155mm cannons menaced the approaches from the sea. Another height, Pointe et Raz de la Percée, also provided defenders with a natural stronghold.

Jack Kuhn, a sergeant with the 2d Ranger Battalion, remembered being summoned from a game of darts in a pub for a special assignment. He and Pfc. Peter Korpalo rode in a Jeep driven by their company commander, Duke Slater, to

London. Enroute, Slater explained that amphibious trucks, officially known as DUKWs ("ducks" to GIs), were to be fitted with 100-foot extension ladders. The intention was to mount a machine gun on a small platform atop the ladder. When the DUKW crawled up onto land, the ladder would rise and extend, lifting a Ranger and the weapon. From that height he could provide covering fire for those Rangers ascending the cliffs.

"I was taken to a large factory," said Kuhn, "where I met with firefighters, military personnel from the British forces, and two British soldiers who would drive the DUKWs. I learned the fundamentals of the ladders and the British Lewis machine gun. The British were very high on the concept and we worked together with great enthusiasm, through trial and error, to make the systems function. In the first experiments I walked up to get acquainted. I had climbed cliffs from one hundred to three hundred feet, and this was a scary proposition. I would much prefer to hold a rope. Then I stood on the platform while the ladder was extending, giving me a hundred-foot free ride. We had a communications system so that I could speak to those on the DUKW and they could answer.

"On a cloudy, cold day with a pretty heavy sea running we gave the vehicle a trial run. The two British soldiers and I went out on the water, turned about and came ashore. That answered my first questions, whether the duck would float. Then the Lewis gun was mounted, and with me on the platform, they raised the ladder, extending it its full hundred feet. I fired the machine gun and everything worked to perfection. Feeling the experiments successful, Korpalo and I returned to the battalion with our DUKW. I believe altogether we had four of them on D day."

"On May 20," said Bob Edlin, a lieutenant who had won

Rudder's approval as a Ranger recruit by his commonsense declaration that if surrounded and out of ammunition he would surrender, "the 2d and 5th Ranger Battalions moved into the marshaling area at Weymouth on the English Channel. The weather was beautiful, sunshine; we knew the time was getting close for the invasion. The first four days were pretty much carefree. We could go into any nearby town, do just about anything, drink, gamble, or whatever. We had the usual arguments with the paratroopers of the 101st Airborne. On May 25, the party was over. We were locked in the marshaling area for a briefing. The area was surrounded by barbed wire. Armed guards, MPs and British, were stationed outside the fence. We were ordered not to communicate with them. We couldn't have any conversation with anybody who wasn't more or less imprisoned in the compound. In fact, we felt more like prisoners than we did invading troops.

"We were briefed by Colonel Rudder on the complete invasion, including the roles of the British, Canadian, Americans, paratroopers, 29th Infantry Division, the 4th and 1st Infantry Divisions, and what the Ranger Battalions were to do. We were told the date, time, and location of the invasion. I can remember someone saying, 'Hitler would give ten million dollars to know what I know.' "

Captain John Raaen Jr., a West Pointer who graduated in 1943 as an engineer officer, grew up in the same Fort Smith, Arkansas, neighborhood as William O. Darby, his senior by about ten years. "I heard of Bill Darby most of my life. When the article in *Life* magazine came out about Darby and his Rangers, I wanted to be one, too." While on maneuvers with armored engineers he learned of the new Ranger battalions being organized, so he volunteered.

Assigned to the 5th Ranger Battalion, Raaen took an almost instant dislike to Maj. Max Schneider, the CO of the

5th and one of the few Rangers in England who had combat experience in North Africa and Sicily before coming to England to work with Rudder. Raaen said, "He wanted to command the 5th but he was stuck with a love of the 2d Rangers. He was often insulting to us and always extolling the quality of the 2d's officers and men while deriding us. I commanded Headquarters Company and had much to do with Schneider." According to Raaen, "Prior to boarding the *Prince Baudouin* [his D-day vessel] we had many training sessions on sand tables and maps that had no names on them. Not until we boarded the *Baudouin* were the names uncovered so we could see the exact location of the invasion."

Behind the barbed wire of the marshaling area Sgt. Bob Slaughter of the 29th Division realized, "This was serious business. Brand-new equipment was issued and new weapons had to be zeroed in on the firing range. Unlimited amounts of ammo were given for target practice. Bayonets and combat knives were honed to razor sharpness. Food not seen since leaving the United States was fed to us, and it was all-you-can-eat. Steak and pork chops with all the trimmings, topped off with lemon meringue pie, were items on a typical menu. One of the wags said, 'They're fattening us up for the kill.' The officers became a bit friendlier and it seemed that the men were kinder to each other. First-run movies were shown; *Mrs. Miniver* with Greer Garson and Walter Pidgeon was one of my favorites. Touch football, softball, boxing, reading, and letter writing were popular pastimes. Bible verses were must reading for most of us and prayers were said many times a day.

"New Yorker Francis 'Skeets' Galligan put on a Broadway skit, *Yankee Doodle Dandy*, portraying himself as George M. Cohan. Skeets, agile and a fair tap dancer, concluded the routine by jumping high in the air and clicking his feet together. Semi-nude hoochie-coochie dancers grinding hips to a beat on a tight canvas cot brought smiles and cheers from a captive audience."

Captain Norval Carter, a thirty-three-year-old battalion surgeon with the 115th Regiment of the 29th Division, a psychiatrist by training, who volunteered for the Army Medical Service, wrote home to his wife Fernie, "We shall hit our objective in the morning. Today is Sunday and we are practicing loading our rubber life craft. Letters from various generals have been read to us showing their faith in us and telling us our mission is to go in very fast and hold what we get *at all costs*. Religious services were held for the last time today. There was probably 100 percent attendance. Most of us have a strong spiritual feeling about this affair. We realize we are up against a well-trained, well-equipped, and a well-disciplined enemy who will resist and counterattack with great zeal. But we realize we are fighting for a way of living that is fundamentally right in the eyes of God and man, and the ideals of the enemy are wrong. . . . Fernie, my sweetheart, I feel that I shall see you again. You and the boys. But if I don't I want you all to remember that my love for you cannot be said or put on paper. It can only be felt. You have meant everything to me that is good and happy. . . . May God help us in our mission."

A 1940 graduate of Presbyterian College in South Carolina, George Mabry, as a reserve officer, went on active duty with the 4th Infantry Division stationed at Fort Benning, Georgia. He subsequently earned a regular-army commission. Mabry had moved up from a lowly platoon leader to the post of S-3 of the 2d Battalion of the 8th Regiment. His responsibilities included preparation of the boat-loading tables to ensure that the proper number of troops, equipment, vehicles, and supplies were allocated for the available landing craft.

"Eventually all personnel were briefed on where we would land and the specific tasks for each battalion and company. Security at Torquay became even stricter. We had only one man in the battalion administer a self-inflicted wound to avoid combat. He shot himself in the foot. During one meeting between officers of the 101st Airborne Division and the 4th Division, Colonel [Robert] Sink chided Colonel [James] Van Fleet, 'Be sure, Van, that members of the 8th Regiment hurry and make contact with my troops at the causeways that cross the inundated area behind the beaches because we have other objectives to capture.' Colonel Van Fleet's reply was 'Bob, you just be sure your troops get there, because mine certainly will be there.' "

# 9

# Overlord Overtures

AT THE END OF MAY AND DURING THE FIRST WEEK OF JUNE, AT a great sacrifice of life, the Allied armies finally ruptured the Gustav Line and bore down on the Italian capital. The forces trapped in the Anzio environs broke out. The various legions picked up their pace, spurred not a little by the competition to be the first in the Eternal City. Clark, in particular, wanted his Fifth Army to beat out any British unit. The Allied high command also believed an announcement that Rome had fallen combined with the D-day invasion would radically dampen German morale.

Howze remembered, "We went up a valley, the 1st Armored Division units working with the 3d Infantry. At one point infantry of the Hermann Goering Division came into the sights of the tankers and they killed a lot of Germans. We just sat in our tanks and killed Germans trying to get beyond where we were to establish a defensive position." The swift ebb and flow of battle bedeviled efforts to avoid the peril of friendly fire. American armor complained that the Air Corps bombed and strafed their units seven times in a single day. When told the ground forces were not properly reporting their positions, Howze retorted that there were Army liaison spotter planes over the tanks and the messages simply were not reaching the proper authorities.

"We made twenty-five miles a day," he recalled. "Get in a firefight every so often, kill a few and lose a few then go on. I'd lose patience. I'd tell my tanks, damn it, there is nothing out there, just get on the road. They'd run two miles and then a mortar would blow up and they'd get cautious and fan out. It was a hard go, the terrain was so broken it made bad tank country." To trundle over the misshapen ground, the tankers improvised, using bundled oil drums and poplar trees to fill deep troughs in their path.

Michael Davison, of the 1st Battalion of the 45th Division's 179th Regiment, recalled, "We had very tough fighting on the breakout. One day on the road that led to the capture of Rome I had nineteen battalions of artillery firing on my battalion's front—every single battalion of the division, battalions from the Corps artillery and from neighboring divisions. The casualty rate was high in the first couple of days. We fought like hell for three or four days getting out of Anzio. It began to ease the third day and on the fourth we had been passed through by another regiment."

Bill Kunz, still in a Naples hospital ward at the time of Diadem, said, "We knew when the 'breakout' from the beachhead occurred, as the wounded were stacked up in the hallways and any other spaces they could find. I learned later my division sustained 995 casualties the day of the breakout and 665 the following day. My injury maybe was really the million-dollar wound."

On the heels of the armor spearheading the advance on Rome came the Special Services Force. This unit was composed of survivors of the three Ranger Battalions and Canadians, and led by USMA graduate Brig. Gen. Robert Frederick, who had the authority to enter Rome. On the morning of 4 June, Frederick halted at the city's outskirts because of mobile antitank guns that repulsed the tanks. When II Corps commander Gen. Geoffrey Keyes demanded why Frederick did not advance, the head of the SSF explained the problem. Keyes, a protégé of Patton, blandly asserted that Clark expected to be in Rome by 4:00 P.M. "Because he has to have a photograph taken." Although the SSF and a recon platoon from the 88th Division, followed by a motley group of Allied troops, surged into Rome starting at dusk, Clark could not publicly celebrate the victory until the next day. The ceremonial occupation degenerated into a farce when the Fifth Army's senior party lost itself in the maze of the city's streets until an English-speaking priest pointed them in the right direction to Capitoline Hill. Furthermore, it was a triumph not over a defeated army but one that retreated to new defensive positions north of Rome.

During the first days of June, with Overlord scheduled to begin on the fifth, the airborne contingents bedded down at the airfields. The huge fleet, numbering 5,000 vessels, milled about in the Channel waters. The weather refused to cooperate, with rough seas matched by a turbulent night sky. Eisenhower accepted a twenty-four-hour delay while meteorologists formulated a prediction for the following night. Troops who had been aboard the lurching ships for several days coped with seasickness. The airborne forces settled in for another twenty-four hours of waiting.

Ed Jeziorski of the 507th Parachute Infantry Regiment said, "Normandy would be my first combat. As foolish as it sounds today, I, among many, felt relief that we would be committed, and excited over the prospect of tangling with

Jerry to show what we could do. I felt let down when we were told the invasion was held off for a day. While in the hangars, before moving out to the planes, we gathered around a small radio as the 'Berlin Bitch' came on. Her words still live with me. 'Good evening, 82d Airborne Division. Tomorrow morning, blood from your guts will grease the bogey wheels on our tanks.' Then she played tear-jerking songs."

Dave Thomas, a battalion surgeon in the 508th Parachute Infantry Regiment, was among the thousands behind the barbed-wire fences. "I was always an odds player and won a lot of money playing poker. This night I wasn't doing that well at the table so I thought I might as well go hit a lick with Jesus. I sat down in the last cot; the place was sold out. Chaplain James Elder was really getting the troops in. As I sat down, he said, 'Now the Lord isn't particularly interested in those who only turn to Him in time of want.' I thought, what the hell am I doing here? I got up and went back to the poker game, but still didn't do all that well. Some time later, back in England, after Normandy, I told Chaplain Elder about the incident. He was mortified."

Bill Dunfee, recalled, "I was disappointed and let down when the mission was postponed twenty-four hours, I was emotionally ready to go. I did my sweating before a mission. Once airborne I was apprehensive but became very calm and accepted whatever was to come."

Turk Seelye, like Dunfee already a veteran of combat with the 505th, recalled the same uneasiness. "We had spent a couple of days and nights living in barracks close to the landing strip. We spent the time getting our equipment ready, sharpening knives and bayonets, and in general having feelings of apprehension of what was to happen next. On the third or fourth of June we had been billeted in the airport hangar itself. Our beds were blankets spread on the concrete floor. We were issued the grenades, ammunition, and other supplies that we would carry. Briefings consisted of studying maps and using sand tables, as well as showing each unit the scope of its particular mission. That's when we had learned that the invasion would take place in Normandy. Other activities at the airport included shooting craps and playing poker, using the French invasion currency, watching a movie in the evening, and attending religious services."

Matthew Ridgway, the 82d Airborne leader, said, "About forty-eight hours before D day, they told us what they had just discovered. The 91st German Division had been moved into our drop zone. [Clay Blair's book, *Ridgway's Paratroopers,* reported the intelligence on the 91st actually came to the attention of the strategists on 25 May.] Bradley asked what will you do. It was too late to change things or planes. My chief worry was enemy air interference. I was confident there would be no planes or night fighters but we might come over unlocated and unneutralized concentrated flak. We would be down so low we would be just sitting ducks."

In the G-3 section (Divisional Plans and Operations) of the 82d Airborne, Tom Graham, of the 505th Parachute Regiment, noted constant revisions. "It was a day and night project because of changes made where we were supposed to jump. Aerial photos would come in to the war room and things had to be changed. No one knew exactly where we were going to drop until shortly before takeoff."

Both the British and American airborne operations were designed to forestall any German deployment of reserves against the soldiers storming onto the beaches. The beneficiaries of the paratroopers from the U.S. 82d and 101st Airborne Divisions, as well as glidermen, would be the GIs from the 4th Infantry Division on Utah Beach. No airborne forces would be deployed behind Omaha Beach. Gavin, among others, believed the flat ground behind Omaha would expose the paratroopers to the crush of an expected advance by German armor. The area picked out for the elements of the 82d straddled the Merderet River five to ten miles behind Utah Beach forming a rough triangle whose perimeter measured about ten miles. The major objectives included the town of Ste.-Mère-Eglise, which sat astride a crossroads and a rail line that connected Cherbourg in the northwest with Paris.

The 101st Airborne Division under Gen. Maxwell Taylor would form a racetrack-shaped position parallel to Utah only two or three miles behind the beach. The 101st's troopers and their glider component, drawn from the 327th Glider Regiment, were expected to hold a coastal road that ran toward Carentan, a known stronghold of enemy reserves. The flight plan for all U.S. airborne components carried them on a southwest course toward the Channel Islands of Guernsey and Jersey. There, a submarine-borne beacon light would signal the transports to veer east over the Cotentin Peninsula for the final run to the appointed areas.

For recognition purposes, the troopers in the 101st Airborne carried tiny noisemakers, spring-steel crickets of the type usually included in boxes of Cracker Jack caramel popcorn. One click was the challenge and two snaps was the appropriate response during Overlord. General Maxwell Taylor, the former Screaming Eagles commander, explained, "It rose out of my experiences earlier in the Mediterranean and from our Eagle [practice] exercise in England. There was so much dispersion in Sicily," said Taylor, "that I realized we needed some method of identification behind enemy lines. Eagle convinced me more than ever. We needed a little noisemaker a man could carry in his hand. The cricket seemed just right."

While the 7,500 men of the 101st clicked together in Normandy, the troopers of the 82d Airborne, according to Gavin, relied solely on the passwords of "Flash" and "Thunder." "There was a lot of gadgetry around," Gavin responded, "and a lot of it didn't make much sense. In Normandy, the 82nd used only an oral password. It's always more important to carry more ammunition . . . to stay alive . . . to fight . . . to get there. I even cut the fringes off the many maps I carried so there'd be more room for ammunition. I myself carried 156 rounds of ammo, four grenades, a knife, a rifle, and a pistol, in case I had to fight my way through enemy territory, which once I did."

Of the top U.S. airborne commanders, only Gavin was a fully qualified paratrooper who had earned his wings at jump school. When the 82d and 101st leaped in Normandy, the most senior commanders, Ridgway and Taylor, had only jumped once or twice. Taylor's deputy, Gen. Don Pratt, could only join the division on D day as a glider passenger. Another novice jumper was the commander of the 101st's airborne artillery unit, Gen. Anthony McAuliffe.

As Lt. Homer Jones and his platoon prepared to board their plane after hearing a message of good luck from Eisenhower, Jones said he felt impelled to address the troopers. "I had tremendous respect and feeling for them. In the paratroops the normal walls between officers and enlisted men broke down. You did everything the men did, and I often finished marches carrying a mortar or machine gun. There were lots of country boys, poor kids, ones with different backgrounds, and they'd all become close. I looked at them and realized there were a lot I wasn't going to see again. This would be a final goodbye. I said, 'I'd like to add a few words.' I began, 'We've been together a long time . . .' and then it got to me. 'Oh shit!' is what I said.

"Trooper Japhet Alphonso said, 'That's okay, Lieutenant. We know what you mean.' "

For both divisions, pathfinders, equipped with the Rebeccas-Eureka system and signal lights, would jump first to guide in the more than 13,000 men. Their aircraft roared down the runways and lifted off while the skies were still light, before the midnight prefacing 6 June. Because of double daylight saving time, darkness arrived very late. The first pathfinders touched down as early as ten minutes into 6 June.

The flak thrown up by the defenders drove most pathfinder-bearing planes off course. As a consequence less than one-third of the 120 troopers assigned to guide in their fellows achieved their targets. Even those who reached the proper place operated on the edge of disaster. German soldiers, alert to the presence of strangers, made the use of illuminating devices suicidal. Radios were damaged or malfunctioned. From the beginning, plans for a strategically effective airdrop went awry. The enemy, gradually aware of extensive activity overhead, filled the skies with exploding shells and bullets. Pilots ferrying the airborne units then sought to evade the fire. Simple navigation errors compounded the growing disarray.

Ridgway, somewhat overstating the case, claimed, "These kids that were flying the troop carriers, C-47s, they hadn't much flying training. They had done the minimum number of hours in the air. The glider pilots still less and so what happened was to be expected. I had fifty-four planes in my serial and they were using only these little violet lights, no navigation lights at all."

Tom Poston piloted a C-47 packed with paratroopers. "D day, it was black, pitch black. I think it was one A.M. when we crossed the coast of Normandy. The moon was bright through the clouds, it was *gorgeous*. We came in, drifting down through those clouds, plane after plane after plane after plane, down through this pitch-black dark and then there's a flaming 'Tee' there that those brave guys that go ahead of the drops set out there and that's the target for the paratroopers. But, oh, my God, they were dropping paratroopers from hell to breakfast because the formations were so spread out. Pilots don't like to fight prop wash too much [the air eddies created from the propellers of nearby aircraft].

"The ideal thing is to come in at 400–500 feet, drop the paratroopers. They just go bustling out, the chute opens, slows them, and they hit the ground. That's ideal because nobody can pick them off. But the guys [pilots] behind them don't want to go in at 400–500 feet because they're fighting the stick like crazy, trying to fly in formation, flying in the prop wash. So they stack and the next group comes in twenty feet higher than the first group. By the time the last groups are dropping, those guys are coming in at 1,000, 1,500 feet in the air, hanging there.

"I don't know what the Germans could see from the ground but we couldn't see anything. It was pitch black when we went in. But when we left it was a *sea of flame*. Everybody woke up down there and went, 'What the hey!' Boom! Boom! Boom! Antiaircraft and machine-gun fire, tracers all over the sky, every which way. The tracers look like they're coming right at you. You'd see a flare coming right at your nose and then it trailed off to the side."

Wallace Swanson, an Oklahoma State football star in Company A, 1st Battalion of the 502d Parachute Regiment, described the ensemble he wore. "The parachute jumpsuit had these baggy pants with large front and rear pockets, two each, plus two more big, front-side pockets. One could easily carry twenty-five to fifty pounds of necessary ammunition, K rations, and personal items. The jacket had four pockets, two on the upper chest, and two lower that went to hip level. These were also wide enough for more stuff. I carried an officer's Colt .45 and a .30-caliber carbine. My favorite was the .45. I was quite accurate with it up to fifty feet. While I used the carbine numerous times, my second choice for combat was the semiautomatic M1 rifle. I had an escape kit with some hacksaw blades, a compass, a map of France, and a knife. Most of the men in my jump stick had a similar kit. An inspection before we left prevented anyone from throwing away items necessary for survival and got rid of any beer or liquor in canteens.

"There was little conversation during the flight. The leaders checked to see that the individuals for whom they were responsible were ready and alert to what they were to do. Most of the talk was along the lines of 'Are you ready?' and 'This time it's for real.' Maybe among a buddy-buddy group of two or three there was a laugh over a remark from one of the comedians on the plane. I dozed off for a while during the flight and saw many others relaxing in similar fashion. My feeling was, get some rest while you can because we might be on the go for many hours through the next day or two. With all that combat equipment on, one snuggled into the most comfortable position possible, sitting up, leaning against others or the fuselage supports. A few stretched out nearly flat in the middle of the aisle and hoped no one would step on them.

"Although I was a platoon leader and second in command of the company, I did not have any info on the flight rendezvous area after takeoff nor the path to our destination. In general I understood we would rendezvous over England, head south in a safe, tight pattern until we would gradually turn east to cross the Cotentin Peninsula well above Ste.-Mère-Eglise, north of Carentan, south of Foucarville to our drop zone. The ground of the Cherbourg or Cotentin Peninsula was in darkness, in contrast to the Channel waters, which reflected the moonlight. I knew we would jump soon. As we crossed the lower portion of the peninsula, we came under antiaircraft flak fire. Visibility was good with moonlight and scattered clouds. I could see ground fire coming up at our planes. I could hear bullets or pieces of flak hitting the fuselage of the plane but so far as I know, none pierced it or came into the troop area. Two or three bursts of flak came pretty close; we saw the bright explosion lights from the doorway. Occasionally the blast of a cannon or an artillery battery from below reached our ears, but we could hear very little from the ground because of the roar of wind blowing past the door.

"The pilot took two severe and one slight maneuver to escape the antiaircraft fire. When the green light went on, I heard the crew chief yell, 'Green light! Jump!' Our plane was probably at the right airspeed, 95 to 100 mph, when I jumped. But because of the evasive actions we were probably down to 500 to 800 feet. Once outside and dropping, I could see very little because almost everything was dark. The sparse light from the moon and stars scattered, showing only vague outlines. What I could clearly see were tracer bullets coming up from gun positions and flak bursts that exposed things with a blast of light.

"When I jumped I wondered where I would land since I couldn't affect whether it would be a low area, a rise, hill, bank, or whatever. To manipulate a chute, one needs a reason or a purpose, such as an obstacle. In any case, I had practically no time to try and guide my chute. It was jump;

plop open, then me swinging in the air. I had only pushed back my helmet from over my eyes because of the jerk of the chute opening and then checked to see that I had not lost any of my equipment when I hit the ground, probably five seconds after I left the plane.

"Actually, I landed in three or four inches of water covering a grassy area. My chute collapsed; I collected it and hid it. The moonlight enabled me to see the outline of certain terrain features such as higher hills, trees, and bushes. Because the more elevated ground lay on one side, I figured out it was to the west and near the first target for our mission, the big offshore guns that the Germans would use to protect the beaches. When daylight came a few hours later, I saw that we were only a few hundred yards from that objective. Further study of my map indicated it was less than a mile to our second important mission, capture and holding the right flank of Utah Beach at Foucarville.

"I took about fifteen or twenty steps and suddenly felt I had stepped into a bottomless pit. I went down in water over my head. Hanging onto my equipment I managed to crawl up the bank of what was a drainage ditch by clinging to the tall weeds, grass, and brush." Shortly after touching down and soaking himself, Swanson began collecting his troopers. With a number of men from his own platoon and the company plus some stragglers from other outfits, he directed a line of march toward the gun emplacements.

Platoon leader Bernard McKearney with E Company of the 502d looked out. "It was a clear night over the Channel. The invasion fleet below appeared as toy boats. Everything seemed so unreal. I had to keep reminding myself that this was it, the day for which we had waited and sweated so long. The men were very quiet. Some dozed, others were on their knees watching history being made below. Then landfall. Fog swirled in. Then the ack-ack started coming up. It didn't look a bit deadly. Strangely enough I thought of July Fourth. One burst clipped us in the wing. The plane lurched and nearly threw me out of the door. Then the warning red light. Stand up and hook up! No dramatics, no shouting. The men's faces were grim and tight. I tried to relax them by kidding a little. Then the green light. I shouted, 'Let's go, girls!' and I piled out.

"The air was criss-crossed with tracers. I couldn't see a soul below. I was over an orchard. I slipped frantically to miss the woods under me. Oh, God, don't let them catch me in a tree. I hit with a thud. I could hear shouting in German and English. With all of my equipment, I would have been helpless in my chute. I tried to keep cool. I gathered up my chute and ran sixty yards before plunging into some thick undergrowth. I placed three hand grenades in front of me and took off my equipment. After some hesitation I started out. Someone challenged me with his cricket. I fumbled for mine. I had lost it! I started swearing at him in good old Jerseyese. I knew an American GI would recognize it. He did and burst out laughing. It was our company exec, Lt. Ray Hunter, a Carolina boy.

"Finally, we collected a force of about sixty men. All this time we had no idea where we were. We had become hopelessly separated from the rest of the battalion. The men were wonderful. After about an hour we were fired upon by a German machine gun. Someone yelled, 'Stay down, Lieutenant Mac,' and then I heard an American Tommy gun chatter. One of our boys, Staff Sergeant Brosseau from Boston, said, 'Come on, I just erased them.' It was the same all through the campaign. The men fought like veterans from the very beginning.

"As it was just getting light, I was looking for some place

to hole up. There was sporadic firing going on all around us. I was getting worried. These men trusted my judgment completely. Finally, we came to a little village. As it was surrounded by a stone wall, I decided to move in. As we approached, we were challenged in English. Inside the place we found a medic captain from our own battalion and three aid men. These were the unsung heroes of the paratroopers. Since we had three or four men shot up and in bad shape, I was mighty happy to see the medics. We set up a perimeter defense around the village and remained tight until dawn. With typical Irish luck, I had stopped just short of a battery of eight German fieldpieces."

"On the night of June 5," says Lou Merlano, elevated to corporal when his Company A of the 502d had entered the marshaling area, "we marched out to our planes and there was an eerie silence about us. There seemed to be a smell of death in the air. We were all fully aware of what the twenty-to-thirty-mile-per-hour winds would do to our jump pattern. When word finally came down the jump was canceled, we were all happy about the situation. When we got the go signal for June 6, I had my M1, musette bag full of rations, ammo and grenades, an infraray gun about three feet long to use for Morse Code communications, and a map case. I expected to jump last, but Sergeant Perko, in charge of the radio and whom I was to help, saw how heavily I was loaded and moved me to second place in the stick. The rest of the guys in the plane were riflemen.

"The formation of the flight was tremendously impressive. I could look out the window and see the beauty of it. Few of us dozed off. There were conversations about how much we hoped the talk about French gals was true. There was a good feeling about the whole operation. During all our briefings in the marshaling area, I clearly remember how this would be like a sneak attack in the pitch of night. However, after we started across the peninsula from west to east, it became like night and day all at one time. For a while we could see planes alongside us. When the antiaircraft shells and stuff began to come up, the pattern scattered.

"Now I saw no other planes. I know of no shells hitting our ship. The first plane, the one with our CO, Capt. Richard Davidson, supposedly was hit and went down in the Channel after only half the men got out. Captain Davidson, the rest of his stick, and the C-47 crew were lost. In my plane, only eight of us landed on the ground. I presume the rest, including Sergeant Perko, who had given me his position in the jump, had dropped in the Channel and drowned. There were no instructions from the pilot, crew chief, or jumpmaster about what was happening. All I remember is 'Go! Go! Go!' I must have jumped at about 300 feet because after one and a half oscillations and I hit the ground with a thud. I was in Normandy, in a field marked *'Minen.'* At the time I did not know it was a dummy minefield and I moved very cautiously. I crept through the field toward a little farmhouse I spotted.

"When I got out of the field, I ran toward the house where I met a man and a woman. They apparently were farmers who seemed jubilant to see an American. They quickly poured me a glass of Calvados. They were anxious to help and I pulled out my map, asking for directions to St. Martin-de-Varreville where our objective, the German artillery, lay. Not speaking French, I couldn't understand what they said but they pointed in a direction of an awful lot of firing. I figured I must be about three to five miles from St. Martin-de-Varreville. I heard quite a number of planes in the area, so I left the house and headed where I thought [there] was some action. I jumped over a fence and lo and behold, I was in an area infested with German soldiers running about the court-yard. From a loft a machine gun fired at planes, probably now flying east back to England. There was much firing, much commotion everywhere. I would have to say that at this point I was terrified, realizing that I had nowhere to go except into the German hands. I sat quietly and devoured my little code book."

Bill Dunfee, with Company I, 3d Battalion of the 505th, remembered, "There was a bright moon, but it was very foggy. As our flight crossed the coastline, all hell broke loose. We were receiving antiaircraft fire in abundance. Machine gun, 20mm cannon, and AA artillery was bouncing us around. The pilot took evasive action, adding to our problem of a stand-up position. It was not a pleasant ride and it seemed to take forever to our DZ. I felt machine-gun bullets penetrate the aircraft wing. Someone shouted, 'Let's get the hell out of here,' but no one moved. At about 0200 hours, the green light finally came on. It did not take long to empty that airplane.

"Jim Beavers and I were in the middle of the stick and the equipment bundles were to be released when we jumped. When my chute opened, I figured I had it made. We were still drawing AA fire but I was out of that flying coffin. Looking around I spotted Jim Beavers next to me and our equipment bundle off to one side. When I looked down, I saw C-47s flying *below* us. That scared the hell out of me and I started cussing. Those rotten bastards were trying to kill us. They had jumped us at over 2,000 feet and now dove down on the deck. I didn't want to be turned into hamburger by our own Air Force. That had happened during regimental maneuvers in the U.S. when a plane lost flying speed and dropped down, running into three of our guys and killing them.

"While descending, I regained my composure because it appeared we were going to make it down in one piece. I had told Jim I would meet him at the equipment bundle. He landed on one side of a hedgerow and the bundle, and I on the other side. By the time Jim joined me I had the bundle unrolled and the bazooka and ammo out. We loaded up and headed for Ste.-Mère-Eglise. It was easy to locate. That's where most of the firing was coming from."

Turk Seelye, a rifleman and first scout for Company E of the 505th, toted the full load: His M1, ammunition, grenades, gas mask, a pick mattock entrenching tool, and some intimate personal items—twenty-four sheets of toilet paper, a French phrase book, tablets to purify water, a bill-fold with invasion currency, toothbrush and tooth powder, a bar of soap, a spare pair of undershorts, two pairs of socks, a handkerchief, and a safety razor with, optimistically, five extra blades. "The name on our plane was *Miss Carriage*, and no sooner had I sat down on the aluminum bucket–seat benches than I had to urinate. There were no latrines on these flying boxcars. So I had to get up, be helped down the boarding ladder, and then relieve myself under the wing. It is not an easy task when bundled up in parachute straps and equipment. The 'nervous pee' syndrome was shared by al-most all. There was a steady file of troopers going up and down the boarding ladder. As we neared the Normandy coast, the jumpmaster, seeing the red warning light, issued the order to stand up and hook up. At this point, each trooper attached his own parachute static line to the steel cable that ran the length of the plane. When one jumped out the door of the aircraft, the static line pulled the parachute from the backpack, causing it to be exposed to the propeller blast and open properly. The next order was, 'Sound off for equip-ment check.' Then each trooper checked with his hands the static line and other equipment of the man standing directly in front of him. When my turn came, I shouted, 'Number six, okay!'

"The cruising speed of the aircraft was about 150 mph. I could see very little standing in the aisle, trying to look out the small windows. I did see some tracers whiz by, and also what appeared to be a burning plane on the ground. As we neared the drop zone, the pilot flashed the green light and the whole stick of sixteen troopers exited in less than thirty seconds. The pilot, no doubt anxious to return to safety and comfort in England, failed to reduce the speed of the aircraft to the normal jump speed of ninety miles an hour.

"After I left the door, the plane nosed downward and I watched the tail pass a few feet over my head. Then, as the prop blast forced air into my chute, I got the strongest opening shock ever. The chute opened with such a violent jolt that a Beretta pistol I took from an Italian naval officer in Sicily was torn loose, along with my new safety razor. Since I reached the ground in no more than half a minute, I estimate the altitude of the plane was no more than 325 feet, very low.

"I was shaken up a bit, nervous and scared when I hit the ground. I immediately rolled up my parachute, stuck it in under some bushes along with the reserve chute and then put together the three pieces of my M1—trigger assembly, barrel, and stock. I put a clip of ammunition into the chamber and fixed my bayonet. I heard automatic weapons and saw some tracer and antiaircraft bullets headed skyward. The first human sound was a cry for help from a squad member. Two others from my group also heard the voice and found our friend, Maryland J. Golden of Tallahassee, Florida, lying on the ground, unable to move. His left leg was broken. He received a shot of morphine and we carried him to the protection of a hedgerow to await medics.

"We walked in the darkness seeking other Americans. Somehow I became separated from the other two squad members and I was alone in a French farmyard. I used my cricket for identification and happened to run across three Yanks from another airborne unit. We moved about still looking for other Americans and trying to avoid contact with the enemy. We saw none of either. But in the distance we heard the sounds of war. At dawn we came across several troopers who seemed to know what was going on. We joined with them and walked the several miles to Ste.-Mère-Eglise, site of the C Company [505th Regiment] command post. The company occupied an open area about the size of a football field. We spent the day setting up a perimeter defense."

James Gavin had elected to jump with the 508th Parachute Regiment. "I was asked to act as his G-3," said Tom Graham.* "William Walton, a *Time* correspondent, had put on an army uniform and was on the plane. Captain Hugo Olson, the general's aide, was also part of our stick. We had all been shocked to hear that four men from Headquarters Company of the 1st Battalion had been killed even before takeoff when a grenade one was carrying exploded.

"As we crossed over the Channel and into France, the general kept contacting the pilot and copilot, and he went up and down the aisle assuring everyone as he passed that everything was all right. He told us we had run into some fog, but that the flight was going according to plan. When we neared the DZ, I looked out the window and saw the river, but things did not look quite right in terms of where

*In his book, *On to Berlin*, Gavin notes, "Lt. Thomas Graham and Capt. Willard Harrison [also aboard] were picked for their combat experience and reputation for toughness and courage in combat."

we were supposed to be. The green light went on and all went out the door with Gavin, as the leader in the plane, first. It was a moonlit night and you could see quite a distance once the chute opened. You could see others dropping close by.

"All at once, firing from a château on one side of the river streaked toward the bundles, which had lights on them, and then at paratroopers. It was an odd scene when the quiet of the night was broken by the guns. As I came close to the ground I thought I was looking at a big pasture. It turned out to be water with grass growing up through it that broke the shine of water. I had never made a water landing and I didn't know how deep this would be and what it would be like. As my feet came down and struck this grassy water, I pitched forward as my parachute pulled me to my knees in water that was above my waist. I stood up but when I had gone under the water I lost my helmet. I fumbled around for the helmet and found it quickly. My rifle was wet, my map case wet, and my pockets full of water. I was anxious to get to a shore that I could see some distance away. Meanwhile, the firing grew heavier with tracers tracking other chutists and gliders now coming down. When I reached the dry ground, there were some other troopers there along with General Gavin."

According to Gavin's recollection, when he gave the signal to exit the C-47, they were more than half a minute beyond their scheduled time to leap. The stick with him, as well as many others, came down several miles east of their drop area. Not only were the American paratroopers misled by the ineffectiveness of the pathfinder operation and the intense antiaircraft fire that drove the C-47 pilots off course, but they were betrayed by faulty interpretation of reconnaissance photos. During the spring thaws and rains, the two principal rivers, the Merderet and Douve, had poured over their banks. The aerial photos indicated the length and breadth of the flooding, but not the depth. The tall grass that grew up through the water fooled observers into believing the swampy area was at most a few inches deep. "Ground here probably soft" was the optimistic conclusion of the report. In fact the water was over a man's head.

A considerable number of troopers, burdened with chutes, laden with weapons and extra ammunition, and toting heavy radios, with equipment stowed in bags strapped to their legs, fell into the deep ooze and drowned. Many of the equipment bundles with precious bazookas, machine guns, and mortars also disappeared into the marshy depths.

The party that included Gavin and Graham moved away from the river while the gunners in the château targeted the marshes. Graham remembered, "The general had seen a glider halfway under water. He said there was a 57mm gun in the glider and asked if I would take three or four troopers to see if we could retrieve the weapon. I didn't have to ask for volunteers. They were all willing. We waded out to the glider in the water. We could not raise the front end. It was wedged into mud and grass. The occupants apparently had gotten out through the side of the glider.

"Unable to lift the nose, we reported back to General Gavin. He told us he'd take a group down the road toward the château and take them under fire if we would try again to remove the 57mm. We started for the glider and the fire from the château became so intense I didn't think we could even get there. We made it without being hit but we still could not budge the nose.

"Gavin directed us to leave the area, and rightfully so, because the Germans had begun closing in on us with heavy fire. We crossed through open water and the river itself; you could not tell when you actually left the flooded field and were in the stream. I looked back while we were partway across and the bullets from the Germans were kicking up water and sometimes you heard them go overhead but you never knew how close."

Gavin surmised that he had dropped several miles northeast of Drop Zone N, the target plotted for the Red Devils. He was on the far side of the wide expanse of water sluiced from the Merderet by the Germans to impede invaders. Furthermore, the troopers he collected were not from the 508th but mostly belonged to the 507th. Gavin led his small force toward the la Fière Causeway across the Merderet, because, "It was a terribly important causeway. It was really the only feasible way to get across the Merderet all the way from Montebourg down south." Movement in this direction by enemy forces would place them directly behind Utah Beach.

But before Gavin could take command at la Fière, the situation lay in the hands of lesser figures much closer to the objective. Among the handful of troopers in the vicinity was the 507th's Raider Nelson. Nelson was one of the relatively small number of paratroopers to land near the designated drop zone. "Our objective was to use the Merderet River, which ran parallel to the beach, as a defense line preventing German reinforcements from reaching the beachheads. Each of us carried an eleven-pound antitank mine below the reserve chute. This was to be buried about fifty feet from the river. We would then dig in along the river. But because of our wide dispersal upon landing in the dark, this plan was not implemented. I was separated from my company and in the darkness found other lost troopers. There was no enemy in our area but plenty of small-arms fire around us. We set up a defensive perimeter and by early light had gained several more troopers, but still none from my company. An officer took charge and we started to march single file, spread out, along a road. The second man in front of me was hit by sniper fire and from then on, enemy resistance built up."

Trooper Ed Jeziorski of the 507th recalled: "My light machine gun was in a pararack under my plane's belly. I carried eight clips of ammo in my cartridge belt plus two bandoliers draped over my shoulders, one Gammon grenade [a British device using plastic explosives], two fragmentation grenades, a phosphorus grenade, an antitank mine in my musette bag, a bayonet, a jump knife strapped to my right boot, two antitank rifle grenades and my trusty M1 rifle with 'Jean' carved into the stock. When I jumped over the Rhine later, I carried Jean IV.

"It seemed like eternity before we were able to get above treetop level. There was little or no talking. I had a certain amount of tenseness but I know it was not fear. Instead I was apprehensive as to what lay ahead. I did say a prayer, asking God to let me do the job for which I had been trained, and not to let my buddies down. We had been briefed, no lights or smoking, but I had a momentary lapse and lit a cigarette. [Lieutenant] Parks yelled instantly, 'Put that goddamn cigarette out!' Someone else then said, 'Do we really have to go?' That brought some real and some fake laughs and the tension eased. As we came over Normandy, the whole sky lit up with sheets of multicolored antiaircraft tracers. Parks had us stand and hook up. We were bouncing and heaving from side to side as our ship tried to dodge the tracers. I lost my balance, went down and somebody had to help me up. Our plane was taking violent evasive action and hadn't slowed a bit when the green light flashed. Parks shouted, 'Let's go!'

"We shuffled out as fast as we could behind him. Just as I cleared the door and before my chute popped open, a great ball of red fire and black smoke erupted directly underneath me. Without thought as to how ridiculous it was, I shouted a warning, 'The bastards are waiting for us!' I pulled my knees up to make myself as small a target as possible; the bullets were crackling that close. I pulled on my risers to try and slip away from the fire. I landed near the hamlet of Hebert, nowhere near the intended drop zone. As soon as I hit the ground, a machine gun began covering me, very closely. Everytime I moved, the gunner opened up on me. I must have been pretty visible because of a burning plane nearby. I pulled my jump knife and cut the leg and chest straps. I rolled over and as a clip was already in my M1, I eased off the safety, then squeezed off a couple of shots at the Jerry gunner. I don't think I hit him but his firing ceased.

"Working my way toward a large hedgerow, I heard a good bit of thrashing about. As the sound came closer, I came close to pulling the trigger. But I called out softly, 'flash.' Quickly, the response was 'thunder.' It was my assistant gunner, Grover Boyce. All of a sudden, the world was a lot more friendly. Our stick had jumped right on top of a German concentration. Some were immediately surrounded and had no choice but to surrender while still in their harnesses. Lieutenant Parks was captured but escaped to rejoin the regiment. My squad leader, Greg Howarth, became a POW, as did Jack Kessler and Marshall Griffin. But Boyce and I teamed up with Dante Tonneguzzo, who later was awarded a DSC, and our aid man, Andy Manger.

"We moved on, trying to hook up with other troopers. Germans fired at us and we scrapped back. We took a prisoner and the firefight eased off. As Doc Manger was interrogating the Jerry, the whole left side of his face disappeared. Apparently, one of the Jerries still hidden in a building was not about to let our prisoner give us any helpful information. We stretched the Kraut out on the ground and Doc gave him a heavy dose of morphine. He was turning gray and his eyes were glazing over when we left him.

"We found a parapack, opened it up, and it had a light machine gun with two boxes of ammo. It was just like old home week. Boyce said, 'Here come the Krauts.' About two hundred yards away advanced a small line of Jerries with a machine gun in the center. They spotted us about the same time we saw them. Their gunner went into action fast and Boyce and I scrambled to get a belt loaded. Most of their bursts went over our heads. I know my fire was a helluva lot more accurate, but damn that gun of his could throw a bunch of lead in a hurry. They broke off the scrap and we didn't go chasing them."

C. B. McCoid commanded B Company in the 507th's 1st Battalion and was scheduled to lead his unit in the vicinity of Amfreville, a village west of the Merderet. "Our C-47, with six jumpers and six bundles in pararacks mounted on its underside, was heavily laden. It struggled to get into the air. It seemed about to go down at one heart-stopping moment. A couple of men cursed with relief as the plane steadied and resumed climbing. I spent much of the flight in the pilots' cabin of the C-47 leading B Company's part of the formation. As the coast was neared, the pilot ordered the crew chief to open the jump door. I shook the men awake. Attaching my static line to the anchor-line cable, I stepped to the open door to watch the coastline north slip beneath us.

"All was as it should be. We were droning along at about 125 to 130 knots and holding an altitude of some 800 feet. The formation was intact. Then the red light came on. The order to 'Stand up and hook up' was issued. The heavily burdened men struggled to their feet with difficulty, most receiving and giving pulls and pushes to get in place in line. Meanwhile we flew steadily toward Drop Zone T. The ground was dimly visible below, with tree lines and open fields identifiable without much trouble. I felt we would surely be able to drop on target.

"Suddenly, we passed over a bank of white fog or smoke, extending north along the midaxis of the peninsula, which totally obscured the ground. We may have taken as much as half a minute to cross this surprise—it seemed much longer. But once we did, the action began. Machine-gun fire was coming from everywhere. The tracer rounds arced slowly toward us and then flashed by with a sharp, ripping sound that turned into uncountable cracking noises as they came close. This was our first experience with the German MG 42 and its amazingly high rate of fire.

"Now the area was being lit up by fires I associated with crashed aircraft. Just how many I cannot say. At the time I would have said ten although there may have been as few as five. Sticks of open parachutes started to appear in the illumination, including some that seemed headed into the flaming wreckage. A low bang then exploded beneath our ship, as if a 37mm or at least a 20mm antiaircraft round had struck. I felt a sharp pain at the right knee and a sudden loss of my ability to stand. As I fell to the floor, so did the entire stick. We had been battle damaged and were crashing, or so it seemed. The plane leveled out at 200 to 250 feet. Its speed was so high it was shaking and we may have reached 150 knots. The sprawled troopers untangled themselves and regained their feet, under the urging of the NCOs and by the help of medic John Vinski.

"I tried to use the rear bulkhead intercom to reach the pilot and order him to get into drop posture. The system didn't work. The crew chief was useless, or dead. He lay curled up against the bulkhead and didn't respond to prods and shouts. Knowing that the Bay of the Seine was coming up fast, and getting the stick out safely would be a near thing, I stepped to the door, salvoed the six parabundles, and shouted, 'Let's go!' I got out, followed quickly by O'Neil Boe, the company runner and the others.

"We seemed to exit the C-47 at treetop level. Our chutes opened so violently that any gear that was not fastened exceptionally firmly on our persons simply tore away and disappeared into the darkness. In my own case, almost every item not encompassed by the T5 Parachute assembly belly band, and the reserve parachute was gone. Anything in my jump pants pockets burst through the reinforced bottom seams. I lost K rations, canteen, spare magazines of carbine ammunition, three grenades, a folding-handle entrenching tool, and my musette bag along with its contents of a Hawkins mine [a British antitank weapon], toilet articles, spare socks, and underwear.

"Fortunately, we carried our individual firearms under the reserve chute, so I had my carbine with its inserted ten-round magazine on landing. The other items I still possessed were maps, escape kit, switchblade jump knife, first-aid packet, and the Gammon grenade. I also still had on the Mae West life vest that I gladly tossed away after I was down. I landed on a stony road about one-third mile south of the small village of St. Martin-de-Varreville. This, after oscillating wildly under my canopy and crashing to the earth on my knees. Stunned initially, I soon was able to check my injuries. I found I had a crushed right kneecap where a wound already existed from the antiaircraft round that hit our plane. I still had my chute on. It was tough to remove in the darkness. I thought it impossible for me to stand, so I wallowed around in a web of harness, canopy, and suspension lines on the road. Finally the reserve and belly band were off, the snaps unfastened, and I was free. More important, my automatic carbine was in hand, although with only one magazine. As I took inventory of the few items still with me, a series of low-flying aircraft passed over at very high speeds. Although these seemed to be ours, they were headed on many azimuths and probably lost.

"I wished them well but I had a problem of my own. The sky above was fairly light so anything higher than one's self tended to be visible in dim outline. The road was a sunken one, placing me in the darkness. A shadowy figure approached from the south. As he came up, I could make out his bayoneted rifle, as well as the shape of his coal scuttle helmet. By this time he was on the dike, or berm, on the east side of the road. Without any thought beyond, 'characteristically shaped helmet,' I thrust up on my good knee and shot him dead.

"There was nothing heroic about the act. We had an intensive series of classes on enemy equipment and the *Stahlhelm* [steel helmet] was easy to remember. My reaction was an example of useful training. Now, perhaps because the dead man was not alone, I had to get going and damn quick. Since there was no way of knowing where I was, any direction seemed as likely as another. By crawling over the dike, I got into a large field with a bunch of curious cows. By now I had found it possible to hobble along by keeping my right leg stiff and swinging it from the hip.

"I made slow progress for about fifty yards before I reached a dense hedgerow, through which it was impossible to pass. Now, with the first light breaking in the east and in considerable pain, I abandoned caution. I returned to the road leading north. Shortly, two Germans appeared immediately in front of me. Neither bore weapons or wore headgear and they seemed disoriented. Because I had only nine rounds left in my carbine, I decided to bluff them and capture them, if possible. About the only useful German phrase I remembered just then was *'Hände Hoch,'* had a magical effect. They turned in alarm, with hands raised. I don't know whether they or I were closer to wetting trousers. Certainly they didn't have the look of elite troops. It later turned out they were Russians who had been impressed into German service.

"When we moved forward we came to the outskirts of what I subsequently learned was St. Martin-de-Varreville. Now I was really scared. Some desultory fire was coming from several directions; I had no way of knowing the situation. I forced the Krauts to lie down in a ditch, which they were glad to do. I then hobbled forward to the edge of the village and met a group of privates from the 502d Parachute Infantry. They informed me that the rest of the built-up area was clear and they were checking out the last few houses. I was happy to turn my prisoners over to them. Then I slowly made my way through a typical Norman farm village with its stone structures and piles of manure. In one building was a battalion-level command post. I reported in."

Private Jim Kurz, as a member of B Company's 1st Platoon, 508th Parachute Infantry, said, "When the red light came on, we all stood and hooked up. Corporal Theis was the last man and I was right ahead of him. He turned around and I checked his chute and anchor line. Then I yelled, 'Fourteen o.k.!' He checked my chute and yelled, 'Thirteen o.k.!' I did the same for Wolfe's chute; he was twelve. As the plane broke out of the clouds, the call, 'One o.k.!' came. The green light went on. Lieutenant [Homer] Jones yelled we were over water. After a few seconds' delay, he shouted, 'Let's go!' All of the troopers left the plane. We had jumped at a very low altitude, maybe 300 to 350 feet. When my chute opened, I hit the trees and hung there. I got my knife

A rescue launch plucked from the water a sailor who jumped overboard from the shattered battleship *West Virginia*. (National Archives)

During the infamous Death March after the fall of Bataan, captives improvised litters for those unable to complete the hike to a prison camp. (National Archives)

The U.S. carrier *Yorktown* listed badly after being hit during the Battle of Midway. (National Archives)

Battle-weary and malaria plagued, leathernecks from the 1st Marine Division relaxed behind the lines on Guadalcanal while fresh forces relieved them. (National Archives)

P-40s flew off the deck of a carrier to support the ground forces in North Africa. (National Archives)

Working with a Sherman tank, infantrymen expanded the beachhead on Bougainville in the South Pacific. (National Archives)

Shattered palms and flame-thrower smoke marked a marine assault upon a sand-banked blockhouse on Tarawa. (National Archives)

Torpedo bombers from U.S. carriers ranged the skies over a Japanese armada in the South Pacific. (National Archives)

Near Italy's Rapido River, an antitank squad defended against an enemy counterattack. (National Archives)

Crewmen aboard the U.S. Coast Guard cutter *Spencer* watch a depth charge explode during a successful attack upon a German submarine, the U-175, which menaced a North Atlantic convoy. (National Archives)

During the bomb run of B-17s from the 94th Bomb Group over Berlin in May 1944, *Miss Donna Mae* drifted beneath another Fort as it released its 500-pounders. The camera in the aircraft dropping the ordnance captured the images.

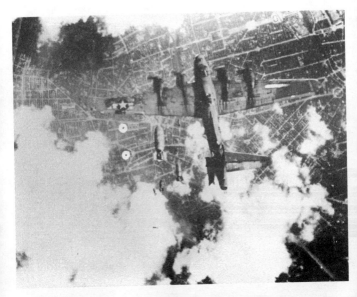

The doomed *Miss Donna Mae*, still level, has lost the elevator and the plane soon plunged to earth. There were no survivors. (Wilbur Richardson)

Half-drowned soldiers in the English Channel on D day were hauled on an inflatable raft to Omaha Beach. (National Archives)

In September 1944, U.S. infantrymen first broke through the formidable German defensive wall known as the Siegfried Line. (National Archives)

The aircraft carrier *Princeton* suffered a mortal blow from a suicide raider during the Battle of Leyte Gulf. (National Archives)

*Boyd's Boids*, a B-17, managed to stagger back to England before it crash landed and broke apart. (Dick Bowman)

Troops fought house to house to capture Cologne. (National Archives)

On Iwo Jima, marines crawled over the black volcanic ash deposited by Mt. Suribachi, whose summit overlooked them and provided a deadly observation post for the enemy. (National Archives)

The capture of the Remagen Bridge over the Rhine hastened the Allied advance into Germany. (National Archives)

Soldiers in an amphibious truck broached the last formidable natural defenses of Germany in March 1945 as they crossed the Rhine River. (National Archives)

Marine Corsair fighter planes operated from landing strips in the Philippines to provide ground support for army troops. (National Archives)

Flames threatened to explode a Navy Hellcat fighter aboard the carrier *Enterprise* after an errant antiaircraft shell aimed at a kamikaze sprayed the deck with hot shrapnel. (National Archives)

Struck by a kamikaze off Okinawa, the aircraft carrier *Bunker Hill* spewed fire and smoke as more than 350 men died and another 250 were injured. (National Archives)

out, cut my harness, and dropped to the ground. It was pitch black and I landed in a bunch of stickers. I had only been two feet off the ground.

"I started along the line of flight; planes were still flying overhead and you could see tracers going up to them. I heard a sound in front of me and ran into Private Wolfe. He had broken his leg. I told him I would return with a medic. When I reached the edge of the field against a hedgerow, I found Lieutenant Jones and part of the stick. The medic who jumped with us was there. We went back to Wolfe, who told us he had heard others nearby. We discovered Theis and one other man. All three had broken a leg. We put them in a hedgerow ditch and left them. The only reason I wasn't hurt was I had landed in the tree and been saved the shock of hitting the ground."

Sergeant Bud Warneke, mortar squad leader, said, "I looked around the hangar at the troopers of Company B who nineteen months ago were mostly recruits. Now they were ready to jump into combat as a family. I knew we were the best trained we could be and capable of beating the Germans in battle. Our morale was high. We had a meal fit for a king and then went blackface, using soot from the stoves in the kitchens. I waddled out to our plane. I had a Mae West in case we had to jump into the Channel. The reserve chute added extra weight and bulk but it would be useless because of the altitude we jumped at. My squad loaded into the plane with the company commander, Capt. Royal Taylor, who would be jumpmaster.

"A few minutes before takeoff, the battalion commander's runner came to the plane with a bicycle and cargo chute attached. He informed us that Colonel [Herbert F.] Batcheller wanted us to drop the cycle into Normandy so he would have transportation. We had our plate full of bundles but Captain Taylor said okay. As our plane joined the formation before crossing the Channel, I thought about what guys from the 505th had told us about what it would be like jumping into combat. I thought about where and how we were to assemble. I reminded myself of the sign and countersign, 'flash' and 'thunder,' and the cricket issued. [Although Gavin would insist no one in the 82d Airborne used the devices, Warneke's memory contradicted him.] I reminded Captain Taylor to release the pararack bundles under the C-47 when the green light came on. There wasn't much talking among the troops but a lot of smoking. All the men prone to air sickness had taken preventive pills.

"We reached the English Channel and Captain Taylor had the troops stand up and hook up. In case we were shot down we would have a chance to get out. In the middle of the Channel we looked out the door on a beautiful moonlit night at a sight no one will ever see again. Ships, so many ships, it looked as if you could walk from England to France without getting your feet wet. About this time, Captain Taylor or I asked what the hell are we going to do with the damn bicycle. Simultaneously, we kicked it into the Channel without hooking up its chute. Flying between the Jersey and Guernsey islands we could see the German antiaircraft gun flashes. The flight was in good formation until we reached the coast of Normandy where we ran into a thick fog. The formation broke all to hell. It seemed as if they speeded up. We were now under heavy German fire; it seemed as if we were engulfed in red and green tracers. Now, I was scared.

"The red light came on. Captain Taylor was standing in the door and said something like, 'I don't know where the hell we are.' The green light came on, he jumped and I bailed out right behind him. It took only a second to realize somebody was mad at us. It seemed unbelievable that I would live through this night. We had jumped at 400 feet or less because it could not have been more than thirty seconds before I'd gone through an apple tree. My canopy had draped around and caught the top. My feet barely touched the ground for the easiest landing I ever had. Using my jump knife, I cut myself out of my harness.

"Using the sign, countersign, and cricket, the first trooper I found was Captain Taylor. He was lying in a ditch beside a hedgerow and injured from the jump. I saw one of our bundles about fifty yards away and wanted to recover it. Taylor told me to forget it because it was covered by German machine-gun fire. Taylor instructed me to roll up the stick, then find Lieutenant Jones and tell him he was now acting company commander. It tells you something about Jones when you realize he was not the senior lieutenant under Taylor.

"I oriented myself by the aircraft still flying overhead, which gave the direction our troops should land. It was about 0230 when I started moving in and around the hedgerows. (We had not been briefed on finding hedgerows as thick or high as these.) In about an hour I found most of my stick and by luck stumbled upon Lieutenant Jones and our exec officer with about half of B Company. We realized we had jumped several kilometers from our drop zone and our objective.

"We waited and searched for others until Lieutenant Jones said it was time to go. He organized us into two platoons. He designated me as one platoon leader. Lieutenant Jones had us ground our heavy musette bags so we could travel faster—I never saw it again—on our way to our objective, the causeway at the Merderet River. On the way, I saw troopers in trees, shot while still in their harnesses. It was dog-eat-dog, and anger for the Germans turned into hate.

There were American and German dead everywhere you looked."

"The three planes with my platoon," said Lt. Homer Jones of B Company, of the 508th, "had managed to stay together. In fact, when we came through a break in the clouds over Normandy, they almost ran into one another. After I got out of my chute on the ground it was surprisingly quiet. We used the recognition signals of 'flash' and 'thunder.' Later, though, one of my guys told me he heard someone running toward him and called out 'Flash' and the other trooper answered, 'Flash, my ass. They're right behind me.'" After his superior, Royal Taylor, assigned command to him, Jones headed his roughly seventy men in the direction of the Merderet Causeway.

Paratrooper Bill Dean said, "It was past 3:00 A.M. when we got to the la Fière Causeway, leading to one of the two bridges over the Merderet. Here, the rigors of the preceding day and night made us first sit down and not long after, lay down in a ditch and go to sleep. After a two-hour fitful doze, we were joined by Lt. Homer Jones, who was leading another small group of B Company men. Lieutenant Jones had met our regimental commander, Colonel Lindquist, who ordered him to attack and take the la Fière Manoir, a group of strongly defended buildings that guarded the approach to the road and bridge over the river."

Battalion surgeon Dave Thomas, still smarting from indifferent success at the poker table, enjoyed a brief moment of optimism in the sky. "In the nice bright moonlight, as far as I could see behind me were echelon upon echelon of C-47s, each filled with a bunch of troopers. I thought, boy, this is going to be a piece of cake. We are really organized. We turned to the coast and hit a cloudbank. When we came out of it, the airplane I was in was the only one I could see in the sky. When the flight hit those clouds they just split up like a bunch of ducks being shot at.

"Trying to find out where we were, I kept looking down and finally I saw a stream. I was jumping number two, behind the battalion commander, Colonel [Henry] Harrison, and I said, 'That has to be the Merderet. Let's get the hell out of here.' We jumped and I landed in a field. As I got out of my chute, I saw something white. I crept up to it, a cow chewing its cud. The first guy I ran into was Bill Ekman who'd been the exec in the 508th but when Gavin was promoted to a brigadier they made Ekman CO of the 505th [the regiment of Bill Dunfee]. Ekman wanted me to come with him and one of his battalions that was moving on Ste.-Mère-Eglise. I said no, I would follow the railroad line, which was west of where I came down near Beuzeville-la-Bastille. I picked up about nine or ten troopers and then bumped into a group with Colonel Harrison and a red-headed major from the 507 with thirty or forty men. Soon, we were fighting on the edge of the Merderet, which was flooded, and on our other three sides were hedgerows. These guys had been kicking a little ass before I got there because they had a lot of German prisoners. But there was no place for us to go and the enemy was all around.

"We took positions manning the ditches and hedgerows and threw the captured Krauts some entrenching tools. We told them to get out in the orchard and dig in. They had the dirt flying soon. I had one patient, a trooper in a ditch with his leg almost blown off, except for his patella tendon. I had very little to work with, a small kit, a few instruments, a bit of morphine but no way to anesthetize him. I said, 'Son, it's like the days in the Wild West. You're going to have to bite the bullet and I am going to have to separate the leg.' I cut the patella tendon and put a dressing on it. He never whimpered. We put the wounded in a little farmhouse. There wasn't much we could do for them. We didn't have a one of our equipment bundles, only what we carried."

Like their subordinates, Generals Maxwell Taylor and Matthew Ridgway plunged into a miasma of confusion far from their objectives. Taylor said, "I dropped halfway between Ste.-Marie-du-Mont and Vierville, just west of the highway connecting the two villages. I landed alone in a field surrounded by the usual high hedges and trees with a few cows as witnesses. The rest of my stick went into an adjacent field and it took me about twenty minutes to find anyone. The area into which I wandered was covered with field fortifications, newly constructed but fortunately I encountered no Germans. Gradually, I picked up a few men of the 501st and later contacted General McAuliffe, who had a group of artillery personnel with him.

"Still under the cover of darkness, we worked our way eastward for about a quarter of a mile and finally halted in an enclosed field where we began to gather stragglers. It was here that I first ran into Colonel [Julian] Ewell [CO of the 3d Battalion, 501st Parachute Regiment]. We outposted the field and sent out patrols in all directions. They, however, learned very little in the darkness and were driven back by enemy fire that seemed to be on all sides. Colonel [Gerald] Higgins [Taylor's chief of staff] soon turned up with Lieutenant Colonel Pappas the division engineer." The concentration of big brass and the paltry number of enlisted men caused Taylor to remark, "Never in the history of military operations have so few been commanded by so many."

Matthew Ridgway landed in a pasture bordered by the ubiquitous hedgerows. "I felt a great exhilaration at being here alone in the dark on this greatest of adventures." After challenging a shape in the dark that proved to be a cow,

Ridgway spotted another figure. "We had these little crickets and I had one in my hand but I didn't use it. I used the challenge of 'flash.' " The respondent was company commander Willard Follmer, by some lottery-size long shot, the same man Ridgway first encountered in Sicily. Ridgway was no lucky talisman for Follmer, however, for the captain had fractured his right ankle in Sicily and now in Normandy he broke his right hip.

Ridgway was in no better position than Taylor or Gavin to exercise true command and control. Instead of conducting precise well-planned maneuvers, the troopers initially performed like gangs of desperadoes, buccaneering through the countryside. The dispersion of the airdrop sowed great confusion among the enemy as the invaders seemed all over the place and difficult to pin down. During the darkness the parachutists ravaged communications by blowing telephone wires, to add to the disorder among the Germans. The defenders themselves had also lost much of their command and control, particularly because Erwin Rommel was back in Germany on a joint venture to visit his family and plead with the Führer for more resources.

For those coming to Normandy by glider, conditions were at least as chaotic. At 12:19 A.M., pilots of the tow planes at Aldermaston Air Base throttled up and the gliderborne troops began their trip toward Normandy. "Lieutenant Colonel Mike Murphy was in the lead glider to my immediate left," remembered Vic Warriner, "and to my right in the four-ship echelon was Capt. Jack Willoughby, CO of the 434th Group. The takeoff was uneventful except for the fact it seemed to take much longer than normal for Murphy's glider to become airborne." Warriner, at the time, knew nothing of the installation of heavy metal plates in Murphy's glider. These were to protect his passenger, General Pratt, and seriously compromised its flight dynamics.

"Our takeoff," continued Warriner, "was smooth and we quickly pulled into formation on the leader's wing. My copilot was Robert (Bob) V. Kaufman. He was more than qualified to pilot a glider himself but agreed to sacrifice that spot so that we would be assured of having a competent replacement if something happened to me. My glider was important because we carried part of a top medical team from the 101st Airborne who would immediately set up a field hospital upon landing. Captains Charles O. Van Gorder and Albert J. Crandall, and several medical technicians were in my glider. In addition we carried a two-wheeled trailer loaded with medical supplies that was to be towed by the jeep carried in General Pratt's ship.

"The flight proceeded as envisioned but the night was so dark, we never knew when we left England and headed southwest, out to sea. The weather wasn't really that bad but occasionally rain would splatter against the plexiglass windshield. Bob and I alternated flying for it was rather a long haul for one pilot, considering the stress. [Contrary to some published accounts, none of the gliders invading Normandy lacked a qualified copilot.] We knew when we made the rendezvous with the submarine stationed in the Channel for we made a ninety-degree left turn to head east-southeast toward the coast of France. And sometime later we made another slight turn to the left that lined us up directly with the Normandy area. From this point on, the trip became much more exciting. As we approached land we could see several fires burning that we thought had been ignited by the pathfinder crews for the paratroops. Wrong! They were bonfires built on top of flak towers by the Germans to help them stay warm on a chilly night. We encountered heavy machine-gun fire but it was mostly inaccurate and caused very little deviation in our planned route. At one time I thought we had been hit, for the controls suddenly were very stiff and unresponsive. I glanced at Bob and he was flying the glider, too. He grinned sheepishly and let go of the wheel.

"When we were at about 500 feet, the light in the dome of the tow plane signaled for us to release. I could see the one from the plane towing Mike Murphy flash at the same time. Even though it was still dark, there was enough light for me to see Murphy release and immediately turn left in a steep climb, using the velocity of the tow to gain enough altitude. He disappeared into the black sky. His actions puzzled me for during all our training and briefing it was stressed that we were to maintain level flight when released until the glider slowed enough to reach its normal gliding speed.

"With Bob calling out the speed and altitude, we descended into darkness. Finally, we could see the vague outline of a row of trees and I put the glider into a slip to kill off excess altitude. We actually brushed the tops of the trees as we went in. We touched down almost immediately and I put the glider up on its skis and applied full brakes. It seemed that instead of slowing down, we were gaining speed. As we hurtled through a herd of terrorized dairy cattle, I could see through the darkness the end of the field coming fast. Luckily, we slowed up enough so the crash was only minimal. We hit a large poplar tree on my side of the cockpit and only hard enough for me to end up with my chin against the trunk of the tree.

"Even before the plexiglass stopped falling, Captain Van Gorder asked if everyone was okay. We were, and all I got was skinned knees from the bark of the poplar. We had been on the ground for an interval of perhaps only fifteen seconds when we heard a tremendous crash close to our left side as a glider smashed into another huge poplar at deadly speed. The impact actually shook the ground. At the very same moment, we spotted the blackout lights of vehicles traveling along a little dirt road just beyond the nose of our glider. We knew they were Germans for the briefing had stressed that no Allied vehicles would move before dawn. The convoy of three vehicles halted by the glider that had crashed next to us. A couple of soldiers emerged and entered what remained of the glider. We could see their flashlight beams as they poked around the wreckage. Soon they left in their vehicles and disappeared down the road.

"Van Gorder said he was going to the smashed glider to see if he could help anyone, although he doubted anyone could have lived through such a crash. He had no more than stated his intentions when we heard another glider thump down in the field and rumble toward us. As it got close we noticed it was up on its skids and gradually slowing down. I then realized that the field we picked sloped downhill severely and was covered in lush, wet pasture grass. The incoming ship hit the tail of our glider, but with little speed, did minimum damage and injured no one. Meanwhile, Captain Van Gorder ran toward the stricken glider.

"The rest of us started to pull away the latest arrival from our tail so we could move it away from the tree and perhaps raise the nose to get the medical supplies out. Our efforts were to no avail. Van Gorder returned and told us it was Mike Murphy's glider. Two of the people aboard, General Pratt and copilot Butler, were dead. Murphy was seriously injured and Van Gorder doubted he would survive. Only General Pratt's aide came through relatively uninjured." Pratt died, apparently of a broken neck, either from the impact of the glider against the tree or as a result of his jeep shifting forward to crush him.

"I learned later," said Warriner, "about the sheet iron on the cargo compartment floor. It completely upset the balance of the glider and constituted a gross overload. And that's why he used so much runway to get airborne. Years afterward, Murphy told Van Gorder, 'It was like trying to fly a freight train.' He hit the landing field like a meteor. Combine that with the downhill slope of a wet, grassy field and they had no chance of avoiding a crash. It's a wonder anyone survived. Murphy never complained publicly about a disaster for which he was not to blame. Ironically, the measures Pratt's staff took to guarantee his safety actually killed him."

In the dark pasture Warriner and the other able-bodied crews pitched in to unload their cargo. "After that we were on our own and took off trying to establish contact with the rest of our glider pilots. We had all been issued the clickers. The whole Normandy peninsula that night sounded as if it had been hit by the greatest cricket infestation in history. And it wasn't unusual to hear someone shout in the eerie darkness, 'Don't shoot! I lost my Goddamn clicker!' "

At the moment of D day, still the youngest man to earn his glider pilot wings, Pete Buckley flew Glider 49 in the same Glider Serial (52 CG 4As altogether) as Warriner. "Thirty minutes before takeoff the engines of the tow ships started up. The muffled noise and throbbing from their motors spread around the field like a distant, approaching thunderstorm, and contributed to our uneasiness. We all climbed aboard trying not to show our true feelings. My own were that in roughly three and a half hours I might be dead. It was a very sobering moment and I wondered why I had been so foolish as to volunteer for this job. When I first went into the glider program, nobody had ever explained to me how gliders were going to be used.

"My copilot was F/O Bill Bruner. Our passengers were

Pfc. Paul Nagelbush, Pfc. Stanley Milewiski, and Pfc. Russel Kamp, antitank crewmen from the 101st Airborne. The cargo included their 57mm antitank gun, ammunition, entrenching tools, a camouflage net, rations, and some supplies. Our tow ship gunned its engines and started down the runway through a light rain shower and into the black of night. As the wheels of the glider left the ground, someone in the back yelled, 'Look out, Hitler, here we come!' This helped break the ice for a moment, after which no one said a word as I trimmed the glider for the long flight ahead.

"For the next three and one-half hours, we would be alone with our thoughts and fears. It wasn't too bad for me because I was busy flying the glider. But the airborne men in back and Bill Bruner, with nothing to do, must have been going through hell with their thoughts. We settled into position behind the C-47, keeping the faint blue formation lights on the top of the plane centered up in line between the glow from the tow plane's engines' flame dampeners. The longer you stare at them, the more your eyes start playing tricks. I turned the controls over to Bruner occasionally so I could look away and refocus my eyes again. An added problem was the extreme turbulence from the prop wash of the forty-eight planes ahead of us.

"Shortly after we crossed the coast of France, small-arms fire and heavier flak started coming up at the planes in the front of the formation, These intensified as we came closer to our landing zone. It looked like fluid streams of tracers zigzagging and hosing across the sky, mixed in with heavier explosions of flak. You wondered how anything could fly through that and come out in one piece. After the lead ships had passed over the Kraut positions and woke them all up, we at the tail end of the line began to be hit by a heavier volume of small arms fire, which, when it went through our glider, sounded like corn popping, or typewriter keys banging on loose paper.

"I tried to pull my head down into my chest to make myself as small as possible. I tucked my elbows in close to my body, pulled my knees together to protect vital parts of my manhood and even was tempted to take my feet off the rudder pedals so they wouldn't stick out so far. I really started to sweat it out. A few minutes after crossing the coast, and before we reached the glider-release point near Hiesville, the group plunged into some low-lying clouds and fog banks. All the planes started to spread out to avoid collisions. This caused many of us to land wide, short, or beyond our objective when we got to the cutoff point. In a very short time, too soon for me, the moment I dreaded arrived. The green light came on in the astrodome of the tow plane, indicating we were over the LZ and it was time to release. At this moment, I had a very strong urge not to cut loose. I'm sure I wasn't the only one who felt this way on that night. It was dark; everything but the kitchen sink was coming up at us from the Germans below, and that tow rope, as long as it was hooked up, was my umbilical cord. The steady pull signified safety, and a nice ride back to England out of this mess, if I hung on. I quickly put this thought out of my mind and waited about ten seconds before I released the tow rope.

"As soon as the rope disconnected from our glider, I made a 360-degree turn to the left, feeling my way down through the darkness. I held the glider as close to stall speed as I could. It is almost impossible to describe my feelings. I knew the ground was down there but I couldn't see it. I didn't know if I was going to hit trees, ditches, barns, houses, or what. And all the time, the flak and tracers are still coming up. The only thing for sure was that Krauts were shooting at me and they were going to be right there, waiting for me when I climbed out of the glider. They say fear has no bounds and at this point in my life, I was in full agreement.

"Finally, out of the corner of my eye, I noticed a faint light patch that looked like an open field, outlined by trees. By this time we were so low that we had no choice in the matter. There would be no chance for a go-around. With a prayer on my lips, and a very tight pucker string, I straightened out my glide path and headed in, while Bruner held on full spoilers. We flared out for a landing, just above stalling speed and touched down smooth as glass. How lucky can you get.

"Just as we thought we had it made, there was a tremendous, bone-jarring crash. We hit one of those damn ditches that the Germans had dug across the fields. This ditch was ten to twelve feet across, five to six feet deep, with water at the bottom. The main purpose was to prevent gliders from landing in one piece and it sure worked with us. We plunged down into the ditch and when the nose slammed into the other side, the glider's back broke as it slid up over the opposite bank. The floor split open and we skidded to a halt in the field on the other side. For a split second we sat in stunned silence and then I breathed a sigh of relief because none of us seemed injured. We bailed out fast because there was rifle and machine-gun fire going off in the fields around us. Fortunately, none seemed aimed at our area at the moment. It took us almost thirty minutes to dig the nose of the glider out of the dirt so we could open it up and roll out the .57mm antitank gun. Midway through this task, the Germans set off a flare right over our heads. Lo and behold, we saw Glider Number 50, piloted by F/Os Calvani and Ryan, on the other side of the ditch without a scratch on it. They were carrying the jeep to tow our antitank gun.

"You're supposed to trust the tow pilot but I did hesitate and it was a good thing, because I still landed about half a mile short of the LZ. If I had let go at the first signal from the tow plane, I would have come down in the swampy area that the Germans had flooded, where many paratroopers and glidermen drowned in the dark."

Transport pilot Tom Poston noted, "We dropped paratroopers, went home, refueled, got the gliders hooked on, went back, and dropped them. It was extremely ill advised. The hedgerows there are very tall and the fields are not all that big. So the poor bastards in the gliders get released and here they are looking at a little patch, surrounded by these high hedgerows. It was a disaster. We had guys come back—Creasy, I think his name was, a glider pilot. He hung upside down in a glider that flipped over, with everybody in it dead as a doornail and the Krauts were checking. He was hanging upside down pretending to be dead. After the Germans left, he crawled under the glider [until] the Americans took that piece of earth."

# 10

# Daylight at Omaha Beach

FOR ALL OF THE SOUND AND FURY OF THE NIGHT, THE ENEMY still seemed uncertain whether this was to be a full-scale invasion and where it would take place. The landings were scheduled for "nautical dawn," an astronomical designation based on the position of the sun when it is two and one-half degrees below the horizon. With double daylight saving in effect, the first faint streaks of light appeared at 3:00 A.M. But those ashore could not have seen the vast fleet more than nine miles away nor could those on board pick out the coastline. Admiral Alan Kirk, the U.S. fleet commander, said his ships opened up at 6:00 A.M., but those vessels hitting the British beaches commenced firing as much as half an hour earlier. By the time the first shells from the naval guns crashed down among the German installations, the landing craft packed with the first waves for the forty miles of beaches had rendezvoused at sea and started for the shore.

At about the same hour, the huge armada of U.S. and British warplanes began opening bomb bay doors to unload their explosive cargoes. But a thick overcast hung over the ground, obscuring targets. Fearful of another deadly deluge of friendly fire from the planes working at high altitudes, the U.S. Eighth Air Force obtained permission from Eisenhower to ensure they did not hit the GIs. Aiming at Omaha Beach, 329 B-24 heavy bombers dumped 13,000 bombs, all of which missed both the beach and the enemy defenses behind it. Tons of high explosives fell as much as three miles inland. At Utah Beach, medium bombers relying on visual sightings achieved only slightly better results. Prior to D day, however, Pointe du Hoc, where the intelligence experts believed the German artillery threatened both the fleet and the beaches, had been visited several times by bombers. Because concentrated efforts might tip the Nazis to the area chosen for Overlord, these attacks were infrequent and more in hopes of delaying full operation of the battery rather than destroying it. The Ranger assignment to climb and conquer Pointe du Hoc's defenders was accepted with confidence by Rudder, but a high-level officer in Overlord planning declared, "Three old women with brooms could knock the Rangers off the cliff."

Those committed to the attack reacted with resolution and anxiety. Medic Frank South with the 2d Ranger Battalion had entered a marshaling yard near Dorchester. "There was an intelligence tent set up with a detailed sand model of the Pointe du Hoc cliff and the objectives down to gun emplacements, bunkers, tunnel works, and minefields. Stereoscopic slides gave us pictures in 3-D. Each of the noncoms was instructed to copy the layout of Pointe du Hoc on cigarette papers that could be destroyed easily or swallowed if necessary. At sea," said South, "I did not go through any religious preparation, but I did repeatedly go over the plans and where every item of equipment or supply was in the huge pack I had. I compulsively and repeatedly inspected and cleaned the .45 Colt automatic I buried in the pack, and I sharpened my knife. All the while I chatted with the Combined Operations medic with whom I stayed in the ship's surgery during the night.

"Most of the men and noncoms remained quite sober, reviewing their mission and checking their arms on board the ship. Some did a bit of gambling. Morale was high and most of us felt confident in our abilities and those of our comrades. There was one exception. Our recently appointed battalion commander had been drinking a bit too much. He either originated or supported the opinion that the assault group of the 2d Rangers was being sent on a suicide mission and that there was no chance we would survive. Communicating this sort of notion would have been devastating. Word of the problem was sent to Rudder on a nearby ship. He immediately transferred to our *Ben Machree* and assumed direct command of the Pointe du Hoc operation."

Ranger Sergeant Jack Kuhn, who had experimented with the machine gun mounted atop a firefighter's ladder, was aboard HMS *Amsterdam*. "I could not envision myself going into combat. It seemed so detached from me, as if it were happening to someone else. The one thing I feared was not being able to face the test. I didn't want to coward out. Then everyone else said the same thing, and I was okay. I never had the apprehension that I would be killed or wounded. As tension mounted, Tom Ruggiero, who had studied acting, and I decided that a skit was needed. We had put on short, crazy ones as gags during training, and with Bill Hoffman and Bob Fruhling we put on a show and it helped. Sometime after, when I got into my bunk, I lay there and listened to my men talking. They all expressed anxiety at not being able to face the unexpected, and were fearful of running."

"I was never seasick," said Len Lomell. "But after a couple of days on the ship, I was getting a bit stir crazy. I am a Protestant but wasn't particularly religious. I never saw anybody praying. We had so much to think about in performing our job; there didn't seem to be time for prayer. I had a good relationship with Father Joe Lacy, the Catholic chaplain assigned to the Rangers. I made everyone in D Company [2d Ranger Battalion] attend services, usually. Late on the eve of D day, I was in a hot poker game in the mess hall when someone announced a midnight mass by Lacy. Here I was with a good hand and I figured I'm entitled to a few more minutes, so I said I'm staying. Three of the eight guys at the table got up and went. The next morning, all of them died."

Battalion surgeon Walter Block told his diary: "This is the last entry to be written before D day. If something happens to me, see that my wife Mrs. Alice Block gets this book. Kiddo—I love you."

Now as dawn crept over the coast and the 2d Ranger Battalion bounced in the choppy Channel seas, a more sustained fury broke over Pointe du Hoc. Naval salvos and aerial ordnance pelted the target. The barrage was to begin twenty minutes before H hour, at 06:30, and end with the arrival on Beach Charley of the 2d Ranger Battalion. Naval guns would remain available for support through communications from a shore fire-control party accompanying the Rangers.

The 2d and 5th Ranger Battalions acted under the overall command of Rudder with Lt. Col. Max Schneider serving as his deputy. From his 2d Battalion, Rudder deployed boats bearing men from E and F Companies for landings on the eastern or left side of the precipice while D Company struck from the other direction. The plan for the Rangers envisioned that if Rudder and his group scaled Pointe du Hoc successfully, they would advise the 5th Ranger Battalion and Companies A and B of the 2d Battalion still in their landing craft, by means of colored rockets or a radio message. Max Schneider's outfit would then follow Rudder's people up the cliff and pass through inland. If that assault on Pointe du Hoc failed, Schneider would head his men toward Dog Green Beach with the aim of breaking through the Vierville-sur-Mer coast exit at that point.

"We put on a show of confidence boarding our assault crafts, ready to be lowered into the water," says D Company's Jack Kuhn, who had turned over his fire-department ladder job to another Ranger. "We tried to impress the British sailors with our seeming disregard for what was coming. They kept calling out, 'Give them what for, Yanks.' Our departure from the *Amsterdam* went smoothly. But the moment we hit the water it was apparent this was to be a most hazardous trip. The seas were high and rough. The swells were big and the winds shipped the water into massive rollers, tossing our crafts severely. These were the smallest boats I had ever seen used. When you stood up, the upper part of your body was exposed to the enemy and the elements. There was very little room in the heavily loaded craft. Men who had never suffered seasickness did that day."

The boats were roughly twelve feet wide, thirty feet long, with seating along the sides. In the middle sat the boat team leader, a second in command, and a radio man. D Company traveled on three craft; one commanded by Duke Slater, a second under Lt. George Kerchner, and the third led by 1st Sgt. Len Lomell. Said Kuhn, "Almost as soon as we left the mother ship, the men became apprehensive about the boats sinking. First Sergeant Len Lomell and I, at the rear of the boat, discussed this possibility. Well aware that we were already shipping water, we instructed the men to start bailing, using their helmets. Nobody had much, if any, sleep the night before. The guys were sick, cold, and turned apathetic. Lomell and I verbally forced them to keep bailing water. Captain Slater's boat was very low in the water, in danger of foundering. It was losing speed and dropping back from the formation.

"As soon as I mentioned it to Len, we saw the boat start to go down. We didn't want our men to see it so we pretended to spot the Pointe and told them to keep watch. I don't know if anyone else was aware that the Duke was now out of the invasion. I wondered whether we should try to rescue him but the time lost would have made us late. Len and I agreed the mission came first. It was his decision to make and personally I felt I was deserting our commander. We spotted our fighter planes overhead and saw the navy ships blasting the shoreline and inland. We saw the rockets projected. We had never seen these before. I realized now that we were taking part in the greatest battle in history and felt proud to be in it. As we got closer, it became my job to arm all six rockets that would carry our ropes up the cliff. When I armed them I saw that everything was underwater or very damp from being exposed. I doubted they would fire at all.

"Still trying to see Pointe du Hoc, I noticed the boat was taking on less water and realized we must be much closer to the shore. The swells subsided slightly. When I armed the rockets, I had leaned my Thompson submachine gun against the bulkhead. Now I couldn't find it. I yelled to Sheldon Bare, a young man from my hometown, who was bailing water, if he could find it. Bare groped around in the knee-deep water of the boat, found my weapon, and handed it to me. I fired into the air and it worked fine. Later in the day,

Sheldon Bare would suffer a bullet wound in the neck, then returned to the company only to be hit again. About this time, we spotted a cliff jutting out into the Channel and it looked just like the pictures of Pointe Du Hoc. But the lead boat turned right and started a course parallel to the cliff and the shoreline. We surmised we had come toward the wrong site—Pointe et Raz de la Percée [a good three miles east]."

Rudder, in the lead landing craft, discovered the error and directed the flotilla toward Pointe du Hoc. But the assault was behind schedule. Instead of the Rangers being the first to strike the Normandy coast, that dubious honor fell to Sid Salomon leading Company C of the 2d Ranger Battalion and the 116th Infantry of the 29th Division, targeted for Dog Green Beach and the promontory mistaken by the helmsman for Pointe du Hoc. "When we boarded the *Prince Charles*," said Salomon, "Colonel Rudder shook hands with company commander Ralph Goranson, the other platoon leader, Lt. Bill Moody, and myself. Rudder said, 'You've got the most dangerous mission.' There had been detailed planning. We looked at postcards, travel material on what was a resort area. We had sand tables. But we never met with anyone from the 29th [Division] to go over the mission.

"In all our training, we had never gotten on a landing craft with all of the weapons, ammo, food, and other supplies required for the actual invasion. Suddenly, we found ourselves so jammed in that I couldn't sit down. I stood behind the steel doors in the bow. Our two landing craft looked forlorn and lonesome as they splashed forward toward the shoreline. I was looking ahead when suddenly I heard pings on the side of the boat. It was machine-gun fire from the shore. There were splashes around the craft, whitewater cascades, then concentric circles as shells landed in our vicinity. I saw a barge with rockets. They made a tremendous amount of noise, a huge whoosh and then the shells burst like fireworks. But every one fell short, splashing down right at the water's edge. I saw no flashes erupting on the cliffs."

Salomon continued. "The British sub-leftenant nodded to his helmsman, who opened the throttle a notch. The intensity of the pings against the outside of the steel hull increased. Everyone kept his head down. When the words 'Get ready' were passed, everyone inched forward a little. All were tense. The sub-leftenant had his hands on the ropes that would release the catch for the steel ramp. 'Now!' he called out, and the ramp flopped down into the water. I immediately jumped off the landing craft, the men following one to the right, the next left. I knew [the] first [person] off was the safest since the guys aiming didn't know when the ramp would go down and it takes a second or two before they squeeze off a shot. My section sergeant, Oliver Reed, right behind me, was hit in the stomach. I was in water up to my chest and I pulled Reed out from under the ramp to keep him from being crushed.

"I told Reed, 'You've got to go on your own from here.' I was running across the sand, with the mortar section behind me, when a mortar shell exploded. It wiped out those around me, killing or wounding them. Some pieces of shrapnel hit me in the back and knocked me flat. I thought I was finished. My platoon sergeant ran up to me. I was about to turn over my maps to him when bullets kicked up sand in my face. I jumped up and ran to the base of the cliff, which gave some cover against the machine guns.

"In the shelter there, I took off my shirt and jacket. An aidman sprinkled on sulfa powder and said, 'That's all I can do now, Lieutenant.' So we started up Pointe et Raz de la Percée. The Germans threw grenades down while the Rangers returned small-arms fire. First, two men inched up, using ropes, hand- and footholds. Then another pair followed them, while the men at the bottom continued firing at the top, taking off some of the pressure and direct attacks on the climbers."

Turning his gaze to the beach for a moment, Salomon beheld bodies strewn about, blood in the sand. He saw some wounded crawling toward shelter with looks of despair upon their faces. Others who tried to get back on their feet went down again from enemy bullets. At the water's edge, bodies rolled back and forth in the ebb and flow of the Channel.

The second boat, with Goranson, Moody, and the remainder of C Company, took a direct hit in the bow as it reached the beach. A number of Rangers were killed or wounded from the blast but the two officers at the rear of the craft remained sound. Observing the carnage and the enormous casualties among C Company, Salomon thought the invasion had failed. The still able-bodied Rangers, including Salomon, Moody, and Goranson, mounted to the top, joining the remnants of C Company. Salomon counted nine men from the thirty-nine packed aboard the landing craft only minutes earlier. Nevertheless, the Rangers doggedly advanced. Moody led an assault that cleaned out a battered stone building housing some enemy gunners. In a shell hole, Salomon and Moody met to determine their next moves. "We were shoulder to shoulder," says Salomon, "I was pointing toward a series of trenches when suddenly he rolled to one side, a bullet struck him directly between his eyes. I told Ralph [Goranson] I was going ahead. Stooping down and with two men, I walked through a series of trenches. We worked our way to a dugout. A white-phosphorus grenade was tossed in and when the Germans came out, the Rangers turned their Tommy gun and rifles on them. Farther down the line we silenced a mortar crew. Then we withdrew back to the rest of the platoon. C Company now held Pointe et Raz de la Percée."

The choreography for conquest of Omaha Beach called upon the 1st and 29th Infantry Divisions, including amphibious tanks, and with the aid of the Rangers companies, to head for the shore at H hour, 6:30 A.M. The naval and aerial barrage on the defenders would blast off forty minutes before. The parade toward the 7,000-yard-long, crescent-shaped strand was to be led by amphibious tanks, followed by more armor to be put shore from landing craft, and then the first 1,450 infantrymen. Those first soldiers were expected to provide adequate protection for demolition task forces assigned to clear and mark lanes for the main body of troops to be ferried onto the beach.

Bob Slaughter of the 29th Division, with his fellow GIs from the 116th Regiment, heard the steady drone of bombers in the darkness overhead. "We saw bomb explosions causing fires that illuminated clouds in the dark sky. We were twelve miles offshore as we climbed into our seat assignments on the LCAs [Landing Craft Assault] and were lowered into the heavy sea by davits. The Navy hadn't begun its firing because it was still dark. We couldn't see the armada because of the dark but we knew it was there.

"Prior to loading, friends said their so-longs and good lucks. I remember finding Sgt. Jack Ingram, an old friend from Roanoke. He had suffered a back injury and I asked him how he felt. 'I'm okay. Good luck, I'll see you on the beach.' Another Roanoker, a neighbor and classmate, George D. Johnson, who'd joined the army with me, asked, 'Are your men ready?' I couldn't imagine why he asked me but I answered yes. Sergeant Robert Bixler of Shamokin, Pennsylvania, joked, 'I'm going to land with a comb in one hand,' running his hand through his blond hair, 'and a pass to Paris in the other.' The feeling among most of the men was that the landing would be a 'walk-in affair' but later we could expect a stiff counterattack. That didn't worry us too much because by then the tanks, heavy artillery, and air support should bolster our defense until the beachhead grew strong enough for a breakout."

"All of us had a letter signed by the supreme commander, General Eisenhower, saying that we were about to embark upon a great crusade, etc. A few of my cohorts autographed it and I carried it in my wallet throughout the war. The message was also read over loudspeakers. "We loaded into our assigned stations on the landing craft and were lowered by davits. The Channel was extremely rough and it wasn't long before we had to help the craft's pumps by bailing with our helmets. The cold spray blew in and soon we were soaking wet. I used a gas cape [a plastic sack for protection against skin irritants] as shelter. Lack of oxygen under the sack brought seasickness.

"As the sky lightened, the armada became visible. The smoking and burning French shoreline also became more defined. At 0600, the huge guns of the Allied navies opened up with what must have been one of the greatest artillery barrages ever. The diesels on board our craft failed to muffle the tornadic blasting. I could see the *Texas* firing broadside into the coastline. Boom-ba-ba-boom-ba-ba-boom! Boom-ba-ba-boom-ba-ba-boom! Within minutes giant swells from the recoil of those guns nearly swamped us and added to the seasickness and misery. But one could actually see 2,000-pound missiles tumbling on targets. Twin-fuselaged P-38 fighter bombers were also overhead protecting us from the *Luftwaffe* and giving us a false sense of security. This should be a piece of cake.

"A few thousand yards from shore we rescued three or

four survivors from a craft that had been swamped and sunk. Other men were left in the water bobbing in their Mae Wests, because we did not have room for them. About 200–300 yards from shore we encountered artillery fire. Near misses sent water skyward and then it rained back on us. The British coxswain said he had to lower the ramp and for us to quickly disembark. Back in Weymouth these sailors bragged they had been on several invasions and we were in capable hands. I heard Sgt. Willard Norfleet say, 'These men have heavy equipment, you *will* take them all the way in.'

"The coxswain pleaded, 'But we'll all be killed!' Norfleet unholstered his .45 Colt, put it to the sailor's head and ordered, '*All the way in!*' The craft kept going, plowing through the choppy water, until the bow scraped the sandy bottom. I thought, if this boat doesn't hurry and get us in, I'll die from seasickness. I had given my puke bag to a buddy who already had filled his. Minus the paper bag, I used my steel helmet.

"About 150 yards from shore, I raised my head despite the warning, 'Keep your head down.' I saw the boat on our right taking a terrific licking from small arms. Tracer bullets were bouncing and skipping off the ramp and sides as the enemy zeroed in on the boat that had beached a few minutes before us. Had we not delayed a few minutes to pick up the survivors of the sunken craft, we might have taken that concentration of fire. Great plumes of water from enemy artillery and mortars sprouted close by. We knew then this was not going to be a walk-in. No one thought the enemy would give us this kind of opposition at the water's edge. We expected A and B Companies to have the beach secured by the time we landed. In reality no one had set foot in our sector. The coxswain had missed the Vierville church steeple, our point to guide on, and the tides also helped pull us 200 hundred yards east. The location didn't make much difference. We could hear the 'p-r-r-r-r, p-r-r-r-r' of enemy machine guns to our right, toward the west. It was obvious someone down there was catching that hell, getting chewed up where we had been supposed to come in."

The "someone catching hell" on Dog Green was Company A, which like much of the 116th, a Virginia National Guard unit, contained men who had grown up with one another. The GIs from battalion headquarters that followed A Company ashore were shocked to see their beach empty of living men. Slaughter remembered, "The ramp went down while shells exploded on land and in the water. Unseen snipers were shooting down from the cliffs, but the most havoc came from automatic weapons. I was at the left side of the craft, about fifth from the front. Norfleet led the right side. The ramp was in the surf and the front of the steel boat bucked violently up and down. Only two at a time could exit.

"When my turn came, I sat on the edge of the bucking ramp, trying to time my leap on the down cycle. I sat there way too long, causing a bottleneck and endangering myself and the men to follow. But the ramp was bouncing six or seven feet and I was afraid it would slam me in the head. One man was crushed and killed instantly. When I did get out, I was in the water. It was very difficult to shed the sixty pounds of equipment, and if one were a weak swimmer he could drown before he inflated his Mae West. Many were hit in the water and drowned, good swimmers or not. There were dead men floating in the water and live men acting dead, letting the tide take them in. Initially, I tried to take cover behind one of the heavy timbers and then noticed an innocent-looking Teller mine tied to the top. I crouched down to chin-deep in the water as shells fell at the water's edge. Small-arms fire kicked up sand. I noticed a GI running, trying to get across the beach. He was weighted down with equipment and having difficulty moving. An enemy gunner shot him. He screamed for a medic. An aidman moved quickly to help him and he was also shot. I'll never forget seeing that medic lying next to that wounded soldier, both of them screaming. They died in minutes.

"Boys were turned into men. Some would be very brave men; others would soon be dead men, but any who survived would be frightened men. Some wet their pants, others cried unashamedly. Many just had to find within themselves the strength to get the job done. Discipline and training took over. For me, it was time to get the hell away from the killing zone and across the beach. Getting across the beach became an obsession. I told Pfc. Walfred Williams, my number-one gunner, to follow. He still had his fifty-one-pound machine gun tripod. He once told me that he was so strong from daily cradling an old iron cookstove in his arms and walking around with it. I felt secure with Williams on the gun. A Chicago boy of nineteen, he was dependable and loyal. He loved the Army and didn't believe a German weapon could kill him. I didn't think so either. We were both wrong. Enemy shrapnel killed him six weeks after D day. Part of me would die with him.

"Our rifles were encased in a plastic bag to shield them from salt water. Before disembarking, because I wanted to be ready, I had removed the covering and fixed the bayonet. I gathered my courage and started running as fast as my long legs would carry me. I ran as low as I could to lessen the target, and since I am six feet five, I still presented a good one. It was a long way to go, 100 yards or more. We were loaded with gear, our shoes full of water, our woolen, impregnated clothes soaked. I stumbled in a tidal pool of a few inches of water, began to stumble, accidently fired my rifle, barely missing my foot. But I made it to the seawall.

"I was joined by Pvt. Sal Augeri, and Pvt. Ernest McCanless and Williams. Augeri lost the machine-gun receiver in the water. We still had one box of MG ammo and the tripod. I had gotten sand in my rifle so I don't believe we had a weapon that would fire. I felt like a naked morsel on a giant sandy platter. I took off my assault jacket and spread my raincoat, so I could clean my rifle. It was then I saw bullet holes in my jacket and raincoat. Until then, I didn't realize I had been a target. I lit my first cigarette. I had to rest and compose myself because I became weak in the knees."

Already dead were many of Slaughter's childhood playmates and brothers in arms in the 116th. In the preinvasion hours, his D Company commander Capt. Walter Schilling had confided to a fellow officer, "I don't believe I will make it." He was right. A German 88 slammed into his landing craft killing him instantly. In fact, the COs from three of the four 1st Battalion companies perished without ever setting foot on dry land, along with sixteen of the other junior officers. Dead, too, were Sgt. Russell Ingram, who shrugged off a back injury in order to participate; Cpl. Jack Simms, who stuffed himself with bananas in order to achieve the minimum weight; the Hoback brothers from the hamlet of Bedford, Virginia; and T.Sgt. Ray Stevens, another Bedfordite whose twin brother, Roy, had waved off a handshake as they walked up the gangplank on the eve of the invasion. "I'll see you at Vierville-sur-Mer," said Roy, but he would never lay eyes on his twin again. Because the regiment originated in southwestern Virginia, the first wave enrolled a number of young men from Bedford, and 23 out of a total population of fewer than 4,000 died on that first day at Omaha Beach.

Bob Sales, who donned the 29th's National Guard uniform at fifteen, had, upon his return from Ranger training with Bob Slaughter, received the post as radio operator and bodyguard for B Company's leader, Capt. Ettore Zappacosta. "About 100 yards from shore, the English coxswain said he couldn't get us in closer. As the ramp lowered, enemy machine guns opened up firing directly into our boat. Captain Zappacosta, a great leader, was first off and the first hit. Staff Sergeant Dick Wright was second and he also was hit as he left the boat, falling into the water. A medic was third and I didn't see what happened to him. I was fourth, caught my heel in the ramp and fell sideways, out of the path of that MG 42, and this undoubtedly saved my life. All of the men who followed were either killed by the Germans or drowned. So far as I know, no one from my craft was ever found alive."

Sales dumped his heavy radio in the water. A log bearing an unexploded Teller mine drifted by and Sales clung to it as the tide carried him to the shoreline. On the beach he saw the badly wounded Sergeant Wright succumb to a sniper bullet in his head, and then the battalion surgeon cut down by a machine gun. "I crawled on my belly, using the dead and wounded as a shield." But when he saw some other B Company men sheltering themselves by the seawall he started to administer help to the wounded. "I kept crawling back to the water's edge, dragging out still-living men. You can't imagine how helpless it was to be lying on that beach and those snipers shooting everything that moved."

Felix Branham, with Company K of the 116th, climbed into a landing craft at 0420. Like Slaughter, he and his mates quickly found the Channel rough, with rain and spray soaking them, the swells turning many men ill. "Each time a boat hit the water, it joined a circle that became larger and larger.

We circled around until finally we headed for Normandy. One guy in my boat raised up and looked over the side. We weren't within machine-gun or rifle range and there was only an occasional artillery shell that would splash down. We were getting near enough and the sky lightening enough to see the contour of the bluffs and skyline. They looked just like Slapton Sands. He was disgusted and said, 'Goddamn, another dry run. I thought this was the real thing.'

"About fifty yards from the beach, we hit a sandbar parallel to the shore. Back at the marshaling area, we had been told there was a sandbar there and were not to let anyone stop there and lower the ramp to let us off. We were to make them close it up. The two fellows from the Navy moved to let down the ramp but Lieutenant Lucas, our boat-team commander, hollered, 'No, no!' He ordered the coxswain to go over the sandbar sideways, as we had been instructed. Unfortunately, some of the guys in my company, in another boat team, didn't remember their homework and left the landing craft when it reached the sandbar. With all of the heavy equipment they had, with the waves coming, and the tide rising a foot every ten minutes, they drowned. Other boats stopped at the sandbar and were demolished; seasick men who'd stayed on board were blasted to smithereens.

"I got out in water at the top of my boots. People were yelling, screaming, dying, running on the beach; equipment was flying everywhere; men were bleeding to death, crawling, lying everywhere, firing coming from all directions. We dropped down behind anything that was the size of a golf ball. Colonel [Charles] Canham [CO of the regiment] was screaming at us to get across the beach, and Lieutenant Cooper and Sergeant Crawford also were urging us off the beach. I turned to say, 'Let's move up, Gino,' to Gino Ferrari, but before I could finish the sentence, something spattered all over the side of my face. He'd been hit in the face and his brains splattered all over my face and my stuff. I moved forward and the tide came on so fast it covered him and I no longer could see him. Canham previously had a BAR shot out of his hand. The bullet went through his right wrist and he wore a makeshift sling. His bodyguard, Private First Class Nami, followed closely behind the colonel, keeping his .45 loaded. Canham would fire a clip and hand the gun back to Nami, who would inject another into the weapon. Back in training we used to call Colonel Canham everything not fit to print. When he took command of the 116th, he made life miserable for us. We thought he would be another rear-echelon commander. After seeing him in action, I sure had to eat a mess of crow."

Antitank squad leader Bill Lewis was twelve miles offshore on an LST when he and his crew with their weapon loaded aboard a DUKW for the trip to the beach. "We had never trained on a DUKW," says Lewis. "The DUKW was like a truck and we had a big load on. The guy driving it was busy trying to keep it heading in. If we got into a trough, we were going to turn over. He let the waves coming from behind push it along.

"When we got to the metal obstacles there was a man hanging on one. He hollered for help. We couldn't control the DUKW very good and when we got close to him, Lieutenant Van de Voort yelled, 'We're out here to kill people not save lives. Jump, if you want on this damn thing.' He leaped and came on board. Then we sheared a pin and lost power. We were adrift in the Teller-mine area and going right into them, sideway. They were sticking out two or three inches above the water. We hit one mine more than once, kept bumping it, but the salt water had deteriorated it. It didn't explode.

"It was about thirty minutes after the first wave and they started to machine-gun the DUKW. We jumped out and there went the DUKW with the AT gun and everything else. When I jumped out, I could stand on my toes except when a wave crashed over me. The natural assumption was the closer you went toward the shore, the more solid it would get. That wasn't true because sand had built up around some obstacles and I stepped off into a hole. I kept paddling. I wasn't about to go back the other way but just kept coming in. The water around me was dancing to that damn machine-gun fire."

Lewis and another man managed to run to the seawall where, cold and scared, they lay until a third man piled in on top of them. "He said, 'Is that you shaking, Sarge?' I said, 'Yeah, damn right!' He answered, 'My God, I thought it was me!' I could see him and he was shaking, all right. Both of us were. We huddled there, just trying to stay alive. There was nothing we could do except keep our butts down. There was no place to go and the automatic fire became heavier. Everyone coming up could see that seawall, so they got on top of you, piling up and trying to get below the damn thing."

The Rangers intent on capturing Pointe du Hoc recognized the costs of their delay. "Now we realized we would land late," said Kuhn. "The enemy would have time to regroup after the bombing attacks. The landing would be contested heavier than expected. To save time, instead of our boat rounding Pointe du Hoc to land on the right side of the cliff, we went in to the left of the Pointe. It was time to fire our rockets and I prayed for success. I pushed the switches and all of them fired. I couldn't watch where my ropes landed as I was busy under the cover of the boat sides, firing the rockets. Later, I learned that three of the six made the cliffs."

Len Lomell, in the same boat with Kuhn, recalled that as the flotilla maneuvered for its run toward the shore, "It was cloudy, foggy, dawn breaking. When we got within a mile, I could see a little dark line across the horizon. Then our rockets lit up the whole sky, the biggest display of fireworks you would ever see. Boom! Boom! Boom! Thousands of explosives and as you got closer the louder the booms. I said to the men, 'Guys, look on this as a big game, hit them fast and hard and keep moving faster. Never stop, because that's when they're going to pinwheel you.''

"The ramp was dropped presumably where you could stand. But there was a bomb crater eight to ten feet deep I stepped into and I got soaked." As he emerged, Lomell swiveled about to take stock of his boat team. "I felt a burning sensation in my left side. I spun around and didn't know who it came from. I didn't see anyone shoot me. But behind me was a Ranger, Harry Fate, with whom I had a nasty confrontation a few days earlier. It was my idea to break him from the rank of sergeant because I didn't think he was hacking it the way he should.

"At the time Harry said, 'You know, Top, what they do with first sergeants in combat.' I made light of it at the time, but here I was the first guy shot. Fate was about fifty feet away and I yelled at him, 'You son of a bitch.' But he protested, 'Honestly, Len, I didn't do it.' We couldn't waste time to sort this out—later Fate and I became very good friends—we went hell-for-leather up the cliff. The Germans held up some of the guys behind us but, using two sections of ladder on the sharpest incline, we got to a portion of the cliff that was bombed out. We started to use a rope. The first guy up, Lieutenant [Gilbert] Baugh from E Company [2d Ranger Battalion], took a bullet that went through his hand.

He was hurt badly and said to me, 'I can't get up. Keep going, Lomell, keep going!'

Lou Lisko, assigned to Headquarters Company and responsible for communications, breakfasted on a single pancake and a cup of coffee before embarking. "Seventy yards from the cliff, a Ranger who was sitting across from me was hit by a bullet in the upper left chest. He lost a considerable amount of blood and started groaning and moaning from the pain. Bullets from machine guns and rifles were flying from the top of the Hoc and nobody dared help him. Another Ranger sitting by my side got sick. Though we all had paper bags under our field jackets near the throat in case of vomiting, this man did not have time to reach it. He threw up all over my left leg, my carbine, and radio equipment. That made me sick, too. I vomited into my paper bag and threw it overboard.

"When our LCA 722 came close to the beach, the Rangers began disembarking. I watched and saw some of them jumping neck-deep and unable to walk. The two Rangers ahead of me jumped and disappeared, so I decided to go to the left. I fell chest-deep with all my equipment, radio, ammunition, carbine. At the same time bullets were hitting the seawater around us. I struggled toward the base of the cliffs, not far away but so difficult to reach."

Lisko managed to get to the base of the cliffs and set up the radio. "After being so scared about this terrible ordeal, we were so emotional that we lost all our saliva. My tongue was stuck to the roof of my mouth. My friend, Steven, gave me a stick of chewing gun and we chewed until we had some saliva and were able to talk. We could see Rangers climbing the cliffs, pulling themselves up on ropes and aluminum ladders. The Germans were throwing hand grenades, the potato mashers, because they were shaped like that kind of cooking tool. It had a wooden handle and a canlike container with explosives. We looked back at the sea. Our LCA 722 was stuck on the sand and couldn't return to the transport. Then we saw two British sailors come out of it and start running toward an LCA moving out. Steven and I yelled as loud as we could that there was an injured Ranger in 722. They heard us and although they had almost reached the outgoing LCA went back to ours to bring the Ranger out. While a machine gun fired at them, they carried him, one by the knees and the other by the arms. Later we learned the Ranger was wounded twice more but the sailors escaped any injury.

"Although our radio was set up, we couldn't contact anybody. I went to inform our communications officer, Lt. Ike [James] Eikner. As I started to move to find him, a machine gun and a rifleman on the left flank fired at me. First I thought I saw pebbles; then I realized they were bullets. I ran fast and jumped into a crevasse. Eikner was there where he couldn't be seen and he had twelve German prisoners. One of the prisoners stood up, as if he wanted to escape. The lieutenant and I grabbed our carbines and said, 'Halt!' When we stood, we exposed ourselves and drew fire again. Eikner shouted, 'Down!' but I was already down. One bullet struck the cliff between our heads. That's the way it would be for two and a half days with German soldiers everywhere. You never knew when you would be fired on by a German who was in a position a Ranger had not reached."

All along the narrow ground beneath the towering precipice, Rangers struggled to make their way up. In some cases, climbers ascended thirty or forty feet on a rocket-launched rope only to fall to the beach as their grapnel gave way, a rope slipped, or was cut. Attackers dropped back as the enemy hammered at the vulnerable Americans occupied with scaling the wall of earth, clay, and stone.

The Rangers from LCA 668 tried to exploit the success of the three rockets fired by Jack Kuhn that carried two smooth ropes and one with toggles to the heights. To expedite the ascent, he ordered that sections of extension ladders be put in play. They reached high enough for agile Rangers to scramble the remainder of the way by free-climbing over the debris caused by the bombardment. "We were shot at as we climbed," says Kuhn "but it was possible to get some cover by climbing behind chunks of cliff dislodged by the shelling." The innovation of a machine gun elevated on a fire ladder was one more casualty of circumstances. Only one DUKW bearing the gear got far enough onto the beach to deploy the weapon. For the most part, individual Rangers, using rifles, submachine guns, and BARs doggedly exchanged fire with enemies who showed themselves while shooting or flinging grenades.

Lieutenant George Kerchner of D Company recalled departing the *Amsterdam* at 4:30 A.M. He noted in his diary, "Heavy seas, began bailing immediately. Motor launch led us to wrong point. Sailed along under machine-gun fire, bailing all the time." Some years later, Kerchner amplified his terse first recollections. "We passed not far from the large warships. About five o'clock, the battleship *Texas* started to fire. It was a terrifying sound, the fourteen-inch guns shot far over our heads but still close enough for us to hear and feel some of the muzzle blast. When we were a little better than half way in, the rocket craft fired their barrages, salvos of ten or fifteen at a time. It, too, was terrifying, one continuous sheet of flame going up from the rocket-firing craft. How could anybody live on the beaches with all this fire landing there from the warship and the rocket-firing boats. Our air force bombers were overhead; we couldn't see them because there was a low overcast in a dull gray sky with clouds down to one or two thousand feet. But we could hear the bombs dropping on the shore and see them exploding as we came closer to the shore.

"We had been told these landing craft were unsinkable. They had large air tanks along both sides, supposed to support the craft even if holed by a shell. At first we did not worry about shipping water. The heavy seas hit the ramp in the front and washed right over the top, and shortly we had six to twelve inches of water in the bottom of the boat. I saw the one boat from D Company [Duke Slater's] carrying a group of men with whom I was very friendly sink because of shipping water. That convinced me our landing craft were not unsinkable. We began bailing with our helmets and managed to keep us afloat, even though we were taking on a lot of water as the boat speeded up."

Acceleration was vital because of the navigation mistake. To Kerchner, the change in course seemed "a catastrophe. We were due to land at 6:30 on the dot. In the forty minutes before that time, the heavy bombers would drop their sticks on the Pointe and the *Texas* would deliver several hundred rounds. Then medium bombers would plaster the area and only three minutes before 6:30, fighters would strafe the Pointe. The attacks were designed to keep the defenders pinned down, so they wouldn't see us approach the Pointe. They would be kept from the edge of the cliff. Otherwise while we were climbing they could cut our ropes before we even managed to get halfway up the cliff.

"Although we were about half a mile offshore and sailing parallel for half an hour under fire by German antiaircraft guns, 20mm and 40mm, none of the men in my boat were wounded. I believe several other craft were struck, one sunk.

As we neared Pointe du Hoc I looked at my watch and saw it was 7:00 A.M. and we were far behind schedule. All of the preparatory fire on the Pointe had been lifted. The Germans who were in their underground shelters were now coming out and starting to look about to see what was happening. As we turned to make our approach, I looked up and saw Germans standing atop the cliff. I thought, this whole thing is a big mistake. None of us will ever get up that cliff because we are so vulnerable. The Germans could just stay back from the edge and cut the ropes.

"When we were about twenty to twenty-five yards offshore, I gave the order to fire our rockets. All of them fired and five actually cleared the cliff. Some other landing craft had a great deal of trouble, firing too soon or, because the seas had wet the ropes and made them too heavy, they couldn't clear the cliff. The ramp was lowered immediately after the rockets fired. It was our hope and desire to run right up on the beach for a dry landing, not because we were afraid of getting wet but because if we were soaked it would have added weight to carry while climbing. The British navy man had promised to put us down dry but suddenly we ran aground with the ramp dropped. The officer said, 'Everybody out.' Looking ahead, I could see fifteen or twenty feet of water, a muddy, dirty gray stretch. The entire area was marked by craters, shell holes from the guns on the *Texas* and the bombers.

"We had run up on the edge of one of these shell craters as I discovered almost immediately. I figured the water was only a foot or two deep because the landing craft drew only about two feet and we could run through it. So I yelled, 'Come on, let's go!' I rushed ahead, first one off, and fell into eight feet of water. It had to be at least that deep because I couldn't touch bottom. When I came to the surface, I started to doggie paddle, keeping my head above water while I tried to reach the beach. The men behind me realized what had happened when I went under and they went off both sides of the crater, getting nothing more than their feet wet. Instead of being the first ashore, I was one of the last. I looked around for someone to help me cuss out the British Navy for dumping me in eight feet of water but there was nobody to sympathize with me. They were all busily engaged.

"I tried my SCR 536 hand radio. It wouldn't work and I threw it down on the beach. Then I realized we were being fired upon by a machine gun off to the left at the top of the cliff, several hundred yards away. Sergeant [Francis] Pacyga, [William] Cruz, and [Lester] Harris were all hit. I don't know how they missed me since I was right next to those who were wounded. I felt rather helpless with my .45 pistol. I picked up the rifle dropped by Harris. My first impulse was to go after the machine gun but I realized this was stupid. Our mission was to get to the top of the cliff and destroy the guns up there. The men all knew what they had to do. They had their ropes, the order in which to climb, and they were all starting up. The only command I gave was for the platoon messenger to stay with the wounded after we got them close to the cliff so they were protected.

"I thought I had better inform Colonel Rudder that the boat with our company commander and a number of men had sunk. I located him about twenty-five or fifty yards down the beach as he was beginning to climb one of the rope ladders. He had his hands and his mind full and did not seem particularly interested in my information that I was assuming command of the company. He told me to get out of there and climb my rope. Getting up the cliff was very easy after all the training we had in England. The shells from the warships and the bomb damage at the edge of the cliff caused dirt and large chunks of clay and shale to fall. You could almost walk up the first twenty-five feet. Using a smooth rope, I had no trouble getting all the way up."

In spite of the loss of boats to the sea, the small arms and grenades of the defenders, and the rigors of the climb, a number of Rangers, like Kerchner, completed the frantic race to get up the cliff in less than fifteen minutes. Within half an hour of setting foot on Beach Charley, the bulk of Rudder's task force moved out in search of their objective: the casemated big guns. (According to Lomell, of the 225 Rangers assigned to assault Pointe du Hoc, about 175 actually reached the top.) To their surprise and chagrin, the battered emplacements on Pointe du Hoc were empty of artillery.

"Upon topping the cliff," said Kuhn, "I was shocked to find nothing that resembled the mock-ups and overlays we had studied prior to D day. The terrain was in complete disarray. Since there were no guns, D Company's second objective was to travel to the highway directly ahead and hold it against the German troops. I was at this time alone, trying to contact my men. As I neared the exit road from Pointe du Hoc, I spotted John Conaboy. We were running from a shell hole to the exit road when a sniper hit Conaboy. We reached a communications ditch and I checked Conaboy. He insisted he was okay and I should go on. I could tell his wound wasn't serious, and not seeing any blood, I asked him where he was hit. He laughed, and said in his canteen. Actually he'd been hit in the hip.

"About ten yards farther, I spotted a column of D Company Rangers where I made contact with Len Lomell. We split into groups to make our way to the road. Heading for the main highway, Len and I walked up the road, scanning it and the hedgerows to our sides. Just as we came abreast of the battered remains of a small French farm building, Lomell grabbed me and threw both of us through the doorway. 'Didn't you see that Jerry kneeling in the road aiming at us?' I had not and went to check him out. I took a quick peek and the German was still kneeling. He was combatwise and figured one of us would probably do this. He fired once and the slug hit the door frame above my head. Len went through a window or a door to cut the Jerry off. I looked again a few seconds later and he was running away. I stepped out to cut him down but the Tommy gun wouldn't fire. When I checked it, I found my clip had been hit right where it inserts into the gun.

"I yelled to Len I was going back to the communication trench where they'd left a pile of our weapons. I retrieved another Tommy gun and then found Lomell setting up the men in the hedgerows along the road. Larry Johnson and I settled down in a very shallow rain ditch that was pretty well hidden by hedge and high grass. We had excellent vision over the three sites we were to guard. Lomell took a position across from us covering the same area. We felt the Germans would probably use an opening in a stone wall across the way.

"We heard movement from behind the stone fence. A German soldier appeared, stood at the opening, looking up and down the highway. Seeing it apparently clear, he came through the wall and ran across the road right up to me. I saw a German burp gun slung across his chest. I jumped up and fired point-blank, hitting him in the chest. My slugs must have cut the strap on his weapon for it fell to the ground about three feet in front of me. The German ran a few steps then dropped.

"Larry Johnson said, 'Hey, Jack, get me his gun.' I leaned

out and picked up the weapon. As I did, I noticed movement and saw another German soldier standing in the opening of the stone fence aiming at me. I had no way to protect myself and felt I was about to be shot. Len saw it all and got the German just as he shot at me. His bullet struck the road near me. For the second time on D day, Lomell had saved my life. I learned the hard way to observe and proceed with caution."

"Because we couldn't stop until we reached the road, we had moved fast," recalled Lomell, "with the wounded men helping one another. Once we set up our roadblocks, there were maybe thirteen of us, Jack and I made up a two-man patrol in one direction, while another two Rangers went the opposite way. I saw some wheel tracks in a dirt lane. We followed them and about 200 yards from the highway, I found the five guns, all in place, pointed toward Utah Beach, but with not a soul around them, not a single guard. It was about 8:30 in the morning and maybe they hadn't realized that there was anyone landing on Utah Beach. But another 100 yards off were a bunch of Germans forming up, putting on jackets, starting their vehicles. I think they were the gun crews getting organized.

" 'Jack,' I instructed Kuhn, 'Keep your eyes on them and if one starts toward here, get him between the eyes.' While he watched the Germans, I took his thermite grenade and the one I carried. I put them in the barrels of two of the guns. They just made a light popping noise that couldn't be heard by the enemy but destroyed the barrels. Then I ran back to the rest of the guys, got their thermite grenades and did the remaining guns. For good measure, I busted out the sights.

"Just as we returned to our hedgerow, there was a tremendous roar, like the whole world had blown up. There was a shower of dirt, metal, ramrods. I figured that a round from the *Texas* or some other warship had hit the ammunition dump for the artillery. When we first came over the top of the Pointe, we were a lot of disappointed guys when there were no guns there. But now, just by a piece of luck, we had found them and were able to destroy the pieces."

Medic Frank South said, "The medics had a problem. It would be impractical for us to carry all the equipment and supplies we would need in our aid kits or simple packs and we did not know when we would be able to retrieve the rest of our materials from a supply boat. We decided each of us would carry an enlarged kit. Because I was the biggest and presumably strongest, youngest, and perhaps the most naive, Block asked me to work with him putting together a very large pack of medical gear and supplies to be carried on a mountain packboard. On its horns I coiled about fifty feet of three-eighths-inch line in case I had to ditch it in the surf and pull it to shore. The pack contained plasma, sulfa-based antibiotics—there was no penicillin yet—drugs, additional instruments, bandages, suture material, and whatever else I could think of. God knows how much it weighed, perhaps sixty-five or seventy pounds. I was a walking aid station and I don't recall any other medic making or carrying such a pack. In addition, I carried my regular aid kit, side arm, knife, canteen, an Argus C-3 camera that I lost in the surf, and a D-ration bar.

"As a medic on the LCA, I was to be the last one off. There was not much conversation around me, a little black humor maybe—'Now if the lieutenant and I get hit, you know who to take care of first, Doc.' Then someone lamented that the army had never issued bulletproof jock-straps. 'After all, I got married just before we left. Could you requisition one for me, Doc?' Approaching the beach, our LCA was able to fire its grapnel-bearing rockets in good order, and most men got off in about two or three feet of water while under almost continuous MG fire from the cliff. Expectably, as the boat load lightened, the LCA rose and shifted its position. When my turn came, I jumped off the ramp into an underwater bomb or shell crater that was over my head. Before either the pack or I became waterlogged, I scrambled out and crawled into a drier crater ashore when I was able to shuck my burden.

"Immediately, there was the first call of 'Medic!' My regular aid kit was still attached to my pistol belt. Opening it, as I dodged the fire from the cliff, I reached the fallen Ranger who had a chest wound. I was able to drag him to an indentation in the cliff face and begin to help him. The call 'Medic!' was now repeated time after time. For a while it seemed as if I were the only one retrieving and working on the wounded, which of course was not so. Block and another medic had worked their way up to the cliff base and were beginning to treat men as fast as they could. However, it was not possible to actually set up a proper aid station on the beach. The highest priority went to scaling and securing the cliff. Also the wounded were too scattered. I worked along the entire beach area, covering all three companies. Block devoted most of his attention to the most critically wounded.

"Although the LCA I was on got its grapnel rockets off effectively, the one with the 1st Platoon [F Company] was in the wrong position to launch the rockets. They were designed so they could be removed and fired by hand, a risky procedure. Sergeant John Cripps took off the LCA four rockets, and while exposed to machine-gun fire from above, mounted them on the beach. He hot-wired and fired one, receiving a blast in the face. With terrific determination, he fired the rest, just as successfully.

"Nearly blinded, almost fainting, Cripps stumbled over to

Block and me. His face, neck, and hands were covered with powder burns and imbedded with black unburned explosives. He said to me, 'Jesus, South, didn't you ever stand too close to a big firecracker?' All we could do was blot his face and neck with water from our canteens and pat on, as gently as possible, some burn ointment I found in the bottom of my aid kit. He immediately left to rejoin his platoon and the attack. For all that courage, willpower, and determination that Cripps displayed while under direct fire, he never was cited or decorated. Very early on, while I was finishing working on someone near our left flank, Sgt. Bill (L-Rod) Petty, his BAR slung across his shoulders, was struggling with a straight rope. It was slippery with wet clay and he was having a terrible time getting a purchase on it and ascending the cliff. During a pause, while he was trying to dry his hands and catch his breath, Block appeared and said in a loud, commanding voice, 'Soldier, get hold of that rope and up the cliff!'

"Petty, face flushed both by anger and his efforts, replied something like, 'What the hell, if you think you can do any better, you can fucking well try!' Short-tempered, Captain Block was stymied by the equally short-tempered Sergeant Petty, one of our most effective noncoms. Somehow Block did control his temper and realize his charge was unjust. He looked at Petty, turned, stared at me for an instant, and then stalked down to the beach where he was needed."

From Pointe du Hoc, Rudder dispatched Rangers to capture other troublesome bastions belonging to the enemy. One was the command post, presumably for the big guns that Lomell and Kuhn found elsewhere; the other was an antiaircraft battery emplacement doing considerable damage to the invaders. In both instances the defenders were too numerous and strongly entrenched to be overrun by the limited number of men Rudder could muster. The German command post, which included a series of underground tunnels, troubled the invaders for many hours, as enemy soldiers disappeared in its warrens only to surface in some protected place and fire. The gun battery, however, yielded to the U.S. Navy. The destroyer *Satterlee*, earlier had help drive off Germans atop the Pointe. Now, with the guidance of a shore fire-control officer it blasted the antiaircraft guns.

When Rudder and his headquarters party achieved the heights of the Pointe, they set up their command post in the revetments of that antiaircraft post. Unfortunately, a round from enemy artillery smashed into their position, wounding Rudder in the arm—down on the beach a bullet had passed through the fleshy part of his leg. The same explosion killed the naval observer. Lou Lisko assumed the responsibility for contacting the warships to enlist their aid. "I had a signal lamp," says Lisko. "I was able to get in touch with the *Satterlee* but the Navy guys were much too fast with their lights for me. Finally, they told me the wave length to use. We began to communicate by radio. When the *Satterlee* used up all its ammunition, the destroyer *Harding* took over. Their fire support saved our necks, breaking up counterattacks."

What the Rangers and all of the soldiers assaulting the beaches lacked was any tactical aid from the air. American fighters either flew air cover for the bombers or else devoted themselves to keeping the inland highways clean of any would-be reinforcements. There were no means of air-to-ground or air-to-ship communications. The absence of coordination sharply contrasted with naval operations in the Pacific, where U.S. Navy warships worked closely with their air arm.

The bloody reception that greeted the Rangers climbing Pointe du Hoc was mimicked by that encountered when A and B Companies of the 2d Battalion attempted to fulfill their mission. Bob Edlin remembered, "The navy had opened up. It seemed as if the whole world exploded. There was gunfire from battleships, destroyers, and cruisers. The bombers were still hitting the beaches. There didn't seem to be any way that anyone could live on the beaches with the amount of firepower laid down by the American forces. As we went in, we could see small craft from the 116th Infantry that had gone in ahead, sunk. A few bodies were bobbing in the water, even out three or four miles.

"I took stock of the men in my boat. They were vomiting on each other's feet and on their clothing. It was just a terrible sight. They were so sick from the action of the waves. There was a deep silence. All the gunfire had lifted for a very short time. The navy was giving way to let the troops get on the beaches. The only thing I could hear was the motor of the boat. It was dawn. The sun was just coming up over the French coast. I saw a bird, a seagull, I guess, fly across the front of the boat, just as if life were going on as normal.

"Then there came something like a peppering of hail, heavy hail on the front of the ramp. I realized it was enemy machine-gun fire. All hell broke loose from the other side, German artillery, rockets, and mortars. It was just unbelievable that anybody could have lived under that barrage. It came in through our boat and the other boats. We crouched in the bottom of the boat in the vomit, urine, and seawater and whatever else was there.

"The assault boat hit a sandbar. We were at least seventy-five yards from shore. I told the coxswain, the operator of the boat, 'Try to get it in farther.' That British seaman had all the guts in the world, but he couldn't get the assault craft off the sandbar. So, I told him to drop the ramp or we were going to die right there. We had been trained for years not to go off the front of the ramp because the boat might get rocked by a wave and run over you. So we went off the sides. I looked to my right and saw a B Company boat next to us with Lt. Bob Fitzsimmons, a good friend, take a direct hit from a mortar or mine on the ramp. I thought, there goes half of B Company. It was cold, miserably cold, even though it was June. The water temperature was probably forty-five or fifty degrees. It was up to my shoulders and I saw men sinking all about me. I tried to grab a couple but my job was to get in and to the guns. There were bodies from the 116th floating everywhere. They were face down in the water, packs still on their backs. They had inflated their life jackets. Fortunately, most of the Rangers did not inflate theirs or they also might have turned over and drowned. I began to run with my rifle in front of me. I went directly across the beach to try to get to the seawall. In front of me was part of the 116th Infantry, pinned down and lying behind beach obstacles. They hadn't made it to the seawall. I kept screaming, 'You have to get up and go! You gotta get up and go! But they didn't. They were worn out, defeated.

   "I continued across the beach. There were mines and obstacles all up and down the beach. The Air Force had missed it entirely. There were no shell holes in which to take cover. The mines had not been detonated. Absolutely nothing that had been planned for that part of the beach had worked. I knew that Vierville-sur-Mer was going to be a hellhole, and it was. When I was about twenty yards from the seawall, I was hit by what I assume was a sniper bullet. It shattered and broke my right leg. I thought, well, I've got a Purple Heart. I fell, and as I did, it was like a searing, hot poker rammed into my leg. My rifle fell, ten feet or so in front of me. I crawled forward to get to it, picked it up, and as I rose on my left leg, another burst of, I think, machine-gun fire tore the muscles out of that leg, knocking me down again.

"I lay there for seconds, looked ahead, and saw several Rangers lying there. One was Butch Bladorn from Wisconsin. I screamed at Butch, 'Get up and run!' Butch, a big, powerful man, just looked back and said, 'I can't.' I got up and hobbled toward him. I was going to kick him in the ass and get him off the beach. He was lying on his stomach, his face in the sand. Then I saw the blood coming out of his back. I realized he had been hit in the stomach and the bullet had come out his spine and he was completely immobilized. Even then I was sorry for screaming at him but I didn't have time to stop and help him. I thought, well, that's the end of Butch. Fortunately, it wasn't. He became a farmer in Wisconsin.

"As I moved forward, I hobbled. Your legs after you have been hit with gunfire, slowly, stiffen. The pain was indescribable. I fell to my hands and knees and tried to crawl forward. I managed a few yards, then blacked out for several minutes. When I came to, I saw Sgt. Bill Klaus. He was up to the seawall and when he saw my predicament, he crawled back to me under heavy rifle and mortar fire and dragged me to the cover of the wall. Klaus had also been wounded in one leg and a medic gave him a shot of morphine. The medic did the same for me. My mental state was such that I told him to shoot it directly into my left leg as that was the one hurting the most. He reminded me that if I took it in the ass or the arm it would get to the leg. I told him to give me a second shot because I was hit in the other leg. He didn't.

"There were some Rangers gathered at the seawall—Sgt. William Courtney, Pvt. William Dreher, Garfield Ray, Gabby Hart, Sgt. Charles Berg. I yelled at them, 'You have to get off of here! You have to get up and get the guns!' They were gone immediately. Sergeant Bill White, my platoon sergeant, whom we called Whitey, an ex-jockey, took charge. He was small, very active, and very courageous. He led what few men were left of the first platoon and started up the cliffs. I crawled and staggered forward as far as I could to some cover in the bushes behind a villa. There was a round, stone well with a bucket and a handle that turned the rope. It was so inviting. I was alone and I wanted that water so bad. But years of training told me it was booby-trapped.

"I looked up at the top of the cliffs and thought, I can't make it on this leg. Where was everyone? Had they all quit? Then I heard Dreher yelling, 'Come on up. These trenches are empty.' Then Kraut burp guns cut loose. I thought, 'Oh, God, I can't get there!' I heard an American Tommy gun and Courtney shout, 'Damn it, Dreher! They're empty, *now*.' There was more German small-arms fire and German grenades popping. I could hear Whitey yelling, 'Cover me!' I heard Garfield Ray's BAR talking American. Then there was silence.

"Now I thought, where are the 5th Rangers? I turned and I couldn't walk or even hobble anymore. I crawled back to the beach. I saw the 5th Rangers coming through the smoke of a burning LST that had been hit by artillery fire. Colonel [Max] Schneider had seen the slaughter on the beaches and used his experience with the Rangers in Africa, Sicily, Italy, and Anzio. He used the smoke as a screen and moved in behind it, saving the 5th Ranger Battalion many casualties. My years of training told me there would be a counterattack. I gathered the wounded by the seawall and told them to arm themselves as best as possible. I said if the Germans come we are either going to be captured or die on the beach but we might as well take the Germans with us. I know it sounds ridiculous, but ten or fifteen Rangers lay there, facing up to the cliffs, praying that Sergeant White, Courtney, Dreher, and the 5th Ranger Battalion would get to the guns. Our fight was over unless the Germans counterattacked.

"I looked back to the sea. There was nothing. There were no reinforcements. I thought the invasion had been abandoned. We would be dead or prisoners soon. Everyone had withdrawn and left us. Well, we had tried. Some guy crawled over and told me he was a colonel from the 29th Infantry Division. He said for us to relax, we were going to be okay. D, E, and F Companies [2d Ranger Battalion] were on the Pointe. The guns had been destroyed. The 2d's A and B Companies and the 5th Rangers were inland. The 29th and 1st Divisions were getting off the beaches.

"This colonel looked at me and said, 'You've done your job.' I answered, 'How? By using up two rounds of German ammo on my legs?' Despite the awful pain, I hoped to catch up with the platoon the next day. Someone gave me another shot of morphine."

# 11

# Getting Off Omaha

Sharing the horror of Omaha Beach with the GIs of the 29th Division were the men from the 1st Infantry Division. Bill Behlmer and his antitank platoon headed for Easy Red Beach with their half-track, *Hitler's Hearse*, up front. "We were to be first off and I was to lead my platoon on Omaha Beach. My driver Stan Stypulkowski, who had come all the way through North Africa and Sicily, sat and talked with me all night. We knew this was it for us. On the way in, another LCT, not far from us, just disappeared. An LCI on the other side with red crosses on the side took a couple of hits. Medics were hanging onto the ramp and in the water. As far as the eye could see was wall-to-wall boats headed for Easy Red near the small town of Colleville-sur-Mer.

"We neared the beach and the ramp dropped. Small arms, machine guns, mortars, artillery raked across the ramp. The Navy CO said we were pulling out to try again. We came back in, and the ramp dropped, I told Stan to gun the half-track. We hit the ground, turned right, and headed down the beach, a big turkey at a turkey shoot. Every gun covering that beach zeroed in on us. We didn't stand a chance. I stood up and turned to the back, told the guys to get out. Stan and I jumped from the hood to the ground. On the way down, it felt as if someone jabbed me in the legs with a red-hot poker. Stan, his arms across his chest, oozed blood. I must have gone into shock, because I drifted in and out. Shells were falling everywhere. But for me the war seemed to have gone away."

Fred Erben, a Brooklyn youth who joined the 1st Division as a seventeen-year-old, was a member of C Company and destined for Easy Red. "As luck would have it," said Erben, "we were in the first wave and hit the beaches at low tide. We were fortunate because we could see the underwater obstacles and skirt around them. However, we hit a sandbar and had to unload. Beyond the sandbar there were obstacles we did not see. Our craft made it out of there in a hurry but some boats that got over the bar, struck the mines and blew up. It was horrible seeing men blown all over the place. Some were swimming ashore. The ones not so lucky floated ashore.

"We had to wade in with all of our equipment: a pair of twenty-pound TNT bangalore torpedoes and ammo. Our flotation devices helped. My squad made it intact, but the beach was rocky and there was no chance to dig in. Many men were hit all around us from the intense crossfire from two pillboxes on either side of us. That's when Omaha Easy Red became known as Bloody Red. We got the word to advance and get the hell off the beach. We had barbed wire and land mines in front. One of my scouts, Private Tripoletti, set his ammunition down on a mine and was killed. This was where the bangalores—we called them stovepipes—came in. They were assembled under fire, one by one, with three-foot lengths pressed into one another until they passed through the barbed wire. The pipes were loaded with high explosives and an ignition cap placed in the last one. A man would lie directly behind the tube, pull the cap, setting off an explosion that caused the tubes to burst sideways, cutting the wires. It also blew up any buried mines. We kept passing them forward and the tubes made a large enough hole for us to pass through.

"This was about twenty minutes after we landed. We inched our way up the hill toward one pillbox. Myself and another man put a charge attached to a wooden pole into the aperture of the pillbox. It sounds crazy but it worked. We moved into a wooded area and went on a recon mission, moving forward to a hedgerow. Peering over it, we saw a group of men on our left flank. Thinking they were another patrol, we waved to them. They waved back; then we motioned for them to come over. They must have realized we were Americans because they dropped down behind their hedge and opened fire. No one was hit at the moment.

"Then they started to drop in mortars on us. We opened up with rifle grenades fired from an adapter on our M1s. I told my squad to withdraw when a mortar shell struck near us. A piece of shrapnel hit me and knocked me out. I came to and heard German voices nearby. They must have thought I was dead and they left. Now I heard Americans but I didn't move. Someone said, 'That's Erben. Is he dead?' Gene Greco came over and bandaged my head. After he patched me up, I headed back toward the beach. It was devastation, littered with bodies, with wounded being tended to. Sunken boats lay on their sides. More troops were coming ashore. Finally one of the medics directed me to a ship, where I saw more bodies being put in body bags."

Fred Erben and his squad were among the very few

Americans to blast an opening for themselves and actually get off the beach and move inland. Most of the men, whether from the 116th, like Slaughter and Branham, the 1st Division or the Rangers detailed for Omaha, huddled below the seawall seeking shelter from the prolonged savage rain of death and destruction.

George Zenie, another 1st Division vet from North Africa and Sicily, was aboard an LCT with three half-tracks, three 57mm antitank guns, and the crews to man them. They also were to come in at Easy Red. "Finally, our LCT landed, dropped the ramp, and we disembarked. It was around noon and we had been scheduled to land between ten and ten-thirty. We followed the two other half-tracks onto Easy Red. Artillery and mortar fire were falling around us. A piece of shrapnel flew through the driver's slit and cut the side of his face. He screamed and stopped the half-track. I put my first-aid gauze against his face, told him to hold it there, moved him over, and drove the half-track down the beach as planned.

"When the whole line halted, I got the driver out and told one of the men to drive, to follow the other vehicles. I helped the driver to an aid station, taking the wounded aboard an LCI. The scene around me depicted the real horror of war. Dead bodies floated in the water and were scattered about the beach. Wounded lay everywhere. All types of equipment were broken and abandoned. A gasoline truck ahead of us was in flames. The entire beach was under constant fire from small arms, mortars, and artillery. The guns of destroyers, cruisers, and battleships were still battering at heavily fortified beach emplacements and pill boxes that blocked the important exits from the beach. A bulldozer trying to clear our exit was a target for enemy fire. Two drivers had been wounded; a third soldier tried to restart the machine. Our line was still contained.

"When I returned to the half-track, another of my men had been wounded, in the buttocks by shrapnel. 'Pappy' Henderson, a sergeant in our platoon, and a very close friend of mine, came along. He was called 'Pappy' because he was a little older than most of us—earlier 30s—and sought after for all kinds of advice. He and I put the wounded man in a blanket and carried him close to the bluff where a first-aid unit was set up in a gully. We left the wounded man there. I told the rest of the men to get into the gully where they were better protected. Pappy and I carried another soldier with chest and arm wounds to the aid station in the gully. Pappy said he was going to see if we could move forward. When he left, I maneuvered the half-track close to the gully. I never saw Pappy Henderson again. To this day he is listed as MIA."

Rifleman John Bistrica, a replacement who joined the 16th Regiment of the 1st Division in England, was forced to disembark in water over his head. He inflated his life preserver to keep himself afloat. Pinned down with others, he remembered, "Our regimental CO, Col. George Taylor, came on the beach and he started to get the officers and noncoms organized, getting us going. He said, 'There are two kinds of people on this beach. Those that are dead and those that are about to die. Let's get out of here!' " [The quote has also been imputed to Gen. Norman Cota, assistant division chief of the 29th Division, or to Col. Charles Canham, CO of the 116th.]

The 1st Division's Lawrence Zeickler, combat savvy after North Africa and Sicily, never succumbed to the optimism voiced by Bob Slaughter and his fellows, who thought it would be a "walk-in." Zeickler, with E Company, also destined for Easy Red, remarked, "We knew the German soldier was a fighter. And especially when we heard Rommel was in charge of the beach, we knew it wasn't going to be a picnic. There is always a sense of fear when you go into combat, particularly before you hit the beaches. Anyone who said he wasn't scared isn't kidding anyone who knows. You should be scared when someone is shooting at you, hoping to hit you.

"The one nice thing about this invasion was we didn't have to climb down the side of the ship. We in the first wave were lowered over the side in our LST without using a cargo net. When we looked over the sides of the landing craft as we started in toward the beach, we could see tanks, some of them still afloat, with the [flotation] rafts holding them up. It was weird to see a tank in the water and floating. Others had gone down; the crews were sitting in their little dinghies after the tanks swamped.

"When we reached the beach, things were not busted up as we expected. The tide was out, and we could see obstacles. The air support had missed the beach, falling inland, and the rockets fell short. We hit a sandbar close to shore and the sailor tried to get us loose to take us all the way in, but small-arms fire and mortars were coming in heavy. Our boat commander, the battalion exec officer, hollered for them to lower the front of the boat so we could get out. The longer we sat there, the more chance we had of being hit by either a mortar or artillery shell.

"I got out of the landing craft but I must have hit a hole at the end of the sandbar because I sank down into the water. We had on the new combat jackets where you only had to pull three or four tabs and you could shed your equipment. But my fingers were so cold I couldn't do it. My helmet flew on the back of my head and was pulling on my neck. As I started down in the water, I thought, 'What the hell, North Africa, Sicily—it seems as though there's nothing to look forward to but being killed.' I thought I'd give up as I went deeper and deeper.

"Suddenly, it came to my mind someone saying that drowning is a helluva way to die. I started to tread water and I finally got my equipment loose and could shed it. I was a fairly good swimmer and made it to shore. My objective was to go to the left with my squad across the beach. I saw men taking cover behind the underwater obstacles. But the tide was coming in now and to stay there was sure death. We started kicking butts to get 'em out of the water, up on shore. Those who were wounded, we drug up behind. Right off the beach was a pile of rocks that looked like a stone fence. We could get down behind it and try to figure out where the hell to go from there.

"When I set my helmet back on my head and put my hand beneath it, there was dried blood. A bullet or piece of shrapnel strafed the top of my head; another half inch I wouldn't be here. Right to the front was a German gun bunker that was supposed to be blown to smithereens but the Air Force wasn't able to do it. All this time, the Navy is coming in, bringing more men, and stuff piling up on the beach. I found Private Ratti and we headed up the beach trying to find the others from our group. We found some medics and they told us the rest of the company had gone up a nearby wadi. The man who had broken the barrier to an exit from the beach was a sergeant from our company, Philip Streczyk. Almost everyone followed him through."

Bill Lewis of the 29th Division credits someone like Streczyk with preparing the way for his departure from the killing ground. "This 1st Division boy who had been in combat, said, I see what they're doing—from the big bunker by the exit. He said, 'Get some fire on that baby.' A shore control man got on his radio but the shells wouldn't even touch it. He [the 1st Division GI] said, everybody get up and start firing on the embrasures and get them back away from that hole. He knew what he was doing. We started firing on the embrasure. He took some men and went up there. I didn't go. They took some bangalore torpedoes and put them under that baby. That was the thing that was murdering us, an 88 or 75mm gun. That stopped the gun, blew it over. He was a 1st Division sergeant who blew it up. He had a big red one on his shoulder."

There were four such exits on Omaha Beach through which the assault companies had been expected to drive inland. The Allied high command had anticipated that even if the big ships and sky fleets failed to demolish the barriers and fortifications defending these openings, the duplex-drive Sherman tanks would overwhelm the enemy. But the rough water ripped away the fragile canvas flotation devices. Seaborne armor sank almost instantly upon launching while still thousands of yards offshore. Of the thirty-two the U.S. expected to launch, twenty-seven quickly disappeared below the waves, many of the crews unable to escape entombment. Just two with the wraparound flotation mechanism actually gained the shore under their own power. Three others made it to land only because an accident aboard the LCT prevented them from trundling down the ramp into the water. On the British beaches, the command realized the sea was too much for any flotation devices and did not attempt to use the amphibious tanks.

Armor came to Omaha Beach later in the form of dual-drive tanks that scuttled across the sea bottom, rather than plowing through the waves on canvas "bloomers." Eddie Ireland, a Calumet City, Illinois, high school grad who chose armor because he didn't care to walk to war, drove the second type of DD tank. "We started out sitting on top of the vehicles. But when we came close to the shore, we were told to get inside the tank. They let us off in water that was about turret-high. I had a camera and I wanted to take pictures of the beach. So I cracked the hatch open and just then we hit a shell hole. Water poured in and I got soaked.

"The tide was in and we rode through the water for quite a bit. The engineers had made a path for us [through the obstacles]. When we did come ashore, the infantry guys had to move the bodies lying at the edge so we wouldn't run over them. The troops were still hugging the shoreline and there wasn't much land between the hill and the water. There was a lot of mortar fire coming down, not so much small arms. We didn't have much trouble there on the beach. But once we got over the hill, we started to catch artillery fire."

The 5th Ranger Battalion's Charles Parker, CO of Company A, Lt. Frank Dawson of D Company, and John Raaen testified to the wisdom of Max Schneider. Lost in the waterborne assault of the Rangers upon Pointe du Hoc were colored rockets to inform Schneider of the success or failure of the mission. A radio carried by Rudder's party would not transmit. Ranger John Raaen, the CO of Headquarters Company, explained that with no information about events at Pointe du Hoc, Schneider had to make a decision. "As we approached the beach, Schneider had a clear view of what was happening on the beach. The survivors of the 1st Battalion of the 116th Infantry were clinging to their very lives in the wreckage of their landing craft and behind the seawall of Omaha Dog Green Beach. As A and B Companies of the 2d Rangers touched down slightly left of the [29th Division GIs] they were hit by enormous fire directed at their LCA ramps. Those Rangers who were to survive went over the side, using the LCAs, DD [dual drive] tanks, other wreckage, and obstacles as a shield against enemy fire.

"We were delayed maybe thirty minutes, and it was about 8:00 A.M.," said Parker. "This is where Max Schneider's leadership and experience paid off. He saw what had happened to the 116th, which was cut to pieces, disorganized; the support elements like tanks, transport, artillery, and supply smashed together in a jumble. The enemy fire from casemated guns, pillboxes, and fortifications was just butchering them. Schneider swung the entire group farther east, from Dog Green to Dog White. We had fewer casualties and the command group was intact. We were the only cohesive force in that vital invasion area. The coxswain of our boat put us off in waist-deep water. He then held his boat in and used his machine gun, trying to suppress enemy fire to give us a better opportunity to cross the beach. I don't think it helped much because the Germans were all shooting from massively prepared positions. Still, it was an incredibly brave thing for him to do.

"We had to get across what seemed an endless expanse of sand and then an area of shingle, small rocks with bad footing. Behind us boats were being blown up and burning, artillery and mortal shells were exploding, machine-gun bullets ricocheting around. The water looked dimpled from the shrapnel and bullets. In addition to Schneider picking Dog White, we got another break. The grass and low bushes that grew on the flat portion of the land behind the beach and up the sides of the bluffs themselves was on fire. Smoke covered the whole area and the Germans couldn't put much observed fire on us. The fire also revealed the mines when the grass burned off. Later I heard the engineers removed about 150 of them from the areas.

"There was concertina wire behind the seawall and we

had to blow that with bangalore torpedoes. The assistant division commander of the 29th, General Cota, came strolling up the beach to where Schneider was. He asked who was in command and then supposedly made his famous line, 'Rangers, lead the way.' Schneider gave the word to us, 'Tallyho,' our planned signal to move out and assemble at the rally point south and west of Vierville."

Ranger lieutenant Frank "Buck" Dawson, a 5th Battalion, D Company platoon leader, occupied a ringside seat during the drive for Dog White beach. "I saw several large ships moving toward the beach. One fired a volley of rockets and I noticed a destroyer had cut across our front between us and the beach and was firing at gun positions as it moved along. Finally, the signal came for us to move out. The LCAs formed a skirmish line parallel to the beach. I could not make out the shore due to the haze and smoke. I began to notice the obstacles. Just ahead were four posts set at an angle with mines attached to the tops. We were just about in them and in the boat no one was talking. I imagine each had his own thoughts of what would happen when the ramp fell.

"We were very lucky. The landing craft was heading straight toward a pole obstacle with a large mine attached to the top and leaning seaward. The skipper on the LCA steered sharply left and the breaking waves just lifted our craft over. We came to a halt in knee-deep water. I could see my immediate destination, a seawall about fifty to seventy-five yards across a flat beach. I was completely pooped from the dash, wet boots, and equipment, with an ammo bag of .45-caliber magazines for my Thompson, gas mask, light pack, and entrenching tool. I was running but still noticed machine-gun rounds hitting near. The ones who stopped to take shelter behind obstacles and stayed at the water's edge were unlucky.

"I saw disabled tanks, one was burning. The noise of gunfire was everywhere, incoming and outgoing. Mortar rounds were falling between the seawall and the water's edge. At the seawall there were other men besides Rangers. You had to push in to get to the wall. I wanted to see what was on the other side. No effort was being made in my sector to get off the beach. I was busy getting my platoon head count and then sending my runner off to contact the company commander, telling him where we were, and finding out any order he might have for me.

"I would not have known General Cota from anyone else. [If Cota indeed said, 'Rangers lead the way,' the man who did as directed never heard him.] The confusion was enormous. When the word 'Go' was given, my two bangalore-torpedo men, [Elwood] Dorman and [Ellis] Reed, set off the charge. Before the dust cleared, I stepped into the cupped hands of my company first sergeant and platoon sergeant and was lifted over the wall through the area just blown. I began my run for the high ground. The ground was very flat, grassy, and in full view of the enemy.

"Knowing I was being fired on, I twice hit the ground, rolled over, sprang up, and continued. I chose to go to my right about fifty yards and then picked a route to climb. The bluff was steep but not a cliff. I knew there were mines in the area but I took a chance. I was alone while climbing the bluff, having outdistanced my platoon following in single file. I hadn't looked back because I was too busy looking forward, right, and left. I knew they were coming behind me; I just had that feeling. Beyond the top lay a battery of rockets that were firing. As I neared the crest smoke started to drift toward me but not enough to block my sight. So far, I had not seen any Germans and I continued to climb, using my hands on the ground to help me. Suddenly, I reached the top, traversed to the right where there were trenches and German soldiers. One, in particular, a huge man came straight at me. He was my first kill. Having a Thompson sub, I kept it hot. Several prisoners came out of a trench and I had them spread-eagle on the ground. By then, members of my platoon took over. One young German emerged with a hand blown off. We were not instructed regarding prisoners. We were attacking in a narrow column so we passed the prisoners back, hoping they got to the rear.

"As I continued along the ridge I saw below active machine-gun positions still firing on the beach. These Germans had not seen my platoon. My BAR man was near and I pointed out the positions to him. But he exposed himself too much and a German crew killed him. I retrieved the BAR and killed that crew. Others in the area were making a hasty retreat toward Vierville." Later, Dawson received a Distinguished Service Cross for his efforts and the two bangalore-torpedo men, Dorman and Ellis, were awarded Silver Stars.

Ranger captain John Raaen contended that in the amphibious aspect of the operation, "Schneider was outstanding. He waited as long as he dared before he diverted to Omaha. He watched the destruction of A and B Companies of the 2d Rangers and then brilliantly diverted to Omaha Dog White. That last move I credit for saving the Omaha beach operation. Without the 5th on the beach, the Germans would have stopped the 29th Division cold (they already had) and swept them back out to sea. Perhaps the 1st Division could have saved the left flank of Omaha, but I doubt they could have done it without the 29th Division's success, which came from the 5th Rangers being in the right place at the right time and in sufficient strength."

Company A, led by Charles (Ace) Parker, meanwhile, advanced upon the bluffs mentioned by Dawson as the eastern anchor of the Ranger line. Parker, with his runner William Fox and a lieutenant from E Company, halted to investigate a field with trees on the far side from them. "We didn't know it," said Parker "but there were snipers in those trees. One of them got us in his sights and we all went down. Fox squatted while the lieutenant and I went prone. A bullet hit Fox in the shoulder, leaving a small blue hole, and then angled down. Another one struck the lieutenant in the right side of his head, blowing out a piece of his skull, leaving his brains partly exposed.

"I kept trying to wriggle out from under my pack while lying flat. It was a huge pack; with enough in it for me to have survived for a month. I finally got my pistol and un-buckled the pack, although, meanwhile, that sniper put sev-eral bullets in it. I rolled over into a ditch and we roped the legs of the two wounded and pulled them into the ditch also. We stayed in that ditch for about three and a half hours be-fore we could get to the rallying point, a château. Every man behind Fox had to crawl over him in that ditch. He waved to everyone and smiled. We gave him a canteen of water and went on our way, on our bellies. There wasn't anything we could do for them. Later, they picked up the lieutenant, who somehow survived, hospitalized him, and he eventually re-gained his ability to speak and function. We didn't know on the other hand that the bullet that hit Fox had ranged down and cut his spine. He died in that ditch."

At the château, Parker counted his troops and discovered he had only twenty-three of his normal complement of close to seventy. Parker reasoned that the remainder of the 5th Battalion must be ahead, on their way to Pointe du Hoc. He led his troops through a series of hedgerows and secondary roads, hoping to catch up with the main body. "We kept switching directions, getting in small-fire fights, killing a few Germans each time, picking up some prisoners. I accepted the surrenders but I really didn't want 'em. We got to a small village, then the Germans started crawling along hedgerows on both sides of us. We could hear them and they were getting behind us. I turned all of the prisoners loose. We retreated at double time until we got well beyond where the Germans were. Eventually, we made contact with the outposted people of the 2d Rangers on Pointe du Hoc." Parker and his slim band now united with the meager forces that included Len Lomell, Jack Kuhn, and George Kerchner.

In his wallet, the chief executive for Overlord, Gen. Dwight D. Eisenhower, carried a brief, hand-written statement. "Our landings in the Cherbourg-Havre area have failed to gain a satisfactory foothold and I have withdrawn the troops. My decision to attack at this time and place was based upon the best information available. The troops, the air, and the Navy did all that bravery and devotion to duty could do. If any blame or fault attaches to the attempt it is mine alone." If his 1948 memoir *Crusade in Europe* is to be believed, he never felt he would need to release this message. There, Eisenhower wrote, "As the morning wore on, it became apparent that the landing was going fairly well." The statement, however, squares neither with the facts nor the reactions of those of his own high command.

Aboard the flagship of the American naval forces, the U.S.S. *Augusta*, Gen. Omar Bradley, as commander of the U.S. First Army, anxiously awaited word on the invasion's progress. In his autobiography he wrote, "As the morning lengthened, my worries deepened over the alarming and fragmentary reports we picked up on the navy net. From these messages we could piece together only an incoherent account of sinkings, swampings, heavy enemy fire, and chaos on the beaches."

Bradley's timetable expected the two assault regiments, the 116th from the 29th Division, and the 16th from the 1st Division, augmented by the Rangers and the waterborne tanks, to have passed a mile inland by 8:30 A.M. But at 10:00, the first report from Gen. Leonard Gerow, commander of the V Corps, charged with the conquest of Omaha Beach, brought gloom and fear. Gerow advised, "Obstacles mined, progress slow . . . DD tanks for Fox Green swamped."

Admiral Kirk and Bradley dispatched aides RAdm. Charles (Savvy) Cooke and Brig. Gen. Thomas Handy for a firsthand look. The latter remembered an appalled Cooke exclaiming, "My God, this is carnage!" Handy was equally dismayed. "It was terrible along that damned beach because they were not only under mortar fire but they were under small-arms fire. The amphibious tanks were all sinking and the beach obstacles blocked access."

The V Corps commander, Gen. Leonard Gerow, asked Handy, "How about it?"

"G, it isn't very good," was the reply. When Gerow pressed for advice on what to do, Handy said he responded, "The only thing you can do and you've got to do, regardless of the losses, you've got to push your doughboys [Handy dated from World War I] in far enough to get that damned beach out from under small-arms fire and if possible, mortar fire, because it's just terrible."

The anxious brass at sea, concerned with Omaha Beach, heard only a series of discouraging words about troops pinned down at the seawall; a beach swept by deadly enemy fire; assault and supply craft milling about offshore because of the failure to open more than six pathways through the honeycomb of mined obstacles. Navy UDTs and Army Engineers trying to blast lanes for the invaders suffered casualties estimated between 50 and 75 percent. Not only did they have to contend with what the foe threw at them but they were frustrated by GIs who clung to the mined obstacles. Detonation by the demolition experts would kill the hapless soldiers. The sole good news from the area was the report that Pointe du Hoc had fallen. Handy remarked, "At Omaha, we just hung on by our eyelashes. For several hours, I don't believe they ever realized how close that things were."

As noon approached, V Corps reported the situation "still critical" at all four of the avenues to a breakthrough on Omaha. Bradley admitted, "I reluctantly contemplated the diversion of Omaha follow-up forces to Utah and the British beaches. Scanty reports from both those sectors indicated the landings there had gone according to plan."

Navy lieutenant Harvey Bennett, serving as assistant gunnery officer for Admiral Kirk aboard the *Augusta*, insisted he saw no evidence of any wavering by Bradley. "I sat very close to him and at no time do I recall his intent to pull troops off the beaches." According to Bennett, the responsibility for bombardment of the beaches, rather than the dugouts, pillboxes, and emplacements guarding the approaches, lay with the U.S. Army Air Corps. "AAC decided on D day that visibility was not suitable. As far as I know, no other command was notified of this omission." Because of this apparent failure to communicate, the shoreline at Omaha Beach remained a pristinely smooth surface without shell holes that might have preserved the lives of those in the first waves.

Bennett also emphasized the serious flaw that marked combined assaults by Allied forces in Europe. "It would have taken more than a joint command to provide the same sort of air support the Navy had in the Pacific. The Army Air Corps and the RAF were basically concerned about their own war against German industry. In no operation in which I have been concerned has there ever been any liaison with the Army Air Corps." In place of a tactical partnership between aircraft and ground forces, the navy dispatched sailors equipped with radios to serve as shore fire-control parties. These teams, acting as forward observers for the ships, accompanied the earliest invaders, including the Rangers' attempt to scale Pointe du Hoc. As soon as minesweepers cleared the seas nearest land, destroyers moved in so close as to risk grounding in order to hammer targets named by the shore fire-control parties. In some instances where the navy personnel were killed or wounded, GIs such as Ranger Lou Lisko assumed the role of liaison with the seaborne gunners.

One of the first sailors to navigate the treacherous Channel waters to Omaha Beach was Dell Martin, coxswain aboard the last of thirteen LCMs (Landing Craft, Mechanized) bearing the spearhead forces around 6:00 A.M. "We circled around waiting to form into a line. I passed alongside a large French ship as she fired some very big guns. As the coxswain, I was in an enclosure by myself. When those shells went over my head, it felt as if someone had socked me in the jaw. My ears started ringing and have ever since. I get a 10 percent pension as a result and the VA also gives me hearing aids.

"It was low tide and the men on our ship got off in knee-deep water after we hit a sandbar. All the obstacles were high and dry. Each boat carried fifty men, half army and half navy. Their job was to blow 100-yard gaps at 50-yard intervals to open lanes for succeeding boats. The army men were responsible for the landward obstacles and the navy the ones in the sea. We ran into very heavy opposition. I understand losses went as high as 85 percent.

"We left the beach and went to a hospital ship to put off a man we had picked up on our way in. He was from one of the amphibious tanks that sank. From there we returned to a rendezvous area, circling about until called to shuttle the 1st Division and Rangers into the beach."

Gil Miller was a member of the crew on one of five boats that made up LCM (fifty-footers) Amphibious Force 88. Traveling under its own power about six miles an hour and pausing once for fuel, Miller was at sea fifteen hours once they departed from England. "Our job would be salvage and we were to go in at Omaha Beach one hour after H hour with the mission of keeping the lanes to the beach open. Six waves were to precede us and they would do any fighting that was necessary. We had a twenty-ton bulldozer that, once dropped off, would push aside anything that blocked the movement of troops or vehicles.

"The obstructions to the beach, crossed steel beams imbedded deep in the sand and with mines on top, were eerie-looking and sinister. I didn't have time to take notice of what was happening on the beach. Once we unloaded the bulldozer, we backed off with a load of wounded. Our starboard engine shut down; the shaft became caught in camouflage netting and the shaft bent in an S shape. It wasn't a big problem, one big engine could do the work of two. I happened to look up for a moment and lost my helmet. I then went down into the well of the LCM and talked to the wounded, passing out cigarettes. An officer called me over and offered me his helmet, saying, 'Here, you need this more than I.' He was badly wounded, his right hindquarter was gone. I went down between the engines and got out of our kit a clean undershirt. We patched him up the best we could. I put on his helmet and it had the bars of a lieutenant or captain on the front. Everytime I passed any of our crew they saluted. With my knife I scraped off the markings. After we passed on the wounded, an LSD repair ship pulled us up out of the water and in half an hour we had a new screw and shaft."

As the engineering officer, Richard Wilstatter, a lieutenant jg on LST 133, was below deck as his ship proceeded toward its position two or three miles off Omaha Beach to await instructions. The invasion plans slated LST 133 for a kind of triple duty. On board were men from the 1st Division with an attached unit of five DUKWs, each packed with seven tons of munitions as well as trucks, jeeps, ammunition, and weapons carriers. In addition, the vessel's personnel included a hospital unit with a pair of navy physicians and roughly twenty pharmacist mates to assist them. An army doctor and his two assistants rounded out the team designated to treat wounded taken off the beach. In its third role, an LST had towed a Rhino ferry (a barge constructed from pontoons) bearing a navy Construction Battalion (CB), more commonly known as Seabees, and its personal tug to the outer anchorage for the fleet off Omaha Beach.

"When we reached our position off Omaha and anchored while awaiting further instructions, it was realized that the situation on the beach was far from 'proceeding according to plan.' A great many ships had been set afire and sunk in the region of the beach. The beach itself was badly infested with obstacles and mines and was still under heavy 88mm and machine-gun fire. Most of the LCTs and LCIs that had hit the beach that morning were casualties there and blocked the further approach of other landing craft. As we learned later from a colonel of the army amphibious troops, the first soldiers had sustained heavy losses and hardly any reinforcements had been able to land.

"Sometime during the day, we received orders to beach at

utmost speed—your cargo urgently needed. We could see that the beach and nearby water were still very much under 88 fire. However, we weighed anchor and proceeded in toward Dog Red. We were stationed at general quarters and in the engine room we received the following, 'All engines ahead flank!'

"On our ship, the 'captain's talker' (an enlisted man with a set of sound-powered phones, who stands alongside the captain where he can instantly communicate with any section of the ship) was a yeoman, married, who when ashore indulged himself extraordinarily and was not an admirable person. On the way to the beach he was very loudly praying to God to protect us/save him and us. Everyone on the phone system was deluged with this outpouring of begging. Then there was a loud voice from some unknown quarter, 'Oh, Allen, shut the hell up!'

"About the time we figured we should be hitting the beach, came the orders, 'All engines stop!' Then immediately, 'All engines back emergency!' Later, I learned we had been approached by a control boat that gave us contrary orders and commanded we retire from the beach at once. We were so close in that it would have been impossible for us to turn, normally, without going on the beach sidewise. We returned to our anchorage area close off the beach.

"Very shortly thereafter, small boats and DUKWs came to us, carrying wounded from the beach. Since we were an auxiliary hospital ship, we received all casualties brought to us. Because all the troops and cargo still remained aboard, our crew vacated their aft quarters for use as bunks for wounded. A makeshift operating room with operating lights was installed on a raised platform on the aft end of the tank deck. A second site for surgeons was a starboard table in the wardroom.

"Somewhere around eighty patients, all on stretchers in the small craft and DUKWs, were lifted through a sling arrangement that raised a litter by electric power. Once aboard, stretcher-bearers took the litter through a hatch from the galley passageway, passed it through the window over the galley steam tables, and then down the ladder into the crew's quarter. Patients so badly injured that they probably could not survive this treatment went immediately into the wardroom for attention. Too much credit cannot be given to a Captain Ely, the army surgeon who worked endlessly and with great skill on these badly shattered men.

"Shortly before dark, the DUKW officer on our LST decided his loads of ammunition must be badly needed and he would try to get through. The captain gave permission for the attempt. The bow doors opened and the ramp lowered. The lieutenant and his five ducks rolled out and headed for the beach. They made it."

Aboard LCI 491, Bill Hughes, a ship's electrician learning his duties on the job, watched about 100 good-humored soldiers settle in on his vessel for the ride to Omaha Beach. "On June 5th we fed them all their last hot meal. We were told to destroy all letters, mail, any papers we carried with us. By 0200 of the 6th we were off the coast of France. The word from the beach all morning was bad. Until noon, the rumor was they were all going to come off the beach and that's why we didn't go in. We were held back and did not land our troops until 1400 hours. It was high tide and none of the obstacles were visible. On the way back, we saw all of them sticking out of the water with bodies, missing their shoes, floating among them. A British LCT broke in half; we pulled out the survivors."

By the time Dick Conley, an officer replacement with the 18th Infantry Regiment of the 1st Division, in the second wave of infantry, arrived, Easy Red was less lethal. "We climbed down rope cargo nets from the sides of the Liberty ships [cargo and troop vessels specially designed for World War II] around 0700. The waves were so high, the LCVPs going up and down, many feet, you had to time the moment you let go of the net to drop into the boat. If you hit it while it was going down, that was okay. But it you dropped while it was coming up, that was not good. Altogether, we had about thirty soldiers.

"We spent four and a half hours in the LCVP [Landing Craft, Vehicles and Personnel]. We were supposed to keep our heads down but everybody had to stand up to take a look at what we were facing, what was waiting. When we looked at the beach, all we could see was a haze of smoke. As we closed in on it, the place was so crowded with debris, wrecked craft, and vehicles that we had a great deal of difficulty finding a place to get in. But we had a good crew that dropped us in fairly shallow water.

"It was about 11:30 and about an hour and a quarter later than scheduled. As the leader I charged off first. It was knee-deep and when I hit it, my feet didn't keep up with the rest of me. I went down flat. But I didn't get any wetter than I already was. As soon as we got ashore, we stripped off the plastic covering from our rifles and carbines and I assembled my platoon. We dropped our life belts and I directed that pole charges, satchel charges, and bangalore torpedoes be discarded because I could see the beach had been breached, we wouldn't need them. I saw my first dead American soldiers as soon as I got ashore. Most were in the water at the shoreline."

Dick Biehl was an infantry replacement with B Company of the 26th Infantry Regiment. He arrived in North Africa too late for an encounter with the *Afrika Korps* but entered combat in Sicily. The 26th was to advance to Omaha Easy Red upon orders from the commanding general of the V Corps, behind the assault waves from its two brother regiments in the 1st Division. Biehl did not feel particularly reassured. "I cannot recall if I was more sick than scared. I was very seasick and frightened. Mentally, I knew I had to accept where I was and what was expected of me. On the way in I could see smoke, some fire, hear shells exploding. Lots of friendly aircraft passed overhead with the black-and-white stripes on the wings and fuselage as we were told they would be. Those planes were somewhat of a comfort.

"About 100 yards from the edge of the water we ran aground. The young officer commanding the vessel wanted us off the ship as soon as possible, so he could back off the sandbar and proceed away from the artillery fire that was hitting the water around the craft. I don't think he was chicken. From his vantage point he could tell wounded were being brought out to his ship to be taken back to England or hospital ships, and he needed to lighten his load and so ordered us off. I am six feet, one-half inches, and as the first one off the ladder on the port side I stepped into water neck-deep. I do not understand how the fellows shorter than I made it. Some things I saw remain quite vivid. I recall two medics, dragging out to the ship we had just vacated, a wounded GI with a hole in his forehead I could have laid my fist in. I saw burning landing craft, a jeep bobbing on the water like a cork . . . a lone sailor who I suppose survived a damaged or sunken landing craft, appearing very confused . . . one of our guys wandering into a mine area but being retrieved okay by two engineers with mine detectors . . . a dead engineer still in a kneeling position with his shovel in his hands, trying to dig into some cover.

"We had a few wounded on the beach but training paid off

as reactions became automatic in given situations. Assigned missions were scrubbed. The resistance was greater than anticipated because the German 352d Infantry Division had arrived just prior to the landings. Those guys were scattered but pockets of resistance were numerous."

Leo Deschamps, a 1st Engineer Combat Battalion replacement, via Algiers and then England, was assigned to a thirty-man assault team. Even though it was H plus 5 hours when his group arrived, the enemy resistance continued. "As the landing craft neared the beach, a shell hit the lowering mechanism and the gate fell down. The Navy [coxswain] told us this was it; he couldn't get any closer. We stepped off 300 yards offshore. As I entered the water, DeLuca stepped into a shell hole. I grabbed him by his Mae West and squeezed the belt to activate the air unit. He bounced back up and treaded water until his feet touched ground. Dave Perlie went to the left up a ravine; his body was found three days later. The others went right. The beach itself was a madhouse; bodies lay where they fell and shouts for medics were in the air. Some corpses were half in and half out of the water and as the waves rolled in the bodies would sway back and forth like dolls.

"There was a depression in the beach, a tank trap, and we had to go through the water a second time to get to the beach proper. A sergeant directed us and we assembled at the battalion command post. We were sitting eating our rations by 1:00 or 1:30 P.M. I am not ashamed to say I prayed all the way in and I prayed also till the next day whenever I had free time."

Sometime after the fire on Omaha slackened, Bill Behlmer regained consciousness. "I heard voices. Sailors were on the beach. One of them rolled me over and said I was still alive. He took me out to the troopship, the *Samuel*

*Chase,* which was now a hospital ship. It was around noon, I later learned. That probably saved my life. The war was over for me. The next morning I was in a hospital in England where they amputated my right leg above the knee due to gangrene. No one was at fault or could have done more for me." His driver Stypulkowski also recovered from his wounds.

# 12

# Utah Beach

To the west of Omaha Beach lay the shelf of yellow sand roughly nine miles in length with the code name Utah Beach. At low tide it was 300–400 yards wide with a low concrete wall inland. Beyond the beach lay the heavily inundated areas into which the troopers from the 82d and 101st dropped. Ordinarily eleven causeways led toward the heart of France but the flooding left only three dry. Once inland, the 4th Infantry Division, with tank and artillery support, would advance over these causeways, secured by the paratroopers against any attempt by German reserves to push the infantrymen back into the sea.

Captain George Mabry and a naval officer designated for the task coordinated the loading of boat teams from his ship onto landing craft. "We ran into trouble when the men began climbing down the nets to the boats below. The Channel was extremely rough and cold. Soldiers climbing down this slippery, cold net, attempting to enter into the small LCVPs bouncing up and down in the pitch-black dark was quite a chore. On two occasions, just before men were to turn loose and jump into the LCVP, a foot would get hung up in the rope and hang the man upside down. The boat would come up and smack the soldier on the shoulder or the head, even while those already in the boat tried to push the man up. You'd see the landing craft high up on a wave, almost halfway to the rail of the ship and then suddenly so far down in a trough you could dimly see it."

The assistant division commander, Terry Allen's former deputy, Brig. Gen. Theodore Roosevelt Jr., had chosen to accompany Mabry's battalion. When the moment for his boat team was about to come, Mabry hastened to notify Roosevelt. "He thanked me," said Mabry, "and then hollered to his aide, 'Stevie, where is my life belt?' Stevie said, 'General, I don't know. I've already given you three.' General Roosevelt said, 'Damnit, I don't care how many you've given me, I don't have one now.' " Mabry and the aide searched and found one for the general. When Mabry asked whether Roosevelt had all his armament, he patted his shoulder holster and responded, "I've got my pistol, one clip of ammunition, and my walking cane. That's all I expect to need."

The assistant division commander expected to accompany part of E Company, scheduled for the first wave. Mabry recalled, "Even though Roosevelt's boat was to be rail loaded, it still required a jump of four or five feet down to the deck of the LCVP. When a soldier reached up from the boat and said, 'Here, General, let me help you,' Roosevelt took his walking stick and lightly tapped the young man on the arm. He said in a friendly growl, 'Get the hell out of my way. I can jump in there by myself. I can take it as well as any of you.' Although tension ran at fever pitch, the remarks brought smiles and a few chuckles."

Compared to Omaha Beach, Utah was less heavily defended. Two casemated positions overlooked the shoreline but only one actually held big guns. The Germans had not completed installation of barriers in the water and there were fewer mines. Underwater demolition teams blew up much of what posed a threat to landing craft. Furthermore, the naval bombardment, in contrast to what happened off Omaha, pounded the shoreline, punishing the existing German positions and also providing convenient shellholes in which foot soldiers could take refuge.

Although Bradley spoke of the assault on Utah going "according to plan," in fact, Utah, assigned to the 4th Infantry Division, did not follow the blueprints, and that deviation had much to do with the success enjoyed there. Nor was it a "walk-in." The commander of the 22d Regiment's 3d Battalion, Lt. Col. Arthur S. Teague, described the initial wave. "We came ashore on LCMs operated by Navy enlisted men. On our LCM [a sailor] remarked this was the third landing in which he had participated and that he didn't mind the initial landing as much as the one afterward because he would have to keep bringing in supplies. Just as we were coming in to shore, I saw a shell fired from up the beach and I knew some of us were going to be hit. I saw spurts of water coming up. I saw one small landing craft hit, and thinking the same might happen to us, I told the Navy man to ram the beach as hard as possible. He held it wide open for about 200 yards and we hit the beach and stepped off on dry soil. A couple of boats behind us—about seventy-five yards back in the water—were hit and then I saw a number of casualties. Many were killed and quite a few wounded.

"I started up by the seawall on the sand dunes and stopped for a moment. I heard someone call me. It was General Roosevelt. He told me we had landed way to the left of where we were supposed to have landed and he wanted us to get this part of the beach cleared as soon as possible. He wanted action from my men immediately after landing and asked me to get them down the beach as soon as I could. This was about 0930."

Roosevelt had quickly realized the helmsmen's errors delivered the initial wave some 2,000 yards south of the prescribed location. Instead of seeking to correct the mistake and shift his forces laterally, Roosevelt, observing the relative ease of the landing, deemed a hookup with the airborne troopers paramount. He ordered the troops to advance inland. Following Roosevelt's directive, a skirmish line organized by Teague rousted some German soldiers. When they surrendered they claimed ignorance of the minefields beyond the beach. Forced by Teague to accompany the Americans over the seawall, the prisoners quickly revealed safe pathways.

George Mabry, with his battalion commander, Col. Carlton McNeely, occupied a "free boat," one that could come in at any stage of the invasion. McNeely decided to arrive behind the third wave, when some idea of the progress of the assault could be determined. "As light began to improve," said Mabry, "the first casualty I saw was a Navy boat that apparently had hit a mine. One sailor was lying on the keel of the boat, holding onto a man who was obviously either critically wounded or dead. That boat had been stationed to mark the lanes for approaching the beach. Soon after, I saw a large transport hit a mine; the front just rose up into the air and bucked like a horse, rocking from side to side. You could see personnel jumping off the ship.

"About this time, the bombers began to bomb the beaches. Wave after wave came parallel to the beach dropping their bombs. Smoke and dust obliterated the area. We couldn't see the shore or any distinguishing features that we had memorized. As bombers went away, naval gunfire opened up. They began to pulverize the beaches and behind them. Rocket ships began to discharge toward the beach. As we got closer to the beach, a German ME 109 fighter came out of the clouds and seemed to me to be diving directly at our landing craft. Right behind that ME 109 came a British Spitfire that fired three bursts of its machine guns. That German ME 109 just disintegrated in the air and the propeller fell right in front of our landing craft.

"The coxswain, a Navy man piloting our craft, kept falling farther and farther behind. Colonel McNeely hollered for him to speed it up and then we slowed down. About this time we passed some of the floating tanks from the 70th Tank Battalion, which had worked closely with the 8th Infantry Regiment in England. They'd been discharged 800 or 900 yards from the beach. Unfortunately, they didn't work too well in the rough Channel. They'd have been fine on a millpond. They were kind of wallowing in the sea and every once in a while you'd see them start to sink. They had a rubber raft and you'd see the crew take it out and jump on it and get away. As we passed the company commander's tank, the crew bailed out, all except the company commander. I assumed he drowned. Later I found out his foot got caught, he went down with the tank, doubled himself up, freed his foot and then swam to the surface and was evacuated.

"When for the third time Colonel McNeely told this coxswain to speed it up and we slowed down again, McNeely pulled his pistol and pressed the barrel against the sailor's head. 'Look, you son of a bitch, I told you to speed up. I'm not going to tell you again. Move it, now!' The young fellow understood. He really moved out. We went through the third wave, traveling fast. I was trying to pick up landmarks; the bombing apparently knocked them down but we figured there was something wrong. The terrain, the beach, didn't look right. We were coming too far to the left, we could see the mouth of the Merderet River and we were supposed to be a thousand yards farther to the right.

"As we approached the beaches the pillboxes became more clear, the tetrahedrons stood out like bristles on a hog's back. We landed right behind the second wave, elements of E and F Companies [of the 2d Battalion, 8th Regiment]. Just as the bottom of the landing craft touched the ground, this coxswain dropped the ramp. He wasn't going any further. Men began to jump off the left and right corners of the ramp. Right ahead of me was this short fellow, 'Smoky' David. He jumped and just disappeared. Seeing this, I jumped in front of the ramp. When I hit the bottom and came up, water was up to my neck. I looked behind and suddenly Smoky David's bald head appeared behind the landing craft. Somehow he had gone under the boat, missed the prop. He got rid of his equipment and began swimming toward the beach. We moved through this water to the beach. We'd been trained that once you hit the beach, you run across that thing; never lie down on it and don't crowd up against the seawall. You've got to push on inland. That was drilled into us.

"Walking through that water, dragging along, we met with something we hadn't reckoned with—right adjacent to our left was Pointe du Hoc, next to the Merderet River. Germans had artillery batteries honeycombed in that Pointe. The Rangers [who were to neutralize the guns] had difficulty and German artillery and mortar fire was raking the beaches. Companies E, F, and G were issued black rockets to signal the navy gunfire to lift from the beach and shift it inland. I saw a black rocket from E Company go off. Later

I saw one from F Company go off. As we were coming ashore, German artillery was just raking the beach. When I and the other fellows heard a shell coming, we'd duck down in water and let it splatter over us. Then try to run again. But when we got to waist-deep or less, you couldn't duck down far and the water was so cold that our muscles had become cramped. You'd run six or seven paces and there was no way you could go farther. You'd hit the beach, lie there a second or two, then get up and run again.

"Just before I got out of the water, Corporal Speck, one of my baseball players when I coached the team at Fort Benning, was lying there. He had been hit in both legs. I reached down to help him but he stopped me. He said, 'Captain, your place is inland. Leave me alone and get moving.' It was a tough thing to do, to leave him there. But he kept insisting my place was inland. I moved forward. Ahead of me was a man carrying like a cloverleaf of 81mm mortar ammunition. This he was to drop at the seawall so that H Company with the mortars would then run down the seawall and gather up the ammunition for their use. As we were struggling to cross the beach, I was standing up trying to run and this man was doing the same. A mortar round came in and hit this soldier right on top of his head. That caused the 81mm mortar rounds to detonate also and this man's body completely disappeared. I felt something hit me on my thigh and it was this man's thumb. It was the only discernible part of a human being you could see. To my left I saw a human stomach lying on the beach. No one dead or alive was near it. It was a stark, grotesque sight." According to Mabry, those on the beach believed the shells falling in their midst belonged to the offshore fleet, but the most damaging artillery came from the defenders.

Mabry knew for certain they had come ashore some 800

to 1,000 yards to the left of their original proposed site because of the location of the Merderet, the absence of the expected number of tetrahedrons, and the abundance of barbed wire in the water. The navigational error happened due to miscalculation of the effects of the weather and speed of the tide. Mabry remembered briefly spotting Roosevelt, waving his cane, urging troops to keep moving.

Although separated from other troops, Mabry now sought to implement the plan devised with McNeely. The strategy called for troops to proceed directly inland over sand dunes, perhaps half a mile, to an inundated area. There, three causeways crossed the flooded low ground. Seizure of these was vital because if the enemy could destroy them and then counterattack while the Americans were trapped between beach and inundated area they would be in serious trouble. He and McNeely divided up supervision of their attacking companies.

"Having finally gotten to the seawall," said Mabry, "I followed a squad of about six men from G Company being led by a red-haired sergeant. As they went over the seawall, they began moving toward a fence. The sergeant started through the barbed wire. A tremendous explosion occurred. Obviously he had stepped on a mine. All six men fell to the ground, some killed, some wounded, some screaming. I ran beyond them because my mission was to follow G Company and ensure that Causeway I was secured. Naval gunfire was now falling inland and German artillery was coming in the area where we were located.

"I was by myself and didn't see anyone else. I began to run over a sand dune and started to receive small-arms fire from some Germans dug in on the sand-dune line. Periodically I would hit the ground and try to survey the situation and pick up the smoke from the German rifles to locate the enemy. After about two short rushes from one sand dune to another, I looked around my feet and noted I was in a minefield. The wind had blown away the sand and uncovered some of them. Having seen the squad killed and wounded by the mine, I thought, if I turn around and try to go back to the beach I'll probably step on a mine. My mission is inland so I'm going to take my chances and continue to move toward the enemy firing at me. I got up, made another dash, landed successfully and safely. The next time I jumped up and ran, the small-arms fire was cracking around me pretty close. I made a long leap to a shell hole I had spied and while in midair, my right foot apparently caught the trip wire attached to a mine. The mine exploded, and the force of it slammed me against the shell hole I was headed for. It numbed my right leg and I thought I had lost a foot. Looking around carefully, I found I had not been touched. My leg was intact. I regained my composure and decided to continue the advance.

"By this time the German rifle fire had subsided a little bit. I assume they thought I had been killed by the mine explosion. I jumped up and ran directly toward the position the Germans were firing from. Apparently I startled them. When I reached the top of the dune line I saw several individual foxholes. The first one was empty but hand grenades and rifle ammunition was all around the edge. I jumped into it and quickly realized this was a rather precarious position because they must have seen me jump into this foxhole. I scrambled out and saw, about eight yards from me, a German in a foxhole who had a hand grenade, a potato masher, in a position to toss it into the foxhole I had been in. I turned on the German and shot him. Germans started getting up on all sides of me; the total count was nine. They raised their hands quickly. I corralled them in a group, I noticed two noncommissioned officers and the others were of lesser rank. I looked over my shoulder toward the Channel. The sight bewildered me. It appeared the entire Channel was choked with ships of all sizes and descriptions. I thought these Germans had a lot of guts to be shooting small-arms fire at even one individual, when they had spread out before them a panorama of the largest invasion force that a human being had ever seen.

"I really did not know what to do with these prisoners. I saw a soldier about a hundred yards away with a bloody cloth wrapped around one hand. He turned out to be Corporal West of G Company I asked where the company was and he told me they were halted by a minefield behind me. I had assumed they were in front of me. I instructed West to escort the prisoners back to the beach and warned him to make a semicircle to avoid the minefield I had negotiated."

Mabry now searched for G Company. After about 300 yards, he met a pair of enlisted GIs, including a BAR man named Ballard, whom he knew to be an excellent marksman. They came upon a huge German pillbox. "Machine-gun fire opened up on us and we dove into a deep ditch nearby. We crawled down the ditch to within one hundred and fifty yards of the bunker. I told Ballard to spray the slits of the bunker with his BAR to determine whether these Germans inside really meant business. He gave a few well-placed bursts and ducked down in the ditch. Two embrasures of the pillbox began delivering machine-gun fire over our heads. This was a formidable emplacement and they meant business. I asked the other soldier if he knew the route back to the beach and could bring back one of the DD tanks and other soldiers."

The first U.S. DD tanks had finally crawled ashore. According to Mabry, about half an hour later, his emissary led in two DD tanks and they began to blast the pillbox. After shells pierced an opening, a white flag poked out of an embrasure. Mabry and Ballard counted thirty-six Germans. The tanks continued to knock off enemy fortifications. Barriers to prevent an exit from Utah fell under the onslaught of the tankers. A flamethrower drove twenty-five defenders from their pillbox, as well as two American paratroopers being held prisoners. Unlike Omaha, the Germans were unable to pin down elements of the 4th Division in a beach killing zone.

Harper Coleman, a member of heavy weapons H Company in the 8th Infantry Regiment, stepped from the transport directly into an LCVP. "Being with the first waves had some advantage. We were not required to go over the sides of the ship. In the water, the small craft began to form groups. We circled under one of the battleships. It was firing the big guns. You could actually see the projectiles going through the air.

"As we moved toward the shore in lines, we passed rocket-launcher ships and they were releasing salvos on the beach, still some distance ahead. It was almost hidden from view by smoke and shell bursts. I saw the craft ahead of ours going up with some sort of direct hit, which left us first. Before we reached the shore, something came through the side of our craft and tore a hole, in one side and out the other. It also ripped a good-size piece from my backpack. I saw a Navy ship lying on its side with many people on the side. We did not stop to render assistance.

"The history books say we landed some distance to the left from where we were supposed to be and this made it one of the easier landings. It did not seem good at the time. We went into the water more than waist-deep. If you're being fired on by small arms and artillery, light or heavy, it does not seem to make much difference at the time. Our first casualty was just behind me with a serious wound to the stomach. A second man was in front of me when he stepped on a land mine. After this we found out that the mines were all marked with a wooden stick. It seems they did not have time to remove the markers or else didn't expect a landing could take place. Those wooden sticks saved many from getting into the mines.

"When we came ashore, we had a greeter. Brig. Gen. Theodore Roosevelt was standing there waving his cane and giving out instructions, as only he could. If we were afraid of the enemy, we were more afraid of him and could not have stopped on the beach had we wanted. Our squad of six was down to four very early, one person on the beach and one when we came to a higher ridge, just beyond the sandy area. We made a left turn as we came over the top of the beach on what seemed to be a path. Moving as fast as we could, we came to a road that led to the beach and this took us through the swamps, which had been flooded by the Germans. We came up on the small town of Pouppeville. This is where we began to see the results of our work, our first dead enemies. Shortly beyond the town, we began to meet some of the airdrop people."

While Coleman, as a member of the same battalion as George Mabry, advanced inland, Mabry, having dispatched BAR man Ballard to escort the prisoners to the beach, grabbed another GI to accompany him toward Causeway I. They reached a point where Mabry noticed a hedgerow that he believed put them close to the objective. However, a field surrounded by a barbed-wire fence, which frequently indicated a minefield, lay dead ahead. "I recalled a piece of intelligence given while in England that stated that if a length of straight wire extended skyward from the corner posts, the minefield was a dummy. On the other hand, if the wire curled like a corkscrew, it was a live field. I saw a straight line extend from the corner post closest to us. I explained to the soldier about the wire and said I would test the veracity of our intelligence. If I hit a mine, the soldier was to head back and contact G Company.

"I crawled through the wire fence and into the field. Talk about walking on eggshells, I was really tiptoeing. I detected no bumps in the grounds and saw no disturbances of the earth, either fresh or old; the minefield was indeed a fake. I motioned for the soldier to follow. We quickly reached the hedgerow and keeping low began to creep down it. I peered over the top and there, only 150 yards away, I saw our Causeway I. At this time we began to hear rifle fire coming from across the flooded area opposite the causeway bridge.

"When we reached a point only forty-five yards from the causeway, we were forced to stop. To get closer we would have to go over the hedgerow to a parallel ditch on the other side. Although there were only two of us, the causeway had to be held at all costs. I decided to make a dash for it and told the soldier to cover me. If I did not get pinned down, I would wave him across. I made it to the ditch, which was filled with nearly two feet of water. I had received no fire, so the soldier promptly followed me. I noticed then that the rifle fire had begun to pick up on the far side of the bridge. We had moved up to a position just thirty yards from the causeway when two German soldiers began running down the road from the direction of village of Pouppeville. I told my companion not to shoot until they got very close to the bridge. When they reached within ten yards of the far side of the bridge, we opened up. Both men fell. Immediately, a squad of seven or eight Germans appeared and moved off the road to their right. They approached the bridge in skirmish formation. They were clearly trying to outflank us and we began shooting at them.

"The gunfire on the far side of the bridge intensified. I felt some of the shots were directed at the same Germans we had engaged. Some of the firing, however, seemed to be aimed at us and had the sound of an M1 rifle instead of a German one. I believed American paratroopers must be closing in from the other side of the bridge. I pulled out my square of orange cloth that identified us as allies and hoisted it on a stick over my head. A few more rifle bullets cracked around but then an orange flag waved back and forth from beyond the bridge. It had to be the paratroopers. All the rifle fire concentrated on that squad attempting to outflank us.

"Several minutes passed and the German rifle fire tapered off and then ended. I decided to run across the bridge to contact the airborne forces. If I didn't get any trouble, I'd wave my companion forward. The soldier covered me as I dashed across. As I ran, I spotted a huge aerial bomb wired for detonation lashed onto the bridge. The Germans we had shot had probably been on their way to blow the bridge. When I reached the far side I saw the two Germans sprawled on the road. They were dead. Several yards away I noticed other German soldiers all around. Some were lying on the side of the road, some in the bushes, and others in a slight ditch a few yards away. One of them appeared to be shaking so I gave him a hard kick in the thigh with my boot. He quickly jumped up and surrendered. Suddenly all the Germans around me began standing up. I gathered them into a group. I had a total of eight prisoners.

"Before I could even consider what to do with them I heard a noise in front of me. An airborne soldier jumped over a hedgerow with his rifle at the ready. I hollered to him, 'Don't shoot, I got some prisoners.' I marched them up to him and he was a member of the 101st Airborne Division. We shook hands and he told me that Maj. Gen. Maxwell Taylor, commanding general of the 101st, was just across the hedgerow and would surely be glad to see me. Seconds later, General Taylor, preceded by two men, crawled over the hedgerow. I saluted and we shook hands. I glanced down at my watch. It was 11:05 A.M. As far as I know, this was the first official contact between airborne troops and seaborne troops. Minutes later, Brig. Gen. James Gavin, the assistant division commander of the 82d Airborne Division, came over the hedgerow along with Lt. Col. Julian Ewell, a battalion CO, and ten airborne soldiers."

Bob Meyer, the BAR man with G Company, 2d Battalion of the 22d Infantry Regiment, stepped from his boat onto the sand of Utah Beach. "Wet feet were the least of our worries. The beach was being shelled by artillery and it was a very serious reminder that someone would like to kill us to prevent the success of the invasion. As we were moving forward, a shell exploded near us and Kinser hit the ground. But if the shell has exploded and you're still going, there is little point of hitting the ground, although it is one's first instinct. I grabbed his shoulder strap and helped him to his feet so we could continue running.

"In one of our early engagements we ran out of ammunition for our BAR. Fortunately, a machine-gun crew gave us some to keep going. The BAR has a crew of three. One is the gunner who carries it, ten magazines with twenty rounds each and some bandoliers of ammunition. The assistant gunner, who has an M1 rifle and bullets for it, plus bandoliers for the BAR, takes over the weapon if the gunner is hit. The third man is the designated ammunition carrier, and he also has an M1 with its ammo, plus bandoliers for the BAR. We started out with something like 200 rounds each in addition to what I had in my ten magazines. But after we ran out of ammunition once, we increased our load to all we could carry. I would take about 600 rounds, plus the magazines to add up to 800 rounds. That meant about forty pounds to carry, plus the BAR, which was around twenty-one pounds. Then there were things like hand grenades, an entrenching tool, canteens and other stuff. I was so heavy that when I stepped down from a little curbing or the like, I often just fell in a heap and had to pick myself up.

"Shortly after we landed," Meyer continued, "we came upon the weapon the GIs named the Screaming Meemie [*Nebelwerfer*], because of the soul-wrenching sound it made when launched. It was a kind of rocket that could be fired right out of the crate and originally they fired them from six barrels. We saw individual ones, about the size of a five-gallon can. When fired from their six-barrel mortar, everything in the circular strike zone could be killed by the concussion alone. If you happened to be where one landed, there would be nothing left to indicate you'd ever been there. We had a scout hit and all we found of him were his shoes.

"We had a person in our company named S——, who was more animal-like than anyone I had ever seen before. When he stood, his arms and hands stretched down past his knees. I never heard him speak. If he had to respond, a sort of grunt was all you would get. It took several trips for him to qualify with an M1, and I wondered if he really did qualify or whether they tired of taking him out to the range. He would sit in the mess hall and with those long arms just reach for what he wanted. Once he reached across Sergeant Garner's plate and Garner stabbed him in the back of his hand with a fork. He didn't even say 'Ouch.' Just became a little more careful where he put his hand.

"There'd been several tries to get him out of the army on

a Section-8 [the regulation that allowed discharge for mental problems], but our captain was convinced he was faking. During our early confrontation with the Germans, S—— was still with us. Bullets were flying everywhere and we were all keeping as low as possible. Suddenly, he stood up and said the only thing I ever heard from him. It was something like, 'To hell with this,' and walked to the rear. We watched him disappear over the little hill behind us as he walked back to the beach. Bullets were everywhere but S—— didn't get hit. God must have been watching over him. We were sure that back on the beach he was seen for what he was, a Section-8, and sent home.

"I think it was at the end of this firefight, when we routed the Germans, that a German SS officer hid in ambush and opened fire with a machine gun, practically cutting in half our captain, Robert Russell, a VMI graduate. Then he dropped his weapon and threw up his hands. This might have gotten him captured, except that, as he put up his hands, he was laughing. It was his last laugh. Our executive officer, Joe Jackson, who weighed 240 pounds with no fat, stuck him with a bayonet and pitched him like a bundle of grain. We weren't too fond of our captain but he was one of us. We were certainly motivated by his death, which we thought cruel and unnecessary. We went through the rest of that German group like a hot knife through butter."

Marion Adair, the surgeon of the 8th Infantry Regiment's 2d Battalion, clambered into an LCVP at 2:30 A.M. In his diary he wrote: "We churn around about 22,000 yards offshore and for a while I think we are lost. Eventually our wave forms and we start toward the beach about dawn. It is terribly rough. We are all drenched, and all but another and myself get terribly seasick.

"We pass Îles St. Marcourf [an offshore spit of land seized

just before the invaders struck the mainland], past battleships and cruisers firing, past rocket LSTs that loose a deafening barrage. There is so much smoke and dust that we can
hardly see. Finally, soaked to the skin, we brace and our boat
touches land. We jump off into three feet of muddy water
and wade to the beach, which is extremely wide at this time
(the tide is just past ebb and coming in).

"We hear shells whining in and think at first it's our own
Navy. But it isn't. The time is 7:00 A.M., thirty minutes after
H hour. I see my first casualty, gunshot wound of the mouth.
We keep working to the seawall, diving into shell holes
every time a shell whines. I get very muddy and my pack
weighs a ton. We see the engineers blowing up the beach obstacles and logs are sailing through the air. Finally, I make
contact with Vic [battalion surgeon Sam Victor] and Chaplain Ellenberg, and we set up a temporary aid station on the
beach. Our next patient that comes was blown up by a mine
and dies. After about two hours, the engineers have blown a
path through the seawall and cleared a path through the
minefield.

"We clear off the beach and work inland. We set up an aid
station just off a little road, eat our rations, and begin to treat
some casualties, including a Jerry. We move south and I'm
glad because the Jerries are shelling the beach quite vigorously. I see my first dead German and we have a few casualties, including Stark, who lost his foot due to stepping on
a mine. We cross the flooded area into Pouppeville where
we run into some wounded from the 101st Airborne and
some Jerry wounded. After this we keep walking to Ste.-
Marie-du-Mont, pass through that town, and follow the
highway toward the Carentan-Cherbourg Highway."

The progress made by Adair indicates the success of the
Utah landings. Malcolm Williams, a North Carolinian who

had tea with King George V, as a member of the 12th Infantry Regiment, was with the later arrivals at Utah. In contrast to Coleman Harper, Williams and his fellow GIs experienced considerable risk just transferring from their LC to the assault boat. "We had to go down a rope ladder with both boats rocking like hell. Everyone was seasick and scared shitless, but we knew what our job was and we were ready to do it. The craft hit bottom and that moment the ramp went down."

Roosevelt was still acting as a kind of host to the newcomers. "He said to us, 'How do you boys like the beach?' After we got off the beach, the trouble started. The heavy equipment on the only open causeway was drawing enemy fire. So we decided to cross the flooded area. We'd been told it was about three to five feet deep and if we stepped in over our heads to swim for about six feet and we would be back where we could walk. We did that until we reached the other side. We could hear machine-gun fire in the distance but it was on the causeway.

"Our first wounded was a major but it wasn't serious. Sergeant Noe, who I always paired off with when digging a hole, had a bullet hit the stock of his rifle, clipping off a piece of wood that struck him in the face. Boy, that got the attention of all of us. The worst thing I saw on D day were some men from the 82d or 101st, tied by their feet, hung up a tree and then cut all the way down their bodies with a knife. I also saw where wounded had been tied to a bed and then the house burned down around them."

Sam Frackman, who manufactured jewelry before being swept up in the draft, said of his voyage to the Normandy shore, "We were crouched low and did not see anything except some planes and we heard the sounds of the big guns from our ships. We were let off in deep water with heavy loads of mortar and machine-gun ammunition we were supposed to deposit on the beach. We had life preservers, but why, I don't know. If you fell over, the preserver didn't help. There were many bodies floating by and a lot of shots being fired.

"On the beach, lines had been marked for the mines. One of my best friends was killed when he ignored the markers. When I had gone about 100 yards inland, I heard crying coming from a crater. I went over to investigate and one of the men from my company lay there with blood spurting from his hip or thigh area. I had no first aid experience and we had orders to move up. I couldn't get a tourniquet around his leg so I called for a medic and went looking for my platoon. Later, I found out he had died and was the first casualty from B Company [22d Regiment].

"Most men just did their job. Some prayed for a 'million dollar wound' and others were too scared to move. As far as our training was concerned, you can shove it. It amounted to a zero. We had on-the-job training and we learned quickly. We learned when to hit the dirt, when to run, where to cross, when to lie still. Crossing a road with the first sergeant leading the way, he was hit slightly by a machine gun. We then waited and ran. On my turn, I ran and then came the machine-gun fire. When I got across, not hit, I looked for a cigarette but they had been shot out of my pocket. My gas mask case had also been hit."

Nathan Fellman, who transferred to B Company of the 12th Regiment in the 4th Division after a sergeant in another unit directed his anti-Semitism at him, was an ammunition sergeant responsible for three jeeps with trailers. For his ride to Utah, Fellman separated from his usual companions and rode in the boat bearing C Company. "There were LCIs to the right and left and we got off in water that was up to my waist. I am six feet tall and while wading quite a distance to the beach, two of us taller men put our rifles across to pull in a very short GI until we got to shallower water. We did not suffer any casualties on the landing. I quickly separated from C Company and began studying my map. I wanted to get to my own unit. I looked up and saw some sand fly in the air. A lieutenant started to give me hell for not taking cover from those 88s. I informed him that I didn't know the sound of 88s. But I decided to get off that sand beach.

"I found myself joining up with some 101st Airborne men. That brought my first combat experience. A sniper fired on us. The paratroopers quickly took cover but before I realized what was happening, three or four more shots came at me. The paratroop sergeant asked me where I thought they were coming from. I pointed out a tree. We all turned our weapons on that tree and fired many rounds. Then the sergeant sent one of his troopers up the tree. He cut down two German soldiers. They were very much dead.

"Shortly thereafter, the sergeant was taking us up a trail when he gave the signal to disperse and take cover. We did while he and his second in command pointed to a barn. The pair of them quickly ran to the barn and threw a hand grenade inside. Before it could explode, five German soldiers rushed out with their hands up and yelling *Kamerad*. The young sergeant lined up the prisoners while we covered them. He asked his assistant what he thought they should do with the Germans. Without hesitation, the paratrooper answered, 'Kill them!' A GI with a small machine gun mowed them down in Chicago-gangster style. We promptly resumed our march.

"On our first rest, I sat down next to the sergeant and asked him how he knew there were any Germans in that barn. He grinned at me and said he could smell them. [Many veterans claim they could detect the odor of the enemy from their diet or the aromas of their uniforms when damp.] I voiced an opinion about shooting prisoners, that if they knew they would get shot, none would ever surrender. He said his landing instructions were to kill all enemy and he merely followed his orders. There were no provisions for taking captives. And none of his commanders had changed these instructions. I shook my head but he told me not to worry. In his mind he did the right thing. But even though I had no love for the Germans I would rather not have had this experience. I never talked about this incident either with my officers or the men in my company."

While the 4th Division was the only infantry organization of its size to cross Utah on this first day, the 359th Regiment of the 90th Division, temporarily attached to the 4th, also was committed on 6 June. As platoon leader for the 359th Regiment, Company A in the 1st Battalion, J. Q. Lynd, a native of Oklahoma, remembered the wet chilly morning when he and his forty companions climbed into their LCVP. "Our grouping contained three craft; we were the middle boat. Almost immediately as our group started the run toward the beach, the LCVP to our right 'blew.' A brilliant flash, thunderous crack of explosion, we ducked, our craft lurched, seemed to lift in a quick bucking motion, then dropped, slapping the ocean surface with a terrific impact. We couldn't fall to the deck, we were wedged together like sardines in a can. We looked to the right—nothing! No LCVP, no debris, no smoke, no nothing! Looked to the left, white shocked faces were looking at us in disbelief! Everybody immediately looked to the front—Utah Beach was approaching. We tensed for debarkation as rapidly as possible, as soon as the ramp dropped.

"Utah Beach was a confused array of metal hedgehog obstacles, crumpled barbed wire, columns of thick black smoke, the pungent odor of burning rubber, bodies of dead and wounded soldiers, scattered equipment and supplies in the sand and signs marked 'ACHTUNG! MINEN.' When we reached the water's edge, we quickly ran zigzag through the smoking debris toward the high sand dunes, dodging a burning jeep, an abandoned tank, and the jagged shell holes in the sand. German artillery was shelling the beach area and some of our soldiers were hit. Our orders were to keep moving, attack, *do not stop*, move to the high ground as rapidly as possible. The units that followed would care for the wounded. Our soldiers obeyed as they had been trained."

The Utah Beach venture was the most successful one achieved by the Americans. Roosevelt had transformed the lemon of a navigation error into something approximating a refreshment for the hard-pressed U.S. strategists. General Handy credited the GIs. "The performance of the 4th Division was remarkable. It was a new division that had never been blooded. We all thought Utah was going to be more of a problem than Omaha—the damned terrain swampy with causeways; one gun at each could stop tanks from coming through."

For the Air Force, D day was almost a milk run, with the major threats coming from midair collisions in the crowded skies and overanxious gunners aboard the armada in the Channel. John Hibbard, a waist gunner and assistant radio operator on a B-17 in the 385th Bomb Group, remembered returning from a mission along the French coast on 5 June, with an alert for the next day. "There was something unusual about the alert. All of us felt it. At briefing time the next morning, 6 June 1944, we found out! Colonel Vandevanter [the 385th CO] addressed us. Everyone was tense with excitement, trying to catch every word. 'Gentlemen, you are about to embark upon a very important mission, the success of which will greatly affect the outcome of this war. Today is the day we've all been waiting for—D day.'

"A cheer went up. This was it! Everyone was bursting with excitement and pride because we were all to be there to help assault the enemy beaches. We made two successful operations that day. One was to bomb gun installations at Caen and one to bomb road junctions and railroad bridges. It was a great day. The *Luftwaffe* didn't dare show itself. We were all out, both the Eighth and Ninth Air Forces as well as the British RAF."

Allied fighter pilots scoured the skies for predators almost entirely in vain. Punchy Powell, in a P-51 that day, said, "The 352d Fighter Group flew several missions on D day, but these were probably some of the easiest we flew. Our job, like most of the fighter groups, was to provide a wall of aircraft from the deck to 30,000 feet in a semicircle about fifty miles south of the beaches to make sure no enemy aircraft reached the shoreline. In this we were successful."

According to Jim Goodson, who interviewed one of two German pilots who managed to break through the cordon, the enemy explained, "We were right down among the weeds and when I got back the tips of my propeller were bent where they struck the ground. Only my wingman and I got through. We got over the beachhead and saw several thousand troops on the beach, several thousand ships at sea, and looked up above at several thousand aircraft. My wingman asked what do we shoot at. And I said, just spray and we'll go home." [George Mabry, however, insisted he saw an ME 109 destroyed by an RAF Spitfire.]

Martin Low, the P-40 pilot caught on the ground at Pearl Harbor in 1941, and whose car was shot up as he sped to the airfield, had the unique experience of having been on the scene for that disastrous start of the war and involved in the biggest single event of the war, D day. Having completed his tour in the South Pacifc, he received a month's leave in the States and then trained P-38 pilots. Low had come to England and the Eighth Air Force. "On June 5, I had a date in town and I took a jeep to drive from the base. The sergeant at the gate had a machine gun and he said, 'Sorry, sir'—I was now a lieutenant colonel—'the base is closed.' I started to argue and he unlimbered the gun. So I went back and saw men from the ground crew painting black-and-white stripes on the planes. [To help the Navy recognize friendly aircraft.] We always expected the Navy to shoot at us and they always did.

"At the briefing we were told it would be an early morning mission. Because the P-38 was easier to identify, we were to be at the bottom of the stack. We had never before taken off in the dark but we had no problem. From the air it looked as if you could walk from Southampton to Omaha Beach. We could not see anything on the beaches, other than explosions and flashes of guns. It was enormously exciting to see the power, the size of what we'd all been waiting for. From June 6 until about ten days later, we flew three missions a day, bombed and strafed anything that moved within fifty to a hundred miles of the coast, mostly trains. We did not do much close, tactical support for the troops. The Ninth Air Force handled most of that."

Bill Dunn, who had started the war as a foot soldier with Canadian troops, gone to the RAF, and finally the Ninth Air Force's 406th Fighter Group, flew a P-47 on D day. "It was black and rainy over England, bloody awful. About 4:00 A.M. we got up, got ready to take off, and thought sure as hell they wouldn't send us off in that rain. But sure as hell they did. Off we went into the black, climbed up through

20,000 feet of soup, three squadrons of twenty-five airplanes each, all hoping we wouldn't run into one another. We all made it, broke out halfway across the pond where it was clear as a bell. Over France the sky was absolutely full of airplanes, all ours. I did about four missions on D day, and three the following day, strafing or striking with bombs, napalm, rockets, areas that requested it."

Martin Garren, a copilot for the 94th Bomb Group and among the youngest aviators to sit in the cockpit of a B-17, recalled their target lay in the Utah Beach area. The schedule mandated bombs-away about fifteen minutes before the first waves were to strike the shore. "That meant taking off around three A.M. and assembling in the dark, which was very hazardous. There was a lot of apprehension because we had never practiced that kind of thing, although we all had experience flying at night. We got off all right and began to form up. The tail gunner had an Aldis lamp, a very bright lamp that he kept flashing to indicate this is the tail of a B-17 here and don't bump into it. We also flew with wing lights, which would have been of great help to German fighters or antiaircraft.

"Soon after we took off, the sun was in the sky, although none on the ground. We could see each other and we turned off our lights. Things were normal. We assembled into our thirty-six-ship formation, then the combat box of our wing, and headed for Utah Beach to bomb the concrete fortifications the Germans had built. I kept looking out and all I could see was our wing, close to 108 planes, and I thought, now they've really screwed up. Then, a minute before we were to bomb, I looked to the right and to the left and out of the high-altitude haze I suddenly saw what looked like the entire Eighth Air Force, maybe 1,500 planes, almost in a line abreast like the kickoff of a football game. We went on and dropped our bombs. We had expected the *Luftwaffe* to put up everything they had because once we got our men ashore— we had two million in England waiting to invade—it would be all over. We did not see a single enemy plane or burst of flak.

"To make sure that nobody mistook who we were when we returned to England, we had a specific course to fly over France and then make a big, wide U-turn. We came over Ste.-Mère-Eglise, where a few hours earlier our paratroopers had dropped. As we were passing over Ste.-Mère-Eglise, I was thinking of what might be happening to the paratroopers—anyone who came swinging down in a parachute was likely to be shot at. Suddenly, we developed a fire in our control panel. Si, our navigator, and Tim, our bombardier, started tearing away insulation. Barehanded, they pulled some wires loose and stopped the fire. We all thought, 'My God, what a place to have to bail out.' We returned to base without further incident. Actually, we were scheduled for a tactical mission later on D day. But they had time lines and you couldn't attack a certain area after a specific hour because our guys might now be there. So after we took off we were called back and landed with our bombs."

According to historian Roger Freeman, "an estimated 11,000 aircraft were in the air over southern England." Only a single U.S. bomber went down because of enemy fire. Two others collided and another crashed on takeoff. Fighter losses amounted to twenty-five planes. Most important, the enemy was unable to move reinforcements and armor to bolster Normandy defenses.

# 13

## Hanging On

BEHIND THE SHORELINE, THE PARACHUTISTS AND GLIDER troopers played a critical role in securing the Normandy turf for the American forces. Of those who entered enemy territory during the dark, early hours of the morning, one of the first GIs to encounter the 4th Division soldiers was paratrooper Lou Merlano, whose C-47 so vigorously changed course to evade flak that Merlano and some of his stick dropped into the Channel.

In his nocturnal wanderings, Merlano had blundered into a German compound. He hid himself until he could chew up the pages for his radio code book and, now, in the last hour of darkness, gathered his wits sufficiently to creep through the shrubbery until he was beyond the immediate vicinity of the enemy. "Around the crack of dawn, I ran into Eddie Stiles and Danny Steinbach. The three of us cautiously searched for others. We finally teamed up with Bob Barnes and Sgt. George Barner with a bunch of people. We now had a complement of a dozen or so troopers. We were still considering our next objectives, such as a crossroads, when we encountered a flight of bombers intent on softening up the beaches for the landing forces. We were caught right smack in the middle. A number of us jumped in a creek for no purpose except we were scared to death.

"After the bombers left, we headed out to the road near us. It was just behind the beach and we could see quite a bit of ocean. Something was going on south of us and we started to destroy whatever lines of communication were still standing. We used hand grenades to blow telephone poles and any wiring around. We split the group in an effort to find the rest of our company and to secure crossroads to the causeway. Stiles, Steinbach, and I took one of them. We brought out carts and anything else we could find that would serve as an obstacle, then took positions in a farmhouse right at one corner.

"In no time at all, the Jerries found us. From inland we received heavy fire, mortars and machine guns. In hopes of confusing the Germans, not letting them know how many people were at this crossroads, two of us went upstairs, while one stayed down below. We would run from window to window, firing our M1s. More and more shells hit the house, practically obliterating it. We took positions in the courtyard, using the craters made by the bombers. Every so often, one of us would sneak out to the causeway just to keep them off guard.

"We felt an ambush was coming and decided I should cross the road, go through the hedgerow to the Channel side, while they held the ends of the yard. There was an eerie quiet and we felt something was abrew. Danny Steinbach first noticed someone coming up the road from the south. Crouched down, we couldn't determine whether friend or foe. Much to our surprise, he was from the 4th Division, proceeding in a crouched position with his rifle at port arms, just as a first scout should. When I surprised him, I screamed and hollered, 'What took you so long.' I said we had expected them at six in the morning and here it was eleven or twelve.

"We were jubilant and I said I wanted to speak with his CO to let him know what was up ahead. I explained to a major that because he had a battalion he should be able to move on and take over completely. The officer asked us to act as point men for him but we felt we should get back to our own outfit. The three of us decided to ride some vehicles that had just come in and I jumped on a tank. I thought we were all together but I soon found myself alone with the tankers while looking for A Company. The first gathering of paratroopers I came across was F Company of the 501. I jumped off the tank and joined them. It didn't take long to get into firefights and sniper chases around the hedgerows. During this period, I saw many of our troopers who had been caught in the trees, butchered. At no time in the marshaling area, where all aspects of combat were covered, was it ever said we should take no prisoners. However, on the scene with so many troopers so brutally killed, without question we had no intention to take prisoners. That happened in numerous skirmishes over the next two days in the hedgerows."

Bernard McKearney, as a platoon leader for E Company in the same 502d Parachute Regiment, was similarly struck by the savagery visited upon invaders. After the drop, he gathered some sixty men and staked out a small village with a stone wall as his group's redoubt. Dawn displayed an enemy artillery position. For several hours, the two forces exchanged small-arms fire. "About ten that morning, a considerable force of paratroopers passed through us and the

Jerries retired. We were assigned the mission of destroying the fieldpieces. I took a demolition squad to carry out the detail. What a scene of carnage! This was my first intimate association with violent death. A man at one hundred yards seemed so impersonal. About ten paratroopers had landed amid the gun emplacements. We had expected sudden death or capture. But not this! Mutilation! Horrible, terrible, vicious mutilation of dead soldiers. Most of the men were slashed about the face and body. One man was wrapped in a chute, a thermite grenade applied to his unholy shroud.

"The men said nothing. Words are so useless at a time like this. We removed the bodies from the trees and covered them with their chutes. Your mind functions oddly under stress. I tried to think of a suitable prayer. All I could think of was my Mass prayers in Latin. So, very slowly, I said, *'Requiescat in pace.'* A solemn Italian boy standing by responded, *'Deo gratias.'* That broke the tension. We moved on to complete our mission and returned to the village.

"All during the day snipers harassed us. One was especially dangerous, wounding three men during the morning. We could pick out his approximate location by the sound of his rifle and the thud of the bullet as it hit. Finally, Sgt. Richard Willburn, a lanky Texan, decided to go after him. He spotted the Jerry up in a tree, wrapped in one of our camouflaged chutes. Willburn's first shot tumbled the sniper from his perch. But before Willburn could reach him, he disappeared. A little French boy, no more than seven years old, took Willburn by the arm and pulled him into a barn. Inside, the sniper cowered and trembled. This Nazi superman presented a very sorry picture."

For Wallace Swanson with A Company, 1st Battalion of the 502d Parachute Regiment under Lt. Col. Pat Cassidy, 6 June presented a hectic series of encounters. Following his landing, Swanson had engaged in small-arms fire exchanges, mostly from a distance, with enemy forces. In some instances the foe were Germans pulling back from the Utah Beach area. "I had started with about sixty-five men with me and was moving north toward Foucarville, a tiny village of maybe eight to ten houses surrounded by farms. I was collecting men and combat gear on the way but as we continued toward the objective some troopers withdrew to go to their own units. My number dropped to about twenty men. Foucarville was our main assignment after the coastal batteries. I suppose the French underground had given the Allied command a pretty good description of what was at and around Foucarville. It was heavily guarded."

Unknown to Swanson, Baker Company GIs of the 502d had already battled the Germans at Foucarville, withdrawing because of the enemy's vastly superior numbers and fortified positions on a knoll overlooking the village. Before backing off, Lt. Harold Hoggard, who took charge of the Americans there after his CO was felled, captured several prisoners. Upon interrogation they revealed the deployment of the Germans. "I could never countenance killing unarmed men," says Swanson, "and prisoners can be a valuable source of information as Hoggard found. He obtained information that enabled us to maneuver our platoons and company-size forces. Later, when a group of Germans surrendered to troopers from C Company, and someone said, 'Let's shoot these bastards now,' their CO, Capt. Fred Hancock, squelched them with, 'Don't you think we've had enough shooting for one day?' That shows how a good dedicated officer can put a stop to the consequences of bitter feelings."

"When I got to Foucarville, most of the Germans had retreated to their fortified spots in the nearby hills. But a wasp's nest of snipers occupied well-protected positions in the village church steeple. Any troopers who tried to cross open areas to get at the snipers were cut down by withering fire from the hillside venues—concrete pillboxes, dugouts, and machine-gun platforms erected up in the trees with deadly sight lines into Foucarville. Hoggard's actions, placing riflemen and setting up machine gun positions, provided us with strong security. What followed at Foucarville was Company A's first organized confrontation with the enemy. Until then, the Germans we encountered were scattered or in flight. Here we needed to be organized into effective fighting forces as squads or platoons. The Germans were always famous for counterattacks and our men had to be ready for that kind of action. Some of our people attached their bayonets, prepared for close contact.

"We had been told that jumping behind enemy lines we would be in situations where an individual or small force would find enemy on all sides of him, and up against rifle and machine-gun fire. We had trained to meet this kind of engagement. Furthermore, we had some very fine soldiers among us. Sergeant Cecil Thelan, our company communications noncom, who had a strong knowledge of explosives and demolition, was in charge of a roadblock to the north. In midafternoon, Germans tried to outflank Thelan's block but, with two machine guns and a dozen riflemen, Thelan's group drove them off. But the enemy now turned a small cannon, sited by dugouts on the slope, toward Thelan's group. On his own, Pvt. John Lyell moved to take offensive action. He crawled up the slope through the brush until he spotted the gun. Holding a grenade in his hand, Lyell yelled for the Germans to surrender and three of them emerged from the dugouts. Behind them came a fourth soldier and Lyell saw him starting to pitch a potato masher. Lyell tossed his grenade, which killed the Germans, but the one thrown at him badly wounded him in the shoulder. He went down.

"For a while we couldn't get to him. Finally, two troopers, Privates Richard Feeney and James Goodyear, covered by fire from Sgt. Thomas Wright, tried to drag Lyell away. Feeney eventually managed to pull the wounded man back while Goodyear and Wright pinned down the enemy. But it took too long to get effective cover fire and by the time we reached Lyell he had lost a lot of blood. He died of his wounds several hours later. He had stopped one spot of enemy fire on us but they were able to replace men and weapons and we couldn't silence that machine gun."

The snipers in the church tower winged a bunch of men at one roadblock. Swanson's people tried to suppress the threat with their own assortment of weapons, while the Germans holed up in the steeple sought to slip away by a side door. Unfortunately for them, a misdropped trooper from the 82d Airborne lay quietly opposite the exit. He dropped them all with several bursts from his Tommy gun.

A German artillery column, racing to reinforce Foucarville, headed for one of Swanson's roadblocks. A well-placed charge blasted the lead vehicle into a pile of flaming wreckage. Two machine guns sprayed the artillerymen in the trucks behind and a pair of bazookas destroyed the remainder of the convoy. But the German soldiers who survived attempted to shoot their way through the small group of paratroopers. They did not succeed.

Rather than remaining in a defensive stance, Swanson and his group began to pound the remnants of the enemy still hunkered down on the fortified hill looking down on Foucarville. "Private Charles, an American Indian," said Swanson, "was an outstanding 60mm mortar man and he hammered the works. I also had several machine guns working the area over. Just before ten o'clock at night, the enemy stopped firing. A white flag was raised. Eighty-seven Germans came out with their hands up, along with the French widow of a soldier killed that day."

Behind the surrender, the startled Swanson and his companions watched an eruption of gunfire in a surprise appearance by a batch of U.S. paratroopers shooting at Germans who elected to flee. Seventeen Americans, misdropped during the earlier hours, had been seized and held by the enemy. Sergeant Charles Ran, an A Company operations noncom, participated in a series of conversations with the captors as the Germans steadily lost confidence in their capacity to resist. Ran informed them that his fellow invaders planned to unleash a huge artillery barrage on the hill at 10:30. As the alleged zero hour approached and the Americans continued to talk up the tale, the garrison became increasingly apprehensive until finally most decided to yield.

But not all of the enemy were prepared to give up. The GIs learned that a considerable number hoped to run off to fight another day. When the main group left their positions, dropping their weapons behind them, the paratrooper prisoners snatched them up and opened fire upon the fugitive Germans. Others also turned their sights on the retreating foe and about fifty Germans died while on the run. Foucarville, strategically important to the western end of Utah Beach, now belonged to the 101st Airborne and, soon, advancing infantrymen from the 4th Division.

Bazooka man, Sgt. Bill Dunfee, of the 82d Airborne, with his buddy Jim Beavers, retrieved their equipment bundle, loaded up, and headed for Ste.-Mère-Eglise. "Jim and I joined a group on the outskirts of the town. Our battalion CO, Lt. Col. 'Cannonball' Krause, ordered all bazooka teams forward. We went to the designated area and were told to stand by. There was a fair amount of rifle and machine-gun fire, but the firing I heard did not indicate major resistance. Ste.-Mère-Eglise did not appear to have a large force in town or else they hauled ass when we started dropping. I was in reserve and didn't observe or engage in the firefights. I believe our men pushed through the town, outposted it, then returned to mop up any enemy bypassed. Considering we dropped around 2:00 A.M. and by 4:30 secured the place, it was quick.

"I was shocked by the sight of the men hanging in the trees. It became apparent they had suffered more than jump injuries. They were cut down immediately. I'm sure each of us said a silent prayer, 'There but for the grace of God am I.' My hatred of the enemy ratcheted up several notches to the point of shoot first and discuss it later. I accepted the enemy as another man fighting for his country but never lost sight that we were there for one purpose, to kill each other.

"Prior to my first day in combat I had accepted the possibility of my early demise. A close friend of mine was killed on D day and that changed my feeling that I possibly would die to a sense that it was probable. My acceptance of my fate was because of what had happened to this friend. I had seen him become emotionally unstable. He had changed from an anything-for-a-laugh extrovert into a subdued and withdrawn shell. He seemed to have a premonition of his death. This was the same man who had exhibited great strength and courage in Sicily and Italy. I assumed that each of us has a breaking point and I prayed I could die like a man and be spared the horror of coming unglued. Personal vanity took over, making death acceptable but certainly not desired.

"I have no idea of any context in which 'Take no prisoners' was issued but it sounds like bullshit to me. We were instructed in the Geneva convention rules of our rights as a

POW, and how we were to treat enemy POWs. No responsible officer or noncom would issue such an order. You would most certainly be court-martialed and spend the rest of the war in Leavenworth. General Maxwell Taylor, who was the 101st Airborne commander in Normandy, was formerly the 82d's artillery commander and then assistant division commander. I don't believe he would tolerate the suggestion of such an order. Most of our field-grade officers and all senior officers were West Pointers. They were career military men and to be a party to such a thing would have ended their careers. At Ste.-Mère-Eglise, we established a perimeter defense, dug in to await the counterattack that came all too swiftly. The enemy really socked it to us with 88s and Screaming Meemies. The 88s must have use timed fuses because we were getting air bursts. The *Nebelwerfers* were so erratic you couldn't tell where the rockets would land.

"We learned in a hurry to cut laterally into the side of your foxhole for a safe place to hide the family jewels. My bazooka became a casualty when shrapnel penetrated the tube, blowing away the firing mechanism. My musette bag was hit, and a Gammon grenade destroyed, but without setting off the Composition C it contained. I acquired a BAR; my .45 seemed inadequate.

"We also found that the safest place to relieve one's bladder was in the bottom of your foxhole. If Mother Nature required further relief you were in serious trouble. We were being shelled almost constantly. During a brief letup, I yelled to Louis DiGiralamo, who was dug in nearby, 'Are you okay, Dee Gee?' His response was, 'If blood smells like shit, I'm bleeding to death.'

"We suffered a number of casualties during these bombardments. The most gruesome came when a rocket landed among three men in a mortar squad. They were all killed but the explosion must have detonated a Gammon grenade in the leg pocket of one man. The secondary explosion blew him to bits. His head, chest, and right arm were all that remained intact. One of our men remarked, 'That's what you call going to hell in a hurry.' He wasn't being callous or unfeeling; his statement seemed appropriate at the time.

"By midafternoon of D day, I Company was ordered to move south toward Fauville. We didn't actually know where we were going nor why. But not too far along the way, fire on the point killed four men, our CO Capt. Harold Swingler, Sergeant Sandefur, Privates Irvin and Vanich. Edwin Jones, the lone survivor in the group, crawled back to us under our covering fire, and reported the news of those KIA. I was really close with both Sam Vanich and George Irvin. Sam and I shared a pup tent in Oujda, French North Africa. He was mischievous, always good for a laugh. George was the strong, silent type, the kind you wanted with you when the going got tough. Their deaths were a deep personal loss. I couldn't help but think of my mortality. Swingler was an excellent leader and could have remained safe in a hospital for his knee operation.

"I don't think Swingler anticipated running into enemy between Ste.-Mère-Eglise and Fauville because our 1st Battalion supposedly held the bridge at la Fière. However, there must have been a corridor between our forces that enabled a German battalion to move in between. The entire situation was in flux those first few days in Normandy. On the platoon level we were pretty much in the dark. At times you get the feeling that nobody knows what the hell is going on."

Battalion surgeon Dave Thomas, with a band of troopers hemmed in by the flooded Merderet and ducked down beneath the hedgerows or in ditches, tried to reach friendly forces. "Using anything we could, blankets, barn doors, tree limbs tied together, we carried the wounded into our aid station. We had German prisoners carrying some wounded who couldn't walk. A machine gunner brought in his buddy who'd been shot. There was a German prisoner who wasn't badly hurt making a lot of racket. The trooper kept telling him to shut up but he wouldn't. The GI said, 'To hell with it!' He stuck his bayonet in the German's guts, threw him over his shoulder, and carried him outside the aid station, dumped him in a ditch, and went back to his machine gun. However, we weren't going anywhere. We were surrounded."

The bridge across the overflowing Merderet at la Fière was critical for the Allies to hold St.-Mere-Eglise, a crossroads town through which German armor would need to travel. Once he had determined his location, Jim Gavin mobilized a patchwork assortment of troopers to seize both ends of the la Fière span. In the peculiar nature of the dispersed airborne drop, the opposing forces in effect surrounded each other. Gavin had maneuvered into a position that placed him on the Channel side of the river. Behind him, however, enemy still defended against the incoming 4th Division. Across the Merderet, elements of the 507th and 508th Airborne Regiments would attack their end of the bridge, while to their rear marched a regiment of German reserves intent on throwing all of the Americans back into the sea.

The 508th's Sgt. Bud Warnecke, whose B Company CO, Capt. Royal Taylor, hurt his leg upon landing, was named a platoon leader by Lt. Homer Jones when Jones assumed the leadership of the eighty men collected. "Our objective," says Warnecke, "was on the west side of the Merderet. But we had landed north of Ste.-Mère-Eglise and the river. We passed through Ste.-Mère-Eglise some time after daybreak when the American flag was flying over the first town on the Continent to be liberated. Chills went down my spine. Shortly after noon, we ran into a strong German roadblock at la Fière Manoir, controlling the causeway and bridge, our objective across the Merderet. We got into our first real fire-fight. The Germans were holed up in a house and several barns. We had more firepower and after what seemed like an hour, the Germans who were not killed waved a white flag, came out, and surrendered. We would have liked to have shot them, but didn't. We treated them as prisoners of war.

"We started through the marshes near the causeway until the water got too deep and then used the bridge before getting concealment and cover from the edge of the causeway to the other side of the marshes. There Lieutenant Jones had the company, now of about sixty men, strung out along a hedgerow with instructions to dig in. We heard tanks coming down the road. All we had were light weapons, really no defense against armor. The order to withdraw came.

"The only route to retreat was by way of the marshes back toward the Merderet. It was an unorganized rout; control over my platoon was impossible. I kept contact with as many men as I could while the Germans fired at random into the reeds. I finally reached the Merderet with about half of my platoon. I didn't think there was a chance to swim the river, even if we were good swimmers. It wasn't very wide nor was there much current. But the banks were very steep. I ordered my men into the river and to move along the bank, using their hands with only their heads out of the water. I was scared, fearful of us drowning, but hoping to find a safe way out.

"The next thing I heard was machine-gun fire coming from a long way off, from a small French Renault tank on the causeway. Like in the movies, the bullets were dancing off the water near our heads. Out of nowhere, a 57mm anti-tank gun blew the tank away. I soon had my men around a bend in the river and out. I took a head count and there were at least two men missing. One of them was Tooley, the squad comedian, who entertained us once by smoking five cigarettes at one time. He had been concerned about going into combat and had asked me to promise him I would take care of him. The promise has haunted me for years. The other fellow who was gone was Forrest 'Lefty' Brewer, a professional baseball player, property of the Washington Senators and at the time he entered the service, playing for the Charlotte Hornets."

Bill Dean, radio man for Homer Jones, was among those engaged in the firefight at Le Manoir and the la Fière causeway. "Le Manoir was a typical Norman house-and-barn combination of stone and concrete, and rather large. The Germans considered it important enough to defend it with a full platoon with many automatic weapons. Our equipment bundles with machine guns and mortars were scattered and lost. We had to make do with what was available. Our heaviest artillery consisted of two hand grenades we each carried hanging from our rifle-belt suspenders. There was one hell of a firefight. Point scout John McGuire, who was beside my right elbow, was shot through the head and killed. I just stared down at him, not wanting to believe what I saw. My shock was short-lived when several more volleys whizzed by my head.

"It was about 2:00 P.M. when Lt. Jones led an inspired attack on the place. By 2:30 P.M., the remaining fifteen or so German troops surrendered. After hastily eating a K ration in the presence of eight or ten dead Germans we crossed the bridge that we had just captured. When we got to the west side of the river, we turned south toward Hill 30 and came under heavy fire from tanks, mortars, and machine guns from our right rear. They had us in a pocket. We couldn't go back across the bridge. Straight ahead or to the right put us in their gun sights. To our left was the flooded river.

"At this point, Lieutenant Jones yelled for us to pull back. When the tank machine guns opened fire, Lefty Brewer and I broke for the water. Brewer had been one of the original cadre when I came to Camp Blanding in October 1942. We all admired and respected him because he had already been through Fort Benning and wore the wings. The Lefty tag remained from his stint with a Double-A baseball team. For some reason, Lefty had memorized every verse of Rudyard Kipling's 'Gunga Din,' and at night in the barracks he would recite them with such enthusiasm that I was prompted to visit the library at Camp Mackall to learn the poem. Now, an instant after we plunged into the water, Lefty Brewer lay face down in the water, dead! I swam the river back to the east shore, like a porpoise going down and up, down and up, because they were firing on me the whole way over and even beyond since I had to climb a ten-foot-high bank to leave the river.

"I lost my rifle, ammunition, and all my gear during the frightful swim. After my breathing returned to normal, I headed north along the river until I came upon a makeshift aid station where twenty or more troopers were being attended to by several medics. The weapons and gear of the wounded had been stacked in a corner of the room, so I went to the pile and reequipped myself. I traveled north again to the la Fière Bridge and recrossed during the night."

The man who led the attack on the la Fière Manoir, Homer Jones, offered an account that differs slightly from those of others involved in the firefight at Le Manoir and the subsequent withdrawal dictated by the confrontation of superior numbers and heavier weapons. "Lieutenant Lee Frigo was with the support group on a hill close by the Le Manoir. I had already worked my way into the basement and the Germans and I had been exchanging fire through what was the ceiling over my head and the floor underneath their feet. Someone, I believe it was Lee, shouted to me that everyone should cease fire in order to let the civilians in the building get out. He spoke fluent French and he arranged the cease-fire. Once the French had left, the firing from the hill and within the house started again, including the exchanges through the floor.

"Lee dashed into the basement, a most welcome sight. There were no other troopers there. The two of us continued to fire up and watch the bullet holes appear above us. We decided they had organized a line and were advancing in an orderly fashion. Since the Germans had bolt-action rifles, there was a pause between volleys. Lee and I figured that during one of those pauses, we could skip to the half of the cellar already covered by the German fire. I may be giving them too much credit for a methodical procedure but in any event they never hit us.

"There was another small room in the cellar; a light machine gun fired on us, cutting my trousers and bruising my leg. I tossed a grenade in and it killed three Germans. Inside there were some barrels spouting what I presume was Calvados from the holes made by the grenades and bullets fired. Frigo and I started up a narrow flight of stairs and just as he was about to toss another grenade through an inside window without glass, we heard shouts that the Germans had surrendered. We escorted seventeen prisoners, leaving eight dead or badly wounded in the house. A couple of the prisoners had been hit in the testicles by our fire coming up from beneath them."

After two groups led by Jones and Lt. Hoyt Goodale pushed across the bridge and causeway Jones quickly realized they lacked the strength to maintain their toehold. "I discovered that Goodale and his people had left. Our right flank was totally exposed. I didn't say 'Every man for himself,'" recalled Jones. "I simply told everyone to get out and get back. Frigo, Bill Dean, and I were the last ones to leave. I swam across, hearing the crackle of small arms in the bulrushes." Jones earned a Silver Star while others received Bronze Stars. La Fière Bridge and Causeway witnessed a murderous series of punches and counterattacks for four more bloody days.

For glider pilots Vic Warriner and Pete Buckley, the remainder of the hours of darkness and the day meant a tense waiting game. Although schooled in combat, they were expected to rejoin air-transport operations. Vic Warriner recalled, "By daylight, we had made contact with and were joined by about a dozen glider pilots. We kept busy unloading gliders and doing messenger work for the airborne. We all realized that the next flight of gliders coming in that evening was going to have great difficulty landing the huge Horsas in the small fields that had destroyed our small CG 4As. We borrowed some plastic explosives from the airborne and blew down the larger trees dividing the pastures so the Horsas could have a longer glide area. That was partially successful but many still crashed that afternoon with severe losses for pilots and passengers.

"I spent my first full night in Normandy in a foxhole in a little French cemetery. It had a stone wall around it and was easy digging. A German 88 blew the front gate off during the night but outside of that it was peaceful. The airborne command had taken over a château for headquarters. We glider pilots gathered there to act as a perimeter guard for as long as was needed. A field nearby served as the area for casualties who were brought in for identification and burial. It seemed like acres of dead, row on row, covered with blankets, or tarps where available. It took away the excitement and enthusiasm I had been feeling and made me realize that this was a pretty rough game we were playing. From the field hospital we heard that [Mike] Murphy was going to survive but his would be a long and painful recovery. I was told by our surgeon, Capt. Charles Van Gorder, 'It looked like Murphy had undergone an explosion inside his body.' "

Pete Buckley, whose glider brought in an antitank cannon, left the gun crew shortly after daylight. "I started on foot to find the 101st Division CP at Hiesville. On my way I stopped a jeep driven by a paratrooper headed in what we hoped was the right direction to the CP. I hopped on the hood and we went up a narrow path between the hedgerows. About five minutes later, some Krauts opened up on us with machine pistol and rifle fire. I fell off and the jeep almost ran over me. I got up and began walking on my own. While still going up this narrow lane I glanced to my left and saw a rectangular opening with a rifle barrel sticking out, pointing at me. I froze in midstep, waiting for the bullet I thought had my name on it. Nothing happened. The gun didn't move. I crawled over the hedge and looked in. It was a complete German bunker, big enough for five or six soldiers. Its sole occupant was a dead German, his rifle poking through the slot. Thank God for the paratroopers who had taken care of him earlier.

"The next German I ran across lay at a crossroads in a pool of blood. He had just been hit by a mortar or shell fragment and was still alive. But his gut was ripped open, his intestines spilling out onto the road. I felt horrible while I stood there watching him die, knowing I could do nothing for him. I had not yet developed the hate for the enemy that would come to me as the day progressed and I saw and heard what they had done to some of our airborne. This German dying on the ground in front of me was a young kid and sure didn't look like a Nazi superman.

"At 8:30 that evening, some of us were asked to go back into the fields to meet and cover the landing of the second serial of gliders. A large force of Horsa gliders were expected by 9:00 P.M. They came right on time and the Germans in the fields around us, who had been playing possum, opened up on the gliders with everything they had. Their heavy AA guns outside the perimeters were firing airbursts over and into the fields while the gliders landed. The fields around Heisville were much too small for these big British gliders and those that weren't shot down, crashed head-on into the hedgerows. Some were fortunate, making it down in one piece. Others came under heavy small-arms fire after they landed. Many glidermen and pilots were killed or captured while climbing out of their Horsas. For an hour or so, it was a god-awful mess."

Glider pilot Tip Randolph had not been a party to the Chicago mission in the early, dark hours of the morning. Instead, he was assigned to Elmira, the evening operation employing Horsas to tote supplies and added weaponry. "I had a jeep, a 75mm pack howitzer, twenty-two rounds of ammunition for it, and five men from the 82d Airborne. Our squadron carried a battery of these guns, six in all, with their jeeps, crews, and ammunition. We were all excited. We were going off to win the war. Before we left Col. Adrien Williams, the CO of the 9th Troop Carrier Command—we called him 'Big Willie'—made a little speech. I have no idea why, but he told us, 'Be good Presbyterians' and finished with 'we'll see you in a few days.'

"The trip was uneventful until we came to Normandy. Over the Channel—it was dusk and with double daylight saving time, visibility was unimpaired—it looked like if you landed in the water, you could take a step either way and put your foot on a boat. They were all headed the same way, toward France. I saw the battleships firing, a lot of stuff was being poured in. There had been some dark and light clouds but just after we turned over the beaches the sky turned black. I could see ahead of me the first echelon of Elmira and about five minutes in, started to see tow ships catch fire. We also saw fires on the ground, tracers flying up.

"It was seven or eight miles inland to our LZ, and when we got the green light it was off we go into the blackness. I thought, there's no way I'm going to make it into the field. I couldn't see anything. All you could do is a 270-degree landing, count five, and then turn the 270 degrees which should line you up. The most important thing now was the altitude. The Horsa had flaps that looked like billboards and could almost put the thing down on its nose, like letting you down in an elevator. We kept watching the altimeter. Flying in the dark there's no sense of where you are until you come level with the horizon. Tracers crossed in front of us, some coming up—that indicated ground fire. We were eighty feet in the air when we finally saw the horizon. We made the decision to drop her on her nose when we were at sixty feet and we felt ourselves brushing the tops of trees in the hedgerows. As we came down farther, we could see streams of light from tracers, people were firing across the field. We set down in the field and went past one glider but didn't hit it. We rolled farther and now could see we were near the end of a field, with less than 800 feet, while we were traveling eighty miles per hour. Bullets hit the Horsa; the sounds were like thuds; in a CG 4A the noise was like a snare drum.

"We came to a stop and got out as quick as we could. One man, the radio operator, sitting in the jeep, had been hit in the arm. When everyone was out and on the ground, I got behind a glider wheel as there was a lot of firing going on. We didn't know who was doing what but figured if they were on our side, they'd stop. We were sprawled there for ten minutes to half an hour when all the shooting stopped. We started to hear the sound of those crickets. Someone put a patch on the wounded man. He was okay, having been hit in the fat part of the shoulder.

"We figured we were near Ste.-Mère-Eglise. What we didn't know was that a division of the Germans that wasn't supposed to be in that area was between us and our objective. Those 75s might just as well have stayed in England. All they could do is move half a mile, and then stay put. They would set their pieces up, ready to fire, then have to knock the gun down, move to another quadrant, but never got a firing order. Meanwhile, a bunch of paratroopers came along and captured the Germans who had been firing at the gliders. Things were so mixed up that Germans were captured just moving down the road not realizing where the GIs were."

From the beach, Max Schneider directed his 5th Battalion Rangers to advance across a blacktop road and sweep southwest toward the Château Vaumicel. Intense machine-gun fire from hedgerows halted the Rangers who sought to outflank the resistance. However, according to John Raaen, Schneider spread out the GIs in the wrong direction. "Clearly, Schneider was completely baffled by the hedgerows. These were like nothing any of us had ever seen before. A hedgerow was a long thick mound of earth, six to ten feet high. On top of the mound was usually a hedge of some sort, old, gnarled, heavy, with huge roots holding the

mounds together. Tanks could not drive through these mon-
sters. The Germans dug holes in the back side of these natural barriers and hollowed out small machine-gun nests and
fighting positions. Because of the natural camouflage and
overhead cover, it was impossible to see these positions as
they fired at you."

After four fruitless hours attempting to move on Château
Vaumicel to the south, the Rangers followed the coastal road
that took them west toward Vierville-sur-Mer where they
contacted the advance elements of the 29th Division. Although the defenders closest to the beach had been eliminated, German soldiers infiltrated through gaps in the lines
to renew their attacks. Buck Dawson, as a platoon leader for
D Company, was on the Vierville Road when a machine gun
opened up. "We failed to eliminate this gun, because they
moved it back through the hedgerows when we attacked. We
withdrew and then sought to skirt the enemy and strike out
for Pointe du Hoc. But as night fell, we were not too far
from Vierville. We dug in, reinforced by elements of the
116th Infantry and other remnants, to form a perimeter for
the beachhead. I had lost only one killed and several
wounded, but an eighteen-man Ranger platoon can't afford
to lose a single soldier. That night at Vierville, I heard a
rumor of the possibility of a pullout, but it was only a
rumor."

Perhaps the most isolated outfit among the invaders were
the Rangers clinging to their small piece of turf atop Pointe
du Hoc. When Lt. George Kerchner finally scaled the
heights he was dumbfounded by the sight. "It didn't look
anything like I thought it would. We had a number of aerial
photos, maps, and sketches of what was supposed to be
there. But the tremendous bombardment from our ships and
planes had torn up the terrain until I could not recognize

things. It was one large shell crater after another. When I headed toward the portion of the Pointe where the guns were supposed to be, the Germans began shelling us from inland. This was my first time under artillery fire and it was a terrifying experience. I kept going in the direction of the emplacements because I felt this was safest. Most of the shells were falling near the cliff edge. I figured inland a way I could be away from shell bursts.

"I began picking up men. Some were from my own company and others from different ones. You would jump into these craters twenty-five feet wide and there might be one or two Rangers there. As soon as a shell had landed, you would get out of the hole, run and jump in the next one. The faster you moved, the safer you felt. I couldn't see any Jerries but saw Branley, Long, and Hefflebower trying to locate mortar targets. About 200 yards inland, I saw a Jerry in a 40mm gun emplacement, the first live one I'd seen. I told Huff to fire at him, but he missed five times. The rest of the men set out for the road. I stayed behind to get the Jerry but I couldn't get a shot at him and left when he turned the AA gun on me.

"I crawled through a communications trench to a house. As I went through it, a shell hit it and a sniper fired at me. I found some E Company men pinned down and asked them where D Company was. They said some of my men were up ahead. I set out up the road as two Jerries came in with hands up. A sergeant reported that the guns were not in the casemates. That eliminated our initial mission. I decided to set off for our second objective, a roadblock along the coastal road running from Grandcamp-les-Bains to Vierville-sur-Mer behind Omaha Beach.

"The men took off in small groups," Kerchner continued. "I followed and as I crossed Pointe du Hoc I dropped into a communications ditch, two feet wide and eight feet deep.

My first impression was, I'm safe from artillery fire. But the trench zigzagged every twenty-five yards. You couldn't see any farther ahead and as you went around a corner you never knew whether you would come face to face with a German. I never felt so lonesome before or after. I became all the more anxious and started to think in terms of my being captured. I hurried to reach the coastal road and the other men. You felt better when there were others around.

"Pointe du Hoc was a self-contained fort. On the land side it was surrounded by minefields, barbed wire, and machine-gun emplacements, all to protect it from a land attack. I don't think the Germans really believed anyone would come from the sea and scale the cliffs. Now we began running into the German defenders along the perimeter of the fortified area. As I came on, I saw one of my Rangers, Bill Vaughn, a machine gunner, and a real fine boy. As soon as I saw him, I realized he was dying. He had practically been stitched across by a machine gun. He wasn't in any pain. He knew he was dying. All I could do was tell him, 'Bill, we'll send a medic up to take care of you.' There was no point in my staying with him since I could do nothing for him."

The "cavalry," in the form of the 116th, never arrived during the day nor that evening, as Bob Slaughter and the others in the Blue and the Gray (29th) Division barely survived their day at the beach. On the Pointe, Ranger lieutenant George Kerchner, who with the remnants of his own platoon, had joined Lomell, Kuhn, and a handful of Rangers in the fortifications of Pointe du Hoc, endured a desperate cat-and-mouse affair with vastly superior numbers of enemy. "About six o'clock," said Kerchner, "we realized we were not going to be relieved by the 116th. The hours had passed so fast that what some call the 'longest day' was to me the shortest. For a while, we weren't even sure that the Americans had not pulled everyone out, gone back to England, and left us there alone. We only knew of a group of Rangers at the CP with Colonel Rudder, where they were also treating the wounded. [We also were aware] that a naval shore fire-control party and a couple from the 29th Division Recon were on hand. Meanwhile, we were about three-quarters of a mile inland and there were a tremendous amount of Germans around, several hundred at least. They had the advantage of knowing the terrain, having underground rooms and passageways. They seemed able to pop above ground, shoot, then duck back down, and come up somewhere else.

"A little later, however, a platoon from the 5th Ranger Battalion, with Lt. [Charles] Parker in command, broke through and joined us around this time. We were so happy to see them, the first men from Omaha Beach. Now we realized the invasion was here to stay and that other men would come forward. Parker and his troops helped contribute to our perimeter." As anticipated, the Germans counterattacked. Said Kerchner, "It was the most frightening moment of my entire life. From all quiet and silent to this tremendous outbreak of firing, exploding grenades, furious yelling. And it seemed there were hundreds and hundreds of Germans running toward us. From their firing, we began to see their outlines; it was not real dark. We started firing and although they did not break our lines, we suffered casualties."

Charles "Ace" Parker from Company A of the 5th Battalion explained his passage to unite with the embattled Rangers on Pointe de Hoc. "We kept switching directions in the hedgerows, and as we did we would meet up with small numbers of Germans, killing some, accepting others' surrender, although we did not want prisoners. About three-quarters of the way to the Pointe, we reached a small village.

Germans began crawling along each side of the road on the other side of the hedgerows. We could hear them and then they began to get behind us. We turned all of the prisoners loose and retreated. We cut off into a field toward the beach and about nine at night made contact with the outposted people of the 2d Battalion. There were three officers there, and since they knew the positions, our men were integrated into the line. When the German counterattacks came and finally broke right into our ranks, some of the 2d Battalion people began pulling out without giving us notice. It was extremely difficult to get our men out, because they were scattered along the line, but we managed."

On the beach, Bob Edlin of the 2d Ranger Battalion, after being knocked down by two bullets and receiving a second morphine shot, had fallen asleep. "When I awoke, it was late afternoon. The sun was shining and there was a lot of incoming artillery fire. The tide was going out, taking bodies and debris. It kept reaching back to pick up another body, but they didn't want to go. They had earned this part of the beach with their lives.

"Other troops were coming ashore, I couldn't walk but as a light tank came by, a wounded sergeant and I got on. They were going up to the Vierville exit. If we went that far, maybe we could find out something about the rest of the battalion. Then the tank stopped. A motionless tank in front of a Kraut pillbox is not a healthy place to be. We bailed off the tank and crawled a few yards. It got popped. Now we were in a hell of a fix. A burning tank a few yards away and we couldn't get to the seawall. Artillery, mortar, and rockets are still pounding away inland.

"I looked at the exit again. The large pillbox was still there, a big stone dinosaur. Because of the heavy artillery fire, people were taking cover under the seawall. They wouldn't come and help us. Finally two black soldiers, part of an engineer battalion, came out under heavy fire and dragged us to cover. They would have made good Rangers. Things began to loosen up as it got toward four or five in the evening. There was still artillery, mortar, and rocket fire on the beach, but it was obvious that we had established a beachhead. As it got toward dark, a boat came in to evacuate the wounded. I was immobilized by this time. A full colonel said they would only take the walking wounded out to the ship. Two or three of the Rangers put me on a stretcher, and they informed the colonel I was the one man on a stretcher who was going to leave. He agreed.

"It was almost dark when we reached the small landing craft. We went out on the landing craft coming up beside a ship. Sergeant Ted James of B Company, 2d Battalion, lost some or all of the fingers from one of his hands. It was impossible for him to climb the ladder. I was lying in the bottom of the boat and just about everyone had gone up except James and me. A German fighter came in, strafing the living hell out of the boat. I saw Sergeant James go up the ladder with no problem. His hand got better in a hurry. Now I was the only one left. The strafing and bombing around the ship became so heavy I thought they would leave me.

"I looked up. It seemed a long distance. There was a red-headed, heavyset American sailor. He said, 'I'll get that son of a bitch.' He dropped a big net, climbed down the ladder, and put me, stretcher and all, into the net, almost single-handedly forcing the Navy to take me. I'll never know who he was but he was a good man.

"All night long the Germans continued to strafe and bomb, it seemed unfair. They took me down into the hospital section of the ship. I was given more morphine, and as I lay there on the operating table, I heard a conversation between an Army and a Navy doctor. One said, 'We're going to have to take his leg off.' The other answered, 'It's not going to get any worse. Why don't we just leave it alone? We don't have time to fool with him anyway. Let's get to the seriously wounded people first. Let's get this man back to England and they can decide what should be done.' Thank God they were busy, because that leg still works.

Sid Salomon, the C Company platoon leader atop Pointe et Raz de la Percée, found the heights lonely after ousting the German defenders. "There was nobody around. We had so many killed. We were supposed to go after Isigny that night, but we had only nine men left from the thirty-one in our boat. The other platoon had ten men. We didn't have a sufficient force for an effective firefight. It wasn't until sometime in the afternoon that I felt that the tide of the invasion seemed to change. Until then it had seemed a failure, but I could look down on the beach and see wave after wave of manpower come in, with tanks firing from the beach. We spent the remainder of the day on the Pointe."

Frank South, the Ranger medic under Captain Block, stayed on the beach for an hour or so after Pointe du Hoc fell. "Block ordered most of the medics to the top, but I was to tend any new casualties on the beach and protect those that couldn't be moved until we had a place for them—which turned out to be the bunker above." Fire on the beach diminished to an occasional outburst as patrols sought out isolated defenders. After helping to move the wounded up to the aid station established by Block, South climbed to the Pointe. The medics there used flashlights until gas lanterns were received. As ammunition ran low, Rudder assigned Block to ration the supply and the surgeon delegated the job to South. "By then many of our men had resorted to German arms because we were so short of ammunition. One supply

LCA had foundered and another pulled out too soon. I was still working in the aid-station bunker at midnight. I do not remember where or if I slept. I doubt that I was thinking any profundity at the moment but instead tended to my job. I did have a sense of wonderment that all this was actually taking place and that we had made it to the top and appeared to be holding on at the time."

While the situation of the Rangers atop Pointe du Hoc was still precarious, things were improving for Overlord. Utah Beach was secure. The airborne forces that remained behind enemy lines continued to repulse efforts to wipe them out. There was no reason, as Bradley had feared, to pull the troops out of the Omaha sector, even though they still struggled to widen their grasp. And to the east, the landings by United Kingdom forces were going reasonably well.

# 14

# The Normandy Campaign Begins

THE "BEGINNING," AS CHURCHILL LABELED OVERLORD, COULD be called a success if establishing a foothold were the sole criteria. By the morning of 7 June, the Allied forces, with the fleet still lobbing huge ordnance at inland targets and the air arms dominant—only 100 German planes operated against the invaders—controlled enough ground to beat off any effort to throw them into the sea. Well over 100,000 Allied troops occupied positions in Normandy (the seaborne gridlock and the aerial-drop confusion prevented precise statistics), with the deepest penetration some eight miles in the British sector and the narrowest as thin as 1,000 yards for the American area beyond Omaha Beach. Inland pockets of airborne GIs and Tommies continued to beat back counterattacks, solidifying and enlarging lodgments on the Cherbourg peninsula.

Casualties among the Allies for that first twenty-four hours included as many as 2,500 on bloody Omaha, fewer than 200 at the less fiercely defended Utah Beach, and 2,499 among the U.S. airborne. Several hundred sailors who went down with their landing craft or were hit by fire as they approached the beaches added to the losses. Because estimates of the dead, wounded, and captured had been pegged as high as 80 percent for the airborne, and from 25 percent upward for others, the numbers were acceptable to the commanders, if not to kin and friends.

For the soldiers now on the continent, 6 June indeed was only a beginning. The Utah Beach losses for D day amounted to only 197 casualties, and these included about 60 men missing from the sinking of a landing craft bearing a portion of an attached field-artillery battalion. (In contrast, the German E-boats that interrupted one of the Slapton Sands preinvasion exercises inflicted losses of some 700 men.) However, in the days that followed, the 4th Division encountered fierce opposition and the KIA, WIA, and MIA numbers rocketed. By the end of the month, the total for the 4th Division mounted to 5,452. Other VII Corps units, including the 82d and 101st Airborne and three infantry divisions brought in by sea, sustained brutal losses.

During the first day or so after climbing Pointe du Hoc or scrambling through the Omaha Beach firestorm, most of the Rangers struggled under similar conditions to those of the airborne forces. Isolated, and operating as small units against severe counterattacks, they clung to their meager portions of French soil. On 7 June, from the command post in a bombed-out German position on Pointe du Hoc, Lou Lisko watched the U.S. destroyers *Harding* and *Satterlee* throwing their weight at the nearby enemy emplacements. German guns responded. Offshore observers decided the Rangers no longer occupied the Pointe. "In the afternoon, several American fighter planes flew in a circle over Pointe du Hoc," says Lisko. "We became very concerned they might think we were Germans and start bombing and killing all of us. I took off my field jacket and waved it. One plane approached so close that the motor was hard on my eardrums. One Ranger had an American flag and started to stretch it out, using stones to keep the wind from blowing it away. A machine gun from the left flank opened up at this Ranger. He fell down but wasn't hit and crawled up again to put more stones on the flag. That enabled the flight leader to see the Rangers were still alive. He flew in a circle several times. We waved at him and he waved back. He and the other six planes left without throwing any bombs or firing any shots. Several hours later, three or four planes returned and pulverized a dangerous target, the machine-gun nest on our left flank. They dropped six or eight bombs on it. The defense of Pointe du Hoc was thus fought by a team that included Rangers, the U.S. and British navies, and the U.S. Air Corps.

"By June 8, we were waiting to be relieved by the Rangers from Omaha Beach who had run into a lot of German resistance. We had run out of ammunition and two Rangers were using a German machine gun. About noon, Schneider and his 5th Ranger Battalion heard the distinctive sound of a German machine gun. They assumed we had been wiped out. In the confusion, they started to fire in our direction with mortars. Tanks attached to the 116th Regiment joined in. After two and a half days of fighting the Germans, now we were being attacked by our own troops.

"Colonel Rudder was yelling as loud as he could to the Rangers to stop firing the German machine gun but he was not close enough for them to hear. My buddy and I were trying to contact the friendly troops over the radio and tell them they were shooting at their own troops. Finally, we succeeded. Colonel Schneider ran out into the open and told his men to cease firing."

Lieutenant Charles Parker from the 5th Ranger Battalion, who received a DSC for D day, was heavily engaged on 7 June with counterattacks. "There was a very nasty fight three or four days later. We had to cross a flooded swamp area where they had the targets painted on their emplacement walls. They could fire two or three mortar rounds from trenches and pits under manhole covers without exposing themselves. They had four years to prepare for us. In the Rangers we practiced an elementary principle. Once you jump off, there's no place to stop until you arrive at the target. If you halt halfway there, then you become pinned down. So we were right among them very soon, working our way down in the trenches using fire and grenades. They started to surrender and a lot of them had been gathered out of their holes but there were several SS men among them. They began killing those who surrendered and that brought chaos. The entire thing had to be done again. One SS officer held a grenade to his head and blew off most of his face rather than surrender. I lost my first sergeant and a dozen other men there."

Subsequently, the Rangers entered a bivouac where they sought to fill their ranks. "I interviewed hundreds of volunteers," said Parker, "and we rejected most of them. Regular-army organizations always hate special units. They didn't know what to do with us. They would use us for smash-and-grab operations. We were to take positions but we never had enough men or firepower to hold them for any length of time." Parker recalled at least four subsequent encounters with the enemy that struck him as equal to the perils of the invasion. "But I went through the entire war and never missed a day at the office."

John Raaen remembered that on D plus 1 orders directed his 5th Battalion Ranger unit to relieve the 2d Battalion at Pointe du Hoc. When he stepped out to the road beside the farmyard where he'd spent an uncomfortable night in a manure-laden haystack, he was pleasantly surprised at daybreak to find that several tanks from the 743d Tank Battalion had arrived. "Suddenly there was a lot of firing directly to our south. A German counterattack of at least company size. I could see through the hedgerow that our troops were being beaten back by a superior force. I could also see that the tanks were doing nothing about it.

"I climbed up on one of the tanks and banged on the turret with my rifle. The hatch opened and the tank commander asked what was up. I pointed out the firefight about 300 yards away and asked that he bring the building the Germans were using for cover under fire. He spoke on the radio, unlimbered his .50-caliber machine gun, and all the tanks began firing. I got his attention again and asked why he wasn't using his 75mm guns. 'Target doesn't call for it. Might hurt friendlies,' was his answer. The 50s must have been enough, for the attack soon died down."

Few American infantrymen, including the Rangers, had practiced coordinated operations with armor. It was another vital skill that GIs learned on the job, at a cost. Not until late in the war did someone think to install systems by which a foot soldier could get the attention of a tank commander by other means than banging upon the turret.

Instructed to contact 29th Division headquarters on the situation of the Rangers, Raaen made his way to the beach command post. Having reported the disposition of the organization, Raaen requested machine-gun and mortar ammunition to replenish the expended supply. Given a barely functioning jeep, Raaen and Jack Sharp, an enlisted man, loaded up and drove along a road that showed evidence of fighting. Occasionally, rounds from unseen adversaries struck the jeep—Raaen counted four hits on his helmet, either by bullets or debris. After distributing their cargo, partly by lying under the jeep and passing back ammunition while enemy fire whizzed overhead, Raaen and Sharp motored toward advance elements. They halted near a huge crater across a road when suddenly a heavy artillery barrage erupted several hundred yards to the front.

"It was clearly enemy fire and it was devastating. Rangers began streaming back across the crater to get away from the fire, officers among them. At first, they were orderly in their withdrawal but soon it became a panic. I stood on the edge of the crater shouting at the men to slow down, swearing at them to stop and reorganize. I knew many of them and calling them by name stopped the rout. My standing there above them as they came out of the crater had a very salutary effect as well." Even the most doughty of troops occasionally broke.

Pressure from the swelling U.S. infantry contingent supported by tanks, artillery, and naval guns offshore cracked the defense at Grandcamp, one of the major objectives for the Rangers. Elsewhere, the invaders encountered similarly stubborn resistance. "We got off the beach well enough," said Charles Mastro from the intelligence section of the 2d Battalion in the 22d Infantry Regiment, "but then we hit a wall." The entire offensive that included the 4th Division shuddered to a halt as an entrenched enemy, backed by the dreaded 88s and Tiger tanks, fiercely defended its turf. Unhappy with the progress, the top brass sacked commanders. Colonel Hervey Tribolet, whom Mastro described as a leader who talked to the lowest privates like a father, was relieved of command over the 22d, although most of his offi-

cers and enlisted men retained confidence in him. "We had
one battalion commander," noted Mastro, "who was not a
leader. Omar Bradley, watching our progress from a hilltop,
relieved him on the spot."

George Mabry recalled that his battalion met sporadic resistance while approaching Ste.-Marie-du-Mont. "Eventually we got into the little village. Once in a while we heard
a rifle with a muffled sound from it. This was coming from
a church in the middle of the town square. It had a very tall
steeple. I dodged around, got myself to the square. There
was a kind of half-track German vehicle with two dead
Germans. The vehicle having turned the corner and the
driver having been shot, it was angled across the street. I
contacted a member of the 101st Airborne who told me
they had some casualties. I asked about the muffled fire
from the steeple. He said, "Oh, sir, that's the first sergeant
up in the church. He shot these two Germans." In a few minutes he appeared and I commended him. I told him to round
up the casualties so that medical personnel would take care
of them. Sitting on the base of a pump in the town square
was a U.S. airborne soldier wounded in the hand and face,
apparently from a hand grenade and small arms. Both hands
were wrapped in bandages and his entire face was covered
with blood-soaked bandages. He was able to mumble
through the gauze covering everything but his nose. It was
shocking to see a man sitting there completely wrapped in
bandages covering every part of the skin that was ordinarily
visible. Yet he was conscious and made no complaint.

"Having passed through Ste.-Marie-du-Mont. it wasn't
long before we met stiff resistance from Germans dug in
along the hedgerows, and the dairy farms that had a stone
wall as well as the hedgerow. I don't recall ever having any
briefing from our intelligence that mentioned the hedgerows

or the formidable obstacles the trees and underbrush on these hedgerows would have on airborne and restrictions upon any vehicle, tracked or on wheels. We soon learned the tactic the Germans would use. We'd run up against a prepared position. The riflemen would lean against the hedgerow and shoot while machine guns would be put atop the hedgerow for enfilade or flanking fire into German positions. The Germans would hold their machine guns in reserve and once we got ours in position, they would run down the field and take a position and give us enfilade fire. We'd be shooting at what [had been] a German machine-gun position, but to our surprise, to our flank would come machine-gun fire. It didn't take long to figure out what they were doing and we began to do the same thing. Fire with MG, then take it down and put a BAR man in the position and run down and move our own MG.

"Daylight at that time of the year prevailed until almost 11:00 P.M. Eventually we stopped to give everyone an opportunity to dig in around 10:00 P.M. We dug in, set out mines, and antitank weapons. But no attack occurred. Apparently, Hitler did not think this was the main invasion force and he held his armor in reserve. In addition, our air force was quite active and caught some German convoys on the road, including some tanks.

"The next morning," Mabry remembered, "we jumped off at first light. We were getting along fairly well until we ran into a complex of dairy farms, each separated by a road and a big stone wall around its house, barn, silos. The Germans had been using these buildings and stone walls for defensive purposes. We began getting a terrific amount of small-arms fire. I was near F Company on the left. We were shooting mortars at these houses and artillery had been brought in. I crawled up by a hedgerow where some of F Company was.

Very close to me was Mickey Donahue, [a highly skilled boxer on a team coached by Mabry while at Fort Benning]. I was peeping over the hedgerow and saw a German run down the field and I shot at him and so did some others. He went down. A tremendous explosion happened close to Mickey Donahue. I had seen a German's arm. I figured the German had thrown a potato masher hand grenade. What I saw was his hand coming down after having hurled the grenade. He stuck his head up and I took a crack at him and I never heard from him again. I crawled down to Mickey and he had been hit. He was bleeding and looked as though he was going to die pretty soon. I dragged him up the little road, turned him over on his back, put his helmet under his head, took out his canteen and put [it] by his right hand. A couple of other enlisted men were there and called for medics. Elements of the company began to move. We crushed the enemy immediately ahead of us and I had to abandon Mickey. I thought Mickey Donahue would die, but some years later I found that he was at the Valley Forge [Pennsylvania] hospital, paralyzed from the waist down.

"Three Germans came running around a stone wall and I hollered 'halt,' they threw up their hands, I made them lie down. If they stood up I knew someone seeing their uniforms would let 'em have a blast. I ran on, telling them to stay there. When I ran inside a courtyard inside a stone wall I noticed a Frenchman making all kinds of signs with hands, indicating someone inside, wounded. I went in with some enlisted men. There was a middle-aged woman and a small boy. The woman had been hit in the abdomen by a shell fragment. She was bleeding profusely. The little boy was sitting in a chair, staring. She was making no noise, other than breathing heavily. I calmed down the man who was quite excited, telling him we'd get a medical person to tend to his wife. I checked later; they assured me this lady was taken care of.

"When we got within 1,000 yards or so of Ste.-Mère-Eglise we met a very stiff defense. The 3d Battalion [of the 8th Regiment] was supposed to be on our left flank as we began to receive quite a bit of fire from that direction. I suggested to Colonel McNeely we try to contact the 3d Battalion. We couldn't reach them by radio so I took two enlisted men with me to see if I could find them. We started up a dirt road and saw many German vehicles on the paved road leading to Ste.-Mère-Eglise. There must have been twenty to twenty-five trucks, strafed and riddled with .50-caliber MG bullets. [This was a convoy shot up by the Air Force.] As we approached, we saw a paratrooper hanging from a telephone line, his feet about a foot off the ground. His throat had been cut. It angered us. The enlisted men made threatening comments. I told them we will never do this, that's what we're fighting against. As we went on we saw a couple more hanging and killed the same way.

"We spied a group of houses on the other side of the road and heard rifle fire from that direction. I figured the 3d Battalion were attacking this group of houses. We got into the big ditch, crawled along it until we noticed some Germans were in the house directly in front of us. Some were looking out of a second-story window, some peeping around the corner on the ground floor. I told [some] enlisted men we'd take 'em under fire and help the 3d Battalion. We sneaked closer behind a hedgerow. I told 'em I'd take the man on the ground floor; the men to take the others. We shot simultaneously. A couple of them fell to the ground. At that time a German on the top floor stuck his head out of the top-floor window. I shot at him; he disappeared. Another soldier stuck his rifle out of the window trying to determine where fire was coming from. I shot at him; he fell back.

"About this time a few rounds of artillery started to land near these houses. I didn't like this artillery, coming from the beach [friendly] area. I told the enlisted men we'd better turn around and get back into our area. We were too far over and too far in front of the 3d Battalion. Just as we started back up the ditch, the U.S. artillery really started coming in. It was massive, flying through the air like a flock of ducks. Rounds hit all around us. We began running back up the ditch. A round hit in a mud puddle, covering us with mud from head to foot. I said, 'On my count to three, let's take off!' We jumped up and ran as hard as we could across an open field toward the 2d Battalion, then flopped down. Meanwhile the artillery was coming in, Brrrmm! Brrrmm! Brrrmm! We ran again. Nobody shot at us because they were taking cover from the artillery. We ran as hard as we could and fell down again with the artillery shells starting to fall behind us. We hit the ground one more time. On the third rush we were able to get out of the artillery concentration, but we were covered from head to toe with mud and dirt. I was visibly shaking when I explained to Colonel McNeely how we'd been caught in that artillery barrage. Since then I studiously avoided getting into somebody's else's area without notifying them.

"I told McNeely about seeing how paratroopers had been killed while hanging from wires and trees. He said he'd seen the same. I recommended that we pass the word to company commanders to inform all officers down to the last enlisted man we did not condone such barbaric behavior. Members of the 2d Battalion would not take out their frustration and anger against German prisoners. Individuals caught doing this would be subjected to a general court-martial. Colonel

McNeely agreed and word was passed to every man to preclude any reprisals. Something like this can get out of hand and it was inhumane treatment, a violation of the Geneva convention."

Eventually united with the 3d Battalion, the GIs of the 4th Division advanced to positions on the left of Ste.-Mère-Eglise. Mabry searched for the airborne commander and troopers directed him to Lt. Col. Benjamin Vandervoort, 2d Battalion, 505th Parachute Infantry. "Lieutenant Colonel Vandervoort was sitting in a wheelbarrow, obviously wounded in his leg, and an enlisted man was pushing him around. He remained in command even though injured. I asked him how secure his position was. He said fairly tenuous with the Germans massing for counterattack. I showed him where our people were. He asked us to move forward and protect his flank. He informed me where he anticipated the counterattack would come. We said we might make a limited, flanking attack, to thwart the Germans who would be surprised to find another battalion in place. He thought it a great idea.

"As luck would have it, the enemy did counterattack head-on. Realizing this, our 2d Battalion conducted a flanking attack and sweep toward the front of the airborne unit. We moved parallel, along a sunken road, worn down by travel, with hedgerows on both sides. The vision of anyone moving up and down this road was obscured. When the German counterattack came across a wide-open field we caught them and began shooting them down in the field. They came running across and reached the sunken road. German bodies were piled up in the road—a sight hard to believe. After they pulled back and we started to dig holes to button up for the night, the troops had to stack German bodies two or three deep in order to have room for a foxhole. On the following morning three Germans gave themselves up, punching GIs to take them prisoners. These live ones mixed in with the dead, feigned being dead before giving themselves up.

"As we attacked inland from the beach we would often run into groups of parachutists. Some were from the 82d and others the 101st. Some would be holed up in a corner of a hedgerow and I'd ask if any enemy were around. No, they hadn't seen any. I asked who's over on right or left; they didn't know. They were waiting, not knowing what to do. I classified those individuals as the nonfighters. Go further and you'd run into another group, walking around, sneaking about, men from a combination of the two airborne divisions. You seen any enemy about? Oh, yes, we had a firefight, killed some. They were out looking for enemy. These were the fighters and the fighters had gotten together. The nonfighters were holed up, eating K rations, waiting. This was not peculiar to airborne; it was typical for infantry, armor, Marine Corps. There is a definite category of individual who will shoot and close with the enemy. There's another group that will shoot but not close with the enemy. And there's a third that will neither shoot nor close."

The bodies piled up rapidly. Much of the diary of Marion Adair, the 4th Division battalion surgeon, is a book of the dead.

"June 7: I set up an aid station in a field where two gliders have crashed and there are casualties. Meanwhile, two more gliders of the 82d crash within fifty yards of where I am, ten men are killed, and as many are wounded. After taking care of this mess, I push on up the road where there are a number of casualties including the Colonel's runner, Tom Sullivan, who has been killed. . . . The woods are full of snipers and a man next to me in the ditch gets shot.

"June 8: Jerry shells our area during midmorning and sets

fire to our ammunition trucks and several vehicles. Fortunately, only several men are hurt. I explore a nearby road and there are more than two dozen dead Germans. I also run across Lt. Vill, killed by rifle fire.

"June 9: . . . the battalion attacks about 6 P.M. and E Company suffers heavy casualties, including the death of Lt. Wilder. We work far into the night, on our hands and knees under blankets, with flashlights. It's gruelling, tiresome and the boys are really in bad shape. . . . This has been one of our worst days yet.

"June 11–20: We hold a defensive position west of Montebourg. We receive our first replacement. Lt. Wilson gets killed and Lt. Couch is wounded. Capt. Haley is hit. We [shifted] place in the line with the 1st Bn and then the 3rd. Capt. Watkins is wounded. . . . I write my first letters home and receive my first mail. We get better rations, a chance to drink cider, and clean up.

"We make a night attack [June 19] commencing at 3 A.M. It's rough going at first but we drive the Jerries out of a dug-in place. . . . Twice we go through an artillery barrage. Lt. Col. Steiner is killed, but our casualties are not too excessive.

"June 22: I am awakened at dawn because a German patrol sneaked in the C.P. and shot and killed Lt. Marquard. Our boys kill five of the Krauts and wound the officer. They reoccupy the crossroad behind us, and cut us off. We are having casualties and I send some back in an ambulance, which is machine-gunned. I also send a jeep back, which is stopped and then permitted to go ahead after a Kraut casualty is removed. I accumulate about twenty casualties during the day which I cannot evacuate. We are shelled thrice and one actually hits the top of the aid station. Shell fragments destroy several units of plasma.

"June 23: Our battalion attacks this afternoon, and E Company sustains about 35 wounded and 15 dead."

"June 25: Chaplain Ellenberg holds a service this morning and I enjoy it. The Lord has been kind."

A day later, Adair drove to the medical clearing station for "a wash and a rest . . . the boys there slip me a shot of real whiskey. Tonight it's mighty fine to sleep under plenty of blankets on a cot above the ground." Returning to the front, Adair passed through the site of one of the earlier battles, a meadow laced with drainage ditches. "There are at least 40 or 50 dead soldiers partially buried in the muck and slime and a few dead Jerries in the rise near the swamp. This was the most depressing thing I saw in all of France."

Already at sea when the first Americans jumped into darkness over France, the 2d Infantry Division, at midnight 6–7 June, prepared to climb down the cargo nets from transports into the landing craft bobbing below. Their destination was Omaha Beach. George Duckworth, a platoon leader with Company F of the 23d Regiment, remembered, "As we were standing by, the Navy crew of our transport distributed steak sandwiches as a gesture of goodwill and good luck. They realized that we could use a morale booster and it was appreciated.

"Company F descended the nets without any real trouble and settled down for the run to the beach. It seemed like an eternity before we grounded just a few yards offshore where the Navy coxswain lowered the ramp and we piled out into knee-deep water and waded ashore as quickly as we could. The distance from the water's edge to the high ground on the far side of the beach was about 200 yards and I think we covered it in record time.

"The higher ground was steeper and more rugged than anticipated, but we finally found a place where we could traverse back and forth until we reached level ground. At the top we encountered considerable confusion among some of the first assault troops, who had just cleared the beach and were behind schedule. Our designated assembly areas had not been cleared of enemy troops. We had to wait for daylight to clear the area so our units could reorganize and proceed with our attack inland.

"We moved forward very cautiously until we came across a narrow blacktop road that ran parallel to the beach and gave us some bearing as to our location. At first light we moved forward through some assault units from the 29th Division that were beginning to withdraw. Evacuation of the dead and wounded was taking place as we prepared for our attack."

Duckworth and his outfit pushed ahead while snipers harassed them. Serious opposition surfaced at a roadblock but still the GIs from the 2d Division progressed until 10 June when ordered to take the high ground in the vicinity of Hill 192. "The area we had to cross was mostly open with little in the way of cover or concealment," said Duckworth. "Company F moved forward with Company E on our left. Everything went according to plan as the troops moved out to the forward slope of the valley, then without warning, all hell broke loose. F Company's position was completely blanketed by enemy artillery, mortar, and automatic-weapons fire. There was no cover or concealment and men were falling like tenpins. Our casualties were so heavy that our advance was halted. We had no artillery or mortar support to suppress the enemy fire. The deadly rain of fire continued until it was obvious that our attack was ended."

After a short discussion with his wounded company commander, Duckworth was ordered to try to outflank the enemy with his platoon. For a brief period the maneuver en-

abled the troops to advance under cover but when they
broke into a clearing, they were spotted and subjected to intense volleys of small-arms fire. Only the fact that they had
come so close to the entrenched defenders prevented an onslaught of artillery and mortars. However, Duckworth and
his people remained pinned down in firefights until dark,
when they retreated. Astonishingly, no artillery backup for
the battered battalion was available even though Duckworth
advised headquarters he could guide forward observers to
appropriate positions.

"Very early the next morning, the battalion received orders to mount a full-scale, all-out, bayonet charge in an effort to break through the enemy and capture Hill 192.
Considering our heavy casualties on the previous day, this
order was a real shocker. Especially to me because I was
aware of the open terrain, the distance to the enemy's positions, and the lack of artillery and mortar support. However,
the word was that the order came from 2d Division headquarters."

The operation was a murderous fiasco for the soldiers
who charged with bayonets fixed. Duckworth said, "We
were deluged by concentrated artillery and mortar fire together with some direct shelling from enemy armored vehicles on the high ground across the valley. This concentration
of high explosives was devastating, men were falling everywhere, some killed instantly by jagged artillery and mortar
fragments, while many others were wounded and screaming
in pain. Before midday it was obvious that our attack had
failed and we had to withdraw what was left of the company."

With all the other officers in the company either dead or
wounded, command passed to Duckworth. "It was not so
much of a shock to find myself the only surviving officer, as

was the realization of the awesome responsibilities I faced in getting the company reorganized, our wounded evacuated, the dead recovered. This while maintaining the morale and combat capability of a unit that had sustained a 50 percent loss of enlisted personnel and most of the officers in its first days of combat." Although still functioning, Duckworth himself seemed considerably worse for the wear. "I was bone-tired, dirty, and sweaty. The entire left side of my combat jacket was ripped and torn away, my canteen had been shot off my left hip, my trench knife, carried strapped to my right leg, had the handle shot off at the hilt, my carbine had a four-inch piece of razor-sharp shell fragment embedded halfway through the stock, my helmet had two deep creases on the right side with a large dent on the left and I had cuts and scratches all over my body, probably from crawling around the company area during the battle."

A few days later, with the American lines almost twenty miles inland, the 2d Infantry Division assumed a defensive stance, exchanging artillery, mortar, and tank fire with a stationary foe. Duckworth's company had dropped to fewer than 100 men when efforts to restore the outfit occurred. "First Sergeant Henry Gratzek notified me that we had fifty replacements coming in. That was good news at first, but less so when I found that they were from a deactivated antiaircraft defense unit, were only armed with .45-caliber pistols, and with no infantry training. I pulled some of my officers and NCOs out of the front line to take them back to a rear area, arm them with M1 rifles, teach them to shoot, and give them some basic infantry tactical training. They were all good soldiers and learned quickly, but time was critical and there was no room for mistakes at the front. As a company commander, it hurt me to have untrained men get

killed or wounded before I even got to know them by
name."

Throughout the war, the system to funnel replacements
for casualties provided mostly unsatisfactory results. Rather
than replace entire units with well-trained equivalents, the
personnel command chose to insert individuals into line
companies. A stateside-bound cadre that would never need
to depend upon recruits for their personal survival taught replacements the rudiments of combat life. There was little
incentive or urgency felt by this cadre who converted newcomers fresh from civilian life into fighting men. They often
lacked the most basic instruction in tactics and weaponry.
By contrast, the first divisions involved in Overlord had all
schooled their foot soldiers in fire-and-maneuver exercises,
how to make the best use of bazookas, antitank grenades,
and working with the modest hedgerows of England. Most
organizations tried to provide some additional training for
replacements before they came under fire, and frequently
paired them off with experienced GIs. That generally did not
compensate for their ignorance of their tools and understanding of how to operate as a cohesive unit. The memoirs
of headquarters staffs and generals in the field show little or
no concern for this weakness, but the comments of junior officers, NCOs, and GIs at the front frequently refer to the in-
adequacies of fresh fodder.

Still harnessed to the 4th Division, the 359th Infantry,
normally part of the 90th, coped with the frustrating
hedgerowed fields of the Cotentin Peninsula. J. Q. Lynd, a
platoon leader of Company A, said of the terrain that "deep
ditches at the base of each hedgerow provided runoff [for
the marshy land with high rainfall]. . . . The narrow trail-like
roads were usually completely overgrown with arching treetops. These formed a cavelike canopy, termed 'sunken

roads.' They effectively hid the well-concealed enemy weapon emplacements from artillery forward observers and aircraft spotters. These boxed-in, solid, earthen-dike hedgerowed fields completely limited tank and armored vehicle maneuver and support fire for attacking infantry. The deep swampy bogs further prohibited heavy tank travel."

The Château de Fontenay, a 200-year-old great house surrounded by massive stone walls, protected a pivotal road junction from the invaders. On 10 June the 2d Battalion of the 22d Infantry, part of a task force directed by the 4th Division, initiated another frontal attack on the château. The violent response of the Germans killed or wounded a great many junior officers, noncoms, and enlisted men. Company L alone lost 159 men in a series of attacks.

Ordered to advance on the château as part of a relief force, Lynd said they had made good progress until "Two flights, each with six B-26 twin-engine bombers, suddenly appeared out of the clouds from the east over Utah Beach. They made a precise banking turn heading right toward us with opened bomb bays. Our lead scout, Pfc. Ebar Manriquez, hollered, 'Bummers! Big Bums!' We scrambled into the deep drainage ditches, jumped into the mud, and then really got a pounding with their intensive bombardment. Then the German artillery at Ozeville renewed firing on us in anticipation of a close follow-up of attacking U.S. troops immediately behind the bombing. One of the big trees toppled across the moat. The large, heavy wooden door in the adjoining stone wall was blown ajar. We clambered out of the ditches, across the downed tree, and through the loose door. Two rapid-fire machine guns were burping at us from the big stone barn. We held up behind the piles of bomb debris but close enough to heave some hand grenades through the near window. Privates First Class Bill Hazuka and Louis

Rossi charged through the dark barn door opening and crash-plunged headlong over a low, circular, stone apple-crushing millstone. The German soldiers fled through the rear door and escaped into the stone-wall maze of the extensive garden tract. Shortly after that, Rossi's foot and lower leg were crushed from an antipersonnel mine near the barn. Private James Lemon and Pfc. Claude Gilbreath were hit with sniper fire. Sergeant Glen Ahrendt, Pfc. Howard Meek, Pfc. Gunder Stavlo were killed. Lieutenant John Sisson's platoon was just about wiped out. Lieutenant Herb Lawson's platoon was hit pretty hard and lost most of S.Sgt. Bill Russell's squad. We attempted to find and give aid to as many of the 22d Regiment wounded as we could stumble across in the darkness.

"About midnight the burning château was an awesome flaming pyre. Two German aircraft flew in from the north and circled twice around the now-vivid, blazing buildings. We couldn't see the planes up in the dark sky but their engine noise was distinctly different from any U.S. airplanes. During each circle, the planes dropped clutches of small antipersonnel, butterfly fragmentation bombs only to the south of the burning château buildings. The German intelligence staff had surmised quite correctly that U.S. headquarters, reserve units, supply, and vehicle concentrations would be around the road junctures south of the château.

"The ingenious butterfly bombs opened precisely at release with the parachute-like shell caps winding upward on the stem as they fell. These shell caps detonated the bombs upon contact with the stem terminal tips. When dropped from a specific altitude the entire bomb clutch would begin exploding as air bursts that detonated fragments about 50 to 100 feet above the ground. These were certainly effective antipersonnel explosives. . . . The casualties numbered almost 200 in wounded and killed among the rear-echelon troops."

Bob Slaughter, who had survived the terror of Omaha Beach, joined the remnants of his 116th Regiment. "Insigny was the division objective and we suspected we were between the 1st and 2d Battalion sectors. We hooked up with others who were separated and organized a leaderless, rabble force that served merely as psychological support. Any friendly rifle or machine gun was welcome. I felt extremely vulnerable and lonely during the early hours after the invasion." Disheartened and uncertain though they were, the patchwork bands of foot soldiers formed from elements of the 1st and 29th Divisions and the Rangers doggedly inched toward the designated objectives. Those innocent of combat received instant educations if they survived.

"Snipers, machine guns, and 88s interrupted movement on the road into Vierville. The column took cover and waited for an officer or noncom with the initiative to collar a few riflemen and clear the obstacle. While lying in the warm sunshine, the rabble smoked K-ration cigarettes or rested. A young rifleman accidently pulled the pin on one of the many hand grenades hanging on his belt. The explosion and shrapnel blew most of his buttocks away. He screamed in agony until an aidman gave him a shot of morphine. Word spread that heat from the sun had ignited the grenade. Many began discarding their precious grenades.

"As we entered the tiny resort village, Vierville-sur-Mer, less than a mile from the beach, sniper and burp-gun fire came from the bombed-out Norman châteaus. We were trained to make every shot count and German targets were hard to find. Smokeless powder was a tremendous advantage. Gunsmoke billowing from our weapons like cumulus clouds helped Jerry spot our positions. We fired in the direction from which rounds came but camouflage and smokeless powder made it difficult to locate the enemy. Following an exchange of fire, three or four enemy soldiers appeared waving white flags, hands over heads, yelling, '*Kamerad!*' With them appeared a young French female civilian whom we suspected of collaboration. Thinking she was one of the deadly snipers, we didn't treat her or the other prisoners gently. I doubt they made it back to the beach alive.

"After the Omaha Beach massacre, I vowed never to take a German prisoner. During the fight for the beachhead, hatred intensified." Slaughter was steadfast in this resolve until a few weeks later when he encountered a young German paratrooper. "His right trouser leg was bloody and torn, the limb almost severed by shrapnel. Remembering my vow taken back at the beach, my first reaction was to put him out of his misery. I believe he sensed what I was thinking. He said, tearfully, '*Bitte*' [please]. He was an impressive-looking soldier and I just couldn't do it. Instead, I made sure he was unarmed and then I cut away his trouser leg and applied a pressure tourniquet. I gave him a shot of morphine, a drink from my canteen, and then lit an American Lucky Strike cigarette for him. As I departed, he smiled weakly, and said in guttural English, '*Danke* very much, may *Gott* bless you. *Gute* luck.' That changed my mind. I still hated the German soldier but I couldn't kill one at close range if his hands were over his head."

Fellow Virginian, Felix Branham, as a squad leader with Company K of the 116th, also hiked through Vierville toward the German strongpoint at Grandcamp on D plus 2. "As we began the attack, we found some 2d and 5th Rangers digging in. They told us they had been stopped cold by a heavy concentration of German fire and two of their support tanks knocked out. There was a company of German infantry in an elaborate communications trench from which they directed heavy machine-gun fire. Several attempts by our company and some Rangers failed to neutralize this fire. Sergeant Frank D. Peregory stood up and began firing his rifle from his hip as he moved in the direction from whence the enemy fire came. Upon reaching the trench, he leaped in while firing his weapon, with fixed bayonet. He paused only to reload and throw hand grenades. Frank soon emerged from the trench with three German prisoners. [Peregory had killed eight of the enemy in the course of his charge.] After handing them over to someone else he leaped back into the trench. After what seemed an eternity, he again emerged from the trench, this time with thirty-two German prisoners.

"I had known Frank for twelve years. He married while we were still in the States, and once told me, 'Felix, I should have married this damned BAR, because I have had more nights with it than I have had with my wife. For his action at Grandcamp, Frank won a Medal of Honor. But six days later, near Couvains, while he attempted to capture a German machine-gun nest single-handedly, he lost his life."

In the vicinity of that village, Branham said the hard ground prevented him from digging in. "Three of us were on watch, two guys would sleep while the other stood guard. We figured if we heard incoming mail, we'd just duck down against the hedgerow. I had just seen a medic not far away and I asked him about a friend of mine from his company. He told me the guy had been killed that morning. I started to feel bad and then everything went black for about ten minutes. You never hear the shell that hits you. A German 88 had landed. My face was streaming blood; my left leg had been torn and something was protruding from my thigh, a piece of shrapnel. I looked over and the other fellow was lying on the ground, his face quiet, his leg lying up over his shoulder. The third man, sprawled on the ground, covered with blood; I could see his lungs or heart on the ground.

"The medic came up and started to patch me up. He used a morphine Syrette above my leg wound, wiped my face clear. There were small pieces of shrapnel in my ear and jaw. I told him, go help the other guys, some are worse off than I am. But he stayed with me until he stopped the bleeding, using a tourniquet above the leg wound. I was carried back to the platoon CP, then a jeep picked me and a couple of others back for a ride to the beach. As they got ready to fly me to England, Major Howie, who became the 3d Battalion CO, said to me while I was on a stretcher, 'You're going home, son.' I answered, 'I'm going back to France.' 'No,' he insisted. 'The war is over for you.' I said, 'You're nuts, sir.' He looked at me and winked."

Frank Wawrynovic, having bolted across the exposed beach "like a deer when hunters are shooting at it," lasted less than two weeks. "When any special scouting mission was necessary, with my Ranger training, I volunteered, or was 'volunteered.' After many close calls, I was beginning to feel like the legendary buck deer back home who, time after time, season after season, escapes the hunters' bullets. But I knew the deer was not eternal, nor was I.

"The morning of D plus 12 arrived and I was still alive. It was the beginning of an unordinary day. We had dug our foxholes near the safety of hedgerows at the outer edge of a large meadow. Other troops were moving forward past us. It was to be a day of rest for us. I was dirty, smelly, and very tired. I looked very ragged since my trousers had been torn to shreds. A week before, when the Germans opened up, I had dived for the ground and I had no choice but to leave part of my trousers and some skin on barbed wire that I didn't know was there. After much crawling on the ground in the days that followed, there wasn't much left to my pants.

"Things were looking better this day. Our cooks finally caught up with us and from one, I got a new pair of trousers. We got our first cooked meal since before we left England and enough water to shave and wash ourselves. As we relaxed and cleaned our weapons, I felt very lonely. Most of my friends were gone by now, either killed or wounded. I realized it was only a matter of time before I, too, would be either killed or wounded."

The following day, the members of Wawrynovic's C Company of the 115th cautiously advanced toward an unseen enemy whom they knew, sooner or later, would challenge them. "There were only two alternatives, one to be killed, the other to be wounded," says Wawrynovic. As he approached one of the ubiquitous hedgerows, a loud noise startled Wawrynovic. He dove for the shield of the earthen and shrub breastworks. A machine gun spattered the ground less than a foot away from his trembling body. A significant force of enemy troops exchanged heavy fire with the C Company GIs. In a highly vulnerable position, Wawrynovic realized his only chance of survival lay in the darkness, still many hours away.

"From one of the patches of weeds and grass in the apple orchard nearby came a loud cry, so loud even the Germans had to hear it. 'Help! I'm bleeding to death.' In the movies I would have rushed to him. But this was the real thing. I knew the slightest movement would bring a volley of German bullets. After he called out again, in a low tone only he could hear I cautioned him to wait until dark for our only chance.

"Everything was quiet for a while. Then he or someone with him panicked and got up and ran toward me. As he reached the open alley between the last row of apple trees and my hedgerow, the Germans opened fire. His limp and probably dead body fell. My cover was broken and I had to act fast. Even as his body toppled, I rose to get over the hedgerow to my right. Fast as I was, the German bullets were faster. I felt their shock and pain. Fortunately, my momentum carried me over the shoulder-high hedgerow and into a ditch beside the road. I lay motionless, face down, thinking that when the Germans saw me, they might think me dead.

"I realized I couldn't wait for darkness now, because I might get weak from loss of blood and pass out. I remembered the advice of an old-time deer hunter back home. 'If you hit a deer and he doesn't go down, don't get too anxious and start tracking him, for he will just keep moving ahead of you. Give him some time and he will lie down and get so stiff and sore that you'll be able to walk right up on him.' Not wanting to get 'stiff and sore,' I understood the danger I was in. I had to get back to my company. I had lost my helmet and rifle. My feet were useless to me. My left shoe was full of blood and blood was running out the top of it, seeping through the bullet holes on each side of my ankle. I thought my lower right leg was broken; there was a deep wound across it. I didn't think I was hurt internally by a wound on the front of my stomach. I padded it as best I could with my first-aid kit, my handkerchief, and the lower part of my shirt, pulling up my trousers and belt. I didn't realize it, but the wall of my stomach had been cut all the way through.

"I removed my pack and cartridge belt as excess weight and started a slow, long, painful crawl back through the dusty ditch. By grasping the clumps of grass with my hands or digging my fingers into the ground, I slid along, inches at a time, my progress almost imperceptible. After many hours of crawling, daylight began to fade. I was getting very weak from exhaustion and loss of blood. I reached a wounded soldier lying in the ditch. He begged me to stay but I felt I had to move on in case the Germans should counterattack.

"When I reached a place where friendly forces were just yards away, and with no shooting for several hours, I began to feel secure and got careless. I thought I had better let my presence be known, so I called for a medic. Very shortly two arrived, the Red Cross bands on their upper arms still very visible in the fading daylight. They stopped by me and the other wounded soldier and both went back saying they'd send up litter-bearers. In a few minutes they returned, accompanied by Captain [Norval] Carter, our battalion medical officer, also identified by his Red Cross armbands. He said it was too dangerous to bring in litter bearers. They checked my wounds and went to the other soldier. I had my head turned, watching them, when from the woods across the road came a long burst from an automatic weapon and all three medics fell to the ground. The Germans had killed all three who were protected under the international law of war. These men answered my call for help and died on account of me. To them I owe a debt I can never repay.

"I was so weak, I knew I couldn't last much longer. But with possible help so close, I could not give up. I pulled myself up to where I was just across the hedgerow from GI voices. I saw a hole through the bottom of the hedgerow, quietly called out, and they pulled me through. It was dark now and I continued to move back, inches at a time. Finally, some unfamiliar American faces came up. As they gathered around me, I felt they were going to help me and I lost consciousness. When I awakened next, I was riding in an ambulance and it was morning."

In a tent field hospital, medical personnel dressed Wawrynovic's wounds and then dispatched him by plane to England. He would spend the next nineteen months in military hospitals and endure a series of operations until his discharge with a permanent disability.

A few days before he attempted to treat Wawrynovic, Norval Carter had written his wife Fernie, "I ache for home and you and the boys—the present circumstances make the ache even more acute. Life is now very precious and dear and home is what life means to me.

"The morale of the men in my battalion is high even though the losses of officers & men have been heavy. We are very tired physically and mentally. Sleep is a rare elixir. Hot meals are non-existent. A bed is a memory. I haven't had my shoes off my feet but once in 10 days. We have been under heavy fire but are giving more than we receive—in other words, we are winning."

On 16 June he wrote his parents, "We have had a few terrible experiences in this battalion and quite a few of us are shaken up. I have never been so nervous and frightened in my life, yet we are able to push on. Some of my aidmen have been killed or wounded & my section sergeant & I were blown off a road by a near-hit from a mortar. Since then I have had bullets all around me but my luck is good. My men have shown admirable courage & heroism in removing wounded under fire."

His final letter to his wife reported, "Today we are resting in an orchard & things are fairly quiet but snipers are 100 yards south of us & I have treated 6 gunshot wounds this morning. . . . Excuse this writing 'cause I am in a foxhole with the litter on a water-can. I have collected a few souvenirs so far from the German dead. They are really well equipped. Their dead outnumber ours. But it is a very sad and distressing thing to see (& smell) so many mangled men. It seems to be so useless for nations to do such things to each other." The following day a bullet snuffed out the battalion surgeon's life.

Side by side with the hard-hit members of the 29th were foot soldiers of the 1st Division. Lawrence Zeickler described his first week in France as "just defensive, trying to teach replacements how to handle their weapons, the mortars and machine guns. Other companies moved up while we got ourselves organized and up to strength again."

John Bistrica, with C Company of the Big Red One's 16th Regiment, had awakened on D plus 1 to find, only yards away, enemy soldiers who surrendered quickly. "As we marched on, the French came out with wine, cognac, brandy, milk. We emptied our canteens and put in whatever they gave us. We were hugged and kissed as we went through the small villages. Mostly, we fought snipers; they did not bring up tanks. The mortars and machine guns from the German 352d Division, whom we were not informed about, were bad. The hedgerows became bigger and thicker and we encountered more and more resistance. Finally, we stopped at Caumont and held. We dug holes in the sides of the hedgerows that were large enough for four men. We patrolled and swapped with the other platoon.

Tom McCann, as a member of an I&R platoon with the 18th Infantry Regiment, also halted at Caumont. "The division had penetrated farther inland than any other one and we stayed in the Caumont area for a week or more while surrounded on three sides by the enemy. In this static position we ran patrols both day and night into the enemy lines. You would be on one side of the hedgerow and the Germans on the other, going in an opposite direction. We had observation posts in houses, churches, on the edges of clearings, any place where we could see what the enemy was doing. A static position like the one in Caumont was hard on the soldiers. It's much better to be on the move. We lost one fellow to a nervous breakdown.

"Because the weather played havoc with shipping in the Channel and destroyed the artificial port, we were short of supplies. We supplemented our C rations by fishing, catching eels, and frying them. I wrote home for some fish hooks and a friend wrote back and asked what I wanted them for when I was supposed to be fighting a war. The hooks came after we had left the area."

Bob Meyer, with the 22d Infantry, swung to the north as the post–D day offensive strove to roll up enemy forces toward the tip of the peninsula. Of particular importance now was the port of Cherbourg. The mid-June gale had destroyed the artificial harbor that had been towed to Omaha Beach and severely handicapped shipments of supplies and replacement troops.

"The Germans sent a bicycle battalion to hinder our advance. However, their G-2 [intelligence section] apparently had no idea where we were. In their ignorance they were moving along in a column with no caution and they ran right into an ambush. Four tanks lay in wait. As the bicycle troops pedaled into this area, two tanks in the roadway, and one on each side in a ditch beside the hedgerows, moved against them, firing all forward machine guns as well as their 75mm cannons. It was a complete slaughter. They were gunned down and then ground up beneath the tank treads. We had all seen dead before but none of us had seen what tanks were capable of. We felt sick as we walked through that carnage. It was hard not to feel sorry for them, even if they were German SS troops."

As the "Double Deuce" trudged forward, Meyer's closest

friend fell victim to a malfunction of his own weapon that put a bullet through his ankle. "After he left it was more difficult for me. We'd done everything together and now he wasn't there. My motivation was very dependant upon esprit de corps. As our numbers dwindled, that feeling faded and each casualty was a personal loss. I had mixed emotions. He was gone but I also felt a sense of relief. I knew where he was and his wound was not life-threatening. Had he been killed, I would have probably gone completely mad before I did."

Subsequently, a German machine gun had ripped away his pants leg before he turned his BAR on the nest. Then he survived a thrust by seven German Tiger tanks, constant shelling by the enemy, and friendly fire. Combat fatigue infected Meyer. "The 8th Regiment moved up and we were relieved. When we started the attack, we had 185 men in our company and when we were relieved, we took 27 men off the line. When we got to the rear, it was dark and some guides led us to foxholes that were already dug. Two of us were taken to an elongated one that would accommodate both of us.

"Everything seemed great but just as we were thinking all was serene, we were almost blasted out of our hole. We were located right under the muzzle of one of our artillery pieces. They fired missions all night, and by morning, I was a crying, babbling idiot. But before they sent me to a hospital, they wanted to know if I could give some instructions to the boy who was to replace me. I tried to tell him about the care and operation of the weapon, but about all I did was show him how to take it apart. Later, I thought about that poor boy. Not only did he have to witness my breakdown, but there was so much more I should have told him about the field tactics of fire and movement, which is what keeps a BAR team alive.

"At the hospital, the first thing I had to do was take off my clothes. I had changed socks and gotten a new pair of pants when the leg of my old ones had been shot off but otherwise they were the same ones I had worn since June 6. The smell was terrible. After a shower they weighed me. I was down to 105 pounds; I had been 165 when we made the invasion. The treatment then for combat fatigue was a drug-induced, deep sleep for seventy-two hours. They were supposed to administer twelve grains in the morning and twelve in the evening to keep the patient in a deep sleep. But someone misread the instructions and they also gave us another twelve grains at noon. When the seventy-two hours ended, we didn't wake up the way we were supposed to. The idea of total rest was supposed to restore your outlook as well as your body. While it went a long way toward the recovery of the fatigued body, the psychological problems remained. I had still lost all my friends; I had still experienced all that blood and gore; I had still been blasted by artillery, theirs and ours.

"I was only slightly improved but according to theory well enough to be sent back to my outfit. I vaguely remember being brought to the company kitchen to wait until I could go up front. The kitchen was well behind the lines and they gave me a hole that was more like a den. It had a cover and I recall huddling in there for what may have been several days. A plane came over real low one day and I don't remember whether it fired or not but I slipped into total oblivion. I have no idea of how long I was away from the kitchen group but I was wandering around in the roadway when a jeep driven by a guy from my company came by. He took me back to a hospital that was an 'exhaustion center.'

They ran me through the sleep therapy again but they were beginning to suspect there was much more to it than originally suspected. I and many others were sent out to provisional companies where it was thought work would restore our sense of well-being better than drugs. We did have resort to sodium amatol, and they sort of left it to the individual to decide when things were catching up to him and he needed the drug. I took it only a couple of times, just to sleep through the night." The labor theory of therapy failed to cure what ailed Meyer. He passed through a series of hospitals before shipment back to the States. The Army discharged Meyer in March 1945 with a 50 percent disability pension.

Taken prisoner late in the afternoon of D day, Jim Irvin, the CO of B Company in the 505th, remained at the German held hospital in Valognes for four days. Meanwhile, other captured GIs were marched farther behind the enemy lines. "Some were killed while on the roads by American aircraft," says Irvin. "I was moved by night. There were twenty-eight officers on a bus taking us to Germany. Some were from other divisions and regiments. Three from the 505th, Bob Keeler, B. Hendrickson, and I escaped. We were the only ones who did; the others spent the rest of their time in Europe as prisoners of war. The three of us were fortunate in that a French family, M. and Mme. Frenais, supplied us with clothing and papers. Together, we started across to Brittany. The French would stop and watch as we went through small towns but the Germans paid no attention to us. On July 1, we separated and on July 4th I met a young boy, Henri Brandilly, who took me to his grandparents' home. I stayed as a family member on their farm until the Brittany peninsula was cut off. On August 15 I returned to England and B Company. My exec officer had taken the company through Normandy, where approximately 70 percent were KIA, wounded, or captured before returning to the base camp in Great Britain."

Bernard McKearney and others from his unit advanced into the countryside. "A more colorful caravan never traveled the rocky roads of Normandy. The men looked more like Gypsies than twentieth-century soldiers. With faces still blackened, heads wrapped pirate-fashion with pieces of camouflaged chutes, and roses behind their ears, they must have seemed very strange to the French. We had horses and carts from the artillery outfit we had captured. Loading up wagons with rations, and mounting our nags, we started out. About twenty men had horses; the rest rode in wagons. I myself had a huge bay. Being a subway kid, I had trouble handling him, but it was much easier than walking.

"The night passed uneventfully but then occurred something that could only happen on a battlefield. Across the road from us was a field hospital and I could see wounded lying on the ground. Major John Hanlon, our battalion exec, who knew both of us, told me my brother Jim was there among the wounded. I was granted permission to go and see him. But before I could leave, word came for the battalion to move. We were to go through Carentan and take positions west of town. Rumor had it that a liaison plane had flown down the main street without a shot being fired. The men were laughing and shouting. This was to be a setup."

To the east of the troopers and glidermen of the 82d, the members of the 101st Airborne indeed drove on the important hub of Carentan. With the beachhead established and reinforcements flooding ashore, the initial defensive posture against a German counterattack shifted over to an offensive. Capture of the Carentan causeway, a long stretch of elevated road that bridged rivers, canals, and a soggy marsh in four places leading into Carentan, would unlock a gate through Normandy and into the heart of France.

The 502d Regiment, "the Deuce," numbering Bernard McKearney, John Hanlon, and Wallace Swanson in its ranks, drew the dubious honor of winning the causeway. The rumor that buoyed the hearts of McKearney and his fellow troopers was pitifully false. Instead of limited resistance they confronted elements of the crack German 6th Parachute Regiment plus pieces of an infantry outfit. The defenders occupied tactically strong positions under the command of a highly skilled German paratroop commander, Col. Friedrich von der Heydte.

McKearney's fantasy cracked and then shattered. "In a long column, with our battalion at the rear, we hit the road. We were strafed and bombed by German aircraft. Our ack-ack downed three of them, one falling end-over-end like a flaming leaf. However, one bomb landed smack on the road, costing I Company a lot of men. We moved slowly during the night. Shots could be heard up front. No one worried especially. Hadn't a plane flown down the main street? Didn't you hear the guy say there was no one in town? We're going to just hold them from the flank. Some other outfit's going from the rear.

"The stories passed up and down the column. Carentan is already ours. We were actually moving toward the beach. Then the word came, 'Dig in.' You could hear it increasing in volume as it passed back. 'Dig in, dig in,' and as it went on by us, it became softer and softer. Then the clink of entrenching tools, not a word while everyone was busy digging. Then another command, 'Moving out.' Muffled curses. 'Why don't they make up their minds?' 'If this is war, I'm turning them war bonds in.' Then the shuffling of feet and we trudged on.

"We had advanced about a half mile when, Whoosh! an 88 was shelling the road. Everyone bit the dirt. To others, dirt's dirt, but to the footslogger, dirt is home, sweet home. The firing up front increased. You could hear the growl of our machine guns, then the snap of Jerry's machine pistol. The rate of fire is so fast it sounds as if someone is ripping heavy canvas. You could pick out two of our guns and three of the Jerries'. They would answer one another back. Then you could almost hear ours talking the Jerries' down. The firing ceased. Back came the word, 'On your feet, moving out.'

"The column had no sooner started up when mortar shells began dropping around us. The firing up front had become a storm of sound. God help the 3d Battalion, I thought. Now the wounded straggled back. At first, just a trickle, but then in groups. Wounded men somehow cling together. By now we were moving from slit trench to slit trench. These had been dug every few yards by the troopers up ahead. We passed through St.-Côme-du-Monte; a cluster of rubble that had once been a village. This was a regimental aid station. I heard someone call my name. It was a lad who had fought on the regimental boxing team that I had managed. I asked him how he was feeling. He said, 'Okay, doesn't seem to hurt much.' After he was evacuated the doctor shook his head and said he hadn't a chance. His middle was all shot up. Ordinary boys do extraordinary things in the most ordinary manner. The wounded don't cry. They seem a little dazed. Many have a surprised, hurt look in their eyes, but they don't cry.

"Just as we cleared the town we came to the first of the four bridges guarding the causeway to Carentan. The Germans had blown the first one. Mortars, 88s, and machine guns were zeroed in on all four crossings. The 3d Battalion had repaired the blown bridge to some extent. The bridges had to be crossed, and the only way was to jump up and run like hell to the other side. One at a time we went over. I timed the man ahead of me. It took him seven seconds. Why I did this, I don't know, but you do funny things in combat.

"Then my turn came. I sprang up and started tearing across when from the other side came a wounded trooper. He had been shot through the neck. In a dazed condition, he just stood up and started to walk back. He was still walking when we passed one another on the bridge. I yelled at him: 'For God's sake, get off this bridge!' He just looked at me with a crooked smile and walked on. The People upstairs must have been looking out for that boy that day." The Fates also gazed benignly upon McKearney, who not only made it across all four bridges without a scratch but also endured the entire war without ever qualifying for a Purple Heart.

Actually, the battle for the causeway and Carentan continued from 8 June through 12 June before the combined efforts of the 101st Airborne's three regiments and heavy support from artillery units finally routed the defenders. John Hanlon, with the 2d Battalion of the 502d, described the engagement as "the most devastating battle I saw. The turning point came when Col. Robert Cole, CO of the 3d Battalion, led a bayonet charge. Because of the noise and confusion, not everyone got the word. And when Cole blew his whistle and started to run while firing, as the signal to begin the assault, only a handful of troopers followed him at first. Cole was awarded a Medal of Honor for what he did at Carentan."

# 15

## Superforts and the Marianas

THOSE ENGAGED IN THE PACIFIC, WHILE APPLAUDING THE successes in Italy and Normandy, undoubtedly felt that they were denied resources vital to continuing the march toward Japan. And they were correct in this assumption; neither Churchill nor Roosevelt and their closest advisors saw any reason to shift priorities. MacArthur had continued to leap toward the Philippines in the Southwest Pacific. Navy brass, particularly Ernest J. King, thought in terms of the Central Pacific, the turf ceded to them when the Pacific was split between MacArthur and Nimitz.

The B-17s and B-24s protected by the P-51s flew the longest distances required for strategic bombing in Europe. Development of the B-29, the supersize edition of the B-17 Flying Fortress, able to travel 1,500 miles, dump a massive load of explosives, and then return an equal distance to a home base, offered a weapon geared to the war against Japan. Richard Carmichael, who had been in a B-17 approaching Pearl Harbor at the time of the Japanese attack and later led the 19th Bomb Group during raids upon the Japanese, had returned to the States to fly a B-29. "We all liked it. It was an easy, honest airplane to fly. It didn't spin out, or do anything you didn't expect. It was just like the old B-17. Both airplanes would get you home under really bad conditions." However, in its first inception, the B-29 engines had a tendency to overheat and catch fire. Carmichael noted, "The engine problem got progressively worse after we got to India because of the heat, humidity, and the dust. When we got to China we had different conditions and we had to fly over the Hump [the Himalaya Mountains]. To get over the Hump was touchy; only one out of five airplanes had radar."

Nevertheless, in the spring of 1944, the first Superforts took up stations in India to fly missions against the Japanese homeland, with a stop in China to refuel. The conditions were daunting. Every gallon needed to refuel the B-29s in China was flown over the Hump. The enormous amount of gasoline burned by the huge planes required a full load of fifty-five-gallon drums loaded on six C-46s or C-47s ferried over the Hump from India. All of the bombs dumped upon Japan also traveled by air over the same perilous route.

Carmichael was on his fifth B-29 mission and over Japan when he fell below the assigned altitude of 25,000 feet. "We were hit on the run-in from the Initial Point to the target, which wounded my central fire-control officer, Chester Tims. It may have started a little fire or something in the back end. There was a little confusion in the cockpit, trying to find out or help do something about what had happened. Instead of turning left, as I should have, out from Yawata-hama over the sea, because it looked like there was more flak and more fighters that way, I elected to turn right, and I kicked my butt all the way through prison camp for making that decision. I was picked up immediately by a Betty, a Japanese twin-engine bomber, above me about 2,000 feet. Nobody saw this plane up above us. We didn't expect to be attacked by bombs. Finally Ed Perry, the navigator, hit me on the leg and pointed up there. When I looked, the bombs were falling from the Betty. All I could do was try to make a steep turn. I always said I missed them all but one. That got us in midship and started a fire in the bomb bay.

"Ed Perry grabbed a fire extinguisher, squeezed himself around the four-gun upper turret that extended vertically all the way down through the fuselage only to find the device empty." Nor could Carmichael get rid of his bomb bay fuel tanks. "I pulled every lever supposed to release those tanks and they wouldn't go. It may have had to do with the temperatures, dust, and all the crap accumulated in India and China. Something could have gone wrong with the electrical and manual release systems. But we couldn't put the fire out and couldn't get rid of the tanks."

Carmichael flew out to sea toward Iki Island while his radio operator tried to contact a submarine stationed offshore for emergency rescues. "We were getting lower and lower and faster and faster and hotter and hotter and burning more and more. We started bailing the crew out a little before we got to the island, because the first three people out of the rear end hit in the water. We lost Chester Tims because he was wounded and he hit in the water; we figured he must have drowned. The copilot hit by gunfire in the water. He was lost, not because he drowned, but because Japanese fighters came around and shot him. They attacked everybody they could in a parachute. The radio operator also was lost. Just as I jumped out, the airplane broke apart and hit the island in two pieces. I landed in a field. The first person I saw was a little Japanese soldier coming toward me. I had a pistol and he had a rifle. Behind him I saw a whole bunch of angry farmers coming with long sticks. I knew I wasn't going to put up any resistance. I let that little soldier, who couldn't have been over sixteen or seventeen—but he had a rifle—come up and gave him my pistol." Several farmers managed to rap Carmichael with staves but the soldier drove them off and along with the seven other survivors of his B-29, Carmichael became a POW.

The difficulties of the arduous haul from India via China to Japan convinced the Air Corps that the conquest of the Marianas Islands, particularly the four largest of the fifteen volcanic atolls—Saipan, Tinian, Rota, and Guam, the former U.S. possession—would bring Japan to within 1,200 miles, a more effective range. Saipan already hosted a new airfield and the Japanese had constructed three more on Tinian. Overall, Adm. Raymond Spruance bossed the operations in the Marianas. Crusty Adm. Richmond Kelly Turner commanded the forces designated for Saipan. The 2d and 4th Marine Divisions composed the basic ground forces for that mission, with the Army's 27th Infantry Division in reserve. The equally irascible Gen. Holland M. Smith of the Marines directed the show once it moved ashore at Saipan

The brutal battles of Guadalcanal, Tarawa, and other sites led the Marines to reorganize their forces. In place of the usual twelve-man squad still employed by the army, the Marines added a leader to a trio of four-man fire teams. Each of these toted a BAR plus three rifles. Extra mortars replaced the less fearsome pack howitzers, adding greater closequarters firepower. From a modest two dozen flamethrowers, the leatherneck divisions now operated 243 portable ones, and an additional 24 longer-range ones on light tanks. Fire as a weapon dated back to British experiments in 1915. During the Italian campaign in World War II, both the British and Canadian forces employed portable, mechanical flamethrowers. American experts in ordnance and armor disparaged placement of a fire cannon on a vehicle. After viewing a demonstration of the British Crocodile tank, which mounted a flamethrower in the place of the bow machine gun, Patton had sneered at the result as a "piddle." In Europe, the leading proponents of armor thought in terms of tank-versus-tank warfare rather than assaults upon deeply imbedded bunkers.

While Crocodiles accompanied British troops to Normandy on D day, June 6, 1944, U.S. soldiers in the invasion of France relied on the individually manned system, a canister of napalm on the back of a soldier who carried a spray hose and ignited the fluid. GIs disliked the weapon, both for its cumbersome weight and ability to attract enemy fire. As early as Guadalcanal, Marines, however, enthusiastically adopted the flamethrower, even though the first versions often failed to produce the requisite conflagration. Negative comment arose from those who labeled the weapon as excessively cruel, while advocates ingenuously promoted the flamethrower as humane since, they argued, it killed instantly. The horrendous loss of Americans at Tarawa and Iwo squelched complaints and Marines continued to employ the devices.

For months, Adm. Marc Mitscher's Task Force 58, composed of fifteen fast carriers and seven new battleships, along with land-based Air Corps bombers, had hammered the Marianas and surrounding areas where Japanese air power might attack invaders. Only a week after D day in Normandy, American battleships stood offshore from Saipan and commenced an impressive bombardment in terms of tonnage. But fear of minefields and shore batteries kept the dreadnoughts at least six miles from the shoreline.

Sixteen-inch shells blasted the island but the gunners received poor advice on targets. The explosions rocked the prominent structures but the low-lying, deadly pillboxes escaped the notice of the spotters and the fury of the guns.

Although the roughly 32,000 Japanese soldiers on Saipan doubled the count by U.S. intelligence, aggressive air and submarine raids destroyed ships bearing materials and heavy weapons essential to erect the most devastating defenses. At the same time, because of the problems encountered earlier, the Marines relied much more heavily upon amtracs, some of which carried artillery pieces. As these swam through the sea they added their 75mm cannons to the chorus from the warships and planes. These waterbugs eliminated the highly vulnerable problem of wading ashore and deposited 8,000 troops on the beach within the first twenty minutes. But not even the steel skins of the amphibians could stop the fierce volleys of shells and small arms from the defenders, who inflicted heavy casualties. By midday, the 6th Marine Regiment, having penetrated only 400 yards, counted 35 percent of its men dead or wounded. When night fell, 20,000 Americans occupied a beachhead no more than 1,000 yards deep. Fortunately, those who were dug in so close to the water were backed by tanks, artillery, and the naval gunfire that erased light-skinned Japanese tanks leading night counterattacks.

While the Nipponese military had fought fiercely wherever they came under attack, the Marianas were a special case even for them. By a stroke of luck, Japanese intelligence knew of the B-29. During a test flight over the Solomon Islands in 1943, a Superfort was shot down. Interrogation of the pilot revealed enough information for the Japanese to realize the capabilities of the airplane. A message from the emperor informed those on the island, "Although the frontline officers and troops are fighting splendidly, if Saipan is lost, air raids on Tokyo will take place often; therefore you will hold Saipan." Thus, fully cognizant of the strategic importance of the Marianas, the Japanese dispatched a fleet of battleships and cruisers to knock out the American armada. Alerted to the threat bearing down on his responsibilities, Spruance asked his deputies if it would be possible to withdraw the transports and cargo ships from harm's way. Turner, remembering how the departure of vessels from Guadalcanal left those on the island desperately short of ammunition and supplies, answered no. Spruance decided to intercept the enemy with Mitscher's Task Force and its fifteen carriers. Valuable intelligence on the approach of the flotilla came from American submarines like the the *Seahorse*, skippered by Lt. Comdr. Slade Cutter, and the *Flying Fish* under Lt. Comdr. Robert Risser while they prowled the Surigao Strait and San Bernardino Strait near the Philippines.

For their part, the Japanese mustered nine flattops with 222 fighters and 200 dive or torpedo bombers. Opposing this were the nearly 500 Hellcats and more than 400 dive and torpedo bombers available to the Americans. Adm. Ozawa Jisaburu's aircraft, because they dispensed with such items as self-sealing fuel tanks and armor to shield the pilots, possessed greater range. Furthermore, the Japanese believed their aerial operations would be enhanced with land-based planes from Guam and Rota. A shortage of experienced and well-trained pilots, however, seriously handicapped the Imperial Navy. The high command in Tokyo had not envisioned a protracted war and the schooling of flight crews lagged far behind American efforts.

Both sides prowled the skies seeking to locate the foe, and Ozawa's searchers picked up the American task force position first. That information paid no dividends. The U.S. system that combined radar with fighter-direction teams, aided by the unintended help from a Japanese scout hovering over the area, dispatched Hellcats in a well-coordinated strike that knocked down as many as two dozen enemy planes with only a single American loss. The surviving marauders met a murderous hail of antiaircraft fire when they came within range of the battleships. Another twelve planes were splashed with only minor damage to one heavyweight.

A second wave of more than 125 planes incurred very heavy losses from American fighters and scored no hits. Similar defeats met two more attacks and, of the 373 aircraft launched by the Japanese, fewer than 100 returned safely to their carriers. With a ratio of almost ten to one favoring the Americans, the encounters became known as "the Great Marianas Turkey Shoot."

Adding to the deadly score, two U.S. subs, the *Albacore* and the *Cavalla,* torpedoed a pair of carriers, including the largest one in the Imperial Navy.

For all of this success, Mitscher's task force still had not made direct contact with the enemy fleet. But late in the afternoon of 20 June, reconnaissance from the *Enterprise* located Ozawa's flotilla, 280 miles away. That was the extreme range for the carrier-based attackers. On their return, the Americans would be required to land at night, a speciality at which they had little or no training. But delay of another day would probably prevent any strike at Ozawa, and Mitscher ordered his planes in the air. The operation destroyed two tankers and a carrier, damaged two more carriers and a battleship. Down almost to the fumes in the tanks, the flyers returned to their flattops, illuminated on Mitscher's orders, even though that could have made them easy meat had any enemy submarines been nearby. While twenty planes went down because of enemy action, another 80 crashed or ditched trying to reach their homes. Intensive search-and-rescue efforts reduced the total of missing air crews to forty-nine.

On Saipan itself, however, the Japanese continued to fight far more effectively. American casualties hovered above 10 percent, an intolerable rate to sustain for any period of time. The inability to gain headway and the maneuvers of the Japanese warships convinced the command to delay the scheduled 18 June landing on neighboring Guam. On 17 June at 3:30 A.M. a counterattack spearheaded by forty-four tanks smashed into the leathernecks of the 2d Marine Division. The Americans, with no armor to speak of, unable in the darkness to summon help from the sea or air, fought as foot soldiers, using bazookas, grenades, and other weapons. In spite of the superior strength of the enemy, the Americans vanquished them, knocking out almost three-quarters of the tanks and killing more than 300 soldiers in a four-hour battle.

In his memoirs, Holland Smith wrote, "Although they resisted from caves and hideouts in the ridges, and tried to harass us at night from bypassed pockets, we dug them out and smoked them out in hand-to-hand combat. With flamethrowers and hand grenades, the Marines ferreted the Japanese out of their holes and killed them. Patrols covered the terrain yard by yard, combing thick vegetation and rocky fastnesses for snipers. It was war such as nobody had fought before; [an obvious overstatement considering Guadalcanal, New Guinea, and Tarawa] a subterranean campaign in which men climbed, crawled, clubbed, shot, burned, and bayonetted each other to death."

Doggedly the Marines thrust toward the major objective, Aslito Airfield. Howlin' Mad Smith threw in his reserves, the 27th Infantry Division with its 165th Regiment first to face the defenders. The insertion of these reinforcements set the stage for further friction between the two branches of the armed forces. Marine doubts about the 27th initially arose during the invasion of Makin Island. In the capture of that island, the division operated under Rear Admiral Turner, called by naval historian Morison a "man of steel," whose command included the amphibious corps led by Marine general Smith. The 27th's CG was Maj. Gen. Ralph Smith. The joint operation of Marines and the 27th at Enewetak again generated negative comments from Morison. He chastised the soldiers. "Too long they were held up by groups of defenders not one-tenth their strength. The men were all right but their training and leadership alike was poor." Under the circumstances, the assignment of the 27th to join the Marines under Howling Mad Smith in the assault upon Saipan seems a dubious choice.

Charles Hallden, with a career in banking and finance, had spent ten years in the New York National Guard and had gone on active duty with the now federalized 27th Division. At Saipan, Hallden held the post of CO of Company L, 106th Regiment. "The first mistake was aboard ship as we sailed toward the Marianas," says Hallden, "for the invasion of Guam. We had maps, photos, landing area, objectives, and general information about roads, buildings, harbor installations, natives, on Guam. All of these were intensely studied. After about a week at sea, plans suddenly changed. We would now participate in the Saipan operation as reserve for the 2d and 4th Marine Divisions there. When we sailed on June 1, there were nineteen alternate plans for possible employment of the 27th. On June 9, they added three more."

With the Japanese artillery, mortar, small arms, and nighttime counterattacks pinning down the two Marine divisions well short of their objectives, the 27th no longer could be kept in floating reserve. One day after the Marines set foot on Saipan, the Army troops arrived. "All previous twenty-two plans," says Hallden, "were now discarded."

The defenders retreated slowly, and after a week of bitter fighting a line of Americans stretched across the island. The two Marine organizations took the flanks while the Army occupied the area between them. This area would become known to the 27th as "Death Valley" with adjoining terrain dubbed "Hell's Pocket" and "Purple Heart Ridge." That set the stage for the great Saipan dispute. "To me," wrote Charles Hallden, "it was a mistake to have a divisional boundary or dividing line along the top, on the eastern edge of Mount Tapotchau. In my opinion, the 27th should have had control of the top of the mountain so it could flush out an enemy in the caves overlooking Death Valley. The Marines made no attempt to clean out these caves and the Army was afraid to fire into the mountain or caves which technically were in the 2d Marine Division zone.

"A third mistake was that the Army could never make contact with the 2d Marine Division on its left even after the regiment sent out an entire company to contact them." As the CO of Company L, Hallden, with only 133 soldiers, relieved two Marine units that included 185 leathernecks. Hallden was disconcerted to find the positions occupied by his predecessors did not square with the locations on maps. He later concluded, "Marine officers never report problems or losses of ground when pulling back, and several I met didn't understand the lines on their maps or were poor map readers. Seldom did they report critical information to higher authority."

In a period of three days, 22–24 June, Hallden and the rest of the 3d Battalion of the 106th Regiment suffered about

100 casualties as the enemy hit them with small arms, mortars, artillery and tanks. "During the entire day of action, June 24," noted Hallden, "Maj. Gen. Ralph C. Smith [division CO] was at the front line keeping in touch with every phase of the critical situation. With his front-line riflemen and small-unit commanders, he studied and tried to solve the terrain puzzle in the area. It became evident that to push forward in a frontal attack, without cleaning the Japs off the cliff side that enfiladed the valley, would mean a heavy cost in lives."

Efforts to break through wrought fearsome costs. Hallden reported, "The L company attempt to seize Hill King [designated objective] had not stopped. It had simply melted away. The commanding officer [himself] soon found himself all alone with none of his assault platoon left." When he finally dodged from cover to cover and safety, he discovered the first and third platoons each numbered only twelve ablebodied men, nominally the number for a rifle squad.

Perhaps the worst of the Saipan experience was the fate of a five-man patrol from Hallden's outfit. "I was requested to send them out through the front lines, with the mission to capture a prisoner for interrogation. They failed to return. Several days after the fierce attack in the vicinity of Death Valley, our men came across the five-man patrol, legs bound with wire, hands behind their backs tied to bend them over, with a bullet hole in the backs of their heads. This was a shock and the troops soon turned angry. They said, 'We'll never take another live prisoner.' I myself was very angry and disturbed by what happened. Prior to this incident we had turned over to battalion intelligence prisoners who surrendered. Word of our take-no-prisoners stance filtered through battalion and the upper echelons of command. An officer from division visited us, stating we were to adhere to the voluntary surrender code. But to put it bluntly, the experience demonized the enemy."

The Marine counterargument to the criticisms of Hallden complained that a late start by the two Army regiments and subsequent inability to advance as part of a straight American line left the Marines on either side vulnerable to flank attacks. Holland Smith chastised the 27th for not moving swiftly enough and its leader Ralph Smith agreed that his outfit had to accelerate its pace. But when the GIs could not achieve the desired results, Holland Smith, commander of the ground forces on Saipan, became choleric over the inability of the 27th Division's pace through Death Valley to keep up with the Marine progress on either side.

Although Holland Smith later professed he considered Gen. Ralph Smith "a likable and professionally knowledgeable man," he advised his superiors, Admirals Raymond Spruance and Richmond Kelly Turner, "Ralph Smith has shown that he lacks aggressive spirit, and his division is slowing down our advance. He should be relieved." The Navy brass concurred and the 27th received a new commander. Dismissal of an Army general by a Marine could be expected to breed rancor among the ordinary GIs as well as the highest circles of the Army.

Nobuo Kishiue, a Nisei member of the 27th Division, explained the dismissal of Ralph Smith: "The Marine General Smith, known as 'Mad Dog Smith' wanted glory. He wanted to finish the campaign in a few days in order to turn the fleet loose. It was said—I did not hear it directly, but from other sources—that he ordered the Marines to advance into enemy fire as they were 'expendable.' Army general Smith wanted more naval and artillery bombardment to soften up the front lines. Saipan was cut off from reinforcements and twenty-four hours did not make a difference in the outcome. The

Army general thought about his troops and because of this, every one of them would have, as they say, 'gone to hell and back with him.' Which is why the Marines had more casualties in all conflicts. I don't care who he is, if a person tells me to cross a field when it is zeroed in, I would tell him to lead the way and I'd follow." The "Marines are expendable" quote may not be factual but Kishiue's sentiments mirror those of many.

Much of the unfavorable comment on the 27th Division stemmed from basic differences in the approaches taken by the Marines and the Army. Morison critiqued, "The Marines consider that an objective should be overrun as quickly as possible; they follow up their assault troops with mop-up squads which take care of any individuals or strong points that have been bypassed or overlooked. Marines dig in at night and attempt never to fire unnecessarily, because night shooting seldom hits anyone but a friend and serves mainly to give one's position away. They allow the enemy to infiltrate—keeping good watch to prevent his accomplishing anything—and when daylight comes, liquidate the infiltrators. Such tactics require good fire discipline of seasoned troops who have plenty of élan but keep their nerves under control. The Army, in World War II, preferred to take an objective slowly and methodically, using mechanized equipment and artillery barrages to the fullest extent, and advancing only after everything visible in front had been pounded down. Army tactics required enemy infiltrators to be shot on sight."

This is, of course, a view from an expert whose main sources and affinities lay with the Navy and Marines and who had the luxury of a military life well removed from foxholes on the front lines. Throughout the way the debate raged over whether one should operate on a "damn the torpedoes, full-speed ahead"—the doctrine accepted by Marine officers. Martin "Stormy" Sexton, a graduate of the 3d Marine Raider Battalion on Bougainville, who warned about being "too careful," said, "An offensive can only be successful it it is conducted in an aggressive, unrelenting mode. In many situations such an attack results in saving lives." There were Army leaders, particularly in the armored forces, like Gen. George Patton, who enthusiastically endorsed speedy advance as a means of minimizing overall casualties, while accepting initially higher ones. Other strategists insisted haste wasted men and pointed to the low losses absorbed by men under Douglas MacArthur's more deliberate campaigns. The body count issue becomes further confused by the nature of the missions assigned to Marines and Army troops—small coral atolls like Iwo Jima and Tarawa presented problems different from the Philippines or Okinawa.

The shift in command of the 27th Division notwithstanding, the battle for Saipan dragged on. Three weeks after the opening rounds, some three thousand of the enemy struck at the 105th Regiment of the 27th in what is believed to be the biggest banzai charge on record. (The word means "ten thousand years," a proclamation by the warrior of willingness to enter eternal life in the service of the emperor.) The soldiers, bearing only small arms, bayonets, and grenades, attacked with such ferocity they burst through the American lines. Behind the shattered lines of the GIs, leatherneck artillerymen used small arms and blasted at very short range with their 105 mm howitzers. Men from the 27th Division's 106th Regiment pitched in along with some Marines. A counterattack by the 106th recaptured the lost ground, but its brother regiment counted almost 1,000 casualties and the Marines lost another 130.

Aboard the destroyer *Downes*, Walter Vogel, who, after

abandoning the doomed *Blue* in the seas around the Solomons, had been wounded again while on another ship, had been an eyewitness to the great Marianas Turkey Shoot. In this action the *Downes* fired its five-inchers steadily, while intermittently plucking fifteen downed U.S. pilots from the water. Now at Saipan, the *Downes* hugged the shores of Saipan to assist the leathernecks and GIs. "The Japs were committing suicide, jumping off the point," said Vogel. "I'd say 400 or more bodies were in the water. We had a spotter plane assigned to us. He spotted five Jap tanks heading for the airfield the Marines took and he called the grid to us. We fired our five-inch armor-piercing shells when he'd tell us up or down so many yards. When we hit one he'd say, 'splash one tank,' and we got all five. Late one evening he was flying along the shoreline and he called us about a pocket of Japs in a cave. He was just circling overhead. When we spotted the cave, we fired phosphorus shells into it. About twenty-five came out burning and naturally the 20mms finished them off."

On Saipan, the 45,000 Marines listed more than 2,300 dead and missing, and an additional 10,500 wounded. The 27th's 16,400-man force recorded killed and missing of more than 1,000, with another 2,500 wounded. In percentages the Marines took more of a beating than the Army.

Morison's remarks about infiltrators seem less supportable. With one incendiary bullet, a single infiltrator on Saipan blew up an ammunition dump, resulting in numerous Marine dead and wounded. The notion that any combat troops could allow enemy infiltrators to freely roam among them until daylight is not credible, and that became particularly true on Okinawa. A case can be made for the strategies and tactics of either branch of the services. But when plans and operations called for cooperation and a unified effort by

Marines and Army, the differences could lead to devastating consequences.

Lying about 100 miles south of Saipan, Guam proved another hard case. Larger and more rugged in terrain than Saipan or Tinian, Guam offered defenders room to maneuver and to spread themselves in ways that avoided concentrated targets for bombers or naval shells. The garrison also profited from the three-day delay forced upon the Americans because of the stubborn resistance on Saipan and the necessity of meeting Ozawa's naval threat.

While UDT [Underwater Demolition team] teams swam in to destroy obstacles barring entry to the beaches, a massive preinvasion bombardment by sea and air preceded the actual landings. Primed to assault Guam were some 30,000 Marines from the 3d Marine Division and the newly activated 1st Provisional Marine Brigade composed of the 4th and 22d Marine Regiments. "Partly because of our failure at Bairoko," said Tony Walker, "higher authority decided early in 1944 to reorganize the four Raider battalions as the 4th Marines, a regular infantry regiment. There had been no active 4th Marine Regiment since it was lost at Corregidor." Walker served as operations officer for the 3d Battalion of the recreated 4th Regiment on Guam. The Army's 77th Division was in reserve.

To the sound of "The Marine Hymn," on 21 July, the first leathernecks loaded into amtracs, and with rocket-armed gunboats and 37mm cannon firing, landing craft sped toward the beaches. They met withering artillery and mortar fire wherever they came ashore, and by nightfall the purchase on Guam extended at best little more than a mile. The standard night counterattack of the Japanese, which employed tanks, grenades, and swords, penetrated the thin Marine lines in several places At 3:00 A.M. they hit a sector of the 4th Marine Regiment commanded by Lt. Stormy Sexton. Although the foe threw mines at the leathernecks, while firing rifles and sticking bayonets into foxholes, Sexton's outnumbered band held off an estimated 750 attackers.

Sergeant Harry Manion, a Marine Raider alumnus, served with a reconnaissance unit attached to the 4th Regiment. "Colonel Alan Shapley had us in his cabin and gave us our first day orders. Push inland as fast and as far as possible. Stay in contact. Get some prisoners. The recon platoon, full of steak and eggs, climbed down into an LCVPT and made for the beach and Mount Alifan. Transferred to an LVY [amphibious tractor] for the final run over the coral to the beach. We took a hit from a small gun on our right flank. Into the water and made the beach. Moved past the infantry. Up a draw, moving a few shell-shocked Japanese out of the way. Moved into a graveyard on a hill. Got fired on by some of our flyboys."

Manion and colleagues were sent forward to tie in between the 22d Marine Regiment and the 4th. "Picked up some ammo and grenades and moved back to the designated draw. By this time it was very dark. At regiment, we had picked up a young 2d lieutenant who was to take over as platoon leader. Recon formed a Vee facing the enemy. Three of us were at the apex. Two Johnson light machine guns [were] handled by Privates-first-class Roy Ownes and James Ware. I had a Thompson submachine gun. We were getting settled when we heard some conversation to our right. The men were from a naval gunfire team. The USS *Salt Lake City* was about to send up some rounds. Overhead came a star shell. In the light we could see an entire Japanese army about a grenade throw ahead of us. I went back and found the lieutenant. He thought we shouldn't get excited. Pulled his poncho over his head. He was either crying or praying, maybe both. The cruiser started firing some heavy explosives. The Japanese were yelling and running toward us. Recon moved up to the near flank of the 4th Regiment. The Japanese came through. We could see them very clearly and threw grenades and fired ammo until our barrels were too hot to touch. Next morning there were many bodies in the draw. No doubt the cruiser's shells did a yeoman's job. Gunnery Sergeant Cutting took the lieutenant back with a few men to get ammo and water. It's amazing how much water a person can drink in a firefight. We never saw that lieutenant again."

Merrill McLane already had four years as a Marine when he graduated from Dartmouth with a reserve commission in 1942 and was a platoon leader in F Company of the 4th Marines. "A few days after our landing, a tragic event occurred in the platoon. At night, when in combat, we remain in our foxholes which we dig before dark. Two men sleep in a hole, taking turns staying awake. No one leaves the hole until daybreak. If someone has to go to the bathroom, he has to do it in his helmet and then scatter it with his arm outside the hole. Anyone observed crawling, walking, standing, or running is considered to be a Japanese, and is to be shot at without warning. This is because the Japanese favor nights for their fighting, and they are very skillful at using darkness, much more than we are.

"That night we were all in our foxholes by dark and I had made my rounds of each one, chatting with all of the platoon. In the foxhole with me was Sergeant McCain. Everyone was expecting a counterattack to try to push us back into the sea, or at least to the beach. Nothing developed early in the evening, and I had dozed off while McCain remained awake.

"Sometime around midnight, I was awakened by a rifle

shot near our foxhole. No other sound followed. McCain, a veteran of the New Georgia campaign, whispered to me that he was worried and would like to crawl to where the shot had come from. My concern was that he would be fired at by other members of the platoon. We discussed it and I gave permission. Before he crawled away, I passed the word around in a low voice what McCain was doing. He wasn't long in returning. He told me that ———— had got out of his foxhole and been shot and killed by ————. What a shock!

"There was nothing further to do except to stay alert for an attack and wait until morning. When it was light, the body was removed. I talked with the platoon member who had done the shooting. He was experienced and well liked by the other marines. I had two problems. Should the man who had fired be punished? Second, what kind of a letter should I write to the parents of the lost marine? I solved this at once. It would be the same as parents of other platoon members killed on Guam; that he'd been lost in combat and no mention of the incident that caused his death.

"I needed guidance about the other problem. I talked to the company commander who informed the battalion commander, who called back with word that the situation should be handled at company level. The company commander talked it over with me, finally saying the decision was mine. There was no time to give a lot of thought to the matter. The company would soon be moving out. I shuffled about headquarters for a few minutes and reached my decision. No official action would be taken nor would what happened appear in written reports. The man who had done the shooting would remain in the platoon in his old position.

"After McCain and I informed him of this and reassured him that what he had done could have been duplicated by any one of us, I added there would be no further discussion of the subject. McCain passed the word around the platoon. It was one of the most difficult decisions I ever had to make and I'm pleased to say it was correct. Although the marine we lost that night was not forgotten, the platoon operated smoothly during the remainder of the campaign."

On 22 July, when the Marines began to advance through the positions of the Japanese. Gen. Roy S. Geiger, in charge of the ground forces, had already committed his reserves from the 77th Infantry Division, a well-schooled organization with a background of desert, mountain, and amphibious training at various locales in the U.S. The 305th Regiment went ashore behind the 1st Provisional Marine Brigade near Agat. Dick Forse, who'd attended radio school, was attached to Cannon Company and part of a crew on an M8, an armored, self-propelled 75mm that the men called a tank even though its protection was limited to high steel sides.

"I felt apprehension going into combat but was super alert. My insides jumped at fire in our direction or any sustained fire. Sometimes I started to sweat. I had a small feeling of security surrounded by the steel side of an M8. I hoped the Japanese didn't have anything larger than machine guns. That first afternoon, the platoon sergeant and I were digging our slit trench. It was halfway completed when two artillery shells, incoming, exploded about seventy-five yards away. Both of us dove to the ground. The platoon sergeant was closer to the slit trench so he jumped in there. I was headed there also but there wasn't room for both of us so I just hit the ground where I was. My cartridge belt twisted and my canteen was in the front. I landed so hard the canteen knocked the breath out of me. As I tried to recover, the platoon sergeant was yelling, 'Oh, God, oh, God!' We remained prone and when there were no more shells we got up to finish the trench.

"A few minutes later, two more shells exploded. I thought they were close and we both hit the ground in the same places. This time I was the one yelling, 'Oh, God, oh, God!' The sergeant looked at me with eyes big as cups. He thought I'd been hit. When it quieted down and the trench was completed we went back to the company. We'd been digging sort of an outpost and when we returned, we found the lieutenant had changed his mind. The slit trench wasn't even used. We were usually up soon after daybreak. I was seldom the first out because if there were snipers, I wanted them to use up their ammo at someone else.

"After breakfast rations we'd start the M8 and work usually in support of the 1st Battalion of the 305th. Most days were spent attacking, which meant going forward, sometimes in a skirmish line, sometimes in columns, depending upon the terrain. When they hit resistance, we were committed, depending on whether we were close by if they needed the tanks. Usually we fired machine guns unless the resistance was tough. Then, if we had a good field of fire, we'd use the 75. After that spot was cleared, we'd continue on the attack.

"In the late afternoon, we would eat when we could. When we stopped for the day, we'd all dig in as part of the battalion defensive perimeter. Our driver slept under the tank with one other man from Cannon Company. The other three of the crew either slept in the tank or pulled guard, one hour on, two off. If the situation was considered dangerous at night, the driver stayed in the tank with guards on either side of the turret. There was seldom any combat at night.

"We acted like a tank infantry team. One infantry spotter on each side of the M8 as it moved forward. The squad followed and surrounded us at times. They used us as an outpost, ahead of the line at night. We had a machine gun or a

BAR section with us, plus three or four riflemen dug in nearby. Our artillery fire was very good and fierce, although sometimes the impact was too close for comfort. Air support looked and sounded very good. Generally, it consisted of bombing and strafing Japanese positions several times by eight or more planes. Mostly it was naval aircraft used to break up Jap resistance. We seldom had naval gunfire after the first day of combat. On Guam we were never under attack by Japanese planes."

A former sportswriter, Ed Fitzgerald wore the six stripes of a first sergeant in Service Company, 307th Infantry Regiment. On 21 July, 1944, a nervous Fitzgerald, whose responsibilities were administrative rather than combative, joined the other GIs in "endless, queasy hours circling offshore before we were sent in. When they finally told us to move up topside, we watched the shelling and the bombing in awe. They told us there were four battleships and three heavy cruisers out there where we couldn't see them, relentlessly firing broadsides of shells ranging from five to sixteen inches. We could see a long line of slender, graceful, quick-turning destroyers patrolling a steady beat to protect the big ships, and turning spitefully every once in a while to fire their own guns at the island. Agat Bay and Agat Village stood in plain view. Clouds of black smoke and leaping sheets of red flame showed the ferocity of the attack. 'There won't be anything left alive on that island by the time you guys get there,' said a sailor standing near me. That's what he thought. It was our first lesson in the exaggerated confidence the Navy had in the effectiveness of offshore shelling. What we found out was that when it started the Japanese went into their elaborate caves, and when it stopped, they came out and started shooting. They fired their rifles and lobbed their mortars down on us from high ground and even opened up with artillery pieces that they had made room for in the same caves they hid in.

"But before we learned this hard lesson, we had to go over what is considered the greatest barrier reef in the Pacific. Our landing craft couldn't go over it, so we had to walk over it. We lost a lot of men before we ever got close enough for the Japanese to shoot at us. Everybody was carrying a lot of weight. It was a helluva long distance from the boats to the beach. Some men were too seasick to keep themselves upright, some stepped into holes in the reef and disappeared from sight. The first worry we had, in the boats and after we got out of them, was that our own planes would aim short and hit us. They were coming in right over our heads. But when we saw the first guys go down in the water without a sound and we reached for them and they weren't there, we realized our biggest worry was just making it to the beach without drowning."

Following orders, Fitzgerald and his associates settled in about five hundred feet beyond the beach line. They dug in for the night. "I learned another lesson that first night," said Fitzgerald. "Some people could stay in their holes, but some of us had to move around the company area and deliver messages and the orders that the colonel gave the captain to give the lieutenants and me. That's what Charlie Bauer's two silver bars and the bars our lieutenants wore, and my six stripes were for. I 'volunteered' a lot of people to do things during the war. I made up my mind that was what I was there for.

"Guam was our high school. Everything before that was kindergarten or grammar school, or if you want to give weight to things like the obstacle course and the infiltration course and amphibious training, junior high school. On Guam we learned the big thing wasn't getting mail or something hot to eat, but staying alive. Charlie and I stood on a hill above Agat on the second day ashore, talking to a warrant officer, Warren Pepple, when the first Japanese planes hit us. They were the first we'd ever seen and suddenly they were right over our heads. Machine-gun bullets came first and then shells, digging deep, angry holes in the dirt around us. We threw ourselves down. Pepple got hit in his behind by a shell burst.

" 'Don't worry,' I told him. 'You're only bleeding on the side of your ass.' Charlie called for an aidman while I gave Pepple a drink of water and rubbed some of it on his sweaty face.

'He needs help,' Charlie said to the medic. 'No, he doesn't,' the medic said after a minute of working on him. 'He's dead.' "

"Our regiment [the 306th]," recalled Buckner Creel, a twenty-year-old platoon leader, "landed on the second day on Guam. Our first night on Mount Alifan was a disaster. Much panic and indiscriminate firing of individual weapons. No enemy could be seen, just shadows and strange noises in the jungle. In our own company headquarters, Pvt. John Loughead was killed by his own foxhole mate when Loughead stuck his head up and was silhouetted above the foxhole. This was quite a personal loss to me. Loughead had been a trifler and always in trouble. But during training in Hawaii he had developed into a good soldier. Although there was the officer–enlisted man relationship, we had developed a closeness and he was slated to become my radio operator.

"I believe training took over and allowed me to cope with my normal fear as I reacted automatically to situations. In addition, I had added responsibilities. I was not only exec for the company, but also had taken command of the 1st Platoon. One cannot show trepidation and lead troops in combat. The soldiers will willingly follow an assured, confident leader, so any fear had to be 'cooped' up. In our first action, my carbine had jammed. I got rid of it and started to carry an M1. The additional firepower gave me more confidence when actively leading the platoon on our many combat patrols. And my leading gave the troops more confidence in my ability to lead, react, and get the tasks done most expeditiously. In my first two contacts with the Japanese on Guam, I found that I did react immediately and with the proper action. First, while on patrol, we located a group of enemy soldiers in a defilade position. I responded with a hand grenade. It had the desired effect, killing five of them with no losses to us.

"On the second occasion, I rounded a bend in a jungle trail. I came face to face, at a distance of perhaps ten to fifteen paces, with an enemy soldier. We both dropped to our knees and fired. Apparently, I was the more accurate since I am still here and he isn't. Both times instinctive reactions took over and governed the situation."

Three days after the first marines went ashore at Guam, Henry Lopez, a sergeant in C Company of the 307th Regiment, well beyond his thirtieth birthday, waded through three-to-five-foot-deep water onto the black sand beach. "Huge craters, partly filled with water; debris; uprooted, riddled, and shredded coconut trees; destroyed landing craft, and abandoned equipment strewn about testified to the intensity of the invasion. The indescribable stench of death contaminated the air, stinging and offending the nostrils."

Company C hiked a mile and a half to spend its first night on the island. "Out of sheer curiosity men left their holes to see what a dead Jap looked like. In a large shell crater three corpses lay sprawled upwards, their bloated, blackened bodies blown up like gruesome balloons. Hundreds of small, slimy white maggots squirmed on top of one another and ate their way in and out of this stinking, rotten mess. This disgusting sight, as well as the stench, made many men sick and caused them to throw up their recently eaten rations." The outfit pressed on, engaging in desultory small skirmishes with the enemy. "I am not ashamed to say that when I first came under fire I was scared to death. The only way I could cope with the fear was to think of the platoon, keep busy, and not let anyone know my feelings."

Lopez and his company were pushing north after the Americans had breached the beach defenses. "We moved in a skirmish line with visual contact on one side with a marine unit and on our other side was another company from the battalion. Entering very dense woods with heavy undergrowth, the skirmish line became a single-file column. We lost all contact with those on our left and right sides. We found ourselves past our objective. There was some firing from our left flank and rear. Suddenly, we heard a voice demanding, 'Who the hell is firing at us!' I replied, 'Not us.' The voice then asked, 'Who the hell are you?' 'Americans, who the hell are you?'

"Without answering my question, he said, 'If you are Americans, throw up your helmet or come toward me.' I threw up my helmet so he could see it. Whereupon, we were greeted with a heavy volume of fire. I didn't have to think twice. We also opened fire and at the same time took off in the opposite direction. We didn't locate the rest of the platoon or the company that day but did come under mortar fire. We ended up with K Company of the [1st Marine Division] just before dusk and dug in with them. There was Jap equipment in the area where we had been and I believe that the man was a Jap who spoke perfect English and pretended to be a marine.

"We had been told that the Japs would not surrender, which very few did, and to kill them before they killed you, that they would rather die than surrender, so long as they could take you along with them. During our jungle training course in Hawaii, a large sign read, 'If they don't stink, stick them.' The civilians we encountered on Guam were treated with kindness and respect along with medical care and food."

When the 706th Tank Battalion trundled ashore on Guam, William Siegel, as a staff officer for the unit, acted as liaison from the division advance command post. "It was there that I attended all of General [Andrew] Bruce's [77th Division CG] briefings with his staff and the regimental COs. Also, I was able to observe the few Japanese prisoners that arrived. When captured, they were very polite, docile, and humble as a rule. We in our unit never considered the Japanese as demons, but rather as sly and treacherous. Furthermore, our instructions were that if we captured any of the enemy, we, as officers, would be held responsible for their well-being as provided by the Geneva convention."

The third major objective in the Marianas, Tinian, fell more quickly than the others. In eight days, the 4th and 2nd Marine Divisions wiped out more than a thousand Japanese, many of whom preferred suicide to surrender. The expanding Pacific operations involved intensive ground support from naval and marine aviation. Tom Hartman, a Princeton freshman, had taken advantage of the Navy's policy in the spring of 1942 to enlist as an aviation cadet with only one year of college. Trained as a carrier pilot, he recalled, "The Navy had to decide whether they needed fighters or torpedo-bomber or dive-bomber pilots. My straw came up dive bomber. They then asked us to choose between the Marine Corps or the Navy. The Marines sent the most gung ho officer in the Corps. We were on our feet cheering when he finished. I rushed over to sign up."

In the cockpit of a Douglas Dauntless dive bomber, he joined the oldest squadron in the Corps, Ace of Spades, technically VMSB231, which had already fought with distinction at Midway and Guadalcanal, under Maj. Elmer Glidden. "Elmer was a very precise man, a taciturn New England Yankee who was a graduate engineer from RPI [Rensselaer Polytechnic Institute]. He was all business, never much emotion. He was an iron man who flew more dive-bombing missions than any other, anywhere. He was a warrior and a most decent man."

Hartman began his tour stationed at Midway, escorting submarines. As the Japanese Empire shrank, the base for the squadron shifted to the Marshall Islands. Flying out of Majuro, he went on his first combat operation against bypassed atolls in the Marshalls. "The first mission was one of apprehension for the unknown, but we had trained so often it was a relief to go on a mission. I was apprehensive, but like all young guys I thought I was indestructible. We knew how to dive our planes at the target, release the bombs at a certain altitude, pull out against many Gs of force, how to close the dive flaps immediately in order to insure a maximum rate of speed at our low level; how to join up in close formation on the way back in case any fighters appeared. The SBDs were so well armored and so underpowered they were slow. We had to fly in tight formations so that all of the rear seat machine guns could fire almost as one against enemy planes.

"We bombed antiaircraft gun placements, barracks, and other buildings. The return fire was intense and a number of planes were hit but there were no casualties. I was well trained and in a unit with experienced leadership; fear was never my particular concern. Our equipment was superb.

My radioman-gunner was a cool customer and very good at everything. He trusted me as he had to; there were no real controls in the back seat. The strategy and tactics were absolutely appropriate for the task. We dove from 10,000 feet at an angle of seventy degrees. We opened our dive flaps at the top—they helped us control the planes and limited the speed (350 knots) in a steep dive. We released the bombs as we passed through 1,500 feet. We were an accurate squadron. We had practiced hitting circles 150 feet in diameter."

Hartman and his squadron participated in the suppression of efforts to reinforce or support objectives upon which the Pacific command had designs. "In the spring of 1944 we were told to pack up and be prepared to go to the invasion of Saipan once a third of the island was secure. We were to fly close support for the Marine troops. We had not been trained in close air support but our accuracy was legend. Then, late one night, Elmer called us together. Orders were changed because the Army wanted to use P-47s for that purpose." Morale dropped sharply with the breakup of the squadron and particularly for Hartman when his new skipper, a raging alcoholic, directed the pilots to fly one above the other rather than in a formation in which the flyers could see the plane ahead of them. Hartman refused to follow the tactic and the men ignored their commander's order. The drunkard was relieved soon after.

In the wake of the Marianas campaign, the war seemed to pass Hartman's squadron. "We were bored. The worst thing that happened to us was that a finely tuned bombing squadron such as ours never had a chance to help in the real war effort. Bypassed islands were no threat. We lost pilots and gunners for not so much of a reason except we were doing our duty."

# 16

## Breakout

ON THE TIP OF THE COTENTIN PENINSULA SITS THE GREAT HAR-
bor city of Cherbourg. As the most westerly port of France
with the shortest sailing distance from the United States it
figured as a prime objective. The 9th and 79th Infantry Divisions, which entered France shortly after D day, along
with the 4th, focused their attentions upon Cherbourg. Two
stalwart *Wehrmacht* divisions plus other units ringed the
city. Inside, a port and labor garrison acted as a reserve.
Hitler ordered them to fight to the death, and also directed
Rommel to "strike into the rear of the First American Army
advancing on Cherbourg." The Germans fought doggedly
but rocked from artillery, armor, and savage raids by Ninth
Air Force dive-bombers and strafing fighters. Allied battleships, cruisers, and destroyers offshore unloosed tons of destructive explosives.

The most obstinate and formidable obstacle was Fort du
Roule, a bastion carved out of a rocky cliff above the city.
From there coastal guns faced the harbor approach, while

abundant mortars, machine guns, and an antitank ditch defied a landward assault. From the 79th Division's 314th Infantry, Cpl. John Kelly crawled up a slope to set off a pole charge against a pillbox that pinned down his platoon. When the explosive failed to detonate, Kelly repeated his maneuver, destroying a pair of machine guns. A third sortie with grenades convinced the Germans to yield. Lieutenant Carlos Ogden of Company K took charge after his superior was hit. Alone, he climbed a hill to knock out an 88 and blasted other defenses, while absorbing two separate wounds. Kelly and Ogden were each awarded the Medal of Honor but the former died of injuries in later action.

The defenders turned about their gigantic coastal defense guns to fire inland against attacking GIs, including George Mabry and the 4th Division. Mabry, highly gratified by a skillful capture of a pair of two well-camouflaged pillboxes housing these massive weapons, showed his battalion commander, Colonel McNeely, how the GIs of E Company "had crawled up so close, charged by short rushes; it was almost a perfect military formation, these bodies—all killed while the wounded had been evacuated—to attack these positions.

"After we had gone back to the CP, while I was checking something, I missed Colonel McNeely. Someone said he had walked off in that direction, behind a little hill. I went behind the hill and found him sitting behind a tree, with his head in his hands and crying. I sat down beside him and he began to say, 'George, it tears me up to see so many of our fine young men being killed like that.' I agreed with him and then said, 'Colonel McNeely, only by the grace of God there lie you and I. It's tough to steel one's feelings in a situation like this but you must establish some attitude that would preclude death of your comrades and close friends from affecting you so much. The only way I can do it, when we look at these men, whom we served with so long and whose names we know, my attitude is, you German SOBs you killed my buddies, I'm going to get ten more of you for that. Also, remember, you and I could be lying there dead in the next five minutes but we cannot afford to let the death of our friends affect us so much because it will affect our ability to fight.' After talking a while he regained his composure."

Although the overall commandant at Cherbourg surrendered 26 June, some soldiers, obedient to the Führer, fought on in isolated groups, and not until the end of the month did the skirmishes within Cherbourg end. During the siege, the Germans executed a masterful destruction of facilities, blowing up piers, sinking ships, and setting out mines to deny use of the harbor. Three weeks elapsed before repairs enabled the first vessels to unload at Cherbourg.

During the first months, Dick Gangel flew missions out of Foggia. He noted a number of missions in which enemy fighters met them during bomber-escort duty to Northern Italy, Ploesti, and Bucharest. On 5 May he remarked, "Got jumped by twenty-five ME 109s. They had an advantage of 5,000 feet on us. They got Klos and he bailed out. Tuffy Leeman came in on one engine. Lucky that another flight shot one off my tail." A day later, over Romania, he wrote, "Were jumped by six ME 109s. Coleman got one. Chased two to the deck and two flights shot one down. Several of us tossed for the victory but Cardimona won. Blakely also won a toss." Only in the Eighth and Ninth Air Forces did pilots share victories if doubt arose about who scored the kill.

The tide of battle in Europe changed the nature of the air war there. Between the onslaughts of the United Kingdom–based bombers and fighters, and the territorial advances on the continent in both France and Italy, the depleted *Luftwaffe* could no longer dispatch swarms of interceptors to meet the enemy and was forced to operate ever deeper within the Third Reich. Gangel's log increasingly reported "uneventful" missions. On one occasion he described the enemy as "not eager to mix it up." He also raided more ground targets, hitting locomotives, shooting up parked aircraft. "Flying an intruder mission in Northern Italy, I saw a German staff car with a big Maltese Cross on it. I was determined to get it and blew it away. I was so low that I hit a tree and knocked a hole in the wing, but I got home. When we were dive-bombing I could put a bomb in a bushel basket. When I saw all the photographs of the dead soldiers on the beaches at Normandy I couldn't understand why they hadn't knocked out the bunkers from the air."

On 26 June Gangel laconically entered, "Shot down ME 109 after a five-minute chase on the deck." He knocked down two more before his final shuttle mission to Poltava in the Soviet Union. Enroute, while strafing German airdromes, he destroyed one plane on the ground. Others on the mission accounted for forty more. But Soviet citizens hardly showed appreciation. "We visited Kharkov and the people were very antagonistic. We went for a walk and a man and his family insulted us. A guard with us walked over and hit them."

On the long trip back to Foggia, half a dozen fighters attacked his flight 100 miles before they reached the Danube. "Sognier and I fought five of them, each getting one e/a. We had a running fight home with two, due to the need for conserving gas." He completed his tour of sixty missions without a scratch, although he counted a number of bullet holes in his ships. Credited with four victories, he earned an Air Medal with ten oak-leaf clusters and a Distinguished Flying Cross. "I never had any feeling that there was a human being in the other plane."

As fewer enemy aircraft met the Americans in the sky, fighter pilots sought them on the ground, missions conceded more dangerous than dogfights. Jim Goodson, now a 4th Fighter Group squadron CO, engaged in this type of warfare. As May ended, his crew chief had painted fifteen swastikas beside the cockpit of Goodson's P-51 for confirmed kills on the ground. But on 20 June, while spraying an enemy airfield, Goodson was forced to belly in his Mustang.

"After I got shot down," said Goodson, "I was taken prisoner by the Gestapo [Nazi secret police]. "I persuaded them to get in touch with the *Luftwaffe* which sent a party to take me in handcuffs to the interrogation center near Frankfurt. Going there, we had to change trains in Berlin. I asked the officer in charge of me where we were going. He said the Friedrichstrasse Bahnhof. I asked the date and then remembered that 1,000 planes were scheduled to hit Berlin with the main aiming point that railroad station about noon. What time did we get there? About noon!

"We took refuge in bomb shelters. Because I had taken part in planning the raid, I knew who would be leading the different boxes of bombers and my own fighters would be escorting. It's a very different view of the war, when you're up there at 30,000 feet and you see only little flashes and puffs of smoke. You don't think of people. Sitting in an airraid shelter with Germans all around you, and the crashing, deafening noise above you is something else. About halfway through, the all-clear sounded and everyone was about to leave the shelter. I said, 'No, no! It's not finished yet. The second wave is going to come in. They looked at me peculiarly but the officer with me said, 'He knows.' Sure enough, another wave of bombers came over. I saw devastation a hundred times worse than the London blitz which I went through. There were hundreds of bodies of people who had not been able to get into the shelters. It brought home a war that pilots very seldom see. Digging women and babies out of the rubble we had caused was profoundly affecting."

Goodson was caught in Berlin by a raid with an added wrinkle to it. While the main bomber stream headed for the German capital, two wings of the 3d Bomb Division, accompanied by their P-51 shadows, hammered the oil refinery complex at Ruhland, then continued east with the intention of landing in the Soviet Union at Poltava and Mirgorod. The bulk of the two wings reached the Soviet Union. On the ground in Red territory, Harry Crosby, a navigator with the 100th Bomb Group, slept on a hard bench covered with hay, the guest accommodations for the visiting firemen. "That afternoon," he remembers, "a problem developed. German reconnaissance planes droned over the field looking at us. The Russians had no antiaircraft. Russian pilots in American Airacobras went up, and the Germans, apparently Stukas [dive-bombers], went away. Colonel Jeff [Tom Jeffrey, the 100th's CO] was uncomfortable. 'We're naked in front of those guys.' "

He was not the only one disturbed by the sight. On the ground at Mirgorod, Col. Joseph Moller, the 95th Bomb Group leader for the expedition, also became alarmed by the appearance of a German photo-reconnaissance plane. The Americans had been instructed that while at the Soviet airfields, they would be under the local commander. Moller and the 13th Bomb Wing commander requested permission from the ranking officer for their P-51 shepherds to knock the intruder out of the sky. Moller saw a few meager flak bursts that hardly disturbed the spy plane.

"After a lengthy discussion with another Russian, he refused. I asked him why. He replied that if we did shoot down the German plane, it would always be said that we had to defend ourselves on Russian bases. I then asked how he proposed to defend us and our parked aircraft against a probable air attack. He had no answer, except merely to shrug and turn away." Moller and the wing commander persuaded their hosts to allow them to fly to a different location.

Using a road map supplied by the base commander, the Americans took off from Mirgorod by the light of the moon and fled to other airfields. For several days, Moller and his people then waited for bombs and fuel required for the return trip. Crosby and the other airmen circulated among the Soviet soldiers, male and female, admired the prominent bosoms of the latter, heard tales of the vicious battles endured and the murderous behavior of the German occupation troops. They swapped souvenirs, partied briefly and saw nothing of the enemy.

At Poltava Archie Old brought in about seventy-five bombers from his 45th Bomb Wing. "We hadn't much more than gotten on the ground before we were met by a General Permanov, the Russian commander at Poltava and a General [Robert] Walsh, I believe his name was, from our embassy at Moscow. [Walsh's assignment had been to arrange resupply and refueling.] I noticed this aircraft that looked like it was up 10,000 to 12,000 feet, not more than that, and I was pretty sure it was an ME 210. I mentioned to the American general and General Permanov, through his lady interpreter, that the plane could signal trouble. But there wasn't a helluva lot we could do about it. We had empty tanks, and there was no way, if we started to work then, that we could fill those things up and go to some other base. We had been told this was the only base readily available. I questioned that it couldn't be done but I had no authority to challenge any

Russian decisions there. It was their country and their bases. But they said [the Germans] wouldn't come in and bomb or anything like that. But it looked like an awfully juicy target to me, sitting down there with these silver airplanes. It was a moot question. We could never have gotten the aircraft refueled until, probably, hours after the first Germans arrived.

"We were having a pretty big dinner in honor of myself and some of my key staff people from the 96th, the 388th, and the 452nd Bomb Groups, at General Permanov's mess. The dinner was progressing with probably too-frequent toasts to toss off some vodka. They would make a toast, 'Long live Stalin,' and you were supposed to chugalug, toss it off. Then someone else would [say] 'Long live Roosevelt.' We got a report that there were some aircraft coming in from the west. They were bringing reports into General Permanov. Finally, it was pretty obvious that these were German bombers coming in to bomb at Poltava and Mirgorod. Dinner immediately ceased and [people] went down into a bomb shelter. The first German aircraft over the field was a pathfinder, dropping flares. Those silver airplanes stood out like a sore toe. Then the Germans proceeded to bomb; they did a superb job. Of course those silver airplanes, sitting out on the ground with those silver wings, silver bodies, was like shooting fish in a barrel. It was rather insulting. They were using some of the oldest damn equipment that they had available. They wouldn't have dared, I don't think, to go over England with anything like that.

"I could have done something about it but I had been thoroughly briefed that we would cooperate fully with the Russians. I had somewhere around seventy-five P-51s sitting over there at either Mirgorod or Piryatin [another field] and they had been refueled. It was my understanding, we could have put them up and shot down every one of those German bombers before they did as much damage as they did. However, when I discussed this with General Permanov, he said he would have to get in touch with Moscow. I can only presume he did try but we were unable to get permission to put our fighters up. I was not about to put the airplanes up to shoot down aircraft over Russian territory when they had told me I would have to get permission from Moscow to do that. I didn't go into the bomb shelter but walked to the edge of the field. There was no danger as long as you stayed off the field. I stood there watching. My people, the crews, were in an area adjacent to the airfields. We had two or three casualties." While very few Americans were injured, when the last of the unmolested enemy planes departed, only seven or eight of the seventy-five aircraft of the 45th Bomb Wing were flyable. At Mirgorod, the *Luftwaffe* flares illuminated only an empty airdrome, as the 13th Bomb Wing had flown the coop.

The introduction of the first jet fighter, the ME 262, shocked and even frightened many Allied airmen. Some historians insist that the German jet might have turned the tide of the war if it had appeared in sufficient numbers. Development of the first jet fighters was detoured by Hitler's request for modifications to create a swift bomber that could exact revenge upon the Allies. They produced a worthless version and delayed manufacture of the ultimate jet, the deadly dangerous ME 262. However, even without the ME 262, the German air force could deploy the latest versions of the ME 109 and FW 190 in sufficient quantities [the *Luftwaffe* counted as many planes in its inventory as from the previous years] to have battled the Allies, but the severe attrition that began with Big Week had robbed the defense of proficient pilots and created a scarcity of oil and its products. No matter how many jets rolled off the assembly lines in 1944, there were nowhere near enough adequate individuals to fill the cockpits nor fuel for the rocket engines. By the end of the first month following D day in Normandy, the Allied armies had developed their real estate along a front some seventy miles wide and twenty to thirty miles deep. The invaders counted about one million soldiers in France by 2 July, but after seven weeks of fighting, they had bitten off basically the territory expected on only D plus 5. Stout German opposition, aided by weather that favored the defense—it was Normandy's wettest July in 40 years—along an axis that stretched from Caen through Caumont and St.-Lô, thwarted advances. The most frustrating natural barrier was the hedgerow whose berms and thick vegetation defied the batterings of tanks and bulldozers. American engineers, mechanics, and farmboys experimented with contraptions attached to armor. According to Stephen Ambrose in his book *Citizen Soldiers*, the two most successful devices were a bumper for Shermans devised by tanker Lt. Charles Green and a cutting mechanism created by former cab driver Sgt. Curtis Culin.

Bud Warnecke, a platoon sergeant with B Company of the 508th Parachute Infantry Regiment, and among those forced to withdraw through the marshes and Merderet River, soon joined an isolated group with whom he fought for four days. "All our initial objectives were taken and held by makeshift companies and battalions. We were placed in reserve and there I learned our first sergeant, hung up in the trees when he jumped, had been shot and the battalion commander killed during the drop. I also heard of one man from our company evacuated for combat fatigue or, as we called it, 'shit in his neck.' Our seaborne tail caught up with us bringing rations. The black bread and Normandy butter the

Krauts carried had been real good. We unshaven, motley-looking troopers cleaned up."

On 4 July, Warnecke's battalion prepared for an attack near the strategic heights commanded by the town of La Haye-du-Puits, as part of the breakout from the now secure Cotentin Peninsula. Warnecke recalls, "Sergeant Call and I were standing behind a hedgerow being briefed by Lieutenant Homer Jones. A German machine gun cut down on us. I went down as if hit by a sledgehammer and, as I fell, a slug ripped through my canteen. I got up dazed and saw Lieutenant Jones had been hit through the neck. Blood was squirting out both sides and he was in horrible pain. We called for a medic. Jones was saying, 'Let me die! Let me die!' and Sgt. Roland Fecteau, who was nearby, immediately stuck two fingers in the lieutenant's neck and plugged the holes. When the medic came he shot him up with morphine. The spinal cord hadn't been severed and the wound was directly behind it. As Lieutenant Jones was loaded on a stretcher, he was smoking a cigarette and said, 'I'll see you boys in Wollington Park.' [The 508th's home base in England.]

"My wound turned out to be much more superficial. It busted the skin, looked as if maybe two or three bullets just grazed me. The medic threw some powder on it, put a big patch over it and said, 'Well, you got a Purple Heart.' The shoulder turned black and blue but it wasn't enough to get me evacuated. By the time the fighting stopped for us on July 9, we in B Company, which started with 148 troopers, were down to thirty-three."

As a platoon leader for the 90th Division, Lt. J. Q. Lynd grappled with the enemy entrenchments that blocked advances. "Natural vegetative cover, concealment, and camouflage were used with well-prepared observation and weapon 'dig-ins' to attain the greatest destruction of attacking troops. The basic *Wehrmacht* defensive tactics were to block tank and armor advances, halt the infantry with grazing small-arms and MG fire, then to bombard the standstill outfits with destructive artillery and mortar fire. Thus it was absolutely necessary for the attacking [troops] to determine the specific locations and capabilities of the many, varied strong-point, observation-weapon sites before launching their attack . . . in order to exactly adjust preattack artillery and mortar fire to destroy [these] strong-point locations before the infantry attacks. The only means to determine the enemy location and capabilities was by probing with night patrols. This hazardous task was achieved with officer-led night combat patrols that penetrated the enemy lines and found the Main-Line-of-Resistance weapons' layout and strong-point entrenchments."

Patrols of this nature were high-risk ventures. Early in the Normandy campaign, Lynd led one of three such ventures dispatched by his battalion. As landmarks disappeared in the mist hanging over a swampy wooded area, they followed the path of an elderly cow bent on reaching its pasture. "A combat patrol that doesn't know where you are at, which direction you're going, and how to get back, is lost. The only thing that can be worse is getting caught in an enemy shoot-up mouse trap and the dense pea-soup fog saved us from that." Their guide "Granny Bossy" started grazing in the pasture, "fair warning that very shortly we were going to be on our own." Fortunately, the ground fog had begun to lift. "We could now make out the distinctive tree and hedgerow features that we *must know* to get back, without our now beloved Granny Bossy."

"We picked up our azimuth reading again and began a very cautious trek roving among those hedgerows. Granny

Bossy had put us in enemy territory for sure. It was still pretty foggy and we tried to be a noiseless part of the landscape. Abruptly we smelled the unmistakable, sharp, pungent smoke odor of a German cigar or pipe. Then there was the stink of fresh human feces. Behind the hedgerow to our front, a diesel engine started up, revved up, idled some moments. We could hear a chain clinking, then it accelerated again. Most likely that had been stuck in the mud, probably one of their 88mm pieces."

Lynd and his companions cautiously retraced their steps through the pasture and then along the path taken by Granny Bossy. They reported to headquarters their meager information. The bodies of all of the eleven men in the two other patrols were discovered a few days later. One of them had been led by a newcomer, "An instance of higher HQ thoughtless, costly blunders," remarked Lynd. "Newly assigned replacement officers were extremely limited in capabilities for effective patrol action, even with daylight missions. Reconnaissance patrols absolutely require individual soldiers operating as a dedicated team with total confidence in their buddies. One goof can completely wipe them out." The perils of patrols often induced men to fakery, moving only far enough to conceal them from superiors and then returning with bogus information.

Lynd mentioned that the Germans behaved slightly better than Americans when dealing with the bodies of the foe. Speaking of the corpses of the missing patrols, he noted, "The men had been stripped of equipment and personal effects, but the enemy did leave their ID dog tags intact. . . . U.S. GIs in the follow-up support units were not equally respectful for an identification of the German dead. They would strip the enemy corpse of everything that could be sent home (free postage) as token souvenirs, including the

German disk ID tags. As a result almost three fourths of the German soldiers killed in France are interred as unknown."

During the first week of July, Lynd's division absorbed devastating damage. His battalion under Capt. Leroy "Fireball" Pond managed to penetrate enemy lines around an objective listed as Hill 122 and bring in artillery that sustained the outfit even though it was cut off from the other regiments by the opponents. During this battle a machine gun shattered bones in Lynd's left arm and chest, necessitating evacuation to a hospital in England. Severe as the casualties were in this engagement, brothers in arms from the 357th Regiment sustained their highest single-action losses when a German counterattack almost annihilated two companies.

Along the Allied front, the 2d Infantry Division set about to occupy Hill 192, a 140-foot-high elevation on the right flank of St.-Lô. George Duckworth, as CO of F Company, 23d Infantry, flew over Hill 192 in an artillery spotter plane to survey the enemy front-line positions. "I could see the enemy in foxholes, machine-gun emplacements, trenches, and their armored vehicles. I could also plainly see enemy troops looking up at us and firing small arms at the plane." Duckworth also saw a heavily wooded approach, lined with the ubiquitous hedgerows and crossed by stream beds. Intelligence described dugouts that ran as much as twelve-feet underground and constructed so the Germans could sit out artillery and mortar barrages, and when the fire lifted, to pop up like jacks-in-boxes to confront any advances.

On the other hand, the Americans enhanced their artillery capability. The VT, or proximity fuse, placed in the nose of a shell, relied on a miniature transmitter and receiver that detonated the shell at a predetermined distance from its target rather than upon impact or at a set time after being fired. The device used a radio beam that, upon striking a solid object, reflected back to the receiver, which then tripped the fuse switch. Proximity fuses made artillery shells lethal to anyone above ground and stripped away the protection ordinarily afforded by trenches or foxholes. The technique of Time-on-Target (TOT) added devastating effects. In a TOT barrage all of the artillery pieces fired with synchronization. This delivered simultaneously explosions of all shells whether in the air or at point of contact. TOT, with both proximity fuses and the usual impact-type ordnance, would precede a coordinated tank and infantry assault by Duckworth's battalion.

According to Duckworth, the officers and key enlisted men when briefed reacted with enthusiasm. "It was almost as if the air was charged with electricity. The constant shelling we had endured, the daily casualties, and our intensive training were at an end. We were exhilarated at the thought of engaging the enemy with the prospect of inflicting heavy casualties as a measure of revenge for the pounding we had taken. After several delays because of bad weather, at 0500 on 11 July, the 2d Division artillery, supported by four other attached battalions, opened fire on Hill 192. The noise was deafening as we watched the fiery explosions. Dust, smoke, brush, rocks, and debris of all kinds erupted over the entire surface of the hill and the surrounding area. This tremendous concentration of firepower continued for approximately an hour and it did not seem possible that there could be anyone left alive in the targeted area. When the firing ceased, the tanks made their initial run and then returned for us.

"As we charged into the enemy front-line positions, we found many still in foxholes, dugouts, and hedgerow positions. Even though they were somewhat dazed and deafened by the artillery bombardment, they were able to bring a heavy volume of small-arms fire down on us. As well-trained, veteran troops they held their ground and fought almost fanatically as we closed in and overran them with our tanks and infantry. It was a fierce, no-quarter-asked and no-quarter-given battle, often man-to-man with rifle butts, bayonets, and trench knives. There were no enemy offers of surrender and I do not recall that we took any prisoners in the initial penetration of their defenses. Some may have surrendered or been taken prisoner after we moved forward.

"Our artillery and tanks gave us a definite advantage and Company F's men fought with ferocity and grim determination as we followed the tanks and broke through line after line of defense, often cutting them down from the rear before they could recover. The tanks, with their plowshare attachments, were awesome and a complete surprise to the enemy. When a tank hit a hedgerow at full speed, the plowshares threw dirt, rocks, brush, and other debris into the air. The tanks then roared on into the next field or open area and, once through, opened fire with the cannons and machine guns on the next hedgerow to the front.

"As the battle progressed, enemy troops were plowed out of their hedgerow positions and fortified bunkers, while others were covered up in their foxholes. One five-man machine-gun squad was plowed completely out of the corner of a hedgerow as the tank burst through and ran over them. One of my BAR men braced his gun on top of a downed tree stump and mowed down a line of enemy troops before they knew we had penetrated behind them.

"The assault on Hill 192 was a textbook attack, with the full power of artillery, tanks, and infantry working together as a team. It came down to face-to-face, hand-to-hand combat with cold steel and it was kill-or-be-killed in our area. By 1200 hours we had completely destroyed the enemy front-line positions and by nightfall consolidated our own. Casualties had been heavy but Company F was still an effective fighting force and morale was high. Later, an intelligence report stated we had virtually wiped out the entire 9th Parachute Regiment."

Despite overcoming the hedgerows, the twelve divisions of the U.S. First Army bogged down in front of St.-Lô. General Omar Bradley scripted a plan named Cobra. The strategy envisioned an opening gambit of intensive bombing across a patch of ground three and a half miles wide and one and a half deep, starting with a road that ran from Périers to St.-Lô. In his memoirs, Bradley wrote, "Indeed, it was this thought of saturation bombing that attracted me to the Périers road. Easily recognizable from the air, the road described a long straight line that would separate our position from that of the German. *The bombers, I reasoned, could fly parallel to it without danger of mistaking our front line.*" [Italics Bradley.]

Until drafted for a role in Overlord, the invasion and conquest of Normandy, the Eighth Air Force had pursued its own objectives, the strategic goals designed to knock the enemy out of the war by demolishing the inventory, production, and distribution of the tools of combat. The preparations for D day and the missions flown on 6 June had been the first tentative attempts of United Kingdom–based air units and the American ground forces to focus on the same objective, the German forces in the field. Even here, the airmen in the big bombers were mostly not engaged in direct support of ground forces but in a more general collaboration. The responsibility to play a tactical role in a specific campaign like Cobra was something new. Unlike the Navy, the Air Corps had neither trained nor practiced for this sort of function.

Early on the morning of 24 July, Cobra started in earnest. The most forward of the Nazi troops noticed that the Americans, for no obvious reason, had withdrawn from the field to positions behind the line of the Périers highway. Shortly thereafter, the German infantry heard aircraft, invisible through a thick ground haze, overhead. The poor visibility—the operation had already been postponed three days because of overcast—prevented almost two-thirds of the 903 planes from reaching the target. Some held their ordnance because they could not see the target and the others obeyed a recall. Those bombs that were dropped exploded mostly in a no-man's-land although, by error, some hit U.S. troops, killing twenty-five and wounding more than sixty.

On 25 July, with the skies clear, the Eighth Air Force, preceded by fighter groups from the Ninth Air Force, carrying high explosives, fragmentation bombs, and napalm, struck with the full fury of more than 1,500 heavyweights. After they departed, Ninth Air Force medium bombers and fighters rained down tons more of devastation. For the German soldiers it was an awesome demonstration of what bombers could achieve in a tactical situation. Commander of the crack Panzer Lehr Division, Lieutenant General Fritz Bayerlein, reportedly said, ". . . back and forth the carpets were laid, artillery positions were wiped out, tanks overturned and buried, infantry positions flattened, and all roads and tracks destroyed. By midday the entire area resembled a moon landscape, with the bomb craters touching rim to rim. . . . All signal communications had been cut and no command was possible. The shock effect on the troops was indescribable. Several of my men went mad and rushed round in the open until they were cut down by splinters. Simultaneously with the storm from the air, innumerable guns of the American artillery poured drumfire into our field positions. . . ." Bayerlein remarked that 70 percent of his soldiers were "either dead, wounded, crazed, or dazed." But again, a number of bombs exploded in U.S. positions, most notably among troops from the 4th, 9th, and 30th Infantry Divisions.

Heath Carriker, a North Carolina farmer and former draftee into an armored unit, had switched to flying. His first combat mission was Cobra. "According to my best memory, the Army [ground troops] would outline an area four miles by one mile astride the German front lines, by firing different colored smoke shells one mile apart showing the beginning of the bomb drop. An all-out effort by the Eighth Air Force heavy bombers and medium bombers from the Ninth Air Force would bomb in squadron formations beginning at the smoke line and ending one mile deep. Two-hundred-fifty-pound antipersonnel bombs were used so that great craters would not result in hindrance to Army equipment [e.g., armor] and, second to kill and demoralize enemy troops. It was reported to us that the bomber stream was to be about eighty miles long.

"The next morning at the group meeting for briefing for another mission, the map showed the American armor and troops many miles past the starting point. The breakthrough was successful. This was a very satisfying and proud moment for me and the beginning of a feeling of power and eagerness for more of the same. Later, we were told that our bombs had killed American soldiers, including General [Lesley] McNair; very sad and a dampener of our spirits." Successful as it had appeared, the first close-in support by the big bombers to the ground troops was, as Carriker recalls, a disaster for some U.S. units, specifically the 9th and 30th Divisions. Several hundred men were killed or wounded. Among the dead was McNair, chief of the U.S.

Army ground forces and the most senior man with the forces astride St.-Lô.

The painful friendly fire results at St.-Lô are traceable to blunders, ignorance, and perhaps bad luck. The blueprints drafted by Omar Bradley specifically directed that the attack pathway follow a horizontal route centered on the Périers road. Disturbed when he learned of the slaughter of Americans on 24 July, Bradley had demanded an explanation. To his outrage, he was informed that instead of following the generally east-west line of the battlefield, the raiders flew north to south, perpendicular to the front. The American First Army commander had contacted Air Chief Marshal Sir Trafford Leigh-Mallory, head of the Allied Expeditionary Air Force, for further explication. In Bradley's account, Leigh-Mallory said, "I've checked this thing with the Eighth [air force] and they tell me the course they flew today was not accidental. They are planning to make it a perpendicular approach over the heads of your troops."

"But why, I [Bradley] asked, when they specifically promised us they would fly parallel to the Périers road? That road was one of the reasons we picked this spot for the breakout." Leigh-Mallory had responded that it would require two and one-half hours to funnel 1,500 heavy bombers down a narrow path like the road, to say nothing of the time demanded if one included the hundreds of fighters and medium bombers. And if Bradley insisted on his approach, the mission for 25 July would need to be scrubbed in order for the Eighth to brief the crews that perpendicular was now out and horizontal in. Bradley says he was "shocked and angered" by the answers, for they seemed a breach of good faith in the agreed-on plan. Against his better judgment, he consented to the north-south vector rather than postpone Cobra further.

With the bomber stream operating along a perpendicular axis, the 1,500 planes indeed could dump within a far shorter period of time than if they had to come in almost single file to the designated zone. Bradley reasoned that the road provided a clear marker to guide the bombardiers from dropping on the friendlies but, somehow, no one had ever pointed out to him that such a path would weaken the effect because it would lessen the concentration over a period of time. On the other hand, given the vagaries of the European weather, dependence upon a landmark seen from 12,000 to 18,000 feet up—altitudes described by some airmen as their distance above the target—would also seem rather chancy. Nor does anyone seem to have considered what the wind might do to the guideline color smoke shells, particularly over a period of time, as squadron after squadron from the eighty-mile-long bomber stream queued up for its shot.

Herb Shanker, the engineer/top-turret gunner with the 303d Bomb Group, agreed that the perpendicular approach to the front enhanced the opportunity for error. He noted, "We carried cluster bombs that opened and released twenty-pound bombs after leaving the plane. The propwash scattered those twenty-pounders all over the place. We had three hit our wings."

Despite the Third Army breakout, the top generals remained dubious about closely coordinated ventures with the Air Corps. According to Bradley, Eisenhower said he would no longer involve heavy bombers in tactical situations. "I don't believe they can be used in support of ground forces. That's a job for artillery. I gave them a green light this time. But I promise you it's the last." And it would be until the ground forces needed them again.

The ferocity of Cobra's saturation bombing literally blew open the gateway for the American advance and the ground troops poured through the shattered German lines for what would become known as the St.-Lô breakout. Harper Coleman, in the 4th Division, recalled that a three- or four-day respite brought shower tents, new, clean uniforms, and kitchens with hot meals. Trucks then bore Coleman and his colleagues to the area near St.-Lô. "The Germans fought for every inch of ground. Everything was destroyed, all buildings, bridges, and equipment of all kinds. The roads and fields looked like a junkyard, dead animals in all of the fields. Some civilians had not been able to escape. Occasionally we would find dead ones in buildings.

"During this period, we lost quite a few people. How anyone made it I still do not know. I saw one of the battalion commanders killed by a sniper as he stood near our position. A member of our squad was killed by a sniper and a bullet came across my shoulder, cutting the top of my hand. We came across a column of German troops caught in an artillery barrage and still on the road when our tanks went through. They did not have time or take time to move any out of the way. It was not a pretty sight but I don't think we gave it much thought. Sometime in this period, I saw a wounded German begging for water. One of our lieutenants seemed to have lost all control. He said, 'Water, hell!' and shot him in the head."

Robert Johnson, son of a former North Carolina tenant farmer, had enlisted in the Air Corps shortly after Pearl Harbor and become a crew chief for B-17s in the 401st Bomb Group. He spent seven months servicing the bombers. In April 1944, with D day two months off, Johnson said, "Word came around on the bulletin board asking for ground crewmen to sign up for active combat duty. Me still being only a twenty-year-old kid, I thought it a great idea." Assigned to the 4th Armored Division, Johnson informed an officer that his experience with the vehicles used to tow B-17s indicated he could drive a tank. He trained for a month, learning how to handle a Sherman. "In July, after the invasion of France, we were going toward St.-Lô. A German colonel with a company was holding a huge concrete pillbox. He had defeated everything that had tried to take his fort until us 4th Armored tanks rolled against him. He was soon taken."

The almost continuous infusion of fresh forces such as the 4th Armored Division imperiled the entire *Wehrmacht* forces along the western front. For two days, a thin crust of the German defense had held up an advance of the 4th, 9th, and 30th Infantry Divisions west of St.-Lô. But the overmatched defenders could not sustain their resistance, particularly after the 2d, 3d, and, 4th Armored Divisions battered enemy strongpoints.

Captain Tommy R. Gilliam was an Indiana University ROTC graduate, with Company B, 2d Infantry Regiment, 5th Division. He participated in the St.-Lô breakout where, after fierce fighting against a veteran German outfit, they captured their objective and then made a forced march to position themselves for support of the British at the Vire River. "It was around midnight and we were moving along a country road with about five yards between each man, men on both sides of the road. Company B was the advance guard and I was marching with my first platoon which was providing the point. The road, more a rutted trail, was thick with dust and the small amount of noise from the occasional clank of equipment was muffled as we entered a dark and foreboding woods, described on our map as *Le Forét Militaire*. The forest was dark and heavy and we were marching with trepidation, not knowing what to expect around the next turn of the trail.

"My first sergeant, Tom Miller, a Regular Army veteran with close to twenty-five years of service, was on the opposite side of the road, and I could tell that even his normally unemotional visage was concerned with our security. At almost the center of this forest, we were startled by the sound of people clapping, quietly and gently but continuously, as we marched along the road. For several hundred yards we could make out the shadowy figures of French men, women, and children, apparently from a village in the woods, on both sides of the road. They were here at midnight to welcome us and thank us. No words were spoken. The applause was not loud enough that it would have attracted attention from more than a few feet away, but it was continuous as the company passed through the area.

"It was an eerie feeling, but also a deeply emotional one. It was our first welcome from the French people [the division had been in France for nearly three weeks], almost as if the ghost of Lafayette was saying *'merci'* through the hands of these French peasants. Although there were to be many more welcomes, most with cheering, flowers, wine, and kisses as we spearheaded the Third Army across France, none was as heartwarming or as poignant as the one we received from the villagers of the little town somewhere between Vidouville and the Vire River."

On 4 August, Patton's Third Army included Leonard Loiacono, of the 5th Division's 50th Field Artillery Battalion. During the next twenty-seven days, Loiacono traveled 700 miles in a race through France. "The infantry rode with us in our trucks," said Loiacono, explaining how foot soldiers managed to keep pace with armored divisions that spearheaded much of Patton's sweep. Other GIs climbed on tanks, tank destroyers, jeeps, ambulances, and anything tracked or wheeled that could carry them forward. Loiacono recalled a similar welcome to Gilliam's. "Going through towns, the civilians would cheer and give us anything from flowers to bottles of wine. Some places we went through, men would be shaving the heads of girls who were friendly with Germans, or the girls would be walking out of town, nude, baldheaded, carrying only a handbag."

As the VII Corps sought to wipe out the remaining, but still potent, German forces from the Cherbourg Peninsula, along the line running from St.-Lô through Périers to the Channel, battalion surgeon Marion Adair chose a house for an aid station. He dispatched his sergeant to bring up the rest of the medical section. His diary reported: "About 10 P.M., I sit on a wall next to the road, reading my map and watching the vehicles go by. Suddenly, something slams behind me about ten feet away and blows me onto my feet. Then my right leg gives way, and it is bleeding. I have to lay in the ditch. I expect more shells but none come. When the smoke and dust clear a bit, I get my breath. I see a couple of men and shout for an aidman. They are too befuddled to help. But it doesn't matter because Vic [Samuel Victor] and the boys come running up.

"By this time, I'm hurting like hell, until I get the morphine syrette. The boys bandage up my thigh (right), left buttock, and back and make out the EMT tag. I'm put on a litter and start back on a jeep to the collecting station. We're slow going back because we are meeting 3d Armored Division vehicles bumper to bumper. Fresh replacements with clean uniforms are going forward. One asks the other if I am a German and I rise up and say, 'Hell, no! I'm an American.'

"I get to Company A station and Captain Smith and Captain Scuka see me. I get sulfadiazine and am then loaded into an ambulance and taken to clearing station. There Captain Miller anesthetizes all my wounds and pulls the clothing out of them. He also gives me tetanus toxoid, a clean dressing, and an initial dose of penicillin. 27 July: . . . After an interminable ride I get to the 44th Evac. Hosp. about 2 A.M. At dawn they X-ray me and I lay around all morning, quite uncomfortable on a litter. In early afternoon, they take me to the O.R. and give me pentathol. I go to sleep easily and when I wake up, I feel good—almost inebriated.

"The surgeon who operated tells me no fragments were removed, only debridement done. I have five wounds on my back. He dissected into one as far as my right subclavian artery, then gave up the search for the fragment. I have a wound on my left buttock and the one in my right thigh is fairly large . . . none of the fragments were removed as it would have involved extensive exploration into the remaining muscle. All the wounds are packed with petrolatum gauze. I am most uncomfortable. . . . Later they bundle me into an ambulance and off I go. I stay all night at an airstrip and it's a tough night." Adair underwent months of work repairing the damage before his return to the U.S. for more treatment. In December 1945, he received his honorable discharge.

The rush through the Germans at St.-Lô by Patton's armor, coupled with the advances achieved by First Army, now commanded by Lt. Gen. Courtney Hodges, pinched the already retreating *Wehrmacht* between the Americans, the British Second Army, and the Canadian First, driving from the east pincers. Hitler, who had held in abeyance his strongest armored reserves in the mistaken belief that the main invasion was yet to come at Pas de Calais, had compounded his blunder with one as memorable by ordering an attack upon the Americans between Avranches and Mortain. Unfortunately for the Panzers, 7 August, in contrast to much of the summer weather, dawned with full sunshine and few clouds. The main American outfit, the 30th Infantry Division, could clearly see the massed attackers and summoned a concentration of artillery. Simultaneously, the P-47s streaked through the sky to unleash a torrent of rockets and bombs. The air cover expected from the *Luftwaffe* hardly left the tarmac before Allied predators fell upon them, rendering their contribution nil. German forces renewed their assault, but the GIs of the 30th Division repulsed any efforts to advance. The defeat broadened the avenue for Patton. The only route for escape or reinforcement lay in the Falaise Gap, a corridor less than thirteen miles wide.

Although Eisenhower, only a few weeks before, had dismissed the use of the heavy bombers for ground support, the strategists called upon the big planes to stop German traffic in both directions, trapping the tens of thousands being enveloped in the Falaise Pocket, and blocking off any attempt to relieve the pressure on the beleaguered troops. While not at the same close-in level as at St.-Lô, the mission again had a tactical purpose rather than a long-range strategic one.

Irwin Stovroff, having bombed major targets, D day, Munich, Hannover, and Peenemünde, had completed thirty-four missions on 13 August when his 44th Bomb Group was posted for his last combat flight, a road junction near Rouen, a choke point for enemy movement in either direction. "It was supposed to be a milk run—easy in, easy out," says Stovroff. "Hell, we'd never be out of sight of the English Channel. I'd already packed my footlocker that morning at the base. I was supposed to go to Northern Ireland to be an instructor when I came back."

Stovroff belonged to the crew of the *Passion Pit*, a B-24 given that name in honor of a basement bar of the Santa Rita Hotel in Tucson where the men training together under pilot Lt. John Milliken relaxed when on pass. Bombardier

Stovroff described the trip to the Rouen target as "a long, straight bomb run, no evasive action. We never dreamed there would be antiaircraft like that that day. But the time they hit us, we were at about 18,000 feet. Our number one and two engines were on fire. I toggled the bombs through the bomb-bay doors so they wouldn't explode. We all saw the flames and it wasn't long before we got the word to bail out. The bomb bay doors were still open so everyone could get out there.

"I put my chest chute on. We didn't wear chutes when flying because we had so damn much clothing, heavy equipment that you couldn't move around if you had a back chute on. We did wear a harness to which we hooked our chest chutes. We had practiced on the ground how to put it on. But I'd never jumped before. There was no hesitation on my part or the others."

In a Liberator in the squadron behind, John McLane Jr. saw the heavy and accurate flak burst within the formation that included *Passion Pit*. "I was looking directly at it when one of their planes [*Passion Pit*] started to burn. The plane fell out of formation. As I looked directly at it, there was a monstrous explosion and the plane disintegrated before my eyes. The motors were torn from the wings and went tumbling through the sky with their props windmilling as they fell. The wing, fuselage and tail were torn to shreds. As the pieces of aluminum drifted and twisted while they fell, with each turn, the sun reflected off their surfaces back to my eyes as if they were mirrors. The most spectacular sight was the tanks that had been torn from the wings. The gasoline did not explode but rather burned in huge orange flames streaming out behind the tanks as they fell in wavy fans to the earth below."

McClane assumed all the occupants perished in the fiery

detonation of *Passion Pit*, but everyone including Stovroff had already exited when *Passion Pit* blew apart. "I landed right in the front lines," said Stovroff. "I hit a fence coming down, got up and got out of my parachute. Germans were coming in all directions. I threw away my dogtags, which had an H [for Hebrew, as his religion], and I threw away my .45 pistol. I put up my hands and surrendered.

With the *Luftwaffe* no longer able to protect the German ground forces, the American dive-bombers, primarily in the form of P-47s and, to a lesser extent, P-51s, wreaked havoc with the Nazi legions in their bunkers, and savaged anyone on the road in retreat or trying to reinforce the defenders. The Germans referred to their tormentors as "Jabos," a short version of *Jäger Bomber*—hunter-bombers. They learned to work closely with ground observers. Stephen Ambrose quoted Capt. Belton Cooper when a pair of Panther tanks menaced his unit. "Within less than 45 seconds, two P-47s appeared right over the treetops traveling like hell at 300 feet. It seemed like the bombs were going to land square in the middle of our area." As Cooper and his men dove into foxholes, the P-47s followed up on their bombs with their .50-caliber machine guns. They apparently exploded a German ammunition dump. "The blast was awesome; flames and debris shot some 500 feet into the air. There were bogie wheels, tank tracks, helmets, backpacks, and rifles flying in all directions. The hedgerow between us and the German tanks protected us from the major direct effects of the blast, however, the tops of trees were sheared off and a tremendous amount of debris came down on us."

Walter Konantz had owned his own airplane since his high school senior year and entered the Air Corps with 250 hours of flying time. As a replacement shipped to the 55th Fighter Group, Konantz discovered, "They had changed from P-38s to P-51s only a few days before my arrival. At the 55th we had another ten hours of tactics, formation, and strafing practice before our first combat mission." The log of Konantz's early sorties suggests the still-prominent role for fighters in aid of the campaign through France during August. On the eighth of the month, his first time on the aerial battlefield, he served as one of the chaperones for B-17s hammering the Romilly-sur-Seine airfield south of Paris. He described the affair as "uneventful." On 12 August he participated in a pair of ground strafing and dive-bombing ventures. In the first he noted at the time: "Southern France. Destroyed one locomotive and damaged several boxcars—lost two pilots due to flak. Time logged: 3:15." He wrote of the second mission in the Verdun-Nancy area, "Destroyed 15 ammunition railcars and a city water tower. Aircraft badly damaged by flying debris from exploding ammo cars but made it back to base. Dented the leading edges of the wings and tail as well as knocking off the propeller spinner. Lt. Gilmore shot down by flak. Time logged: 3:15." On 13 August he reported, "Dive-bombing and strafing south of Paris—Hit a railroad station with my two 500 pound bombs and strafed a German staff car. Time logged: 3:00."

Patton, dubious about the value of air support while in North Africa, now relied heavily upon the Jabos. He expressed confidence that they could ward off any attacks upon his flanks. The Third Army commander gloried in his role, speeding about in a jeep, constantly popping up to figuratively boot his forces in the rear end, exhorting, demanding them to move forward ever faster, Thor hurling multiple thunderbolts at the enemy. Success emboldened him to entertain grandiose strategic visions. If he could head due east to Paris, then dash northwest, the Third Army would seal off a huge chunk of territory, trapping more prisoners than bagged in North Africa. Eisenhower and Bradley—now Twelfth Army Group head and Patton's boss—focused on Brittany rather than what they considered a highly risky venture. Their more limited objectives would include the port of Brest, as well as shutting down Lorient and St.-Nazaire, the two biggest hives for U-boats. In spite of his reassurances, they worried over Patton's exposed flanks. Intelligence intercepts gleaned from ULTRA, the code-breaking system, hinted at a counteroffensive. They foresaw an acute gasoline shortage for his armor. Indeed, to keep the vehicles rolling, the Third Army stole fuel from stores reserved for other organizations, impersonated officers from the First Army, bribed quartermaster people with truckloads of souvenirs, and salvaged captured materials. The "midnight requisitions" reduced shortages, but the supply pipeline could not keep up with demand. The Red Ball Express itself consumed huge amounts of fuel. A thriving black market seduced greedy American soldiers who siphoned off vital oil, gas, and food rations as well as amenities like cigarettes and coffee.

Unable to scold, cajole, or steal the necessary resources, Patton grudgingly accepted the mandate of his superiors, grousing, "Brad and [Courtney] Hodges [First Army chief] are such nothings. Their one virtue is that they get along by doing nothing." Patton's army dutifully advanced as far as Le Mans, then veered west to pinch off the entire Brittany peninsula.

Even this did not fully exploit the potential for victory. To close the escape roads, Canadian troops advanced on Falaise but were slowed by strong enemy resistance. With Field Marshal Montgomery's acquiescence, Bradley agreed to use Patton's XV Corps to pinch off the Falaise Gap. The Americans began to work their way toward the objective when again Bradley erred on the side of caution. He halted the advance for fear the two Allied forces would collide. Some 35,000 enemy soldiers, albeit bereft of heavy weapons and armor, escaped. Still, 50,000 German soldiers went behind the POW wire and perhaps 10,000 more died during the campaign.

The decision to restrict Patton's sweep was partially due to a genuine fear that he would overreach. To those who expressed worry over his vulnerable flanks, he snapped, "Forget this goddamn business of worrying about our flanks. . . . Some goddamn fool once said that flanks must be secured and since then sons of bitches all over the world have been going crazy guarding their flanks. . . . Flanks are something for the enemy to worry about, not us." He denounced any effort to hold one's position instead of "advancing constantly." But in the eyes of some military experts it reflected a difference in philosophy. The traditional view was based upon the conquest of territory. Patton, however, never wavered in his belief that the way to win was by killing; his speeches are replete with references to eliminating the opposition— whether by their deaths or by capturing them. Like the Marines in the Pacific, he advocated blunt force, head-on confrontation, arguing that in the long run it would kill more enemy and cost fewer American lives. It was not a simple issue; the top political and military leaders undoubtedly recalled that the failure to occupy Germany in World War I allowed the Nazis to argue that the Fatherland had not been defeated. Unconditional surrender in Europe was unlikely unless Allied soldiers tramped the *strasses*. In the Pacific Theater, areas were bypassed because there was no value to planting the flag, but the prevailing sentiment held that only invasion of the homeland would squash the Japanese empire.

Absent a call on the heavyweights for ground support, the B-17s and B-24s again concentrated upon strategic objectives. A major, and dreaded, target was the heavily defended synthetic oil complex at Merseburg, well over 300 miles east of the coastline. Bill Ruffin, from a broken family in a tiny Kentucky coal mining town, saw Merseburg from the air on four occasions and of all his destinations came to fear it most. "My first mission, July 28, was to Merseburg as they say, 'the flak was heavy enough to get out and walk on.' I did not realize the danger. I didn't know that these little black clouds that suddenly appeared around our plane were there to destroy me until we returned to base and counted the holes in our plane. I soon learned that if I could see the red center of those little black clouds, I could count on some damage. On very rare occasions, I could hear and feel the explosion of those shells and knew we had suffered some major damage. On one such occasion, three feet of nose section was blown away, wounding our navigator and bombardier. They were dragged up into the pilot compartment where after being attended to, the navigator sat on the hatch to stop the air coming through. The German 88 was a remarkably accurate weapon, particularly at 25,000 feet where the B-24s were normally assigned, while we in B-17s drew 29,000 to 31,000 feet."

Ruffin, like so many of those who entered the European war in its final year, speaks more of flak than he does of the enemy fighters. Although the latter appeared sporadically and in lesser numbers than earlier, the casualties among bomber crews continued to be substantial as the enemy invested heavily in antiaircraft batteries, both fixed and mobile. The percentage of losses had fallen well below the double digits of Black Thursday to 2 or 3 percent and occasionally less than 1 percent. But with thousand-plane raids now commonplace, hundreds of young men died, disappeared, or were maimed each week. The Air Corps hoped to balance its payments in blood with a shutdown of the enemy war power. Indirectly, the savage exchanges aided the Soviets because even before D day the mammoth aerial attacks on the industrial areas forced the Germans to deploy guns, ammunition, and troops away from the eastern front.

# 17

# Dragoon

AT THE TIME OVERLORD WENT ON THE DRAWING BOARDS, A companion piece, Anvil, was plotted for southern France, deploying troops drawn mainly from the Mediterranean theater. When the Italian campaign bogged down at the Rapido, before Cassino, on the Anzio beachhead, the Allied forces could not provide the resources to mount an invasion of the two proposed sites, Brittany or the Riviera coastline. Anvil required more fine-tuning to harmonize with the efforts in Normandy. In fact, Winston Churchill had always opposed Anvil. The British leader prophesied catastrophic casualties, although intelligence reports indicated sparse German troops in the area. The Americans correctly perceived that Churchill's real objective in Italy was to drive up into the Balkans and block the entry of the Soviet Union into the region.

Eisenhower, the American Chiefs of Staff, and Roosevelt insisted upon Anvil. The only concession was to rename it Dragoon to allay the British prime minister's worry of a breach in security. The final scenario rejected Churchill's plea for an assault in the Bay of Biscay, closer to the main Allied forces already in Normandy, and fixed upon the Riviera from Marseille to Nice. As in the cross-channel attack, airborne elements under the code of Albatross would drop during the night of 14–15 August to wall off the beaches from reinforcements.

Dragoon initially committed elements of three U.S. infantry divisions, Free French armored units, and both British and American airborne. Among the regiments listed for Albatross was the 517th Parachute Regimental Combat Team. Introduced as ground troops north of Rome late in June, the 517th had been lightly blooded and gained a reputation for itself as carousers with minimum regard for some of the niceties of soldierly behavior.

In addition to the infantry-trained troopers, the 517th included a field artillery battalion equipped with pack howitzers, and a combat engineer company, all told about 3,000 men. A few troopers arranged for the 1944 equivalent of a Mohawk haircut. Almost everyone applied liberal amounts of green and black greasepaint, from tubes bearing the logo of the Lily Daché cosmetics company, to their faces for camouflage and prevention of reflections that might alert the enemy to their presence.

Assembled at the Orbetello airfield, the 3d Battalion heard an address from CO Mel Zais. "I told them, and I really meant it, that I would much, much rather be in our position than that of anybody on the ground, because we knew where we were going, where we were coming in, how many of us there were. We knew what we were going to do, and we had the advantage of having the initiative. Meanwhile, those on the ground would have descending upon them at night, out of the heavens, innumerable people. Those on the ground had only three alternatives. They could lie still and be captured. They could run and probably be shot. Or they could shoot at us and if they got one or two, they would be lucky but they would never live after that because all of our attention would be directed toward them. I told this to all of my men. Of course they were up, high, just cheering." Some, like engineer Allan Goodman, however, regarded Zais's declamation as just a "Knute Rockne style pep talk." Neither Bill Boyle nor Dick Seitz, who commanded the 1st and 2d Battalions, chose to make any speeches to their people.

Something of a special meal was served; boneless chicken from a can and three cans of beer were issued to each trooper. There was debate about whether to drink it on the spot or carry it along. Most, like Phil Di Stanislao, opted for the bird-in-hand approach. The troopers of the 1st Battalion watched a movie, *Stage Door Canteen*, a highly improbable romance between a soldier on leave and a celebrity appearing at a Stateside canteen. Before the last reel, however, the loudspeakers called upon them to report to their planes. The pathfinders, like Dick Robb and Jack Burns, toted the Eureka system.

Said Robb, "In practice and total darkness, we had jumpers landing on us, breaking the Eureka's antennae. On one drill I landed twenty feet from the Eureka operator and I was the twelfth man out." The pathfinders also bore special lights mounted on a tripod that created a five-foot-by-three-foot target area in the drop zone, as well as luminous panels to aid a daylight glider landing. This also showed wind direction. The teams took two of everything in the belief that redundancy compensated for any mechanical or electronic malfunction.

While waiting to take off, an extra beer ration was served.

"About ten o'clock," said Robb, "Lieutenant Fuller stood up, and with a slight weave and a bit of a slur said, 'Lesh go over thish one more time.' Someone said, 'Oh shit, Lieutenant, we've been doing this for a month. If we don't know it now, we never will.' He said, 'Right, so let's have another beer.' We gathered at the planes around 11:30 for a midnight takeoff. I put a can of beer in each side pocket of my jacket. Jim Kitchin was ahead of me. He was laughing and fumbling with his gear and couldn't get his foot up to the first step onto the ladder. The crew chief boosted him up into the plane. The Air Corps types thought it a riot we were all so smashed we couldn't get into the planes without help. We were having a ball, too. However, I can assure anyone that a flight time of 3 hours and 30 minutes, and an altitude temperature drop of fifteen or twenty degrees, did a lot to sober up all concerned. The adrenaline and fear of what was in store added much to the process. Vasoconstriction from the latter, plus the beer, gearing up, and flight time left almost no chance to pee. There were thirty-six fellows almost in tears begging to get out of the three planes to perform the mission. Later, I suggested to Lieutenant Fuller that beer might be one of the surest means to eliminate jump refusals."

To confuse potential hostile reception parties, six aircraft hauled six hundred rubber parachute dummies and dumped them to the north and west of Toulon, well away from the actual drop zones. Battle noise simulators, devices that exploded upon hitting the ground with a sound resembling rifle fire, accompanied the dummies to further convince the enemy. Planes also scattered tons of metal strips that would deceive enemy radar. The official Allied report claims that German radio transmissions indicated the tricks fooled the enemy, but events conspired to confuse all sides.

Altogether, the 405 C-47s under Troop Carrier Command lifted off ten Italian airfields with 5,630 paratroopers bound for southern France among these, the largest single outfit was the 517th Combat Team. Not only were its three major combat components aboard but also some men not ordinarily considered as ground forces. From the Service Company, eighteen parachute riggers volunteered to accompany the combat team. They were assigned to assist the 460th Parachute Field Artillery in setting up howitzers. In the tradition of airborne, the two chaplains, Protestant minister Charles Brown and Roman Catholic padre Alfred J. Guenette, went along.

As the flights of aircraft bearing troopers from the three Rome airfields droned toward their targets, the Pathfinders prepared to descend. The strategists had arranged for boats spaced thirty miles apart in the Mediterranean to provide checkpoints for the air crews. These enabled the planes to make their landfall accurately. Unhappily, as their planes flew over the coastline, a heavy fog obscured the ground. Navigational problems due to poor visibility, shifting winds, and perhaps some pilot error, handicapped the Pathfinder operation. The entire affair was jeopardized. Even after the results of the overall operation were recorded, Troop Carrier Command boasted this was the most successful drop of the war with 85 percent accuracy. In fact, only four out of ten of the flights of planes unloaded their sticks anywhere near their DZs.

Robb recalled, "The Pathfinder pilot-commander, who led the Normandy Pathfinders, advised us that he could not locate our DZ exactly. The beer we consumed had nothing to do with the fact that we landed about six miles from the DZ. And when we were immediately discovered by a company of Germans, we got into a running firefight that gave us no chance to guide in the other planes." His companion Jack Burns was wounded as he touched down but managed to free his weapon and wipe out his attackers. Without the Pathfinders and the Eureka-Rebecca system to guide them, the pilots relied on their airspeed and the navigational checks they managed to make before the fog blotted out the ground

The contingent that included Engineer Ernie Kosan had been separated from the 517th Parachute Regiment Combat Team. The 1st Platoon of the 596th Parachute Engineer Company was detached from the 517th to work with the 509th Parachute Battalion, a veteran combat outfit that had participated in the invasion of Italy nearly a year earlier. "I was proud to be attached to an outfit with the reputation of the 509th," said Ernie Kosan. "The objective was to secure the bridges into Le Muy for the advancing seaborne troops. It seemed like a simple, classic operation. But we were naive.

"While we waited on the tarmac to take off, we received a welcome bonus, grapefruit juice with a good, stiff shot of medicinal alcohol. Also we were given four condoms and four prophylaxis kits. These had to be shown to the officers as we boarded the planes. Failure to display them would eliminate you from the jump which would then be treated as a case of desertion. On the way to the drop zone we sat quietly on the plane, lost in our own thoughts. We were also completely bushed after the physical exertions and emotional stress prior to boarding the plane. We were discouraged from leaving our positions to look out the door because of the sheer bulk of our equipment. Anyway, the overcast and fog made it impossible to see anything.

"Then came the final command. 'Stand in the door!' The engines throttled back and the nose was dropped and the plane began to shudder. The red light continued glowing, for an eternity it seemed. Suddenly the green light came on. The jumpmaster screamed, 'GO!' The jump seemed like any other, except in this case it was a relief from tension. My chute opened and it was quiet—eerily quiet. There were no shouts, no laughter, no banter. I knew there were others out there but I couldn't see them. We were descending in a dense, cold fog. I assumed the 'prepare to land position' and waited. Suddenly, I heard below noises that chilled me to the marrow of my bones—these were crashing sounds. I thought, God, no, a water landing. I began saying my prayers because very few troopers can survive a water landing. The equipment is like a pair of concrete boots. Add to that the drag of the parachute and you're a goner.

"Then I hit a clump of shrubbery and the ground. It is impossible to describe the feeling of relief upon being safe on terra firma. All was quiet. I freed myself of the riser lines and took off the chute harness. The gas mask went into the bushes. Abruptly, I froze. I heard a crashing sound from the bushes. I couldn't remember the password or countersign. I crouched with my carbine and waited. Incredibly, a British paratrooper came striding through the brush. He saw me and without any preliminaries asked in a normal voice, 'I say, have you seen anything of my chaps?' All I could answer was, 'No.' 'Cheerio,' he said, and disappeared into the woods."

While Dick Robb and his Pathfinder comrades were engaged in a firefight far from the place pinpointed to bring in parachutists, troopers of the 3d Battalion started their journey to the earth. Without the expected help from Robb's team, the pilots could only guess where they should give the green light. In contrast, however, to the Normandy air drop, the ground-to-air fire was not heavy and the airspeed of the aircraft, if not the altitude [because of ignorance of the terrain], was appropriate. Mel Zais, who'd fallen asleep once his airplane took off, immediately sensed a problem. "I jumped as soon as the green light went on. I swung twice in my chute before I hit and I knew then we were in the wrong place because we should have been at 1,100 feet and over a vineyard. It had been nowhere near 1,100 feet and this was no vineyard that I landed in."

Zais was, in fact, twenty-five miles east of his appointed drop zone. "I started to unstrap my chute after taking my pistol out and laying it beside me in case there was any shooting. I could hear thuds from here and there as the bundles from the planes dropped. About twenty yards away I saw a yellow chute. That was one that carried a radio and I knew I must get it because I was in the wrong place. A soldier came out of the gloom, pressing his little cricket for identification. I said, 'Hey, trooper.' A voice answered, 'What do you want?' Then he added, 'I'm looking for a blue chute.' [The color signified a machine gun.] I told him the yellow chute had a radio. He said, 'You can't shoot no radio.' "

At dawn, Zais, using his maps, located himself and determined that his troopers were spread over the landscape in three segments roughly four miles apart. He started collecting troopers and marched toward a road junction through which the enemy could bring reinforcements. "My exec, Bob McMahon, had landed against a wall, ripping open his knee so badly I could see white cartilage. He insisted on walking so I carried his musette bag."

Lieutenant Howard Hensleigh, who had joined the 517th and G Company as a platoon leader in November 1944, was part of Zais's lost legions. Having tossed two bundles with bazookas from his plane, he also lost his dinner for the first time in a plane. But he avoided serious injury even as he caromed off a tree onto a couple of rocks. "I got the chest snap, leg straps, and bellyband unbuckled, just as they taught us in jump school, pulled the M1 out of the bag, and assembled it, inserting a clip, and putting her on safety."

Hensleigh started to round up men from his scattered stick. Aided by Sergeants John Podalac and Charles Boyer, Hensleigh accumulated seventy to eighty enlisted men. One of them discovered a house. "After placing five or six men behind cover. I banged the big brass knocker on the door. When I heard a female voice in French from the balcony just above, I said, 'American parachutists' in my bad French. The house seemed to shake. Soon half a dozen men and women greeted us with kisses on both cheeks and strong handshakes. We went in, had a glass of wine. I asked where Le Muy, the town we should have landed near, was. They showed signs of distress and, through a conglomeration of sign language, English, and French, told me we were thirty-three kilometers away." The column continued to swell, although the most senior officer was 1st Lt. Ludlow Gibbons of Company H. The battalion Headquarters Company commander, Capt. Joseph McGeever, appeared with several troopers. McGeever had met up with eighty Brits and, between the GIs and the Tommies, a German truck convoy bearing infantrymen had been wiped out. The union of the two American groups brought the total to 400 troopers heading for their assembly area near Le Muy.

The 2d Battalion, led by Dick Seitz, came down closest to their drop zone. "I saw fog over the water as we approached the French coast," recalls Seitz's exec, Tom Cross. "Then I saw some islands, then more fog. When the green light came on for 'go' I really wasn't certain we were over land, so I prepared for a water landing, or tried to, but I really couldn't.

I had too much equipment on. I never saw the ground but, unfortunately, I grazed a tree and then landed unevenly in a ditch. I thought I sprained my right leg but I broke it above the ankle. The trench knife strapped to my right boot may have helped snap the leg but now it acted like a splint. It hurt like hell when I started to walk, but the name of the game was to get going. All of us were aware of how the Germans had killed troopers whose chutes caught in trees or were wounded during the Normandy invasion. That was a highly motivating factor toward meeting the rest of the men.

"As I hobbled along, I saw T5 Victor Cawthon, of Headquarters Company's communications platoon, and hailed him. He said he had to find his radio and scooted off in search of the communications bundle. I gathered everyone that I could find and we headed for where I thought the assembly area would be. It was still foggy and difficult to establish our position. A Frenchman on a bicycle wheeled up and I asked him for directions to La Motte in my fractured French. With the greasepaint smeared on our faces, all I did was scare him. Suddenly, a German machine gun started up. We couldn't determine the direction of fire or its location but it was too damn close for comfort.

"I had a sizable force with me, about the size of a company, when I met Dick Seitz. He took over and we marched on our initial objective. I tried to start out at the head of the column but couldn't keep up until they halted because of enemy machine-gun fire. That allowed me an opportunity to hobble up to the front. When we finally reached our objective, I sat down beside a tree. Then I could not get up when it was time to move out. Someone helped me to a nearby château that became an aid station of sorts. A French family took care of us temporarily."

Company A's 2d Platoon under Lt. James A. Reith had

been assigned a movie-style piece of heroics. Remembered Reith, "We were to slip into the *Wehrmacht* stronghold of Draguignan before the enemy realized that Southern France was under parachute attack. We were to capture Gen. Ferdinand Neuling, commander of the LXII Corps. And if we couldn't kidnap him alive, we were to kill Neuling and then get out of Draguignan anyway we could.

"My platoon and I had studied the details of the capture plot for a long time. Neuling's residence was Villa Gladys, a stately old mansion that nestled among a stand of towering pines on the outskirts of the town. From our study of the aged architectural plans, stolen for us by the French underground, and a sandtable reproduction of the house, we knew the site well. We were also well briefed on Neuling's daily routine and personal habits."

From his plane, Reith splashed down into a watery ditch. In the nearby darkness he heard voices speaking German. He struggled desperately to get out of his harness. He was on his back, unbuckling his reserve chute, when he heard footsteps approaching through the underbrush. "Just as I freed myself, I looked up and saw a Kraut aiming a burp gun at me. I pulled my .45 pistol and rolled over just as a burst of machine-gun fire struck where I had been. I squeezed off several rounds and the German toppled over, dead from chest wounds. Knowing the firing would alert his comrades, I hurried away toward the main highway. A glowing red light on an equipment bundle attracted my attention. I headed toward it and saw the dim outline of a paratrooper standing near the bundle, gazing up at the C-47s in the sky. I edged closer to the figure, who remained focused on the planes. Moments later, I grew suspicious of my new-found comrade because the man gave off a fishy odor. I had encountered Germans in Italy who had the same odor, apparently from their diet of smoked salmon.

"I stooped to gain a better look at the man's silhouette. My heart skipped a beat when I discerned the coal-bucket-shaped helmet. He was no American paratrooper but a German. Almost at the same time, he became aware of my presence and his hand flashed toward his P38 pistol. I beat him to the draw, sticking the muzzle of my .45 in his stomach and firing. He let out a gurgling grunt before collapsing in a heap. As dawn came I saw from my watch it was 5:35. I had been in France only an hour but it seemed an eternity. But how could I hope to carry out my mission of capturing the general? I was alone and had no idea of my location, and the Wehrmacht between me and Draguignan were certainly on full alert now that thousands of paratroopers had fallen from the sky. A short time later, I ran into Joe Blackwell, my mortar sergeant, who told me we were at least twenty miles from Draguignan."

As daylight pierced the morning fog, Waco gliders, carrying infantrymen, antitank weapons, and 4.2-inch chemical-mortar units, were now coming in to their landing fields. To forestall such airborne incursions, the enemy had planted a full crop of *Rommelspargel*. Some but not all of the antiglider obstacles had already been hacked down by paratroopers. The gliders plowed into them but by serendipity many poles had been poorly installed. They snapped off wings but acted almost like brakes. Nevertheless, a total of 108 men from the more than 2,250 passengers were injured and a number were killed by crashes.

The combat team's own artillery quickly added its resources to those of the line companies. John Kinzer, the exec of the 460th Parachute Artillery, rode in the same plane as Rupert Graves but when he jumped he touched down on the other side of a ridge from Graves. "I prepared for a tree landing," says Kinzer, "after hearing the bundles hitting trees. I ended up with my toes against a large rock on the mountainside. When I opened the Griswold container, one of my submachine-gun magazines fell out and I heard it bounce from rock to rock down the hillside. Therefore, I proceeded with caution until hooking up with other troopers below. Since I was not an infantryman, I led our first small group walking in front, until the trigger-happy guy behind me fired a shot between my legs. From that point, trigger-happy led and I guided him from behind.

"Upon arrival at our assembly areas I assisted Col. [Raymond] Cato [the unit's CO] in organizing our battalion command and control. The most impressive thing about our operation was the delivery of our major artillery power in one serial of aircraft, rather than breaking it up into batteries in support of battalion combat teams. That gave us coordinated fire support in position on D day. Three of our four gun batteries were in action within twenty-four hours of the landing." It was a prodigious achievement considering that a quarter of the artillerymen and their pieces dropped several miles from their designated area. Everything from weapons through the ammunition piled into small, hand-pulled carts moved only by straining legs, backs, and arms. Phil Di Stanislao, one of the troopers of A Company of the 517th, came to earth well out of sight and sound of his buddies. "I had decided that when the red light lit, if we had passed over the coast, I would discard my Mae West. When I went out of the plane and looked down I said 'Oh, Christ!' I wanted to climb back up the suspension lines of the canopy and retrieve the Mae West. But my landing was dry, heavy, and hard. I didn't see anyone nearby. When I went to get my rifle out of its container, the trigger housing slipped out of my hands. I searched on my hands and knees until I found it. My compass was smashed. I didn't know where north or south was. I tried to locate my position from the pattern of planes overhead but they were going every which way.

"Scattered as we were presented some tactical advantages. We were all over the area, in groups as small as two or three, sometimes even as individuals. As my friend Joe Blackwell, who was a sergeant with a mortar crew, insisted, we all thought we were capable of being officers. We all felt we had the leadership ability. We knew what to do, as a result of both training and ego. And we believed in each other. I came across two or three British troopers and since I was the ranking noncom they followed me. We ran into a group of Germans entrenched behind a huge bramble patch. We killed them. The Brits went their way and I continued by myself. Even though my compass had been smashed, I had lots of maps. In the dark I couldn't find out anything. But with daylight I came across what I could see was a small irrigation canal, and I plotted a route toward my primary target, where we would rendezvous or capture, whichever came first. In my travels I met up with a team from the 460th, pushing and pulling their howitzer. I stayed with them a bit, helping them move toward their target.

"I headed for where I was supposed to be and ran into Joe Chobot. We were not the best of friends. In Toccoa [Georgia] one night, while I was charge of quarters, I went to his barracks and told him to turn the light out. He told me to shove it and we had at it outside. I believe I bruised him pretty badly and he was never warm toward me. But situations like this make strange bedfellows. Together, Joe and I started up the path of a wooded, not very steep hill. He ran ahead and suddenly dashed back. 'Goddamn, there are Germans up there.'

"The two of us hit the ground, preparing to fire. Then they rolled concussion grenades down the path, little black eggs. One rolled almost against my head. I did a complete flip-flop and it exploded near my boot. My foot went temporarily numb but it wasn't a fragmentation grenade or I'd have had it. I asked Joe how many there were but he said he couldn't tell. I said, 'Let's stand up, fire into the area, and then haul ass.' They rolled a few more grenades at us, all concussion. I could never figure out why they didn't use fragmentation ones and didn't fire. We stood up, emptied our rifles and then scrammed." Di Stanislao gave up on reaching the primary objective and decided to head for the secondary target.

Jim Reith had reluctantly abandoned any hopes of kidnapping the enemy commander. Instead, he rounded up a large band of troopers until he brought fifty to sixty soldiers to an assembly area. There the party united with a band of troopers including Erle Ehly from the 1st Battalion Headquarters Company and C Company's top gun, Capt. Charles La Chaussee. The group set its sights on a position that would block Highway N7, a vital artery that led to the beaches. Along the way, Reith led a patrol into the woods after sniper fire harrassed the advance. He came upon an entire stick of British paratroopers whose chutes failed to open. Reith counted bodies horribly mangled from the impact of their falls. Apparently, some breakage in the static-line cable caused the terrible accident. The American safeguard of a reserve parachute would probably have saved all of them, but only U.S. troopers wore a spare.

Captain Walter Plassman, the 3d Battalion surgeon, with a Sergeant Harvey and six other medics, traveled with I Company. John Chism, a newly recruited assistant battalion surgeon, Daniel Dickinson, who quit a safe spot in a military hospital to become a paratrooper, and a half-dozen medics accompanied G Company. Plassman noted, "I carried two aid kits strapped to my legs, two canteens of water, one unit of plasma, and my musette bag with medicine strapped below my reserve chute. I could hardly get in the plane. Four bundles with plasma, litters, and other stuff were loaded on the pararacks beneath the wings but we never found them. We landed far from our objective and those who could walk left to join the main forces. About six men and myself were unable to do more than hobble. One man had a fractured leg. My left knee had banged against a rock wall next to a road. With the help of two civilians, we managed to reach Montoroux, which was about one kilometer off.

"I set up a casualty station in a building that had been a TB sanitarium. There were only three cots there but people brought in mattresses. While I was there, I met a French dentist who happened to be visiting his in-laws. He was great. He managed to scrounge food and water for us. Another very helpful person was the local priest. Things were quiet except for a few artillery rounds that fell quite close. That night, around 1:00 A.M. about twenty-five German soldiers came into the town. They had one old truck and they were part of an engineer company. Their captain spoke some English. He said we should stay put and later they would try to evacuate us to their hospital. The Germans remained all day. They had one wounded man with them, a gut shot. I examined him but explained I could do nothing except give him morphine. He died in a few hours. That night, around 2:00 A.M. they pulled out, taking their dead man."

After medic Charles Keen and rifleman Melvin Biddle touched down they had no idea of their location and as they wandered about "trying to find where in hell we were, or someone who knew," they came across other troopers.

"Near daylight, we met Captain [William] Young [the battalion's S-3]. About thirty of us started out to see just what we could tear up. First we passed under a long string of heavy, cross-country electric cables running from the coast to the interior. Young must have been out of his mind because he sent a man up the high metal towers to cut the one-inch cables with a pick mattock. The poor fellow hit once and then raised himself up and really gave it a whack. When he hit the second cable a flame or spark jumped from the overhead cable about a foot, sounding like a cannon.

"The man's body went rigid. He fell stiff as a board to the ground, bouncing off a small building and knocking off some of the tile roof. His feet were still on the metal support of the tower when he stopped falling. The next thing I heard was 'Keen, see if you can help him!'

"I knew nothing about electricity so I used a tree limb to free him. But even then I knew it was all over for him. His helmet was still on and when I removed it, it was hot and burned black. All the hair on his head was burned off. His skin was black. There was no heart or pulse beat. Our leader decided we should attack the cables with a rifle grenade. That failed and we also lost some of our crowd who apparently did not like the direction of our leader."

The remainder of the group pressed on until they bumped into a young Frenchman. "I was chosen to ask him where was the railroad. *'Où est la gare?'* is what I think I said. He answered with a long series of French words and hand gestures. I confessed I had no idea of what he was saying. Trooper John Garcia, a 110 percent American Indian, who learned a lot of the language at the reservation school, informed me the Frenchman wanted to know what state in America I was from. So much for my college French course."

Making do as best they could, Keen and company piled into the back of a flame-spouting, smoky, charcoal-burning truck. The driver headed for the village of Les Arcs. "At the edge of town we disembarked because no one knew whether the Americans, the FFI or the Germans controlled the town. In a very military manner we crossed through the streets until stopped by a man who spoke perfect English. He had come there after World War I from Boston.

"He explained to Captain Young that the land beyond the railroad bridge was in German hands. In the middle of the bridge sat a burning 75mm howitzer that had belonged to our own 460th. Later we learned that a crew from the 460th had assembled the gun after their landing and were pulling it through the town when the Germans hit them. Our commander decided we would all climb aboard the fire-belching, charcoal-burning, slow-moving truck and storm across the bridge to carry the war to the enemy. While the fireman was stoking the burners of the lorry, I spotted an old man in the uniform of the French foreign legion. He had ribbons down to his belly and he was waving his arms, yelling 'Suicide!' 'Suicide!' My French may have been poor but suicide happens to mean the same in French and English. I took one look at Captain Young, then looked at the old, decorated legionnaire. Without another moment's hesitation, I climbed over the side of the truck and down to the street. All of the other troopers followed.

"God, observing our predicament, saw fit to have Colonel Boyle appear, from God only knows where, and assume command." Keen, like De Stanislao, Chism, and others, marvels still at the omnipresence of Bill Boyle. They insist he invariably surfaced at moments of crisis and, in fact, wherever he happened to be of a moment, firefights broke out. That Boyle stepped on stage at Les Arcs at that moment was almost a miracle, considering the start of his role in Dragoon. When the group of aircraft ferrying his troops was perhaps twenty to twenty-five minutes from the drop zone, Boyle glanced out of the open door of his C-47. The formation of some fifty planes seemed in order. He turned his attention to his stick and the equipment bundles that included the vital radio gear necessary for communications. Boyle himself was weighted down with his individual needs, plus a can of machine-gun ammunition. He required every man not a member of a crew-served weapon to bear either a mortar round or the machine-gun ammunition. Officers were included not only because of the value of the extra rounds, but because Boyle also reasoned that if the men saw that officers bore the added weight it would maintain morale.

"When we jumped," Boyle said, "I discovered that my plane was the only one in the sky I could see. The fog bank below me looked like the sea and I started to prepare for a water landing." On the ground, Boyle realized his troops were scattered very widely. In fact, he could find only half a dozen troopers. Fortunately, a pair of French civilians provided directions to Les Arcs, his target. There he discovered the small group that included Charlie Keen. Unfortunately, when Boyle sought to advance toward his objective, control of a rail line near Le Muy, his force of perhaps forty troopers met a strong German attack comprising as many as 400 soldiers. Boyle and his crew fell back to a defensive stance on the edge of Les Arcs.

Ed Johnson became one of the eighteen troopers from C Company dug in at Les Arcs with Bill Boyle's outnumbered band. "We held the town for a day and a half," reported Johnson, "although there were ten of them to every one of us. At the height of one of their attacks, Pvt. Jim Dorman spotted three Jerries coming up the railroad tracks on the left flank about fifty yards away. Depressing his rifle, he let go a muzzle-aimed antitank grenade. It caught the middle man squarely in the back and killed all three Krauts. Patrols led by Sergeant Landsom, Corporals Perkins, and Lathers and Privates First Class North and Shaddoz gained vital information about the disposition of the enemy and the whereabouts of friendly troops." And in spite of casualties, Boyle's forces actually increased as 1st Battalion jumpers sifted into the Les Arcs redoubts.

The enemy took heavy casualties from a machine gun operated by Privates Richard Jamme and Albert Ernst. Boyle deployed Johnson as part of a machine-gun team to guard one avenue leading to the embattled troopers' position. The strategy worked for a while but then German snipers infiltrated some of the taller buildings in town, making the spot untenable. Indeed, the only way to avoid death or capture lay in a retreat. Boyle skillfully extricated his troops. A major reason for the American escape lay in the courageous act of Al Ernst. Both he and Jamme were killed during the Dragoon fighting.

Russ Brami of 517th Regiment, E Company, fortified with dexadrine (other troopers do not recall receiving any amphetamines or other drugs), said, "Using my cricket, the first man I saw was Rupert Graves [regimental commander]. He had banged up his nose. He made me carry a bazooka, the 2.3-inch, which was a lousy weapon. As soon as we could, we started using the captured German *Panzerfausts*. I joined up with some others from E Company and we headed for La Motte. We were on our way when the kid in front got one right between the horns. We started pushing out patrols. With some others I was outposted on a hill where the gliders from the 551st were to come in. We pulled out some of the poles put into the earth to prevent gliders. There were

mines on wires between some. We shot at them but we had
no real tools for removing the poles."

The immediate concerns for Dick Seitz upon the assembly of his troopers were to take over in front of the command
post established at Château Ste.-Roseline and to help break
out Boyle's small garrison before the enemy enveloped it.
On D plus 1, Lt. Carl Starkey led a pair of the 517th's D
Company platoons into Les Arcs from the north. One of the
units then pushed through to contact some of the embattled
Boyle troopers. The still outnumbered Americans hung on,
fending off the enemy with their own small arms and aided
by 4.2 mortars as well as marauding Air Corps P-51 Mustangs that dumped 500-pounders on the foe.

The 596th Airborne Engineer Company not only did not
jump as a unit into Southern France but the 1st Platoon was
parceled out to the 509th Combat Team, an entirely separate
organization. One batch fell at Le Muy, a town designated
for future assault and which lay four miles from the planned
DZ. The jump brought serious injuries to two men, one of
whom was Pvt. Henry Wikins, Ernie Kozan's fellow refugee
from Germany. Heavy mortar fire on the Americans forced
them to pull back. Because of the severity of Wikins's injury, a broken leg, he could not be removed. A day later he
was found dead, apparently executed by the Germans. The
murderers cut off his penis and stuffed it in his mouth, perhaps because they knew he was Jewish since he wore a Star
of David on a chain around his neck.

"This had a profound effect on our attitude toward the
enemy for the rest of the war," said Charles Pugh. As both a
radioman and a demolition specialist, Pugh had made his
jump with a forty-pound radio strapped to him, several
blocks of TNT, and the usual field pack, weapon, and extra
ammunition. With his two chutes, Pugh figures he bore be-

tween 130 and 140 pounds. "My group missed its drop zone more than anyone else. About sixty of us landed some thirty miles off. We marched, mostly at night, and after three or four firefights with Germans trying to retreat, we contacted the main unit on D plus 2. We ate K rations but we had all the wine we could drink, which came from the French people as we marched through their villages. We also picked up some potatoes, tomatoes, and onions, even an occasional chicken while traveling on foot."

Weary 3d Battalion troopers, having marched more than twenty miles along mountain roads, plunked down their exhausted, sweating bodies on the slopes by Ste.-Roseline. Sprawling under anything that would shield them from the sun, the men expected to have a night to recover their strength. However, Rupert Graves believed any delay in the operations around Les Arcs might jeopardize the entire mission. He ordered the 3d Battalion to attack.

Bereft of sleep for as much as thirty-six hours, H and I Companies led the assault. Cato's 75mm howitzers, bolstered by the 4.2 mortars flown in by glider, poured 1,000 rounds upon the enemy in a period of twenty minutes. To some of the 460th it seemed like a contest to see who could fire the most. Everybody assisted in the loading, including captains and lieutenants. While the guns were still in recoil after firing, another shell was being loaded for almost immediate refiring. German prisoners later asked whether the victors had belt-fed howitzers.

The troopers jumped off a few minutes after 8:00 P.M. It seemed unlikely that anyone could have withstood that avalanche of fire, smoke, white-hot phosphorus, and shrapnel. But Zais's forces met stiff fire. The attack bogged down as the Americans hugged the ground. Zais, said, "I knew I had to get them to move up into position, to cross the line of departure. I was just breaking out into the open and I kept walking. When I walked out there and said, 'Come on, let's go. Everybody get up,' the firing for whatever reason stopped."

There were two companies up ahead that had halted in their tracks. "First Sergeant Gaunce had been shot in the throat and when Lieutenant Freeman went to help him he was hit in the belly. Then a third man went down. I thought, 'Boy, this is bad. I wasn't sure what to do. Everytime someone tried to get up on the railroad embankment ahead they were shot. I called for mortar fire from the chemical battery that had come in on gliders because the 460th with its pack 75s couldn't get the right angle.

"My S-3 had been injured and the acting S-3 was a kid named Ludlow Gibbons, a great youngster but getting very nervous. 'Colonel, I'll do anything you want to do, but this is suicide.' I said, 'What would you suggest?' He answered, 'We can't go over the embankment. Gaunce has been killed. Freeman has been killed.' He sounded almost hysterical.

"I said, 'We'll do what we've got to do. They're not going to shoot if all of us appear at once.' The mortars put down a barrage and then we attacked. The enemy came out running, hands up. There were about eighteen of them and they all surrendered." The citation that accompanied his Silver Star award stated that Zais "completely disregarded the enemy fire and moved out into the open in direct observation of the enemy, shouting to his men to continue forward. Inspired and encouraged by the actions of their battalion commander, the men rose to their feet and continued the attack with vigor." The Germans surrendered and among the trophies were a handful of GIs from the 45th Division who had been captured.

Ed Johnson from C Company and part of the original

band with Bill Boyle which had almost been destroyed at Les Arcs was among the victory party that occupied the town. "I confess my view of the enemy changed when we took about fifty German military students prisoners. They were just kids, like us. Their small equipment bags spewed out pictures of their loved ones, just as ours would have. We turned them over to the French FFI where I am sure the sentiment was different."

All along the front the Germans died, surrendered or retreated. British troopers captured Draguignan and Reith's intended victim, General Neuling. From out of the hills came several hundred members of the 517th; these were men who'd been listed as missing and were feared dead or prisoners, but who, in fact, had fought small skirmishes with the enemy on their own, or on some occasions tied in with scatterings of the FFI. Actually, few members of the 517th found the French helpful for much more than intelligence. "If you saw them around waving their weapons," remarks Di Stanislao, "you could be pretty sure the enemy was long gone."

Contact with armored units of the 45th Division in the vicinity of Le Muy marked the success of Dragoon. The soldiers who had waded ashore on the Riviera had linked up with the airborne forces holding the interior. John Forrest was with the group controlling Highway N7 when they observed armored scout cars working their way along the road. "At first we thought it was another German attack but then we recognized them as from the 45th Division. When the lead one pulled up, a red-haired soldier stuck his head out and asked, 'Does anybody here know "You Are My Sunshine?" I can sing the harmony.'"

With hostilities temporarily reduced to the occasional sniper, Howard Hensleigh requisitioned a handful of troopers to scout Montoroux. "I found Doc Plassman with a white uniform, just as if he were a part of the small hospital. All the boys were there and that was a relief since we heard all kinds of rumors how the Jerries had treated them. I made arrangements to have them evacuated by ambulance."

Now that the shooting temporarily died down and the opening phases of Dragoon were coming to a close, the 517th Parachute Infantry units counted the toll absorbed. It added up to 19 dead, 126 wounded, and 137 injured, which is a high 14 percent of the complement. Furthermore, the casualties occured in less than a week of action and do not include the losses suffered by both the 460th Parachute Field Artillery and the 596th Parachute Engineers.

The foot soldiers of the 3d, 36th, and 45th Divisions, all veterans of Italy, who invaded from the sea as part of the U.S. Seventh Army, under Lt. Gen. Alexander M. Patch, met much less opposition. Alongside of them eventually moved six Free Fench outfits of similar size. These units eventually were organized into the French First Army. Both armies became the charges of the Sixth Army Group headed by Gen. Jacob L. Devers. They moved inland smoothly and soon headed northeast while the 517th drew the task of driving east through the champagne country into the torturous terrain that led toward Italy.

Communications Sergeant Harold Taylor of the 3d Division said, "Prior to our landing on the St. Tropez peninsula our heavy navy guns shelled the coastal area. At the same time our aircraft kept the German forces off-guard, strafing them and bombing their defenses. My regiment, along with other regiments of the 3d division, met moderate gun and mortar fire as we came ashore. We made our way up the Rhone Valley. The division, accompanied by French and American divisions, expanded the beachhead over several days into several hundred miles."

"The entire VI Corps," said William Rosson, who left his post as a battalion commander in the 7th Regiment of the 3d to become assistant G-3 of the corps, "followed the Route Napoléon, parallel to the Rhone, covering 300 miles in seventeen days against light resistance by the German garrisons. Near Montélimar, a German column was destroyed by air strikes. They had a lot of horse-drawn equipment. Dead bloated horses were all over the place. Destroyed vehicles and bodies were scattered about. It was a ghastly mess."

The battalion commanded by Michael Davison of the 45th Division was designated regimental reserve for the invasion. "We simply made a walk-in landing," said Davison. "It was not an assault because we were in reserve and the regiment met no resistance on the beach. We had a couple of fairly tough scrapes just in from the beach but they loaded my battalion up in trucks one night and we drove all night to Grenoble up the Route Napoléon. We made bivouac about three in the morning, right alongside of a main road into town. I will never forget the next morning, watching those French girls pedaling by on bicycles to work. The soldiers were really excited. Those French girls were wearing long skirts, but when they rode their bicycles they let those skirts fly right up around their hips. God, those soldiers, they were growling."

His battalion deployed to hold the city of Grenoble while the battle for Montélimar went on. "A German reserve division up the valley was moving toward Grenoble. G-2 claimed its total strength was like 3,500, but I only had 800 guys and I got together with a Commandant Le Barbier of the French Forces of the Interior who had about a thousand men. We decided on a plan in which my battalion would place a roadblock and stop the head of the division. Le Barbier, the commander of the FFI, would take his guys, who were totally familiar with the terrain, up in the mountains and they would circle around to get on the flank of this German column. We would ambush it because the best way to protect the city was to ambush the whole bunch before they had a chance to deploy and assault us. We did it and we captured more than 1,000 prisoners."

# Roll Call

**Adair, Marion.** The 4th Infantry Division battalion surgeon resumed his medical practice in Georgia until retirement in 1990.

**Alison, John.** Air Corps lend-lease consultant, fighter pilot with the Fourteenth Air Force in the China-Burma Theater, an ace, he retired as a major general.

**Allen, Brooke.** Commander of the 5th Bomb Group at Hickam Field, Hawaii, on 7 December 1941, he supervised training of B-29 crews and retired in 1965 as a major general.

**Allen, Terry.** Commanding general of the 1st and 104th Infantry Divisions, he is deceased. His only son, who graduated from the U.S. Military Academy, was killed in Vietnam.

**Altieri, James.** An original Ranger, he has been active in the Rangers Association as well as the World War II Remembrance Society and makes his home in Corona Del Mar, California.

**Andrusko, Ed.** After thirty-three months of service, earning three Purple Hearts with the 1st Marine Division, he expressed no regrets for his experiences. "I saw our countrymen united against our enemies in a worldwide war. The men in my company were my family and friends, our senior NCOs were our parents. Item Company was my home on land or sea. We protected each other and fought for each other. After the war, I felt I could handle anything in the civilian world and took on all challenges, started college a day after my discharge. We returning veterans had pride in our accomplishments, love for our families, and ambition for our future. We assimilated into the civilian world with ease." After a career in electronics, he lives in Colorado.

**Ashe, Walter.** The pre-war-Navy sailor sailed on a number of ships in the Pacific theater, was aboard the first vessel to dock in Korea after the fighting began there, and in 1966 retired after thirty years of service. He lives in Asheville, North Carolina.

**Ashworth, Frederick.** "There's only two guys in the world who have had the experience of essentially being in tactical command of the delivery of an atom bomb in wartime, and I am one of them. You're supposed to get very emotional about it. How did it feel? I didn't feel anything in particular. I guess it is just like so many other experiences. While they are going on, you don't really feel much of anything except that this is a job that has to be done. When you get shot at, you're not scared right then. You are too busy doing what has to be done. You do get scared after it's all over." He retired as a vice admiral and lives in New Mexico.

**Austin, Gordon.** An Air Corps fighter pilot, hunting deer in the Hawaiian Islands at the time of the Japanese attack, he had graduated from West Point in 1936—"I don't remember choosing anything. My father [an architect and veteran of the Spanish-American War] sent me." He retired as a major general.

**Austin, Paul.** Following his stint as a company commander and battalion staff officer with the 24th Infantry Division, he worked for a telephone company until retirement. "I was sick to my stomach, of all those who'd been killed or got wounded. But that's the infantry story. You take the mud, the pain, do without food, do without water, and you keep fighting." He lives in Fort Worth.

**Barron, Frank Jr.** Following his role as a platoon leader and company commander with the 77th Division, he became an executive in the textile industry. He makes his home in Columbia, South Carolina.

**Baum, Abe.** The leader of the ill-fated task force that bore his name went into the garment industry after the war. He retired to southern California.

**Behlmer, Bill.** The antitank crewman with the 1st Division received a prosthesis for his amputated right leg and worked in the aircraft industry.

**Bernheim, Eli.** After combat in the Philippines with the 11th Airborne Division, he worked in the family business before re-entering the service to participate in the Korean War. He retired after more than twenty years to enter business and now lives in Florida.

**Biddle, Melvin.** The Medal of Honor awardee from the 517th Parachute Regimental Combat Team spent nearly thirty years as an employee of the Veterans Administration in his home state of Indiana.

**Bluemel, Clifford.** The commander of the 31st Philippine Division in 1941 survived captivity and retired as a major general. He is deceased.

**Bolt, Jones E.** A P-47 pilot, he recalled the depths of the Great Depression when a man with rags on his feet for shoes asked for a job and his father, a textile manufacturer, had none to offer. "Everybody elected the ROTC [at Clemson University] because we got something like twenty-five cents a day." As a prisoner of war he struggled through the infamous march from StalagLuft III to Moosburg and said, "We found out that Hitler had ordered all of us shot. Goering [Hermann, the Nazi *Luftwaffe* chief] refused to carry out the order." He retired as a major general.

**Bouck, Lyle.** He became a chiropractor in St. Louis.

**Bower, William.** The Doolittle Raid pilot who reached China and escaped capture remained in the Air Force until he retired as a colonel.

**Boyle, Bill.** Commander of the 1st Battalion of the 517th Parachute Regimental Combat Team, he recovered from his wounds in the Ardennes, and served in Korea before retirement. After a few years in security he went back to school, and opened a business in accountancy. "My first company commander after I graduated from West Point told me, 'You take care of the men and they will take care of you.'" He lives in Saratoga Springs, New York.

**Buckley, Pete.** A glider pilot for D day in Normandy, Market Garden in Holland, and Varsity across the Rhine, he studied commercial photography under the GI Bill. "I came home ten years older than I should have been and I had enough of flying." His home is in Connecticut.

**Bulkeley, John D.** The 1930 United States Naval Academy graduate awarded a Medal of Honor after he helped MacArthur leave the Philippines aboard a PT boat, later commanded torpedo boats during the Normandy invasion, and then finished the war aboard the cruiser *Houston*, reborn after the original ship was sunk by the Japanese. He died a vice admiral in 1998 after sixty-four years of active duty.

**Burchinal, David.** A B-29 test pilot and participant in

raids on Japan, he had worked in a factory and been a union leader after graduation from Brown University before the war. He remained in the Air Force, helping develop the Air University curriculum; held staff posts at upper echelons and retired as a general.

**Caron, George.** The tail gunner on the *Enola Gay* is deceased.

**Carlton, Paul.** After flying a number of B-29 missions against Japan from China and mining the Singapore Harbor as well as the enemy-controlled portions of the Yangtze River, Carlton piloted pathfinder planes from the Marianas. "We would fly upwind over the target precisely dropping our bombs. Then the follow-on force would come in and bomb on our fire, downwind. The survival rate upwind was kind of atrocious." On one such occasion, the headwind reduced the pathfinder's speed to only eighty knots; ten out of the twelve in the operation went down. The upwind approach was abandoned. He retired as a general after running the Military Airlift Command.

**Carmichael, Richard.** He was a 1936 graduate of the U.S. Military Academy, after joining the Texas National Guard at age fifteen. Interviewed in 1942 about a number of subjects including morale, he remarked, "The two main topics, except at the dinner table, were bombing and women. I personally believe that if there were some form of controlled prostitution around an Army camp, it would be the best solution . . . it would control the venereal rate and keep the combat crews a hell of a lot happier." He noted that as a prisoner it struck him that the Japanese "were going to fight to the bitter end . . . the military . . . and the populace went along with whatever the military decided. They put us to work digging tunnels, caves actually, inside of hills not far from where our gardens were. We presumed that this was part of their last-ditch defense system." He left the service as a major general.

**Carpenter, John.** As a 1939 graduate of the USMA, he transferred from the field artillery to USAF, which brought him to the 19th Bomb Group in the Philippines in 1941. After he reached Australia, Carpenter flew missions in the Pacific, and following V-J Day held various staff posts before retiring as a lieutenant general. He lives in North Carolina.

**Carter, Norval.** The 29th Infantry Division battalion surgeon KIA in Normandy left a widow and two sons. Upon the death of Emma Ferne Lowry Carter in 1995, their son Walter discovered several caches of correspondence between her and his father. Walter Carter researched the experiences of his father and discovered in my book *June 6, 1944: The Voices of D-Day* an excerpt from Frank Wawrynovic's account that mentioned the circumstances of his father's death. Walter Carter wrote to me and very kindly allowed me to make use of portions of the collected letters of Norval Carter.

**Chism, John.** The medic with the 517th Parachute Regimental Combat Team left the service to attend college, where he earned a reserve commission and went on active duty as a field artillery commander during the Korean War. He remained in the Army until retirement as a colonel.

**Cochran, Philip.** After he completed his tour as joint leader of the 1st Air Commando unit in the Far East, he trained pilots until the war's end. Physical disabilities forced him to retire in 1947 with the rank of colonel. He provided technical expertise to Hollywood filmmakers before entering business in Pennsylvania. He died in 1979.

**Conver, Milt.** The bombardier with the 303d Bomb Group coped with respiratory infections that limited his missions with the Eighth Air Force. After V-E Day he left the service, entered business in Ohio. He is deceased.

**Creel, Buckner.** A platoon leader with the 77th Division on Guam and in the Philippines, he commanded a company on Okinawa. He fought in Korea, where he was wounded, and then in Vietnam before retirement. He lives in Arlington, Virginia.

**Cutter, Slade.** The former submariner and 1935 USNA graduate retired as a captain and lives in Annapolis.

**Darby, William O.** After the disaster at Cisterna that destroyed three of his battalions, the founder of the Rangers, who previously refused offers to lead regiments, took over the 179th Regiment of the 45th Division at Anzio. Subsequently named assistant commander of the 10th Mountain Division, he was killed by German artillery fire, two days before the enemy forces in Italy surrendered.

**Davison, Michael.** A USMC graduate, the former staff officer and battalion commander with the 45th Division earned a graduate degree at Harvard, commanded troops in Vietnam, and headed the army units in Europe before retirement as a general. He lives in Virginia.

**Dawson, Frank (Buck).** The 5th Ranger Battalion lieutenant who led pinned-down troops off Omaha Beach on D day entered the reserves following V-E Day, but when recalled for the Korean War elected the service as a career, which culminated in 1968 after a tour in Vietnam. He is deceased.

**DeHaven, Robert.** The USAF ace with fourteen victories retired as a colonel and lives in southern California.

**DeLoach, James.** The 32d Division company officer chose to enter local government after the war and lives in Columbia, South Carolina.

**Duckworth, George.** The 2d Infantry Division officer

stayed in uniform, retiring as a colonel, and lives in New Mexico.

**Dunfee, Bill.** The 82d Airborne trooper worked for a lumber business in Columbus, Ohio, and became a top executive with the organization.

**Dunn, Bill.** The Air Force fighter pilot began his World War II experience as an infantryman with the Canadian Seaforth Highlanders. After V-J Day he advised in China, Iran, and South America during the 1950s before he put in his papers.

**Edlin, Bob.** The 2d Ranger Battalion platoon leader in Normandy, the Cotentin Peninsula, and in the grim winter on the German border held the job of a police chief in Indiana before moving to Corpus Christi, Texas, where he operates an antique auction house.

**Eller, Ernest.** A USNA 1925 graduate and a gunnery officer aboard the *Lexington* at the Battle of Midway, he retired as a captain. He is deceased.

**Ellis, Richard.** A B-25 pilot in the South Pacific who had been drafted in 1940 before enrolling in flight training, he completed 200 missions. He left the service to practice law, but when called up for Korea he stayed on until retirement as a general.

**Emmens, Robert.** After the war, the Doolittle Raid pilot who spent two years as a "guest of the Kremlin" served as a military attaché and in intelligence for the Air Force before retirement as a colonel.

**Engeman, Len.** The 9th Armored Division tank battalion commander who directed the capture of the vital bridge at Remagen remained in the Army until retirement as a colonel. He lives in California.

**Erwin, Henry.** The Air Corps crewman badly burned by

an incendiary and who received a Medal of Honor is deceased.

**Eubank, Eugene.** The commander of the B-17 19th Bomb Group in the Philippines on 7 December 1941, he earned Army wings almost thirty years earlier. He recalled that when Boeing produced the first Flying Fortress he and his associates immediately recognized it was far superior to any competitor's wares. However, while the prototype was being tested in 1935 at Wright Field, Ohio, the plane crashed. "We damned near sat down and cried when the first one was wrecked. In those days the manufacturer had to submit an article [a plane] that was tested, evaluated, and the board decided which one was going to win. If it hadn't been for that accident, Boeing would have won the competition and we would have had the B-17 two or three years ahead of what we did." He retired as a major general.

**Evans, Bing.** An original Ranger who was Darby's sergeant major, he received a commission before being captured at Cisterna. He noted that his experiences as a POW so scarred him that throughout his life he was subject to "black rages." He worked in private industry and now lives in Huntington, Indiana.

**Gage, Tom.** The Air Corps clerk captured on Bataan acts as a clearinghouse for information about prisoners of war from that period and lives in Tulsa, Oklahoma.

**Gangel, Dick.** The P-38 pilot came home from the Fifteenth Air Force in Italy to teach other flyers. After his honorable discharge he became an art director, first in advertising and then for *Sports Illustrated*. He lives in Weston, Connecticut, where he creates sculptures.

**Gilliam, Tom.** As an officer with the 2d Division, he recovered from wounds after a three-month hospital stay in time to participate in the final drives against the Germans.

After the enemy repulsed the unit in a brutal confrontation in the vicinity of Eisenschmitt, Gilliam noted to his superior that for the third time he had wound up the senior company commander in the battalion. He added that the only other officer of that responsibility who was left from their arrival in France on 9 July was home on a forty-five-days leave. Told he was regarded as the best in the division, Gilliam said he replied, " 'Colonel, I am going to be a dead company commander if this keeps up.' We retook the town the next day, but we lost 117 men up there that night. Less than three weeks later I was on orders to return home for a forty-five-day leave. But that three weeks included the second crossing of the Moselle, the closing of the Trier pocket, the crossing of the Rhine at Oppenheim, the capture of Frankfurt am Main, and the memorial service for President Roosevelt aboard ship." He lives in Lakeport, California.

**Goode, John.** The 36th Division officer shattered by the Rapido River experience is deceased.

**Hartman, Tom.** The Navy pilot recalled that while a student at Princeton, in his enthusiastic rush to enlist after the college requirements were lowered, his physical exam revealed possible problems with one eye. He was instructed to return for a second test. "A Navy corpsman was to be the examiner. His first question was, 'Are you another college boy?' I thought that I should drop through the floor. Princeton was like the kiss of death in that milieu. But I admitted my status. He said, 'Princeton! That's great.' He told me he had worked as an usher at the Chicago Opera House and the only company passing through that invited the ushers to their cast parties was the Triangle Club [the university's drama group]! He was so excited that he never gave my eye a look and signed my clearance." Hartman returned to his alma mater to complete his education and then taught at Rutgers. He lives in Princeton, New Jersey.

**Hayes, Tommy.** The Army fighter pilot who fought in both the Pacific and Europe retired as a colonel and lives in Pennsylvania.

**Herder, Harry.** The 2d Ranger Battalion replacement participated in the liberation of the Buchenwald concentration camp. "We were the last replacements taken into the battalion. Barely in my memory is the first job [that] rumor said we were scheduled to do. They were going to put us, a company at a time, in Piper Cubs and fly us over the Rhine. That was washed out when the Remagen Bridge stood. I remember a ballistic company commander. Being nearsighted made me less than perfect and unfit to be a Ranger. The way that man was mad at me was something else. With him, I did not belong. In 1947 I was accepted in jump school and allowed to be a member of the 82d Airborne for three years and they knew I wore glasses the whole time. Even jumped with them taped on once they found out. The helmet jammed them into my nose on 'opening shock.' They remained in my shirt pocket all the rest of the jumps."

Herder on his third military hitch joined the Navy and served as a corpsman for the Marines in Korea. He lives in Hayward, Wisconsin.

**Hill, David (Tex).** The former Navy flyer who enlisted in the American Volunteer Group under Gen. Clare Chennault retired as a colonel and is a resident of San Antonio.

**Hite, Robert L.** The last-minute addition to the Doolittle Raiders, who endured years of captivity, remained in the service after his liberation and worked as an air attaché in North Africa. He retired as a lieutenant colonel.

**Hofrichter, Joe.** The rifleman from the 24th Division entered a family construction business and makes his home in Port Charlotte, Florida.

**Hostetter, Philip.** The battalion surgeon with the 24th Division, after mustering out, opened a practice in family medicine and lives in Manhattan, Kansas.

**Howze, Hamilton.** The 1930 West Point alumnus who spent World War II with armored forces in North Africa and Italy switched to airborne in the 1950s to command the 82d Airborne Division and the Eighteenth Airborne Corps. He retired as a full general in 1965 and died in 1998.

**Jackson, Schuyler.** The 101st Airborne paratrooper worked in construction until his death in 1995.

**Johnson, Fred.** The former National Guardsman called up in 1940 and who fought with the 32d Division in the Pacific said, "I approved of what we did in the war then and still do. There was a sense of duty; you were scared, heck yes. But you just did what you thought you had to do. There was pride in not letting the others down. To bug out would make you ashamed. The worst food was in Buna, bully beef, and small rations, two spoons a day. I came home with malaria, having had three separate attacks." After his discharge he became a Superior, Wisconsin, policeman and then was elected sheriff ten times before retirement. He lives in Arizona.

**Johnson, Leon.** He was in the class of 1926 at the USMA. He led the 44th Bomb Group on the Ploesti raid, where he earned a Medal of Honor, and then commanded a bomber wing with the Eighth Air Force in England. He retired in 1961 as a general and died in 1998.

**Johnson, Robert.** The ground crew sergeant who volunteered for the 4th Armored Division was convicted of a 1971 murder and is serving a life term in North Carolina.

**Johnson, Robert.** The fighter pilot with the second highest number of planes shot down in Europe worked in the aircraft industry after the war. He died in 1998.

**Jones, David M.** The Doolittle Raider who parachuted into China then returned to duty was subsequently shot down in a B-26 during a raid on Bizerte. He became a prisoner of war in Germany. Following liberation he held positions in the Pentagon, with NASA, and other research projects. He retired as a major general.

**Jones, Harry.** The Navy pilot who helped sink the *Yamato* remarked, "I think it was a good idea to drop the atomic bomb because I think the invasion would have killed millions of Japanese. War is hell; stay the hell out of it. We had no business in Vietnam; in my opinion we should stay the hell out of Bosnia. They should have some sort of international police there." He became an FBI agent and now lives in Carlisle, Pennsylvania.

**Jones, Homer.** After the war ended, the paratroop platoon leader left the service but was recalled for the war in Korea. He remained on active duty until retirement and then taught Spanish in public schools. He lives in Florida.

**Kelly, Walter.** The Eighth Air Force pilot who flew the first B-17 raid on occupied Europe later flew missions against the Japanese in the Pacific. He continued his career in the Air Force after the end of hostilities and retired as a colonel. He worked in private industry before retiring to a home in Alexandria, Virginia.

**Kidwell, Vance.** The draftee from Illinois who became a replacement in a supply section of the 2d Armored Division while the outfit was in North Africa was with the outfit when it reached France on D plus 1. He lives in Donnellson, Illinois.

**Kitzmann, Erich.** The *Suwannee* crewman blown overboard after a Kamikaze explosion worked in aircraft maintenance until he retired to Sedona, Arizona.

**Kunz, William J.** The former 3d Infantry Division field artillery hand who campaigned through North Africa, Sicily, Italy, Anzio, southern France, and Germany lives in Illinois.

**Loiacano, Leonard.** An artilleryman, he said, "When the gun was fired it made so much noise that you had to keep your mouth open and if your hands were free you put them in your ears. We would be wet to the skin, cold and in total darkness. Most of the time we got six hours of sleep every other night. One time we went sixty hours without sleep. We were never relieved and always firing for somebody. We dug gun pits and cut down trees [to brace the artillery and cover foxholes] from Normandy to Czechoslovakia." The 105mm howitzer crewman with the 5th Infantry Division had amassed enough points to warrant discharge shortly after V-E Day. "When we were home, the two 'A' bombs were dropped and the war was over. Many years later the bleeding hearts would say what a terrible thing it was to drop the bomb. For all of those people I wish them ten months of combat and then let us hear what they have to say." He makes his home in Yeadon, Pennsylvania.

**Lomell, Len (Bud).** The Ranger sergeant involved in the destruction of enemy big guns atop Pointe du Hoc on D day received a battlefield commission before being wounded a second time. He studied law under the GI Bill and practiced in New Jersey where he makes his home.

**Long, Stanley.** The first P-38 pilot to shoot down a Japanese plane in the Aleutians, he remained in the Air Force, retiring as a colonel.

**Low, Martin.** The fighter pilot, who was at Hickam Field on 7 December 1941 and over the Normandy beaches on 6 June 1944, came home after seventy-five missions in Europe. "I had seen enough of the Army in peacetime to know that it was not for me. I applied to the airlines but they did not think fighter pilots had the right stuff. Because of my experience of war I took up the cause of the United Nations, which I believe is a much more viable method of settling differences." As a civilian he produced commercials for TV and lives in a suburb of New York City.

**Lynd, J. Q.** The 90th Division platoon leader recovered from his wounds and became a research scientist and teacher at Oklahoma State University in Stillwater, Oklahoma.

**Mabry, George L. Jr.** The 4th Division officer finally received a regular army commission in 1944 and by the time the war ended he was the second most decorated soldier of the conflict. He subsequently graduated from the Command and General Staff College, the National War College, and held a variety of command, training, and staff positions. He led a 100-man team of officers and civilians to evaluate operations in Vietnam and later served as chief of staff and assistant deputy commanding general for the U.S. Army Forces in Vietnam. In 1975 he retired as a major general and lived in Columbia, South Carolina, until his death in 1990.

**McCubbin, James.** The fighter pilot now lives in Garberville, California.

**Meltessen, Clarence.** The 4th Ranger Battalion lieutenant captured at Cisterna survived more than a year in the stalags. He remained on active duty after the war, retiring as a colonel. He has compiled an exhaustive record of what happened to his fellow Rangers and their experiences in the prisoner-of-war camps. He lives in California.

**Merrill, Alan.** The 2d Battalion Ranger wounded and temporarily captured near Anzio recovered in a Naples hospital. During his recuperation he met a captain who offered to wangle a transfer to the Air Corps, enabling Merrill to serve out his time as a limited-duty, noncombat soldier. Assigned to the 379th Bomb Group, a B-25 outfit, he learned aircraft recognition while assisting in tow-target practice. He even went along on missions that dumped aluminum foil to foul up enemy radar. But when a batch of replacement gunners failed to arrive, Merrill was pressed into service as a tail gunner beginning in October 1944. He flew twenty-four missions, occupying various positions manning a .50-caliber machine gun. Flak ripped into his airplanes on several occasions, killing other members of the crew, and he survived a crash landing in the sea near Corsica. Blackouts, bleeding from his left ear and nose on his last missions grounded him after his twenty-fourth. He waited several months before orders finally sent him home via Casablanca, where he said he visited bordellos supervised by the U.S. Army with military police on duty.

"I went away a frightened boy. I returned a frightened man. The actual battle of enduring a war in the various types of combat that I participated in was not as riveting an experience as the battles my mind fought daily in the ensuing peaceful years. When the actual fighting was done I had to conquer my own personal, mental war of nerves. I found out much later that I had no control over what happened to the unprepared, mindless, loose ends of my young manhood and the residue of the code of killing or being killed. I don't believe I ever really adjusted to this code of the military survivor. Everything I was taught to do to survive was diametrically opposed to a way of life I had been raised to believe in for eighteen years.

"How does one go about 'unlearning' to kill another human being? This unlearning process comes ever so slowly or it never comes at all. It is your own individual struggle.

No one can do it for you. If this cannot be done, then peace of mind eludes you all your days. In my half century, since World War II and with my battles over, I truly believe that war is like a malignant tumor on the face of mankind." He now lives in Florida.

**Mott, Hugh.** The platoon leader who helped preserve the Remagen Bridge over the Rhine went into politics and in 1949 was elected to the Tennessee State Legislature while remaining active in the National Guard. He retired from the Guard as a major general in 1972.

**Mueller, Arndt.** The 6th Infantry Division battalion commander attended the Command and General Staff College and eventually joined its faculty. He headed the ROTC program at the University of Miami, earned a law degree, and joined the Florida bar.

**Newman, Stan.** The P-51 pilot assigned to the Fifteenth Air Force in Italy redeployed to the States after V-E Day in preparation for the finale against Japan. "I changed my mind about a regular air force career, took a reserve commission, and made it back to start my interrupted college at the University of Illinois. I was one of the first vets back and was like a fish out of water. I really missed the Air Corps life, good pay, great airplanes, and wonderful friends. But I eventually adapted." As a reserve officer, however, he was recalled during the Korean War and flew 100 missions in that conflict. During the war in Vietnam he flew cargo missions to Southeast Asia. He retired in 1983 as a major general and lives in Oklahoma.

**Northrup, Jay.** The replacement officer with the Rangers had been reassigned, but a bout of malaria contracted in Sicily sent him back to the States. After he left the service he entered the field of banking before retirement to Florida.

**Odell, Bill.** The Eighth Air Force pilot involved in the organization's first raid moved first to North Africa and then the Pacific. After he retired as a colonel he embarked on a career as a writer publishing many novels in the mystery, adventure, and Western genres. He lives in Colorado Springs.

**Olson, John E.** After liberation from his Philippine prison camp, the 1939 USMA graduate remained in uniform until retirement as a colonel in 1967. He has done extensive research and writing on the Bataan fighting, the Death March, and Philippine guerrilla movements. He lives in Houston, Texas.

**Paris, Dee.** The 9th Armored Division tank commander retained a reserve commission after the war and made barbershop quartet music his avocation while living in Maryland.

**Poston, Tom.** The troop carrier pilot chose the life of an actor after being mustered out. He appeared on Broadway, and in numerous roles on radio and then television. He lives in California.

**Raaen, John C. Jr.** One of the few West Pointers (class of 1943) to volunteer for the Rangers, his jeep accident in France ended World War II for him. In 1951 he earned a master's degree from Johns Hopkins and then held command posts with various units before retirement as a major general. He lives in Florida.

**Raila, Frank.** The 106th Division soldier taken prisoner in the Ardennes became a radiologist in Mississippi. The emotional outbursts, triggered by his memories of the stalag that disturbed him in the years immediately after the war, subsided.

**Rants, Hanford.** The wireman with the 24th Infantry Division, which fought in the Pacific theater, used the GI Bill to complete his education at Washington State University, then taught in high school before becoming a principal. He lives in Downey, California.

**Robison, Noel (Eugene).** As a replacement, he joined the 90th Division in November 1944, where he served as a runner until his frozen feet disabled him during the Battle of the Bulge. He lives in Claremont, California.

**Rosson, William.** The officer with the 3d Infantry Division, as an honor student in the ROTC program at the University of Oregon in 1940, had obtained a regular army commission. His senior captain instructed a first sergeant, "I want you to make an officer of Lieutenant Rosson." Rosson says, "The training was rather rudimentary and simply wouldn't be accepted today. It was a peacetime oriented affair with more emphasis upon spit and polish, cleanliness of barracks and whatnot rather than combat readiness. I never attended the basic course of the infantry school. I went into the war and learned on the job."

When he visited the Dachau concentration camp after its liberation, he recalled, "I was shaken—so much so that when I left I was literally unable to speak as I drove back to the division. I had never seen such depravity and inhuman treatment." Following his service in Italy and France, Rosson qualified for airborne, was involved in the Vietnam conflict before his retirement in 1975 as a general, and resides in Florida.

**Ruhlen, George.** The commander of the 3d Field Artillery attached to the 9th Armored Division, a 1932 graduate of the USMA, retired on a disability in 1970 as a major general. He lives in San Antonio.

**Salomon, Sid.** The Ranger captain who captured Pointe et Raz de la Percée at Omaha Beach entered the paper products field after the war. He makes his home in Pennsylvania.

**Salter, Cary.** The P-47 and P-51 fighter pilot in the Ninth

Air Force said, "We were shooting down planes but we knew we were killing people, too. I don't know any of our guys who lost sleep over it. We were there to fight a war and the more we killed, the quicker it would be over and the less likely we would be killed." He became a pharmacist, then presided over a wholesale drug firm. Active in the P-40 Warhawk Pilots Association, he resides in Jackson, Mississippi.

**Schueler, Jon.** The B-17 navigator, invalided home for physical and emotional disabilities, became a well-known painter. His autobiography, *The Sound of Sleat*, was published posthumously in 1999.

**Schwarz, Otto.** A prisoner of war after the sinking of the USS *Houston*, he endured years of hard labor, beatings, and lack of food in a series of camps. "We were under strict orders that, whenever a Japanese of any rank approached us, the first person seeing him had to shout in good Japanese and call the group to attention. You then all had to properly bow to the person. You had to bow from the hips down with the face tilting up and facing the person. If you deviated from this at all, you very quickly got bashed."

Schwarz recalled that the British captives treated the problem of sanitation far more casually than the Americans and as a consequence suffered a much greater incidence of dysentery. However, they insisted upon maintaining a military mode. "These guys acted as if they were on regimental maneuvers. The British held regular drills—complete uniforms, full field packs—and they would march up and down the hills, and the officers with their little 'dog-chasers,' the little sticks they carried, would be marching alongside of them." The Americans in shorts and ragged garments refused to salute and an intense dislike grew between the two allies.

Shipped to Burma, Schwarz became part of the gangs constructing a railroad much like that described in the film *The Bridge on the River Kwai*. Along with the prisoners, the Japanese conscripted thousands of local people who, said Schwarz, "died like flies. Entire villages, the entire male populations of villages were just wiped out."

Toward the end of the war, while housed in Saigon, Schwarz and three companions escaped and sought refuge in the French quarter of the city, only to be caught up in the Vietnamese effort to oust the French. Jailed by the rebels along with the French, Schwarz convinced his captors that he was an American and was allowed to return to the Japanese prison camp. A U.S. Army officer parachuted in to the camp and officially freed all of the POWs.

"My service in the Navy and World War II were years of great pride and dedication to America. I have been in the presence of men who have cried openly when hearing our National Anthem, which was picked up by a Japanese radio in Saigon. These were the kinds of men I was privileged to serve with. Despite our disadvantage of being ill prepared, outnumbered, and outgunned at the beginning of World War II, and the horrendous ordeal of three and one-half years as Japanese POWs, we never wavered in our loyalty and faith in our country."

In 1948, Schwarz entered the U.S. Postal Service and on retirement in 1980 held a senior management position. He lives in Union, New Jersey.

**Shapiro, Alan.** After leaving the service, the 87th Division rifleman taught school and now lives in Ridgefield, Connecticut.

**Sims, Ed.** The paratrooper officer with the 504th Regiment went on inactive reserve after being demobilized, but said, "I returned to active duty because good employment was hard to find and I was more oriented toward military life." He retired as a colonel in 1968, then earned a college degree and held jobs with a title company and, later, as a county probation officer. He lives in New Jersey.

**Smith, Robert.** The Air Force B-26 pilot in the South Pacific became intelligence director of the Strategic Air Command during the 1950s, where he pioneered in the use of computers for dealing with intelligence. He retired as a lieutenant general.

**South, Frank.** "The death of FDR [12 April 1945] came as a shock. There was not a dry eye that could be found. I recall leaning against a tree and bawling like an infant." After V-E Day, South's unit became part of Patton's Third Army. For a review before himself and some Soviet officers, Patton ordered clean, pressed uniforms and polished boots, which South considered reasonable. Further instruction to coat helmets with shellac and all arms and vehicles oiled on the surfaces to provide a shine struck the Ranger as foolish because of the prevalence of road dust. "Most of us had long regarded Patton as a bloody popinjay whose exhibitionist streak was witnessed by his dress and pearl-handled revolvers." The medic with the 2d Ranger Battalion used his benefits to study biophysics and physiology. He lives in Maryland.

**Southworth, Billy.** The B-17 pilot completed his tour in the United Kingdom but was killed on a training flight in 1945.

**Stroop, Paul D.** A USNA 1926 alumnus, he retired as a vice admiral and died in 1995.

**Strange, Glen.** The 27th Armored Infantry officer required two years of medical treatment for his wounds before he recovered enough to work in manufacturing. He later became a postmaster in Oklahoma.

**Swanson, Wallace.** The 101st Airborne company commander worked in the petroleum industry and lives in Alabama.

**Taylor, Harold.** The 3d Division GI joined the Fort Wayne police department, put in twenty years, and then operated a part-time cabinet-making shop.

**Thach, John (Jimmy).** The naval aviator says, "Everybody's scared, but it isn't a thing you can let prey on your mind very long because there's always something to do. And you can function just as well, maybe a little better, if you're scared." He retired as a full admiral and died in 1981.

**Turner, William (Pappy).** The army pilot said, "I did not shoot at anyone in a parachute although I had several chances. I figured he had his problems. Also on the ground he could be captured, some information gained. On one occasion, one of the pilots asked me for permission to strafe the Jap in the parachute. I told him to let his conscience be his guide. He broke off, made a pass at the man, but did not shoot." After the war he worked briefly in private industry before signing on with the New York State Department of Public Works and switched to the Department of Transportation. He now lives in Florida.

**Ullom, Madeline.** The former army nurse, taken prisoner in the Philippines, now lives in Tucson.

**Ulsaker, Carl.** The USMA 1942 graduate finished the war with the 95th Division. He collected a master's degree and then taught English at West Point. He retired as a colonel in 1969 and resides in Virginia.

**Uzemack, Ed.** The 28th Division POW returned to a career as a newspaperman and then entered public relations in Chicago.

**Vaccaro, Tony.** Born in the United States to Italian émigrés, the 83d Division intelligence specialist had lived in

Italy for much of his childhood and early adolescence where he developed an abiding hatred of the fascist philosophy. After V-E Day he signed on as a photographer for the military newspaper *Stars and Stripes*, and then as a civilian remained in Europe several more years building a reputation for his photographs. Back in the States he worked on staff for *Look* and the short-lived but influential *Flair* before a long successful career as a freelancer. He lives in New York City.

**Vogel, Walter.** The 1937 enlistee in the Navy started his career in the Asiatic Fleet and served on the ill-fated *Houston* in the first months after the war began. Having survived the sinking of the destroyer *Blue* and other adventures, he was promoted to the rank of chief petty officer and assigned to the destroyer *Hyman* engaged in picket duty off Okinawa. The kamikaze hit on the *Hyman* brought a third Purple Heart to Vogel, but the full extent of his wounds only surfaced several months after V-J Day when he collapsed with ruptured lungs, apparently due to the explosion off Okinawa. He recovered after four months of hospitalization and served on a number of ships including support for the war in Korea. He taught at the USNA as well as other institutions and became a commissioned officer. He weathered an attack of blindness before retirement in 1970. He lives in Tennessee.

**Walker, Anthony.** The Yale graduate and Marine officer remained in the Corps. "I suppose I decided to stay on because I liked the life, was reasonably successful in the war and had nothing else to do, not being qualified or interested in other professions or business." His three sons all became leathernecks. He makes his home in Rhode Island.

**Warneke, Bud.** The paratrooper with the 508th Parachute Regimental Combat Team won a battlefield commission and remained in the service until 1964 when he retired and began a TV rental service. He lives in North Carolina.

**Warriner, Vic.** The glider pilot involved in the D day invasion, and the Market Garden and Varsity operations, completed his education at the University of Michigan and became a real estate developer in Texas. He lives in Fort Worth.

**Widoff, Gerald.** The interpreter with Merrill's Marauders began a career as a violinist with prominent orchestras before starting a chain of music record stores. His home is in New York City.

**Yarborough, William.** The USMA Class of 1936 paratrooper officer, following World War II, held top staff positions at home and abroad until his retirement in 1971 as a lieutenant general. He lives in North Carolina.

# Bibliography

Adair, Charles. Oral History. Annapolis, Maryland: United States Naval Institute.

Alexander, Irvin. *Memoirs of Internment in the Philippines, 1942–45.* West Point: U.S. Military Academy.

Alison, John R. Oral Histories. Maxwell Field, Alabama: United States Air Force Historical Center, 1943, 1944, 1960, 1977, 1979.

Allen, Brooke E. Oral History. Maxwell Field, Alabama: United States Air Force Historical Center, 1965.

Altieri, James. *The Spearheaders.* Indianapolis: Bobbs-Merrill Company, Inc., 1960.

Ambrose, Stephen E. *Citizen Soldiers.* New York: Simon & Schuster, 1997.

Andrusko, Edward. Unpublished Stories. Denver, Colo.

Archer, Clark, ed. *Paratroopers' Odyssey.* Hudson, Florida: 517th Parachute Regimental Combat Team Association, 1985.

Ashworth, Frederick. Oral History. Annapolis, Maryland: United States Naval Institute.

Austin, Gordon H. Oral History. Maxwell Field, Alabama: United States Air Force Historical Center, 1982.

Benitez, R. C. *Battle Stations Submerged.* Annapolis, Maryland: *Proceedings*, January 1948.

Bidwell, Sheffield. *The Chindit War.* New York: Macmillan Publishing Co., Inc., 1979.

Blair, Clay. *Ridgway's Paratroopers.* Garden City, New York: Dial Press, 1985.

Bluemel, Clifford. Private Papers. West Point: U.S. Military Academy Library.

Blumenson, Martin. *Mark Clark.* New York: Congdon & Weed, 1984.

Bolt, Jones E. Oral History. Maxwell Field, Alabama: United States Air Force Historical Center, 1984.

Bower, William. Oral History. Maxwell Field, Alabama: United States Air Force Historical Center, 1971.

Bradley, Omar. *A Soldier's Story.* New York: Henry Holt and Company, Inc., 1951.

Breuer, William. *Geronimo!* New York: St. Martin's Press, 1989.

Budge, Joseph. Unpublished Memoir. Moraga, California.

Buffington, Herman. Unpublished Memoir. Jefferson, Georgia.

Bunker, Paul D. *The Bunker Diary.* West Point: U.S. Military Academy Library.

Burchinal, David A. Oral History. Maxwell Field, Alabama: United States Air Force Historical Center, 1975.

Byers, Dick. Unpublished Memoir. Mentor-on-the Lake, Ohio.

Carlton, Paul K. Oral History. Maxwell Field, Alabama: United States Air Force Historical Center, 1979.

Carmichael, Richard. Oral Histories. Maxwell Field, Alabama: United States Air Force Historical Center, 1942, 1980.

Caron, George R. Oral History. Maxwell Field, Alabama: United States Air Force Historical Center, 1975.

Carpenter, John W. Oral History. Maxwell Field, Alabama: United States Air Force Historical Center, 1970.

Cass, Bevan, ed. *History of the 6th Marine Division.* Washington, D.C.: Infantry Journal, Inc., 1948.

Chandler, P. R. Oral History. Maxwell Field, Alabama: United States Air Force Historical Center, 1943.

Chernitsky, Dorothy. *Voices from the Foxholes.* Uniontown, Pennsylvania: Dorothy Chernitsky, 1991.

Cochran, Philip. Oral Histories. Maxwell Field, Alabama: United States Air Force Historical Center, 1943, 1975.

Cole, Hugh M. *The Ardennes: The Battle of the Bulge.* Washington, D.C.: Center of Military History, U.S. Army, 1965.

Cox, Luther C. *Always Fighting the Enemy.* Baltimore: Gateway, 1990.

Craig, Robert. Unpublished Memoir. Winter Haven, Florida.

Craven, Wesley Frank, and James Lea Cate. *The Army Air Force in World War II.* Vol. 1: vi. Chicago: U.S. Air Force History Office, University of Chicago Press, 1948.

Crosby, Harry H. *A Wing and a Prayer.* New York: Harper, 1993.

Cutter, Slade. Oral History. Annapolis, Maryland: United States Naval Institute.

Dacus, W. E., and E. Kitzmann. *As We Lived It—USS Suwannee (CVE-27).* USS *Suwannee* and its Air Groups, 27, 60, & 40. Reunion Association, 1992.

DeHaven, Robert M. Oral History. Maxwell Field, Alabama: United States Air Force Historical Center, 1977.

Dennison, Robert Lee. Oral History. Annapolis, Maryland: United States Naval Institute.

D'Este, Carlo. *Patton: A Genius for War.* New York: Harper-Collins, 1995.

Duckworth, George H. Unpublished memoir. Farmington, New Mexico.

Dunn, William. Oral History. Maxwell Field, Alabama: United States Air Force Historical Center, 1973.

Edlin, Robert. Unpublished Manuscript. Corpus Christi, Texas.

Edmonds, Walter D. *They Fought with What They Had.* Washington, D.C.: Center for Air Force History, 1951.

Eisenhower, David. *Eisenhower at War 1943–45.* New York: Random House, 1986.

Eisenhower, Dwight D. *Crusade in Europe.* Garden City, New York: Doubleday & Company, Inc., 1948.

Eisenhower, John. *The Bitter Woods: The Battle of the Bulge.* New York: G.P. Putnam's Sons, 1969.

Ellington, Paul. Oral History. American Air Power Heritage Museum, Midland, Texas, 1991.

Ellis, John. *Cassino: The Hollow Victory.* New York: Mc-Graw-Hill Book Company, 1984.

Ellis, Richard. Oral History. Maxwell Field, Alabama: United States Air Force Historical Center, 1987.

Emmens, Robert G. Oral History. Maxwell Field, Alabama: United States Air Force Historical Center, 1982.

Eubank, Eugene. Oral Histories. Maxwell Field, Alabama: United States Air Force Historical Center, 1942, 1982.

Fitzgerald, Ed. *A Penny an Inch.* New York: Atheneum, 1985.

Frank, Richard B. *Guadalcanal.* New York: Random House, 1990.

Freeman, Roger A., with Alan Crouchman and Vic Maslen.

*The Mighty Eighth War Diary.* London: Motorbooks International, 1990.

Gavin, James M. *On to Berlin.* New York: Viking Press, 1978.

Gelb, Norman. *Desperate Venture: The Story of Operation Torch.* New York: William Morrow and Company, 1992.

Gerevas, Larry. Unpublished Memoir. Napa, California.

Golubock, Ralph. *Hello, Pathway: A Bomber Pilot's Memories of Love and War.* Unpublished Manuscript. St. Louis.

Goodson, James. Oral History. American Air Power Heritage Museum, Midland, Texas, 1991.

Grashio, Samuel C., and Bernard Norling. *Return to Freedom.* Spokane, Washington: University Press, 1982

Hagerman, Bart., ed. *U.S. Airborne: 50th Anniversary.* Paducah, Kentucky: Turner Publishing Company, 1990.

Hall, Leonard G. *Brother of the Fox: Company F, 172d Infantry.* Orange, Texas, 1985.

Hallden, Charles. Unpublished Memoir. Madeira Beach, Florida.

Hamilton, Tom. Unpublished Memoir. Santa Barbara, California.

Hammel, Eric. *Guadalcanal: Starvation Island.* New York, Crown, 1987.

———*Munda Trail.* New York: Orion Books, 1989.

Hannon, Philip. Unpublished Memoir. Ellicott City, Maryland.

Hanson, Robert. *Memoirs.* Unpublished manuscript.

Harmon, Ernest. Oral History. Carlisle, Pennsylvania: United States Army History Institute.

Harrington, Jasper. Oral History. Maxwell Field, Alabama: United States Air Force Historical Center, 1981.

Hastings, Max. *Overlord: D-Day and the Battle for Normandy.* New York: Simon & Schuster, 1984.

Hawkins, Ian L. *B-17s Over Berlin.* Washington, D.C.: Brassey's, 1990.

Hechler, Ken. *The Bridge at Remagen.* Missoula, Montana: Pictorial Histories Publishing Company, 1993.

Heinl, Robert Debs Jr. *Soldiers of the Sea.* Annapolis: Naval Institute Press, 1962.

Herder, Harry J. Unpublished Memoir. Hayward, Wisconsin.

Hill, David (Tex). Oral History. Maxwell Field, Alabama: United States Air Force Historical Center, 1977.

Holloway, Bruce K. Oral History. Maxwell Field, Alabama: United States Air Force Historical Center, 1977.

Holloway, James L. III. *Historical Perspective: The Battle of Surigao Strait.* Naval Engineer's Journal, September 1994.

Hostetter, Philip H. *Doctor and Soldier in the South Pacific.* Unpublished Manuscript. Manhattan, Kansas.

Howard, Thomas. *All to This End: The Road to and through the Philippines.* Unpublished Manuscript. St. Charles, Missouri.

Howze, Hamilton. Oral History. Carlisle, Pennsylvania: United States Army Military History Institute.

Hoyt, Edwin P. *Submarines at War.* Briarcliff Manor, New York: Stein and Day, 1983.

Hudson, Ed. *The History of the USS Cabot (CVL-28).* Hickory, North Carolina, 1988.

Jackson, Robert. *War Stories.* Unpublished Memoir. Anacortes, Washington.

Johnson, Robert S. Oral History. American Air Power Heritage Museum, Midland, Texas, 1977.

Kunz, William J. Unpublished Memoir. Rockford, Illinois, 1996.

LaMagna, Sam. *Silent Victory: Fox Company, 169th Regi-*

*mental Combat Team, 43d Infantry Division*. Unpublished Manuscript. Ocala, Florida.

Leckie, Robert. *Strong Men Armed*. New York: Random House, 1962.

Lee, Ulysses. *The Employment of Negro Troops*. Washington, D.C.: Center of Military History, 1994.

Leinbaugh, Harold P., and John D. Campbell. *The Men of Company K: The Autobiography of a World War II Rifle Company*. New York: William Morrow and Company, 1985.

Lynd, J. Q. *Château de Fontenay: Episode tragique de la libération 1944*. Unpublished Memoir. Stillwater, Oklahoma.

———*Legacy of Valor* [Video Script]. South Hill, Virginia: 90th Division Association.

MacArthur, Douglas. *Reminiscences*. New York: McGraw-Hill Book Company, 1964.

MacDonald, Charles. *A Time for Trumpets*. New York: William Morrow and Company, 1985.

———*Company Commander*. New York: Bantam, 1987.

———*The Mighty Endeavor: American Armed Forces in the European Theater in World War II*. New York: Oxford University Press, 1969.

McClintock, D. H. Narrative. Washington, D.C.: U.S. Naval Historical Center, 1945.

McClure, John. Oral History. American Air Power Heritage Museum, Midland, Texas, 1991.

McCubbin, James. Unpublished Memoirs. Garberville, California.

McManus, John. *The Deadly Brotherhood*. Novato, California: Presidio Press, 1998.

Mack, William. Oral History. Annapolis, Maryland: United States Naval Institute.

Manchester, William. *American Caesar*. Boston: Little, Brown & Company, 1978.

Martin, Harry. Unpublished Memoir. Mt. Arlington, New Jersey

Merillat, Herbert C. *Guadalcanal Remembered*. New York: Dodd, Mead & Company, 1982.

Milkovics, Lewis. *The Devils Have Landed*. Longwood, Florida: Creative Printing and Publishing, 1993.

Miller, Thomas G. Jr. *The Cactus Air Force*. New York: Harper & Row, 1969.

Mills, James. Unpublished Memoir. Vandalia, Ohio.

Moore, Ellis O. *Notes on Leaving Okinawa*. Pelham, New York: Privately Published, 1988.

Morison, Samuel Eliot. *The Battle of the Atlantic*. Boston: Little, Brown & Company, 1984.

———*Coral Sea, Midway and Submarine Actions*. Boston: Little, Brown & Company, 1984.

———*The Struggle for Guadalcanal*. Boston: Little, Brown & Company, 1949.

———*The Rising Sun in the Pacific*. Boston: Little, Brown & Company, 1961.

Morton, Louis. *The Fall of the Philippines, U.S. Army in World War II*. Washington, D.C.: Center of Military History, U.S. Army, 1953.

Muehrcke, Robert, ed. *Orchids in the Mud*. Chicago: Privately Published, 1985.

Mueller, Arndt. *Hill 400: The Destiny and the Agony*. Monograph.

Murphy, Robert. *Diplomat among Warriors*. Garden City, New York: Doubleday & Company, Inc. 1964.

Murray, S. S. Oral History. Annapolis, Maryland: United States Naval Institute.

Old, Archie Jr. Oral History. Maxwell Field, Alabama: Historical Research Center, Air University, 1982.

Olson, John E., assisted by Frank O. Anders. *Anywhere, Anytime: The History of the 57th Infantry (PS)*. Houston: John Olson, 1991.

———*O'Donnell: The Andersonville of the Pacific*. Houston: John Olson, 1985.

Patton, George. *War As I Knew It*. Boston: Houghton Mifflin, 1947.

Philos, C. D., and Ernie Hayhow. *1987 History of the 83d Infantry Division*. Hillsdale, Michigan: Ferguson Communications, 1986.

Potter, E. B. *Bull Halsey*. Annapolis, Maryland: United States Naval Institute, 1985.

Potts, Ramsay. Oral History. United States Air Force Historical Center, Maxwell Field, Alabama, 1960.

Prange, Gordon W. *Dec. 7 1941*. New York: McGraw-Hill Book Company, 1988.

Pyle, Ernie. *At Dawn We Slept*. New York: McGraw-Hill Book Company, 1981.

———*Here Is Your War*. New York: Henry Holt and Company, 1943.

———*Brave Men*. New York: Henry Holt and Company, 1944.

———*Last Chapter*. New York: Henry Holt and Company, 1946.

Rants, Hanford. *My Memories of World War II*. Unpublished Manuscript. Downey, California.

Rodman, Gage. Unpublished Memoir. Hurricane, Utah.

Rooney, Andy. *My War*. New York: Random House, 1996.

Rosson, William. Oral History. Carlisle, Pennsylvania: United States Army Military History Institute.

Ryan, Cornelius. *A Bridge Too Far.* New York: Simon & Schuster, 1974.

Salomon, Sidney. *2d Ranger Infantry Battalion.* Doylestown, Pennsylvania: Birchwood Books, 1991.

Samson, Jack. *Chennault.* New York: Doubleday & Company, Inc., 1987.

Schueler, Jon. *The Sound of Sleat.* Unpublished Manuscript.

Schultz, Duane. *The Maverick War.* New York: St. Martin's Press, 1987.

————*The Doolittle Raid.* New York: St. Martin's Press, 1988.

Schwarz, Otto. Unpublished Memoir.

Seibert, Donald A. Unpublished Memoir. Fort Belvoir, Virginia.

Shapiro, Alan. Unpublished Memoir. Ridgefield, Connecticut.

Sherrod, Robert. *Tarawa: The Story of a Battle.* New York: Duell, Sloan and Pearce, 1944.

Sledge, E. B. *With the Old Breed.* Novato, California: Presidio Press, 1981.

Smith, John F. *Hellcats Over the Philippine Deep.* Manhattan, Kansas: Sunflower Press, 1995.

Smith, Robert. Oral History. Maxwell Field, Alabama: United States Air Force Historical Center, 1983.

Spector, Ronald. *Eagle Against the Sun: The American War with Japan.* New York: Free Press, 1985.

Stroop, Paul. Oral History. Annapolis, Maryland: United States Naval Institute.

Svihra, Albert. Transcripts of letters to his family and Diary. West Point: U.S. Military Academy Library.

Teeples, Robert. *Jackson County Veterans,* Vol. II. Black River Falls, Wisconsin, 1986.

Thach, John (Jimmy). Oral History. Annapolis, Maryland: United States Naval Institute.

Tregaskis, Richard. *Guadalcanal Diary*. New York: Random House, 1943.

Ullom, Madeline. Memoir. Washington, D.C.: U.S. Army Center for Military History.

Van der Vat, Dan. *The Pacific Campaign*. New York: Simon & Schuster, 1991.

Walker, Anthony, ed., *Memorial to the Men of C/P Company, 4th Marine Raider Battalion*. Middletown, Rhode Island, 1994.

Ward, Norvell. Oral History. Annapolis, Maryland: United States Naval Institute.

White, W. L. *They Knew They Were Expendable*. New York: Harcourt Brace and Company, 1942.

# Index